lab 5 stud1mw

www.bls.gov - job requirement, salary, job, outlook. skill level

www.onetonline.org

(# will CCNA)

professormesser.com

CASP

MS 08-067

Jamey
Network +

All, People, Seem, to, need, Data, Processing

CompTIA®
Security+® (Exam
SY0-401)

Ports in cheat sheet

Simulations - See + data disk

(2-1, 6-1a - 6-1c

6-2a - 6-2d

7-1 - on the exam
exact one

9-1 - on the exam

10-3 - on the test

13-1 - on test

16-1a & 16-1b ✓ like exam

① Service
about computer

IT
HR
Manager
Company

CompTIA® Security+® (Exam SY0-401)

Part Number: 093022
Course Edition: 1.0

Acknowledgements

PROJECT TEAM

Author	Media Designer	Content Editor
Pamela J. Taylor Jason Nufryk	Alex Tong	Joe McElveney

Notices

CompTIA® Security+® (Exam SY0-401)

About This Course

CompTIA® Security+® (Exam SY0-401) is the primary course you will need to take if your job responsibilities include securing network services, devices, and traffic in your organization. You can also take this course to prepare for the CompTIA Security+ certification examination. In this course, you will build on your knowledge of and professional experience with security fundamentals, networks, and organizational security as you acquire the specific skills required to implement basic security services on any type of computer network.

This course can benefit you in two ways. If you intend to pass the CompTIA Security+ (Exam SY0-401) certification examination, this course can be a significant part of your preparation. But certification is not the only key to professional success in the field of computer security. Today's job market demands individuals with demonstrable skills, and the information and activities in this course can help you build your computer security skill set so that you can confidently perform your duties in any security-related role.

Course Description

Target Student

This course is targeted toward the information technology (IT) professional who has networking and administrative skills in Windows®-based Transmission Control Protocol/Internet Protocol (TCP/IP) networks; familiarity with other operating systems, such as Mac OS X®, Unix, or Linux; and who wants to further a career in IT by acquiring foundational knowledge of security topics; prepare for the CompTIA Security+ certification examination; or use Security+ as the foundation for advanced security certifications or career roles.

Course Prerequisites

To ensure your success in your course, you should possess basic Windows user skills and a fundamental understanding of computer and networking concepts. You can obtain this level of skills and knowledge by taking one of the following LogicalCHOICE courses:

- *Using Microsoft® Windows® 8.1*
- *Microsoft® Windows® 8.1 Transition from Windows® 7*

CompTIA A+ and Network+ certifications, or equivalent knowledge, and six to nine months experience in networking, including configuring security parameters, are strongly recommended. Students can obtain this level of skill and knowledge by taking any of the following LogicalCHOICE courses:

- *CompTIA® A+®: A Comprehensive Approach (Exams 220-801 and 220-802)*
- *CompTIA® Network+® (Exam N10-005)*

Additional introductory courses or work experience in application development and programming, or in network and operating system administration for any software platform or system are helpful but not required. For instance, to gain experience with managing Windows Server® 2012, you could take any or all of the following LogicalCHOICE courses:

- *Microsoft® Windows® Server 2012: Installation and Configuration*
- *Microsoft® Windows® Server 2012: Administration*
- *Microsoft® Windows® Server 2012: Configuring Advanced Services*

Course Objectives

In this course, you will implement, monitor, and troubleshoot infrastructure, application, information, and operational security.

You will:

- Identify the fundamental concepts of computer security.
- Identify security threats and vulnerabilities.
- Manage data, application, and host security.
- Implement network security.
- Identify and implement access control and account management security measures.
- Manage certificates.
- Identify and implement compliance and operational security measures.
- Manage risk.
- Troubleshoot and manage security incidents.
- Plan for business continuity and disaster recovery.

The LogicalCHOICE Home Screen

The LogicalCHOICE Home screen is your entry point to the LogicalCHOICE learning experience, of which this course manual is only one part. Visit the LogicalCHOICE Course screen both during and after class to make use of the world of support and instructional resources that make up the LogicalCHOICE experience.

Log-on and access information for your LogicalCHOICE environment will be provided with your class experience. On the LogicalCHOICE Home screen, you can access the LogicalCHOICE Course screens for your specific courses.

Each LogicalCHOICE Course screen will give you access to the following resources:

- eBook: an interactive electronic version of the printed book for your course.
- LearnTOs: brief animated components that enhance and extend the classroom learning experience.

Depending on the nature of your course and the choices of your learning provider, the LogicalCHOICE Course screen may also include access to elements such as:

- The interactive eBook.
- Social media resources that enable you to collaborate with others in the learning community using professional communications sites such as LinkedIn or microblogging tools such as Twitter.
- Checklists with useful post-class reference information.
- Any course files you will download.
- The course assessment.
- Notices from the LogicalCHOICE administrator.
- Virtual labs, for remote access to the technical environment for your course.
- Your personal whiteboard for sketches and notes.
- Newsletters and other communications from your learning provider.
- Mentoring services.
- A link to the website of your training provider.
- The LogicalCHOICE store.

Visit your LogicalCHOICE Home screen often to connect, communicate, and extend your learning experience!

How to Use This Book

As You Learn

This book is divided into lessons and topics, covering a subject or a set of related subjects. In most cases, lessons are arranged in order of increasing proficiency.

The results-oriented topics include relevant and supporting information you need to master the content. Each topic has various types of activities designed to enable you to practice the guidelines and procedures as well as to solidify your understanding of the informational material presented in the course. Procedures and guidelines are presented in a concise fashion along with activities and discussions. Information is provided for reference and reflection in such a way as to facilitate understanding and practice.

Data files for various activities as well as other supporting files for the course are available by download from the LogicalCHOICE Course screen. In addition to sample data for the course exercises, the course files may contain media components to enhance your learning and additional reference materials for use both during and after the course.

At the back of the book, you will find a glossary of the definitions of the terms and concepts used throughout the course. You will also find an index to assist in locating information within the instructional components of the book.

As You Review

Any method of instruction is only as effective as the time and effort you, the student, are willing to invest in it. In addition, some of the information that you learn in class may not be important to you immediately, but it may become important later. For this reason, we encourage you to spend some time reviewing the content of the course after your time in the classroom.

As a Reference

The organization and layout of this book make it an easy-to-use resource for future reference. Taking advantage of the glossary, index, and table of contents, you can use this book as a first source of definitions, background information, and summaries.

Course Icons

Watch throughout the material for these visual cues:

Icon	Description
	A **Note** provides additional information, guidance, or hints about a topic or task.
	A **Caution** helps make you aware of places where you need to be particularly careful with your actions, settings, or decisions so that you can be sure to get the desired results of an activity or task.
	LearnTO notes show you where an associated LearnTO is particularly relevant to the content. Access LearnTOs from your LogicalCHOICE Course screen.
	Checklists provide job aids you can use after class as a reference to performing skills back on the job. Access checklists from your LogicalCHOICE Course screen.
	Social notes remind you to check your LogicalCHOICE Course screen for opportunities to interact with the LogicalCHOICE community using social media.
	Notes Pages are intentionally left blank for you to write on.

1 | Security Fundamentals

Lesson Time: 4 hours

Lesson Objectives

In this lesson, you will identify the fundamental concepts of computer security. You will:

- Identify the basic components of the information security cycle.

- Identify information security controls.

- List common authentication methods.

- Identify the fundamental components of cryptography.

- Identify fundamental security policy issues.

Lesson Introduction

There are many different tasks, concepts, and skills involved in the pursuit of computer security. But most of these tasks, concepts, and skills share a few fundamental principles. In this lesson, you will identify some of the most basic ideas involved in securing computers and networks.

Just as you begin the construction of a building with bricks and mortar, each security implementation starts with a series of fundamental building blocks. No matter what the final result is, you will always start with the same fundamentals. As a security professional, it is your responsibility to understand these fundamental concepts so you can build the appropriate security structure for your organization.

TOPIC A

The Information Security Cycle

This lesson covers fundamentals of computer security. The most fundamental ideas are the ones that spring from the information security cycle that forms the basis of all security systems. In this topic, you will identify the components of the information security cycle.

To be successful and credible as a security professional, you should understand security in business starting from the ground up. You should also know the key security terms and ideas used by other security experts in technical documents and in trade publications. Security implementations are constructed from fundamental building blocks, just like a large building is constructed from individual bricks. This topic will help you understand those building blocks so that you can use them as the foundation for your security career.

What Is Information Security?

Information security refers to the protection of available information or information resources from unauthorized access, attacks, thefts, or data damage. Responsible individuals and organizations must secure their confidential information. Due to the presence of a widely connected business environment, data is now available in a variety of forms such as digital media and print. Therefore, every bit of data that is being used, shared, or transmitted must be protected to minimize business risks and other consequences of losing crucial data.

What to Protect

As an information security professional, you need to know what information to secure in an organization and why those assets need protection.

Information Security Asset	Why They Need Protection
Data	This is a general term that relates to the information assets of a person, customer, or organization. In a computer system, the files are the data. You need to protect data from getting corrupt or from being accessed without authorization.
Resources	These are any virtual or physical system components that have limited availability. A physical resource is any device connected directly to a computer system. A virtual resource refers to types of files, memory locations, or network connections.

Data

Resource

Figure 1–1: What to protect.

Collateral Damage

As an information security professional, you are directly responsible for protecting an organization's data and resources. If the security of an organization's data and resources is compromised, it may cause collateral damage to the organization in the form of compromised *reputation*, loss of goodwill, reduced investor confidence, loss of customers, and various financial losses. Although you are not directly responsible for customer relations, finances, or the business' reputation, any such collateral business damage that results from a failure of your primary security duties could be considered your indirect responsibility.

Goals of Security

There are three primary goals or functions involved in the practice of information security.

Security Goal	Description
Prevention	Personal information, company information, and information about intellectual property must be protected. If there is a breach in security in any of these areas, then the organization may have to put a lot of effort into recovering losses. Preventing users from gaining unauthorized access to confidential information should be the number one priority of information security professionals.
Detection	Detection occurs when a user is discovered trying to access unauthorized data or after information has been lost. It can be accomplished by investigating individuals or by scanning the data and networks for any traces left by the intruder in any attack against the system.
Recovery	When there is a disaster or an intrusion by unauthorized users, system data is sometimes compromised or damaged. It is in these cases that you need to employ a process to recover vital data from a crashed system or data storage devices. Recovery can also pertain to physical resources.

> **Note:** For additional information, check out the LearnTO **Recognize Goals of Security** presentation from the **LearnTO** tile on the LogicalCHOICE Course screen.

Risk

As applied to information systems, *risk* is a concept that indicates exposure to the chance of damage or loss. It signifies the likelihood of a hazard or dangerous threat occurring.

In information technology, risk is often associated with the loss of a system, power, or network, and other physical losses. Risk also affects people, practices, and processes.

For example, a disgruntled former employee is a threat. The amount of risk this threat represents depends on the likelihood that the employee will access his or her previous place of business and remove or damage data. It also depends on the extent of harm that could result.

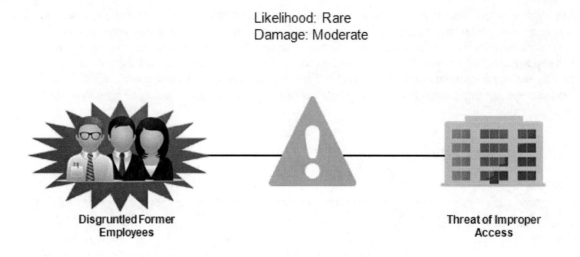

Figure 1-2: Risk.

Risk is the determining factor when looking at information systems security. If an organization chooses to ignore risks to operations, it could suffer a catastrophic outage that would limit its ability to survive.

Threats

In the realm of computer security, a *threat* is any event or action that could potentially cause damage to an asset. Threats are often in violation of a security requirement, policy, or procedure. Regardless of whether a violation is intentional or unintentional, malicious or not, it is considered a threat. Potential threats to computer and network security include:

- Unintentional or unauthorized access or changes to data.
- The interruption of services.
- The interruption of access to assets.
- Damage to hardware.
- Unauthorized access or damage to facilities.

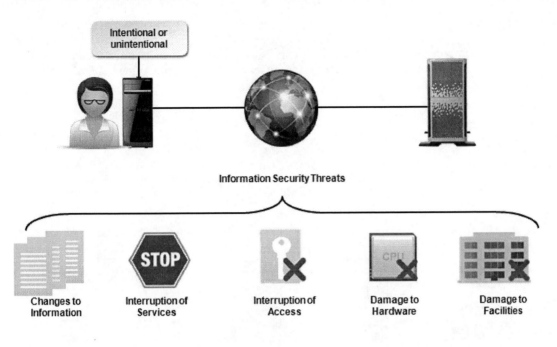

Figure 1–3: A threat.

Vulnerabilities

At the most basic level, a *vulnerability* is any condition that leaves a system open to harm. Vulnerabilities can come in a wide variety of forms, including:

- Improperly configured or installed hardware or software.
- Untested software and firmware patches.
- Bugs in software or operating systems.
- The misuse of software or communication protocols.
- Poorly designed networks.
- Poor physical security.
- Insecure passwords.
- Design flaws in software or operating systems.
- Unchecked user input.

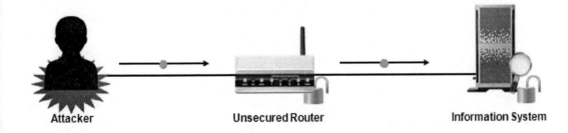

Figure 1–4: A vulnerability.

 Note: For additional information, check out the LearnTO **Recognize Threats, Risks, and Vulnerabilities** presentation from the **LearnTO** tile on the LogicalCHOICE Course screen.

Intrusions

In the realm of computer security, an *intrusion* occurs when an attacker accesses a computer system without the authorization to do so. An intrusion occurs when the system is vulnerable to attacks, and may include:

- Physical intrusions.
- Host-based intrusions.
- Network-based intrusions.

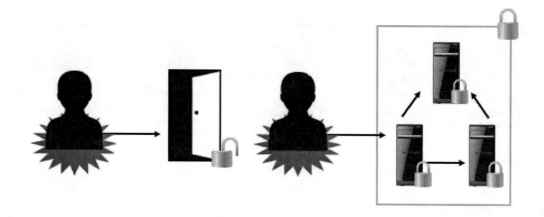

Figure 1–5: Intrusions.

Attacks

In the realm of computer security, an *attack* is a technique that is used to exploit a vulnerability in any application or physical computer system without the authorization to do so. Attacks on a computer system and network security include:

- Physical security attacks.
- Network-based attacks, including wireless networks.
- Software-based attacks.
- Social engineering attacks.
- Web application-based attacks.

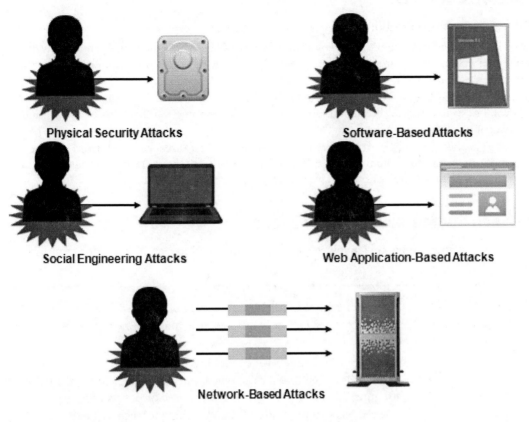

Figure 1-6: Attacks.

> **Note:** Physical security attack, software attack, and so on are terms used in this course to group threats into general categories for ease of discussion. They are not meant to imply that the security industry makes technical distinctions between these broad groups.

Controls

In the realm of computer security, *controls* are the countermeasures that you need to put in place to avoid, mitigate, or counteract security risks due to threats or attacks. In other words, controls are solutions and activities that enable an organization to meet the objectives of an information security strategy. Controls can be safeguards and countermeasures that are logical or physical. Controls are broadly classified as prevention, detection, and correction controls.

Prevention Control

Detection Control

Correction Control

Figure 1-7: Controls.

*Educate
Your users
is the Best
way to Defend
against vulabtions*

Types of Controls

The different types of controls include:

- *Prevention controls*: These help to prevent a threat or attack from exposing a vulnerability in the computer system. For example, a security lock on a building's access door is a prevention control.
- *Detection controls*: These help to discover if a threat or vulnerability has entered into the computer system. For example, surveillance cameras that record everything that happens in and around a building are detection controls.
- *Correction controls*: These help to mitigate the consequences of a threat or attack from adversely affecting the computer system. For example, a security officer who responds to a silent alarm detecting an intrusion and who then stops the intruder is a correction control.

The Security Management Process

The security management process involves identifying, implementing, and monitoring security controls.

Phase	Description
Identify security controls	This involves detecting problems and determining how best to protect a system: <ul><li>Find out when and where security breaches occur.</li><li>Log details of the breaches, showing information regarding the failed attempts, such as typing a wrong user name or password.</li><li>Select the appropriate identification technique, such as a network intrusion detection system (NIDS).</li></ul>
Implement security controls	This involves installing control mechanisms to prevent problems in a system: <ul><li>Authenticate users appropriately or control access to data and resources.</li><li>Match implementation security controls with the management requirements in any organization.</li><li>Install a security mechanism such as an intrusion detection system (IDS) or an intrusion prevention system (IPS) to prevent any attacks on the system.</li></ul>
Monitor security controls	This involves detecting and solving any security issues that arise after security controls are implemented: <ul><li>Run tests on the various controls installed to see if they are working correctly and will remain effective against further attacks on the system.</li><li>Analyze important steps that improve the performance of controls.</li><li>Document each control failure and determine if a control needs to be upgraded or removed.</li></ul>

ACTIVITY 1–1

Identifying Information Security Concepts and Components

Scenario

You are the new security administrator at Develetech Industries, a manufacturer of home electronics located in the fictional city and state of Greene City, Richland (RL). As you are meeting your new colleagues, several of them ask you some questions about security and how it relates to the business.

1. As an information security officer, what are the information security goals that you need to keep in mind while defining the protection you will need? (Select all that apply.)

   ☑ Prevention

   ☐ Auditing

   ☑ Recovery

   ☑ Detection

2. Which of these are vulnerabilities? (Select all that apply.)

   ☑ Improperly configured software

   ☑ Misuse of communication protocols

   ☑ Damage to hardware

   ☐ Lengthy passwords with a mix of characters

3. Describe the differences between a threat, vulnerability, and risk.

   threat - violation of security policy
   vul - open to attack
   risk - danger or loss

TOPIC B

Information Security Controls

You have just identified the components of the information security cycle. Now you can find out how they control computer security. In this topic, you will identify the security controls in more detail and identify how controls are implemented in computer security.

Understanding the basics of the information security cycle is just the first step in discovering how these factors control computer security as a whole. By identifying information security controls and how other security experts use them in the field, you will be better prepared to select and implement the proper controls in your own workplace.

The CIA Triad

Information security seeks to address three specific principles: confidentiality, integrity, and availability. This is called the *CIA triad*. If one of the principles is compromised, the security of the organization is threatened.

Figure 1–8: The CIA triad.

The CIA triad consists of three principles.

Principle	Description
Confidentiality	This is the fundamental principle of keeping information and communications private and protecting them from unauthorized access.
	Confidential information includes trade secrets, personnel records, health records, tax records, and military secrets.
	Confidentiality is typically controlled through encryption, access controls, and steganography.

Principle	Description
Integrity	This is the fundamental principle of keeping organization information accurate, free of errors, and without unauthorized modifications. For example, if an attack on a school system's server occurred and student test scores were modified, the integrity of the grade information was compromised by unauthorized modification. Integrity is typically controlled through hashing, digital signatures, certificates, and non-repudiation.
Availability	This is the fundamental principle of ensuring that systems operate continuously and that authorized persons can access the data that they need. Information available on a computer system is useless unless the users can get to it. Consider what would happen if the Federal Aviation Administration's air traffic control system failed. Radar images would be captured but not distributed to those who need the information. Availability is typically controlled through redundancy, fault tolerance, and patching.

> **Note:** For additional information, check out the LearnTO **Recognize Components of the CIA Triad** presentation from the **LearnTO** tile on the LogicalCHOICE Course screen.

Non-repudiation

Non-repudiation is the goal of ensuring that the party that sent a transmission or created data remains associated with that data and cannot deny sending or creating that data. You should be able to independently verify the identity of a message sender, and the sender should be responsible for the message and its data.

Figure 1-9: Non-repudiation.

Non-repudiation is one way to determine *accountability*, which is the process of determining who to hold responsible for a particular activity or event, such as a log on.

Identification

In security terms, *identification* is a method that ensures that an entity requesting access to resources by using a certain set of credentials is the true owner of the credentials. The investment and effort that goes into implementing a method of identification varies depending on the degree of security or protection that is needed in an organization.

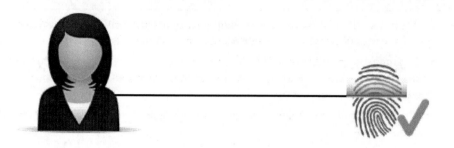

Figure 1-10: Identification.

When a request for access to resources involves providing credentials such as an email address or user name together with a password, identification ascertains whether or not the individual who enters the credentials is also the owner of those assigned, particular credentials.

Authentication

Authentication is the method of validating a particular entity or individual's unique credentials. Authentication concentrates on identifying if a particular individual has the right credentials to enter a system or secure site. Authentication credentials should be kept secret to keep unauthorized individuals from gaining access to confidential information.

Figure 1-11: Authentication.

Authentication Factors

Most authentication schemes are based on the use of one or more authentication factors. The factors include:

- Something you are, including physical characteristics, such as fingerprints or a retina pattern.
- Something you have, such as a token or access card.
- Something you know, such as a password.
- Somewhere you are or are not, such as an approved IP address or GPS location.
- Something you do, such as established keystroke patterns or tracing over a Windows 8.1 picture password.

> **Note:** The keystroke pattern factor is also referred to as keystroke biometrics or dynamic biometrics.

Authorization

In security terms, *authorization* is the process of determining what rights and privileges a particular entity has. Authorization is equivalent to a security guard checking the guest list at an exclusive gathering, or checking for your ticket when you go to the movies.

After a user has been identified and authenticated, a system can then determine what rights and privileges that user should have to various resources.

Access Control

Access control is the process of determining and assigning privileges to various resources, objects, or data.

Access control is how authorization is managed.

Access Control Models

There are four general models for managing access control.

Access Control Method	Description
Mandatory Access Control (MAC)	When you are trying to access a file that is labeled "Top Secret," it will only open if you are a person with access to view Top-Secret files. In this model, access is controlled by comparing an object's security designation and a user's security clearance. Objects, such as files and other resources, are assigned security labels of varying levels, depending on the object's sensitivity. Users are assigned a security level or clearance, and when they try to access an object, their clearance level must correspond to the object's security level. If there is a match, the user can access the object; if there is no match, the user is denied access. MAC security labels can generally be changed only by a system administrator.
Discretionary Access Control (DAC)	When you are trying to access a file that is protected, all you need to do is request the administrator to allow access and then start using the file. In this model, access to each object is controlled on a customized basis, which is based on a user's identity. Objects are configured with an *Access Control List (ACL)* of subjects (users or other entities) who are allowed access to them. An administrator has the discretion to place the user on the list or not, and to configure a particular level of access. Unlike MAC, in a DAC authorization scheme, object owners can generally modify their objects' ACLs.

Access Control Method	Description
Role-Based Access Control (RBAC)	When you are trying to access a file labeled "employee database," it comes up as access denied. This is because your role as an employee does not allow access to files in the HR folder. In this model, users are assigned to predefined roles, and network objects are configured to allow access only to specific roles. Access is controlled based on a user's assigned role. A user might have more than one role assigned at one time, or might switch from one role to another over the course of the user's employment. An administrator can assign to a role only those privileges users in the role need to complete their work. Often, the roles are dynamically assigned at the time access is requested, based on policies and rules determined by the administrator.
Rule-Based Access Control	A set of firewall restriction rules is a Rule-Based Access Control. This is a non-discretionary technique that is based on a set of operational rules or restrictions. For example, an employee may be allowed to log in to a system between the hours of 9:00 A.M. and 7:00 P.M. If the employee attempts to log in at 10:00 P.M. they will be denied access, even if they have the correct credentials. Rule sets are always examined before a subject is given access to objects.

Accounting and Auditing

In security terms, *accounting* is the process of tracking and recording system activities and resource access. *Auditing* is the part of accounting in which a security professional examines logs of what was recorded.

Common Security Practices

Common security practices help implement access controls in ways that provide effective measures for the protection of data and resources. The following is a list of common security practices:

- Implicit deny
- Least privilege
- Separation of duties
- Job rotation
- Mandatory vacation
- Time of day restrictions
- Privilege management

Implicit Deny

The principle of *implicit deny* dictates that everything that is not explicitly allowed is denied. Users and software should only be allowed to access data and perform actions when permissions are specifically granted to them. No other action is allowed.

Figure 1–12: Implicit deny.

Least Privilege

The principle of *least privilege* dictates that users and software should only have the minimal level of access that is necessary for them to perform the duties required of them. This level of minimal access includes facilities, computing hardware, software, and information. When a user or system is given access, that access should still be only at the level required to perform the necessary task.

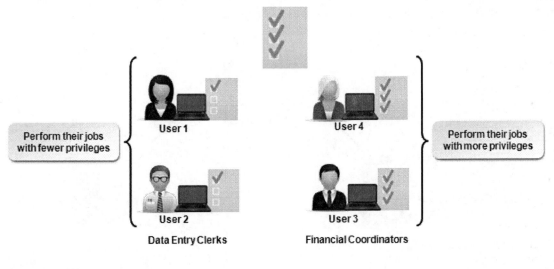

Figure 1–13: Least privilege.

Privilege Bracketing

The term *privilege bracketing* is used when privileges are given out only when needed, then revoked as soon as the task is finished or the need has passed.

Separation of Duties

Separation of duties states that no one person should have too much power or responsibility. Duties and responsibilities should be divided among individuals to prevent ethical conflicts or abuse of powers. Duties such as authorization and approval, and design and development should not be held by the same individual, because it would be far too easy for that individual to exploit an organization into using only specific software that contains vulnerabilities, or taking on projects that would be beneficial to that individual.

For example, in many typical IT departments, the roles of backup operator, restore operator, and auditor are assigned to different people.

Figure 1–14: Separation of duties.

Job Rotation

The idea of *job rotation* is that no one person stays in a vital job role for too long. Rotating individuals into and out of roles, such as the firewall administrator or access control specialist, helps an organization ensure that it is not tied too firmly to any one individual because vital institutional knowledge is spread among trusted employees. Job rotation also helps prevent abuse of power, reduces boredom, and enhances individuals' professional skills.

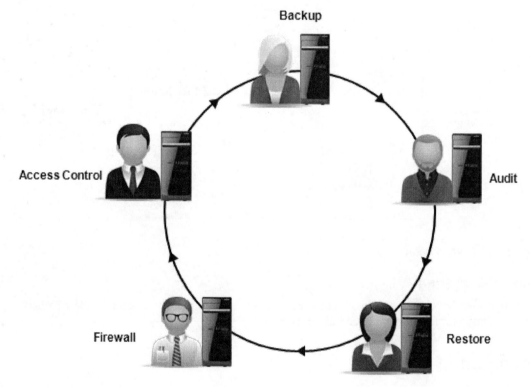

Figure 1–15: Job rotation.

Mandatory Vacation

Mandating employee vacations is a personnel management issue that has security implications. From a security standpoint, *mandatory vacations* provide an opportunity to review employees' activities. The typical mandatory vacation policy requires that employees take at least one vacation a year in a full-week increment so that they are away from work for at least five days in a row. During that time, the corporate audit and security employees have time to investigate and discover any discrepancies in employee activity. When employees understand the security focus of the mandatory vacation policy, the chance of fraudulent activities decreases.

Figure 1-16: Mandatory vacation.

Time of Day Restrictions

Time of day restrictions are controls that restrict the periods of time when users are allowed to access systems, which can be set using a group policy. You can also apply time of day restrictions to individual systems and to wireless access points.

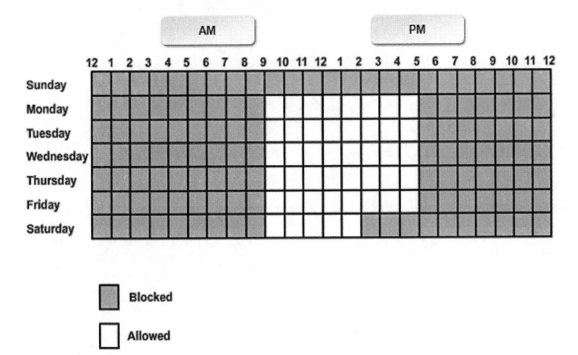

Figure 1-17: Time of day restrictions.

Orphaned Accounts

Orphaned accounts are user accounts that remain active even after the employees have left the organization. Not deactivating these accounts may give an attacker access to the system. Large organizations have found that isolating orphaned accounts can be a very difficult task, creating a potential avenue for attackers.

Privilege Management

Privilege management is the use of authentication and authorization mechanisms to provide centralized or decentralized administration of user and group access control. Privilege management should include an auditing component to track privilege use and privilege escalation. *Single sign-on (SSO)* can offer privilege management capabilities by providing users with one-time authentication for browsing resources such as multiple servers or sites.

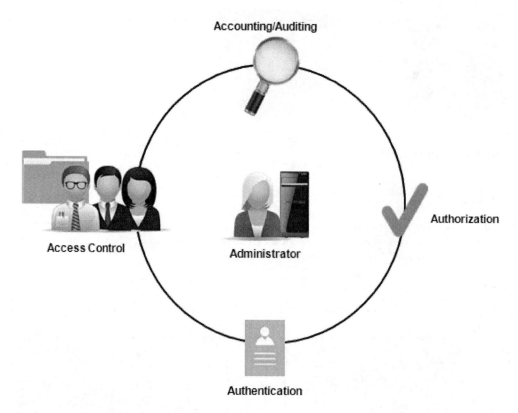

Figure 1-18: Privilege management.

PMI

An implementation of a particular set of privilege management technologies is called a *Privilege Management Infrastructure (PMI)*. The purpose of a PMI is to issue specific permissions and rights to users within the infrastructure. PMI functions in a similar way to Public Key Infrastructure (PKI) in that both have authoritative resources that issue rights or certificates to nodes below them in the infrastructure. Most often, PMI is leveraged alongside PKI because PKI is used to validate signatures for PMI. PMI should follow ITU-T (International Telecommunication Union-Telecommunication Standardization Sector) Recommendation X.509 as the basis for implementation.

ACTIVITY 1-2
Discussing Information Security Controls

Scenario

As a new security administrator, you want to identify some information security controls that you might be able to implement at Develetech Industries.

1. What are the three most fundamental goals of computer security?
   - ☑ Confidentiality
   - ☐ Auditing
   - ☑ Integrity
   - ☐ Privilege management
   - ☑ Availability

2. A biometric handprint scanner is used as part of a system for granting access to a facility. Once an identity is verified, the system checks and confirms that the user is allowed to leave the lobby and enter the facility, and the electronic door lock is released. Which security controls are being used in this situation? (Select all that apply.)
   - ☑ Authentication
   - ☑ Authorization
   - ☑ Access control
   - ☐ Auditing

3. Katie's handprint is matched against a record in the system that indicates that she has been assigned clearance to view the contents of secret documents. Later, at her desk, she tries to connect to a folder that is marked Top Secret, and access is denied. Which type of access control is being used?
   - ● MAC
   - ○ DAC
   - ○ RBAC
   - ○ Rule-Based Access Control

4. At the end of the day, security personnel can view electronic log files that record the identities of everyone who entered and exited the building along with the time of day. Which type of security control is this?
   - ○ Authentication
   - ○ Authorization
   - ○ Access control
   - ● Auditing

5. An administrator of a large multinational company has the ability to assign object access rights and track users' resource access from a central administrative console. Users throughout the organization can gain access to any system after providing a single user name and password. Which type of security control is this?

○ Auditing

○ Security labels

● Privilege management

○ Confidentiality

TOPIC C

Authentication Methods

In the previous topic, you described various information security controls, including authentication, which is one of the primary controls in use. Although authentication always has the same goal, there are many approaches to accomplishing that goal. In this topic, you will list some of the primary authentication methods used today.

Strong authentication is the first line of defense in the battle to secure network resources. But authentication is not a single process; there are many different methods and mechanisms, some of which can even be combined to form more complex schemes. As a network professional, familiarizing yourself with the major authentication methods in use today can help you implement and support the ones that are appropriate for your environment.

User Name/Password Authentication

The combination of a user name and password is one of the most basic and widely used authentication schemes. In this type of authentication, a user's credentials are compared against credentials stored in a database. If the user name and password match the database, the user is authenticated. If not, the user is denied access. This method may not be very secure because it doesn't necessarily identify the correct user. For example, the user's credentials are sometimes transmitted through the network in unencrypted text, making the user name and password easily accessible to an attacker.

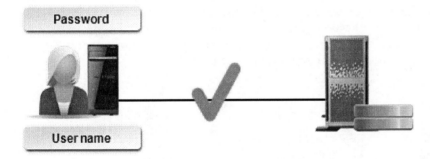

Figure 1-19: User name/password authentication.

Tokens

Tokens are physical or virtual objects, such as smart cards, ID badges, or data packets, that store authentication information. Tokens can store personal identification numbers (PINs), information about users, or passwords. Unique token values can be generated by special devices or software in response to a challenge from an authenticating server or by using independent algorithms.

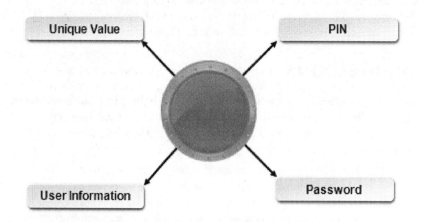

Figure 1-20: Tokens.

Smart Cards

Smart cards are a common example of token-based authentication. A smart card is a plastic card containing an embedded computer chip that can store different types of electronic information. The United States Department of Defense (DoD) has introduced a type of smart card called a *Common Access Card (CAC)* that is used as identification for all its military personnel, contract personnel, non-DoD government employees, and state employees of the National Guard. The contents of a smart card can be read with a smart card reader. Physical tokens like smart cards and CACs are sometimes categorized under the umbrella term *personal identification verification card*.

Biometrics

Biometrics are authentication schemes based on the identification of individuals by their physical characteristics. This can involve a fingerprint scanner, a retinal scanner, a hand geometry scanner, or voice-recognition and facial-recognition software. As biometric authentication becomes less expensive to implement, it is becoming more widely adopted.

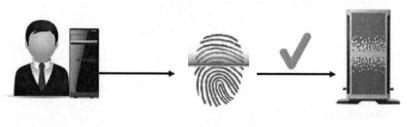

Fingerprint Scanner

Figure 1-21: Biometrics.

Type 4

Geolocation

With more and more mobile devices connecting to networks, *geolocation* provides an extra level for authentication. Users who are attempting to authenticate from an approved location can be granted network access, while users who are trying to authenticate from a location that is not approved can be denied network access.

Internet and computer geolocation can be performed by associating a geographic location with an Internet Protocol (IP) address, Media Access Control (MAC) address, radio-frequency ID (RFID), embedded hardware or software number, invoice, Wi-Fi positioning system, device GPS coordinates, or other information. Geolocation usually works by automatically looking up an IP address on a WHOIS service and retrieving the registrant's physical address.

When the physical location is determined, it can be compared to a list of locations that are approved for (or restricted from) network access, and access to resources can be granted accordingly. Conversely, if a network attack originates from a particular country, packets originating from IP addresses physically located in that country could be automatically dropped during the attack period, while continuing to accept traffic from other areas. Similarly, organizations that do business in certain parts of the world could configure their systems to always deny authentication requests that come from areas outside of their zones of interest, thereby limiting their potential risk.

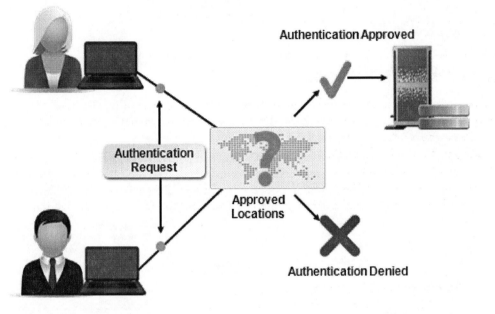

Figure 1–22: Geolocation.

Keystroke Authentication

Keystroke authentication is a type of authentication that relies on detailed information that describes exactly when a keyboard key is pressed and released as someone types information into a computer or other electronic device. Each user has certain tendencies, rhythms, and patterns when it comes to typing on a keyboard, and these can be recorded and measured to compare against future keystrokes.

Keystroke authentication requires the use of a keystroke logger, as well as other measurements such as when a key is pressed and released, the interval between a key release and the next key being pressed, and so forth. All of this data is fed into a series of algorithms that establish a primary keystroke pattern that is attributable to the individual user.

 Note: Some sources consider keystroke authentication to be an extension of biometrics.

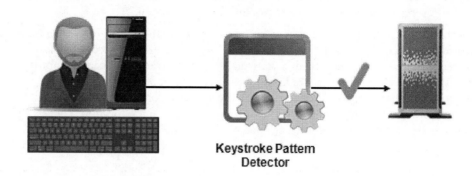

Figure 1-23: Keystroke authentication.

Multi-factor Authentication

Multi-factor authentication is any authentication scheme that requires validation of two or more authentication factors. It can be any combination of who you are, what you have, what you know, where you are or are not, and what you do.

Requiring a physical ID card along with a secret password is an example of multi-factor authentication. A bank ATM card is a common example of this. Keep in mind that multi-factor authentication requires the *factors* to be different, not just the specific objects or methods. So, using a smart card with a VPN token is *not* multi-factor authentication, as both methods are part of the same single factor: what you have.

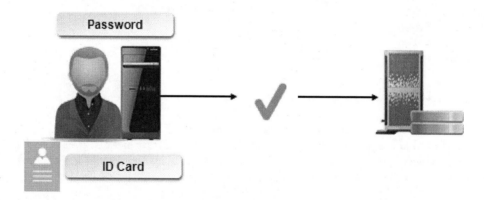

Figure 1-24: Multi-factor authentication.

Mutual Authentication

Mutual authentication is a security mechanism that requires that each party in a communication verifies each other's identity. A service or resource verifies the client's credentials, and the client verifies the resource's credentials. Mutual authentication prevents a client from inadvertently submitting confidential information to a non-secure server. Any type or combination of authentication mechanisms can be used.

Figure 1-25: Mutual authentication.

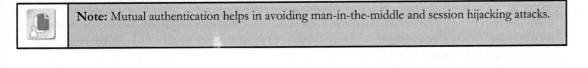

Note: Mutual authentication helps in avoiding man-in-the-middle and session hijacking attacks.

ACTIVITY 1–3
Discussing Authentication Methods

Scenario

As the security administrator, you are planning to discuss various authentication methods with your colleagues at Develetech Industries.

1. Brian works in your IT department. To access his laptop, he inserts his employee ID card into a special card reader. This is an example of:
   - ○ User name/password authentication.
   - ○ Biometrics.
   - ● Token-based authentication.
   - ○ Mutual authentication.

2. To access the server room, Brian places his index finger on a fingerprint reader. This is an example of:
   - ○ Password authentication.
   - ○ Token-based authentication.
   - ● Biometric authentication.
   - ○ Multi-factor authentication.

3. To withdraw money from an automatic teller machine, Nancy inserts a card and types a four-digit PIN. This incorporates what types of authentication? (Select all that apply.)
   - ☑ Token-based
   - ☑ Password
   - ☐ Biometrics
   - ☑ Multi-factor
   - ☐ Mutual

4. What is the best description of token-based authentication?
   - ○ It relies on typing a code.
   - ○ It relies on a card and a PIN.
   - ○ It relies on a user's physical characteristics.
   - ● It relies on a card being inserted into a card reader.

5. What is an example of a "what you do" authentication factor?
   - ○ Fingerprint or handprint recognition
   - ○ ID card and PIN
   - ● Keystroke pattern recognition
   - ○ Geolocation
   - ○ User name and password

6. **True or False? Mutual authentication protects clients from submitting confidential information to an insecure server.**

☑ True

☐ False

7. **How does multi-factor authentication enhance security?**

Layers of defense

TOPIC D

Cryptography Fundamentals

Earlier in the lesson, you identified the elements of security as confidentiality, integrity, and availability. Encryption is one of the most versatile security tools you can use to do justice to these elements. In this topic, you will identify fundamental cryptography components, concepts, and tools.

Cryptography is a powerful and complex weapon in the fight to maintain computer security. There are many cryptography systems, and the specifics of each cryptography implementation vary. Nevertheless, there are commonalities among all cryptography systems that all security professionals should understand. The basic cryptography terms and ideas you will learn in this topic will help you evaluate, understand, and manage any type of cryptographic system you choose to implement.

Cryptography

Cryptography is the science of hiding information. The practice of cryptography is thought to be nearly as old as the written word. Current cryptographic science has its roots in mathematics and computer science, and relies heavily upon technology. Modern communications and computing use cryptography extensively to protect sensitive information and communications from unauthorized access or accidental disclosure while the information is in transit and while the information is being stored.

> **Note:** The word cryptography has roots in the Greek words kryptós, meaning "hidden," and "gráphein," meaning "to write," translating to "hidden writing."

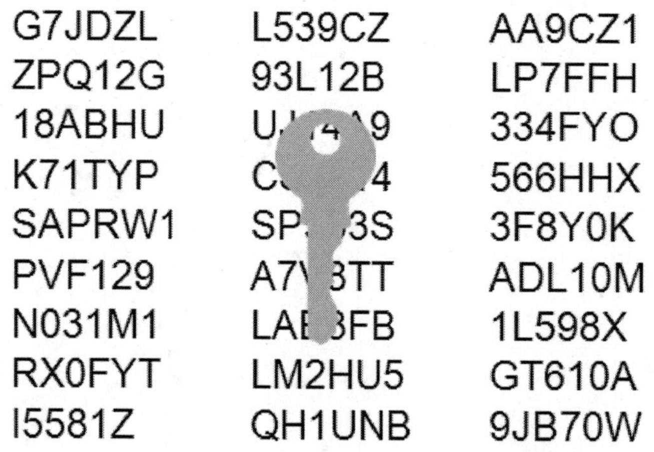

G7JDZL	L539CZ	AA9CZ1
ZPQ12G	93L12B	LP7FFH
18ABHU	U 9	334FYO
K71TYP	C 4	566HHX
SAPRW1	SP 3S	3F8Y0K
PVF129	A7 3TT	ADL10M
N031M1	LA 3FB	1L598X
RX0FYT	LM2HU5	GT610A
I5581Z	QH1UNB	9JB70W

Figure 1-26: Cryptography.

Use of Proven Technologies

Any new technology should be rigorously tested before being applied to a live, production network. Particularly with cryptography, the technologies and techniques should have a well-documented history of investigation by industry professionals.

Encryption and Decryption

Encryption is a cryptographic technique that converts data from *plaintext*, or *cleartext* form, into coded, or *ciphertext* form. *Decryption* is the companion technique that converts ciphertext back to cleartext.

When a message is encrypted, only authorized parties with the necessary decryption information can decode and read the data. Encryption can be one-way, which means the encryption is designed to never be decrypted. Encryption can also be two-way, in which the ciphertext can be decrypted back to cleartext and read.

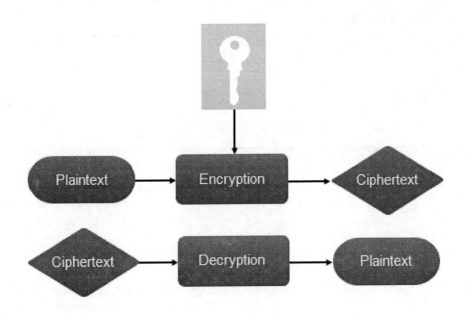

Figure 1-27: Encryption and decryption.

Quantum Cryptography

Quantum cryptography is an experimental method of data encryption based upon quantum communication and computation. A *qubit* is a unit of data that is encrypted by entangling data with a photon or electron that has a particular spin cycle which can be read using a polarization filter that controls spin. If a qubit is read with an incorrect polarization filter, then it becomes unreadable and the receiver will know that someone may actually be eavesdropping. For more information, visit **www.csa.com/discoveryguides/crypt/overview.php**.

Ciphers

A *cipher* is an algorithm used to encrypt or decrypt data. Algorithms can be simple mechanical substitutions, but in electronic cryptography, they are generally complex mathematical functions. The stronger the mathematical function, the more difficult it is to break the encryption. Plaintext, or cleartext, is the original, un-encoded data. Once the cipher is applied via *enciphering*, the obscured data is known as ciphertext. The reverse process of translating ciphertext to cleartext is known as *deciphering*.

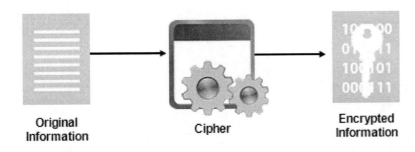

Figure 1-28: Ciphers.

Ciphers are differentiated from codes in that codes are meant to translate words or phrases or act like a secret language, whereas ciphers operate on individual letters or bits and scramble the message.

Cryptanalysis is the science of breaking codes and ciphers.

A Simple Encryption Algorithm

A letter-substitution cipher, in which each letter of the alphabet is systematically replaced by another letter, is an example of a simple encryption algorithm.

Cipher Types

There are two major categories of encryption ciphers: stream and block.

Cipher Type	Description
Stream cipher	A type of encryption that encrypts data one bit at a time. Each plaintext bit is transformed into encrypted ciphertext. These ciphers are relatively fast to execute and do not require much performance overhead. The ciphertext is the same size as the original text. This method produces fewer errors than other methods, and when errors occur, they affect only one bit.
Block cipher	This cipher encrypts data one block at a time, often in 64-bit blocks. It is usually stronger and more secure, but also offers slower performance, than stream encryption. Some common modes of block cipher encryption are: • *Electronic Code Block (ECB) encryption* • *Cipher Block Chaining (CBC) encryption* • *Propagating or Plaintext Cipher Block Chaining (PCBC) encryption* • *Cipher Feedback mode (CFB) encryption* • *Output Feedback mode (OFB) encryption* • *Counter mode (CTR)*

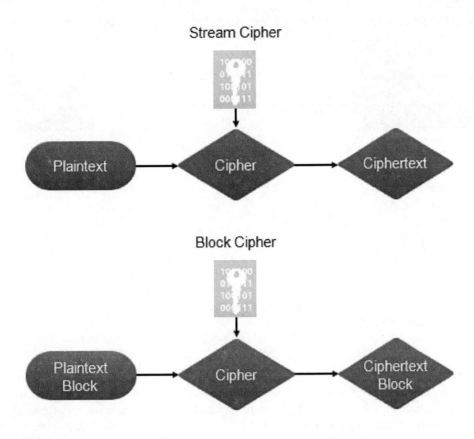

Figure 1–29: Cipher types.

Encryption and Security Goals

Encryption is used to promote and support many security goals and techniques:

*   It enables confidentiality by protecting data from unauthorized access.
*   It supports integrity because it is difficult to decipher encrypted data without the secret decrypting cipher.
*   It supports non-repudiation, because only parties that know about the confidential encryption scheme can encrypt or decrypt data.
*   Some form of encryption is employed in most authentication mechanisms to protect passwords.
*   It is also used in many access control mechanisms.

It is becoming more common to encrypt many forms of communications and data streams, as well as entire hard disks. Some operating systems support whole-disk encryption, and there are many commercial and open-source tools available that are capable of encrypting all or part of the data on a disk or drive.

Steganography

Steganography is an alternative cipher process that hides information by enclosing it in another file such as a graphic, movie, or sound file. Where encryption hides the content of information, but does not attempt to hide the fact that information exists, steganography is an attempt to obscure the fact that information is even present. Steganographic techniques include hiding information in blocks of what appears to be innocuous text, or hiding information within images either by using subtle clues, or by invisibly altering the structure of a digital image by applying an algorithm to change the color of individual pixels within the image.

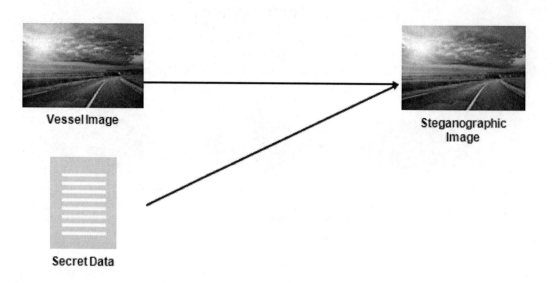

Figure 1–30: Steganography.

Keys

An encryption *key* is a specific piece of information that is used in conjunction with an algorithm to perform encryption and decryption. A different key can be used with the same algorithm to produce different ciphertext. Without the correct key, the receiver cannot decrypt the ciphertext even if the algorithm is known. The longer the key, the stronger the encryption.

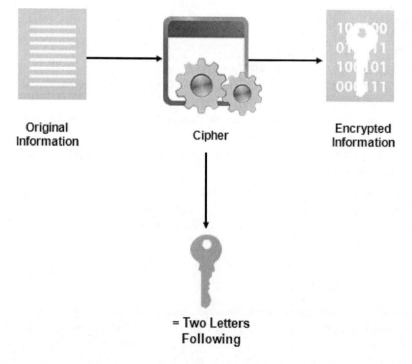

Figure 1–31: A key.

Keys can be static or ephemeral. Static keys are intended to be used for a relatively long time and for many instances within a key-establishment process, while ephemeral keys are generated for each individual communication segment or session.

One-Time Pad — Key Fob example

The one-time pad is an encryption algorithm that was developed under the assumption that if a key was used once, was completely random, and was kept totally secret, then it constituted the perfect method of encryption. However, because the successful use of a one-time pad relies on an absolutely perfect setting to work correctly, one-time pad encryption has very little practical value. It is so named because the earliest encryption involved pads of paper where the various sheets could be destroyed after use.

A Simple Encryption Key

In a simple letter-substitution algorithm, the key might be "replace each letter with the letter that is two letters following it in the alphabet." If the same algorithm were used on the same cleartext, but with a different key (for example, "replace each letter with the one three letters before it") the resulting ciphertext would be different.

Hashing Encryption

Hashing encryption is one-way encryption that transforms cleartext into ciphertext that is not intended to be decrypted. The result of the hashing process is called a *hash*, *hash value*, or *message digest*. The input data can vary in length, whereas the hash length is fixed.

Hashing has several uses:

- Hashing is used in a number of password authentication schemes. Encrypted password data is called a hash of the password.
- A hash value can be embedded in an electronic message to support data integrity and non-repudiation.
- A hash of a file can be used to verify the integrity of that file after transfer.

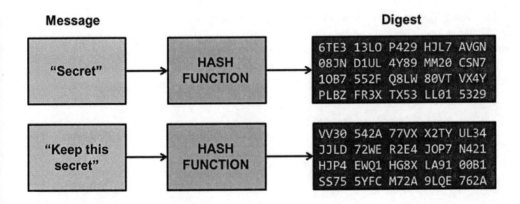

Figure 1-32: Hashing encryption.

Hashing Encryption Algorithms

Some common encryption algorithms are used for hashing encryption.

Hashing Algorithm	Description
Message Digest 5 (MD5)	This algorithm produces a 128-bit message digest. It was created by Ronald Rivest and is now in the public domain. MD5 is no longer considered a strong hash function.

Hashing Algorithm	Description
Secure Hash Algorithm (SHA)	This algorithm is modeled after MD5 and is considered the stronger of the two. Common versions of SHA include SHA-160, which produces a 160-bit hash value, while SHA-256, SHA-384, and SHA-512 produce 256-bit, 384-bit, and 512-bit digests, respectively. Performance-wise, SHA is at a disadvantage to MD5.
NT LAN Manager (NTLM#)	NTLMv1 is an authentication protocol created by Microsoft® for use in its products and released in early versions of Windows® NT. NTLMv2 was introduced in the later versions of Windows NT.
RACE Integrity Primitives Evaluation Message Digest (RIPEMD)	This is a message digest algorithm (cryptographic hash function) that is based along the lines of the design principles used in MD4. There are 128, 160, 256, and 320-bit versions called RIPEMD-128, RIPEMD-160, RIPEMD-256, and RIPEMD-320, respectively. The 256- and 320-bit versions reduce the chances of generating duplicate output hashes but do little in terms of higher levels of security. RIPEMD-160 was designed by the open academic community and is used less frequently than SHA-1, which may explain why it is less scrutinized than SHA.
Hash-based Message Authentication Code (HMAC)	This is a method used to verify both the integrity and authenticity of a message by combining cryptographic hash functions, such as MD5 or SHA-1, with a secret key. The resulting calculation is named based on what underlying hash function was used. For example, if SHA-1 is the hash function, then the HMAC algorithm is named HMAC-SHA1.

Symmetric Encryption

Symmetric encryption is a two-way encryption scheme in which encryption and decryption are both performed by the same key. The key can be configured in software or coded in hardware. The key must be securely transmitted between the two parties prior to encrypted communications, which can prove difficult. Symmetric encryption is relatively fast, but is vulnerable if the key is lost or compromised. Some of the common names for symmetric encryption are secret-key, shared-key, and private-key encryption.

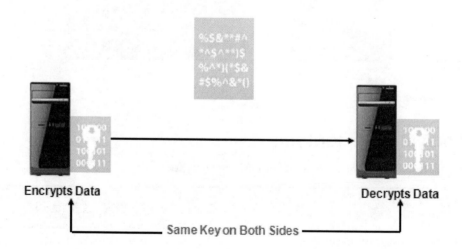

Encrypts Data

Decrypts Data

Same Key on Both Sides

Figure 1–33: Symmetric encryption.

Symmetric Encryption Algorithms

Some algorithms are used for symmetric encryption.

Study this Either you know or Don't

Symmetric Algorithm	Description
Data Encryption Standard (DES)	A block-cipher symmetric encryption algorithm that encrypts data in 64-bit blocks using a 56-bit key with 8 bits used for parity. The short key length makes DES a relatively weak algorithm, though it requires less performance overhead.
Triple DES (3DES)	A symmetric encryption algorithm that encrypts data by processing each block of data three times using a different key each time. It first encrypts plaintext into ciphertext using one key, then encrypts that ciphertext with another key, and lastly encrypts the second ciphertext with yet another key. 3DES is stronger than DES, but also triples the performance impact.
Advanced Encryption Standard (AES) algorithm	A symmetric 128-, 192-, or 256-bit block cipher developed by Belgian cryptographers Joan Daemen and Vincent Rijmen and adopted by the U.S. government as its encryption standard to replace DES. The AES algorithm is called Rijndael (pronounced "Rhine-dale") after its creators. Rijndael was one of five algorithms considered for adoption in the AES contest conducted by the National Institute of Standards and Technology (NIST) of the United States. AES is considered one of the strongest encryption algorithms available, and offers better performance than 3DES.
Blowfish	A freely available 64-bit block cipher algorithm that uses a variable key length. It was developed by Bruce Schneier. Blowfish is no longer considered strong, though it does offer greater performance than DES.
Twofish	A symmetric key block cipher, similar to Blowfish, consisting of a block size of 128 bits and key sizes up to 256 bits. Although not selected for standardization, it appeared as one of the five finalists in the AES contest. Twofish encryption uses a pre-computed encrypted algorithm. The encrypted algorithm is a key-dependent *S-box*, which is a relatively complex key algorithm that when given the key, provides a substitution key in its place. This is referred to as "n" and has the sizes of 128, 192, and 256 bits. One half of "n" is made up of the encryption key, and the other half contains a modifier used in the encryption algorithm. Twofish is stronger than Blowfish and offers comparative levels of performance.
Rivest Cipher (RC) 4, 5, and 6	A series of algorithms developed by Ronald Rivest. All have variable key lengths. RC4 is a stream cipher. RC5 and RC6 are variable-size block ciphers. RC6 is considered a strong cipher and offers good performance.

Asymmetric Encryption

Most Secure

private Keys - news transit

Publc in transt

Unlike symmetric encryption, the mainstay of *asymmetric encryption* is using public and private keys. The *private key* is kept secret by one party during two-way encryption. Because the private key is never shared, its security is relatively maintained. The asymmetric key exchange process is therefore easier and more secure than the symmetric process.

The *public key* is given to anyone. Depending on the application of the encryption, either party may use the encryption key. The other key in the pair is used to decrypt. The private key in a pair can decrypt data encoded with the corresponding public key.

Asymmetric algorithms usually perform much slower than symmetric algorithms due to their larger key sizes.

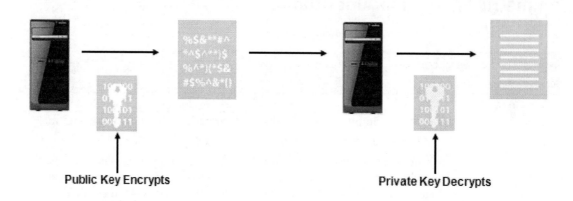

Public Key Encrypts   Private Key Decrypts

Figure 1-34: Asymmetric encryption.

Key generation is the process of generating a public and private key pair by using a specific application.

> **Note:** Asymmetric encryption may be used to exchange symmetric keys for the purpose of providing an extra layer of security.

> **Note:** For additional information, check out the LearnTO **Contrast Symmetric and Asymmetric Encryption** presentation from the **LearnTO** tile on the LogicalCHOICE Course screen.

Asymmetric Encryption Techniques

The following table lists some of the techniques and algorithms used in asymmetric encryption.

Asymmetric Algorithm	Description
Rivest Shamir Adelman (RSA)	Named for its designers, Ronald Rivest, Adi Shamir, and Len Adelman, RSA was the first successful algorithm for public key encryption. It has a variable key length and block size. It is still widely used and considered highly secure if it employs sufficiently long keys.
Diffie-Hellman (DH)	A cryptographic technique that provides for secure key exchange. Described in 1976, it formed the basis for most public key encryption implementations, including RSA, DHE, and ECDHE.
Elliptic curve cryptography (ECC)	An asymmetric, public key encryption technique that leverages the algebraic structures of elliptic curves over finite fields. ECC is used with wireless and mobile devices.
Diffie-Hellman Ephemeral (DHE)	A variant of DH that uses ephemeral keys to provide secure key exchange.
Elliptic Curve Diffie-Hellman Ephemeral (ECDHE)	A variant of DH that incorporates the use of ECC and ephemeral keys.

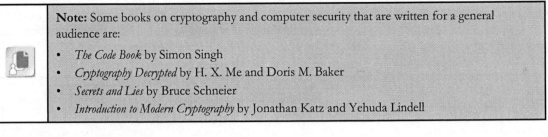

> **Note:** Some books on cryptography and computer security that are written for a general audience are:
> - *The Code Book* by Simon Singh
> - *Cryptography Decrypted* by H. X. Me and Doris M. Baker
> - *Secrets and Lies* by Bruce Schneier
> - *Introduction to Modern Cryptography* by Jonathan Katz and Yehuda Lindell

Key Exchange

Key exchange is any method by which cryptographic keys are transferred among users, thus enabling the use of a cryptographic algorithm.

For a sender and receiver to exchange encrypted messages, each must be equipped to encrypt the messages to be sent and to decrypt the messages to be received. How they need to be equipped depends on the encryption technique that is used. If they use a code, both will require a copy of the same codebook. If they use a cipher, they will need appropriate keys:

- If the cipher is a symmetric key cipher, both will need a copy of the same key.
- If the cipher is an asymmetric key cipher with the public/private key property, both will need the other's public key.

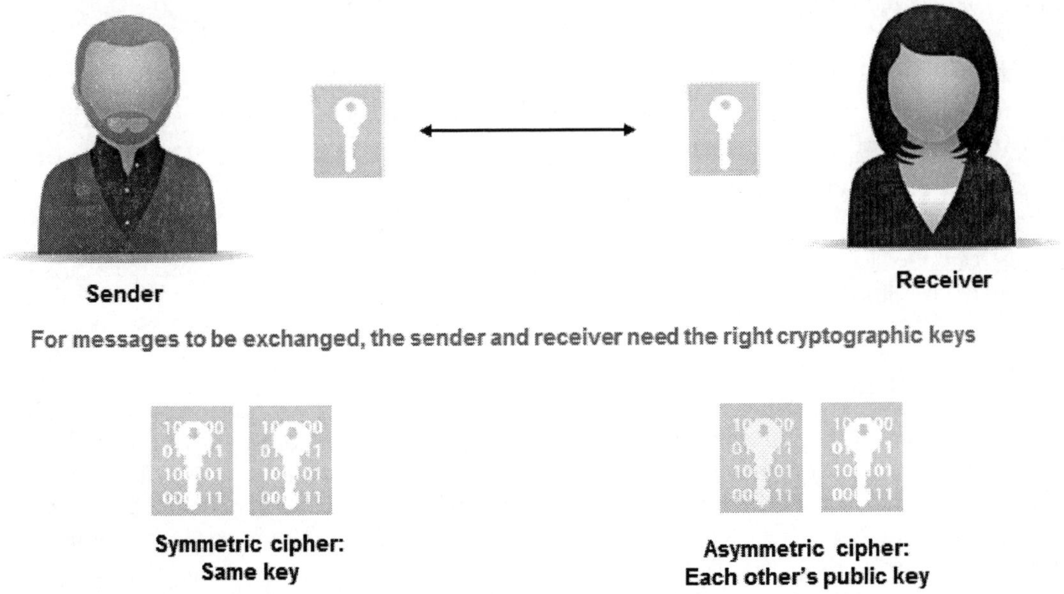

Sender

Receiver

For messages to be exchanged, the sender and receiver need the right cryptographic keys

Symmetric cipher: Same key

Asymmetric cipher: Each other's public key

Figure 1-35: Key exchange.

There are two basic types of key exchanges: in-band and out-of-band. In-band key exchanges use the same path as other data, while out-of-band exchanges use a different path, such as a phone call, letter or email message, or physical meeting. Symmetric key encryption requires out-of-band key exchanges to avoid keys being intercepted.

Digital Signatures

A *digital signature* is a message digest that has been encrypted again with a user's private key. Asymmetric encryption algorithms can be used with hashing algorithms to create digital signatures. The sender creates a hashed version of the message text, and then encrypts the hash itself with the sender's private key. The encrypted hash is attached to the message as the digital signature. The sender provides the receiver with the signed message and the corresponding public key. The receiver uses the public key to decrypt the signature to reveal the sender's version of the hash. This proves

(handwritten note in right margin: "Salting — randomization - adds to the encrypt")

the sender's identity, because if the public and private keys did not match, the receiver would not be able to decrypt the signature. The receiver then creates a new hash version of the document with the public key and compares the two hash values. If they match, this proves that the data has not been altered.

 Note: Digital signatures support message integrity, because if the signature is altered in transit, the receiver's version of the hash will not match the original hash value. They support non-repudiation because the specific encrypted hash value is unique to the sender.

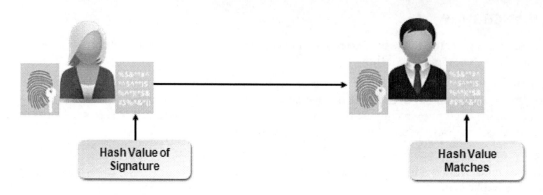

Figure 1-36: A digital signature.

Encryption of the Hash

It is important to remember that a digital signature is a hash that is then itself encrypted. Without the second round of encryption, another party could easily:

1. Intercept the file and the hash.
2. Modify the file.
3. Re-create the hash.
4. Send the modified file to the recipient.

Cipher Suites

A *cipher suite* is a collection of symmetric and asymmetric encryption algorithms that are used to establish a secure connection between hosts. Commonly associated with the Transport Layer Security (TLS) and Secure Sockets Layer (SSL) network protocols, there are over 200 known cipher suites available, each providing varying levels of protection. Cipher suites that use weak ciphers should be avoided; these generally have key lengths that are too short for modern use (such as 40- or 56-bit). Cipher suites with strong ciphers use a 128- and/or 256-bit key length and have no known major vulnerabilities in the algorithm itself.

A cipher suite defines a key exchange algorithm, a bulk encryption algorithm, a message authentication code algorithm, and a pseudorandom function.

Cipher Suite Component	Description
Key exchange algorithm	Determines if and how the client and server will authenticate during the TLS connection handshake.
Bulk encryption algorithm	Encrypts the actual message stream, and includes the key size.
Message authentication code algorithm	Creates the message digest.
Pseudorandom function	Creates the master secret, which is a 48-byte secret that is shared between the two systems being connected.

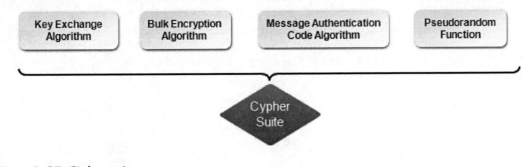

Figure 1-37: Cipher suites.

Session Keys

A *session key* is a single-use symmetric key that is used for encrypting all messages in a single series of related communications. There are two primary reasons to use session keys:

- Some cryptanalytic attacks become easier or more successful as more material encrypted with a specific key is available. By limiting the key's use to only one communication session, you necessarily limit the amount of data that has been encrypted with that key.
- Using session keys can be faster and more efficient than using asymmetric encryption alone. You can still use an asymmetric algorithm to encrypt the secret key for another, faster, symmetric algorithm. This ensures that the key is securely distributed, and it can also improve overall performance.

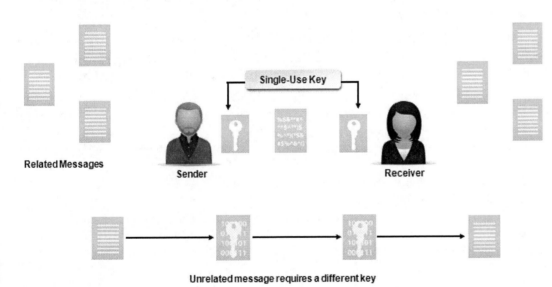

Figure 1-38: Session keys.

Perfect forward secrecy is a property of public key cryptographic systems that ensures that any session key derived from a set of long-term keys cannot be compromised if one of the keys is compromised at a future date. A key that is used to protect transmission of data cannot be used to derive any other keys, and if a key that used to protect transmission of data was derived from some other keying material, that material cannot be used to derive any more keys. Thus, compromise of a single key will permit access only to data protected by that key. DHE and ECDHE are said to provide perfect forward secrecy.

Key Stretching

Key stretching is a technique that strengthens potentially weak cryptographic keys, such as passwords or passphrases created by people, against brute force attacks. In key stretching, the original key is enhanced by running it through a key-stretching algorithm. Enhanced keys are usually larger than 128 bits, which makes them harder to crack via a brute force attack.

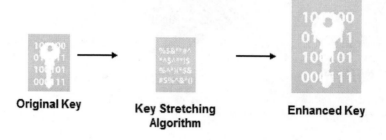

Original Key   **Key Stretching**   **Enhanced Key**
                          Algorithm

Key stretching makes it harder to crack passwords and passphrases.

Figure 1–39: Key stretching.

Key stretching techniques include:

- Repeatedly looping cryptographic hash functions.
- Repeatedly looping block ciphers.
- Where the key is used for a cipher, configuring the cipher's key schedule to increase the time it takes for the key to be set up.

One popular approach to key stretching is to use a key-derivation function:

- *Password-Based Key Derivation Function 2 (PBKDF2)* is part of the Public Key Cryptography Standards from RSA Laboratories. This key derivation function uses five input parameters to create a derived key:

    - A pseudorandom function such as a hash, cipher, or HMAC.
    - The master password used to generate derived keys.
    - A cryptographic salt, or random data added to a password or passphrase to counter against certain attacks.
    - A specified number of iterations for the function to loop.
    - The desired length of the derived key.

- *Bcrypt* is a key-derivation function based on the Blowfish cipher. Like PBKDF2, it uses a cryptographic salt, but it also adapts over time by increasing the iteration count. There are implementations of bcrypt for Ruby, Python, C, C#, Perl, PHP, Java, and other languages.

ACTIVITY 1-4
Discussing Cryptography Fundamentals

Scenario

As Develetech's security administrator, you know that you will need to implement and support cryptographic technologies to help keep company, employee, and customer data secure. Prior to a discussion with the Chief Security Officer, you decide to review some basic concepts related to cryptography.

1. Which algorithm is a hashing encryption algorithm?
   - ● SHA
   - ○ AES
   - ○ RSA
   - ○ 3DES

2. Which of the following is a specific set of actions used to encrypt data?
   - ○ Steganography
   - ○ Key
   - ● Cipher
   - ○ Digital signature

3. True or False? A digital signature is an application of hashing encryption, because the signature is never transformed back to cleartext.
   - ☑ True
   - ☐ False

4. What are the distinctions between an encryption algorithm and a key? — *what is secret after* ↳ *Rules & Instructions*

5. What is a potential drawback of symmetric encryption?
   share a key

6. What makes public key encryption potentially so secure?
   Private key never shared & used to decrypt

7. Considering that hashing encryption is one-way and the hash is never decrypted, what makes hashing encryption a useful security technique?
   Integrity & Non repudiation

8. Which asymmetric encryption algorithm uses a temporary key?
   - ○ RSA
   - ○ RC4
   - ◉ DHE
   - ○ RIPEMD
   - ○ ECC

9. What are the common components of a cipher suite? (Select all that apply.)
   - ☑ Message authentication code algorithm
   - ☐ Ephemeral key
   - ☑ Bulk encryption algorithm
   - ☑ Pseudorandom function
   - ☑ Key exchange algorithm

10. True or false? A session key is equivalent to a static key.
    - ☐ True
    - ☑ False

11. Give at least one example of a key-stretching implementation.

    PBKDF2

TOPIC E

Security Policy Fundamentals

So far, you have looked at increasingly more complex components of security systems. When all the components and requirements of a security system are identified, they are typically documented and maintained in security policies. In this topic, you will identify how security policies are constructed to meet the security needs of an organization.

In most organizations, security policies are the documents that have the greatest influence over the actions taken and decisions made by security professionals. A well-constructed security policy is a great weapon in the fight to preserve the safety and integrity of an institution's technical and intellectual assets. As you pursue your career, you will certainly be called upon to read, understand, and conform to security policies, and you might even be charged with designing, implementing, and maintaining them. Whatever aspect of the security profession you pursue, the fundamental security policy terms and ideas introduced in this topic will always serve you well.

Security Policies

A *security policy* is a formalized statement that defines how security will be implemented within a particular organization. It describes the means the organization will take to protect the confidentiality, availability, and integrity of sensitive data and resources, including the network infrastructure, physical and electronic data, applications, and the physical environment. It often consists of multiple individual policies. All implemented security measures should conform to the stated policy.

Develetech Industries has a password policy that is required for all employees. Each employee is responsible for using strong passwords and protecting those passwords accordingly. The password policy contains guidelines for strong passwords to use and weak passwords to avoid.

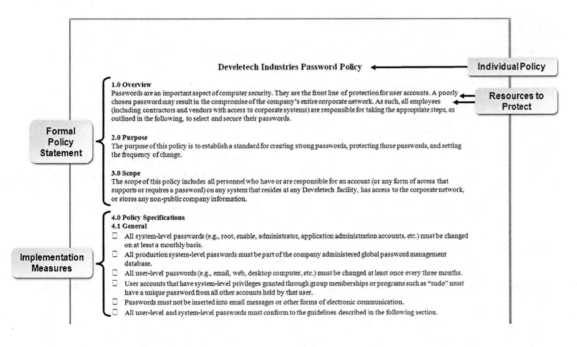

Figure 1-40: A security policy.

A good security policy provides functions similar to a government's foreign policy. The policy is determined by the needs of the organization. Just as a nation needs a foreign policy in part because of real and perceived threats from other countries, organizations also need policies to protect their data and resources. A nation's foreign policy defines what the threats are and how the government will handle those threats. A security policy does the same for an organization; it defines threats to its resources and how those threats will be handled. A policy forms the plan that ties everything together. Without a formal policy, you can only react to threats instead of anticipating them and preparing accordingly.

Need to Know

A security policy should specify who should have access to privileged information and on what basis. Employees should only be able to access sensitive information if it is essential for their jobs.

Security Policy Components

Each subsection of a security policy typically consists of several standard components.

Policy Component	Description
Policy statement	Outlines the plan for the individual security component.
Standards	Define how to measure the level of adherence to the policy.
Guidelines	Suggestions, recommendations, or best practices for how to meet the policy standard.
Procedures	Step-by-step instructions that detail how to implement components of the policy.

Common Security Policy Types

There are several common security policy types that are included in most corporate security policies.

Policy Type	Description
Acceptable use policy (AUP)	States the limits and guidelines that are set for users and others to make use of an organization's physical and intellectual resources. The policy should define what use of organizational assets, such as computers and telecommunications equipment, will be considered acceptable and what will be considered in violation. Acceptable use guidelines must be reasonable and not interfere with employees' fundamental job duties or human rights.
Privacy policy	Defines standards for divulging organizational or personal information to other parties. The policy should specify to what extent organizational information as well as users' personal information will be kept private, and the consequences of violations of privacy. Users should also understand which of their workplace actions and communications are not considered private.
Audit policy	Details the requirements and parameters for risk assessment and audits of the organization's information and resources.
Extranet policy	Sets the requirements for third-party entities that desire access to an organization's networks.
Password policy	Defines standards for creating password complexity. It also defines what an organization considers weak passwords and the guidelines for protecting password safety.
Wireless standards policy	Defines which wireless devices can connect to an organization's network and how to use them in a safe manner that protects the organization's security.

Policy Type	Description
Social media policy	Defines how the organization and its employees use social media such as blogs, Facebook, Twitter, LinkedIn, and others. Although these media can be an effective tool for sharing information and marketing products and services, they can also adversely affect an organization's reputation. A social media policy can be general, dealing with all forms of online collaboration and sharing, or it can contain individual policies for different types of social media.

Regardless of the type of security policy, you are likely to encounter certain issues, such as separation of duties or roles, job rotation, implicit deny, least privilege, need to know, and so forth.

Security Policy Standards Organizations

The SysAdmin, Audit, Networking and Security (SANS) Institute has identified a list of standard policy types and policy templates, ranging from the acceptable encryption policy to the wireless communication policy. To view the complete list of policies from the SANS Institute, see **www.sans.org/resources/policies/**.

There are other organizations, such as the Internet Engineering Task Force (IETF), that provide templates, such as Request for Comments (RFC) 2196 for different security policies. To view RFC 2196, see **www.cse.ohio-state.edu/cgi-bin/rfc/rfc2196.html**.

The International Organization for Standardization (ISO) has published ISO/IEC 27002:2005, which is a standard for information security. To view information on ISO/IEC 27002:2005, see **www.iso.org**.

Group Policy

Windows security policies are configuration settings within the Microsoft® Windows® operating systems that control the overall security behavior of the system. They are found in a policy object in the **Computer Configuration\Policies\Windows Settings\Security Settings** node. The policies can be set on a centralized basis, through a Group Policy in Windows Server® systems, or in the individual policy objects on each computer.

A *group policy* is a centralized account management feature available for Active Directory® on Windows Server systems. A group policy can be used to control certain desktop workstation features within an enterprise, such as specifying that all workstations display the company logo as their wallpaper, or that the default browser should have pre-loaded settings. It is also used to control security features, such as limiting the desktop icons that get displayed, granting permission to access certain servers but not others, or totally locking down a desktop.

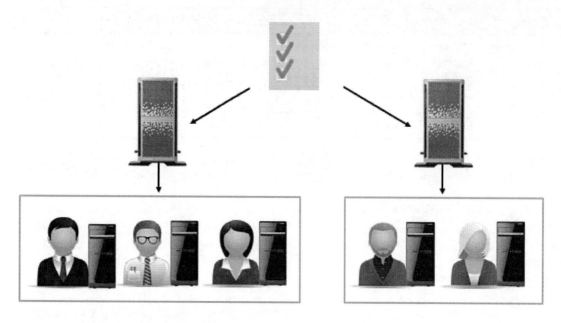

Figure 1–41: A group policy assigned to two distinct sets of users.

Security Document Categories

There are several categories of documents that you will need to securely maintain, so they should be addressed in the security policy.

Security Document	Description
System architecture	Physical documentation about the setup and configuration of your network and systems must be stored securely. Network mapping and diagnostic software, along with the maps and reports that they provide, must also be protected. These can be valuable sources of information for potential attackers.
Change documentation	Changes in the configuration of data, systems, and services are often tracked and documented to provide an official record of the correct current configuration. Changes to documents themselves should be internally noted with the current revision number, the revision date, the revision author, and the contents of each revision.
Logs	System logs, especially those generated by the auditing security function, need to be protected from unauthorized access or tampering. Altering audit or activity logs is one approach attackers might take to cover their tracks following a system breach.
Inventories	Equipment and asset inventories provide a valuable source of information for attackers, whether they plan to mount an electronic attack against the system or resort to physical damage or theft. You should maintain accurate inventories and keep those inventories secure.

Change Management

Change management is a systematic way of approving and executing change in order to assure maximum security, stability, and availability of information technology services. When an organization changes its hardware, software, infrastructure, or documentation, it risks the introduction of unanticipated consequences. Therefore, it is important for an organization to be able to properly assess risk; to quantify the cost of training, support, maintenance, or implementation;

and to properly weigh benefits against the complexity of a proposed change. By maintaining a documented change management procedure, an organization can protect itself from the potential adverse effects of hasty change.

For example, Jane has identified a new service pack that has been released that fixes numerous security vulnerabilities for the operating system on a server. The server that needs this service pack is running a custom in-house application, and significant downtime is not acceptable. The company policy states that a change management form must be approved for all service packs. The form comes back from the approval process with a qualification that the service pack must be tested on a lab system prior to deployment on the production server. Jane applies the service pack in a lab and discovers that it causes the custom in-house application to fail. The application must be sent back to the software developers for testing before the service pack can be applied in production.

Figure 1–42: Change management.

Documentation Handling Measures

Your policy should specify standards and guidelines for the measures you take when handling sensitive documents.

Document Handling Measure	Description
Classification	Many organizations assign classification levels, such as Public, Internal, Confidential, and Restricted, to their official documentation. The classification of a document not only determines who has the right to see or alter the document, but also the correct procedure for storing, archiving, and handling the document. The classification system can also serve as the basis for a MAC access scheme implementation. Employees should be notified as to their security level and should understand the procedures for accessing documents at each level. Also, the classification level should be stated clearly within the document itself.
Retention and storage	Your policy should include standards and guidelines for how long different types of documents are retained to meet legal or policy requirements. You should also have a plan for consistent and secure storage, and retrieval of all document types. Storage recommendations take into account the nature of the information, the physical media on which it is stored, and the security measures for the documents.

Document Handling Measure	Description
Disposal and destruction	There should be a plan for disposal or destruction of outdated documents. Some documents can simply be recycled or thrown away. However, confidential information must have an approved destruction method to ensure that the data cannot be retrieved. The destruction method depends upon the sensitivity of the data and the media it is stored on. It can range from shredding and then burning paper documents, to overwriting the data on a hard drive with pseudorandom numbers.

ACTIVITY 1-5
Examining a Security Policy

Data Files

C:\093022Data\Security Fundamentals\DeveletechPasswordPolicy.rtf

Before You Begin

You have a Windows Server 2012 R2 computer to complete some of the activities in this course.
The computer name is **Server##**, where ## is your unique student number. The server is a domain
controller for domain##.internal.

 Note: Microsoft Windows is the platform used to practice the security concepts presented in
this course. There are also Windows-specific procedures included throughout the course to help
you perform the guided activities. Be aware that there may be other methods for performing the
tasks included in the activities.

Scenario

As the new security administrator for Develetech Industries, you will be responsible for maintaining
and updating the documentation related to security policies, as well as for understanding and
enforcing the policies. Before you can be effective in these new duties, you have decided that you
need to familiarize yourself with the existing policy documents in the organization.

 Note: Activities may vary slightly if the software vendor has issued digital updates. Your
instructor will notify you of any changes.

1. Open the C:\093022Data\Security Fundamentals\DeveletechPasswordPolicy.rtf policy file, and review
   its contents.
   a) Log on to Windows Server 2012 as **DOMAIN##\Administrator** with a password of *!Pass1234*

   b) In the taskbar, select the File Explorer icon [icon] and navigate to **C:\093022Data\Security
      Fundamentals**.
   c) Double-click **DeveletechPasswordPolicy** to open the file in WordPad.

2. What type of policy document is this?
   ○   Acceptable use policy
   ○   Audit policy
   ○   Extranet policy
   ○   Password policy
   ○   Wireless standards policy

3. Which standard policy components are included in this policy? (Select all that apply.)
   ☐   Policy statement
   ☐   Standards
   ☐   Guidelines
   ☐   Procedures

4. How often must system-level administrators change their passwords to conform to this policy?

5. To conform to this policy, how often must regular system users change their passwords?

6. According to this policy, what is the minimum character length for a password, and how should it be constructed?

7. According to this policy, why is "password1" not a good choice for a password?

8. Close the policy file. If necessary, close File Explorer.

Summary

In this lesson, you identified some of the most basic components, goals, and tools involved in securing computers and networks. The information you learned in this lesson will help you communicate effectively with other security professionals you encounter during your career, as well as help you make informed choices as you select, implement, support, and maintain network security measures.

Which of the basic security concepts in this lesson were familiar to you, and which were new?

Can you describe some real-world situations where you used basic security techniques such as authentication, access control, and encryption, or made use of a security policy?

Note: Check your LogicalCHOICE Course screen for opportunities to interact with your classmates, peers, and the larger LogicalCHOICE online community about the topics covered in this course or other topics you are interested in. From the Course screen you can also access available resources for a more continuous learning experience.

2 | Identifying Security Threats and Vulnerabilities

Lesson Time: 2 hours, 30 minutes

Lesson Objectives

In this lesson, you will identify security threats and vulnerabilities. You will:

- Identify social engineering attacks.

- Identify various malware threats.

- Identify software-based threats.

- Identify network-based threats.

- Identify wireless threats and vulnerabilities.

- Identify physical threats and vulnerabilities.

Lesson Introduction

Security is an ongoing process that includes setting up organizational security systems, hardening them, monitoring them, responding to attacks in progress, and deterring attackers. As a security professional, you will be involved in all phases of that process. But, in order for that process to be effective, you need to understand the threats and vulnerabilities you will be protecting your systems against. In this lesson, you will identify the various types of security threats and vulnerabilities that you might encounter.

Unsecured systems can result in compromised data and, ultimately, lost revenue. But you cannot protect your systems from threats you do not understand. Once you understand the types of possible threats and identify individuals who will try to use them against your network, you can take the appropriate steps to protect your systems and keep your resources and revenue safe from potential attacks.

TOPIC A

Social Engineering

When you think about attacks against information systems, you might think most about protecting the technological components of those systems. But people—the system users—are as much a part of an information system as the technological components; they have their own vulnerabilities, and they can be the first part of the system to succumb to certain types of attacks. In this topic, you will learn to identify social engineering attacks—threats against the human factors in your technology environment.

For technically oriented people, it can be easy to forget that one of the most important components of information systems is the people using those systems. Computers and technology do not exist in a vacuum; their only benefit comes from the way people use them and interact with them. Attackers know this, and so they know that the people in the system may well be the best target for attack. If you want to protect your infrastructure, systems, and data, you need to be able to recognize this kind of attack when it happens.

Social Engineering Attacks

A *social engineering attack* is a type of attack that uses deception and trickery to convince unsuspecting users to provide sensitive data or to violate security guidelines. Social engineering is often a precursor to another type of attack. Because these attacks depend on human factors rather than on technology, their symptoms can be vague and hard to identify. Social engineering attacks can come in a variety of methods: in person, through email, or over the phone.

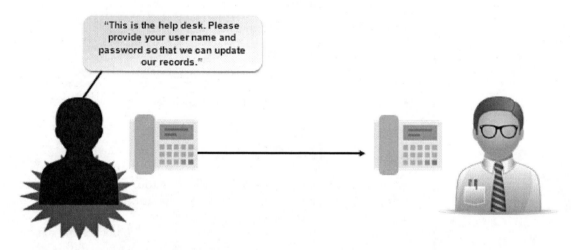

Figure 2–1: A social engineering attack.

Social Engineering Attack Scenarios

These are a few typical social engineering attack scenarios:

- An attacker creates an executable program file (for example, a file with a .vbs or .exe file extension) that prompts a network user for their user name and password, and then records whatever the user inputs. The attacker then emails the executable file to the user with the story that the user must double-click the file and log on to the network again to clear up some logon problems the organization has been experiencing that morning. After the user complies, the attacker now has access to their credentials.

- An attacker contacts the help desk pretending to be a remote sales representative who needs assistance setting up his dial-in access. Through a series of phone calls, the attacker obtains the phone number for remote access and the phone number for accessing the organization's private phone and voice-mail system.

- An attacker sends an executable file disguised as an electronic greeting card (e-card) or as a patch for an operating system or a specific application. The unsuspecting user launches the executable, which might install email spamming software or a keylogging program, or turn the computer into a remote "zombie" for the hacker.

Social Engineering Targets

Social engineering typically takes advantage of users who are not technically knowledgeable, but it can also be directed against technical support staff if the attacker pretends to be a user who needs help.

 Note: For additional information, check out the LearnTO **Recognize Social Engineering Attacks** presentation from the **LearnTO** tile on the LogicalCHOICE Course screen.

Effectiveness

Social engineering is one of the most common and successful malicious techniques in information security. Because it exploits basic human trust, social engineering has proven to be a particularly effective way of manipulating people into misplacing this trust. A social engineer may pose as an authority figure, like a manager or IT administrator, or someone the user is familiar with, like a friend or family member. If the facade is believable enough, the victim will likely let their guard down.

Social engineers also find success in exploiting common human thought processes and behavior. If an attacker convinces a user that they need to log in and fix their account immediately or something bad will happen, the user may panic and fail to exercise critical thinking. Likewise, a social engineer may be able to take advantage of the human tendency to want to belong to groups and defer actions to the wisdom of crowds. For instance, an attacker may be able to fool a user into believing that a malicious website is actually legitimate by posting numerous fake reviews and testimonials praising the site. The victim, believing many different people have judged the site acceptable, takes this as evidence of the site's legitimacy and places their trust in it.

With the rise of personal computing and the Internet, more and more sensitive information is made vulnerable to falling into the wrong hands. Whether it's a bank account that lets a user access their entire finances remotely and instantly, or an intra-organization network that allows users to view confidential information, almost every system can be breached by technological con artists who have tricked the right people. What's more, these attackers can cause a great deal of damage to privacy, property, and finances.

One particular hurdle security professionals find difficult to overcome is strengthening the human element of security. It's relatively straightforward to implement security in software and hardware; you put a control in place to block unwanted access, or you implement a defense to stop a direct attack from breaching your system. However, because social engineering is indirect and deceptive, all it takes is one careless or technologically inexperienced user to compromise your entire operation. Because few organizations properly equip their employees with the knowledge to recognize social engineering attempts, attackers who prey upon human weaknesses are a danger to every information system.

Types of Social Engineering

There are various types of social engineering attacks.

Social Engineering Type	Description
Spoofing	This is a human-based or software-based attack where the goal is to pretend to be someone else for the purpose of identity concealment. Spoofing can occur in Internet Protocol (IP) addresses, network adapter hardware (Media Access Control [MAC]) addresses, and email. If employed in email, various email message headers are changed to conceal the originator's identity.
Impersonation	This is a human-based attack where an attacker pretends to be someone they are not. A common scenario is when the attacker calls an employee and pretends to be calling from the help desk. The attacker tells the employee he is reprogramming the order-entry database, and he needs the employee's user name and password to make sure it gets entered into the new system.
	Impersonation is often successful in situations where identity cannot be easily established. If the employee in the previous example doesn't know the real help desk worker or the help desk number, they may be less inclined to question the request.
Hoax	This is an email-based or web-based attack that is intended to trick the user into performing undesired actions, such as deleting important system files in an attempt to remove a virus. It could also be a scam to convince users to give up important information or money for an interesting offer.
	Like many social engineering techniques, hoaxes depend greatly on the amount of experience the target has with computer technology. An email that tells a user to delete a virus file on their computer will likely be ineffective if the user knows what the file does, or if they know that antivirus software is the preferred method for detecting and removing infected files.
Phishing	This is a common type of email-based social engineering attack. In a phishing attack, the attacker sends an email that seems to come from a respected bank or other financial institution. The email claims that the recipient needs to provide an account number, Social Security number, or other private information to the sender in order to "verify an account." Ironically, the phishing attack often claims that the "account verification" is necessary for security reasons. Individuals should never provide personal financial information to someone who requests it, whether through email or over the phone. Legitimate financial institutions never solicit this information from their clients. When attackers target a specific individual or institution, this social engineering technique is known as *spear phishing*. An attack similar to phishing, called *pharming*, can be done by redirecting a request for a website, typically an e-commerce site, to a similar-looking, but fake, website.
	Both phishing and pharming are some of the most prominent forms of social engineering, and even experienced computer users may be fooled by what appears to be an authority figure.
Vishing	This is a human-based attack where the goal is to extract personal, financial, or confidential information from the victim by using services such as the telephone system and IP-based voice messaging services (*Voice over Internet Protocol [VoIP]*) as the communication medium. This is also called voice phishing.
	Vishing can be more effective than phishing because of the trust that people tend to place in others they can speak to in real time. In addition, users may be too used to traditional telecommunications to know that VoIP identity can be much more easily spoofed due to the open nature of the Internet.

Social Engineering Type	Description
Whaling	This is a form of spear phishing that targets individuals or organizations that are known to possess a good deal of wealth. Whaling targets individuals who work in Fortune 500 companies or financial institutions whose salaries are expected to be high. Whaling is a riskier method for social engineers, as security is bound to be more robust than it is with average users or small companies, and the consequences of being caught will likely be much more severe. However, exploiting the weakest link can result in a huge payoff for the attacker(s).
URL hijacking	Also called *typo squatting*, this is the tactic of exploiting typos that users sometimes make when entering a URL into a browser. For example, a malicious user might register a domain with the URL www.comtpia.org, which has a minor typo compared to the correct www.comptia.org. A user who makes this mistake when entering the URL into their browser will be directed to the attacker's site, which may mimic the real website or contain malicious software that will infect the victim's computer.
Spam and *spim*	Spam is an email-based threat where the user's inbox is flooded with emails which act as vehicles that carry advertising material for products or promotions for get-rich-quick schemes and can sometimes deliver viruses or *malware*. Spam can also be utilized within social networking sites such as Facebook and Twitter. Spim is an attack similar to spam that is propagated through *instant messaging (IM)* instead of through email. With the prevalence of spam filters in email clients and spim blockers in instant messaging services, these techniques are less effective than they used to be. However, the sheer volume of unsolicited messages sent in bulk every day keeps spam and spim viable methods for deceiving inexperienced users.
Shoulder surfing	This is an attack where the goal is to look over the shoulder of an individual as he or she enters password information or a PIN. This is very easy to do today with camera-equipped mobile phones.
Dumpster diving	This is an attack where the goal is to reclaim important information by inspecting the contents of trash containers. This is especially effective in the first few weeks of the year as users discard old calendars with passwords written in them.
Tailgating	Also known as piggy backing, this is a human-based attack where the attacker will slip in through a secure area following a legitimate employee. The only way to prevent this type of attack is by installing a good access control mechanism and to educate users not to admit unauthorized personnel.

VoIP

VoIP is a technology that enables you to deliver telephony information over IP networks. The voice information that is sent over the IP network is in digital form in packets, as compared to the implementation on the Public Switched Telephone Network (PSTN) which includes circuit-committed protocols.

Hackers and Attackers

Hackers and *attackers* are related terms for individuals who have the skills to gain access to computer systems through unauthorized or unapproved means. Originally, hacker was a neutral term for a user who excelled at computer programming and computer system administration. Hacking into a system was a sign of technical skill and creativity that gradually became associated with illegal or malicious system intrusions. Attacker is a term that always represents a malicious system intruder.

> **Note:** The term *cracker* refers to an individual who breaks encryption codes, defeats software copy protections, or specializes in breaking into systems. The term "cracker" is sometimes used to refer to a hacker or attacker.

White Hats and Black Hats

A *white hat* is a hacker who discovers and exposes security flaws in applications and operating systems so that manufacturers can fix them before they become widespread problems. The white hat often does this on a professional basis, working for a security organization or a system manufacturer. This is sometimes called an ethical hack.

A *black hat* is a hacker who discovers and exposes security vulnerabilities for financial gain or for some malicious purpose. While the black hats might not break directly into systems the way attackers do, widely publicizing security flaws can potentially cause financial or other damage to an organization.

Some who consider themselves white hats also discover and publicize security problems, but without the organization's knowledge or permission. They consider themselves to be acting for the common good. These hackers are commonly referred to as *grey hats* because of their moral ambiguity. In this case, the only distinction between a grey hat and a black hat is one of intent. There is some debate over whether this kind of unauthorized revelation of security issues really serves the public good or simply provides an avenue of attack.

White hats and black hats get their names from characters in old Western movies: the good guys always wore white hats, while the bad guys wore black hats.

Categories of Attackers

Attackers have many different motivations, and recognizing some of the different types may help you detect and deter attacks.

> **Note:** There are many ways to categorize attackers, and sometimes there is no firm distinction between one type and another. The important thing to realize is that attacks can come from many sources, and that the motivations and goals for the attacks might be highly subjective, and not necessarily seem reasonable or logical to a rational observer.

Attacker Category	Motivations and Goals
Malicious insider (employees and contractors)	A *malicious insider threat* is a threat originating from an employee in an organization who performs malicious acts, such as deleting critical information or sharing this critical information with outsiders, which may result in a certain amount of losses to the organization. Internal attackers might be fueled by some kind of resentment against the organization, in which case their goal might be to get revenge by simply causing damage or disrupting systems. Or, they might be motivated by financial gain if they want to obtain and sell confidential information to competitors or third parties.
Electronic activist ("*hacktivist*")	The hacktivist is motivated by a desire to cause social change, and might be trying to get media attention by disrupting services, or promoting a message by replacing the information on public websites. The hacktivist also might want to cause damage to organizations that are deemed socially irresponsible or unworthy.

Attacker Category	Motivations and Goals
Data thief	This kind of attacker blatantly steals resources or confidential information for personal or financial gain. They are likely to try to cover their tracks so their attacks are not detected and stopped. Usually in data theft, the attacker exploits unauthorized access or acts in collusion with a disgruntled employee.
Script kiddie	The novice attacker, known as a script kiddie, has limited technical knowledge and is motivated by a desire to gain and display technical skills. The script kiddie will use simple means, such as virus code samples or automated attack tools available on the Internet, to mount attacks that might have no specific target or any reasonable goal other than gaining attention or proving technical abilities. The tools are often known as script kiddie tools and are often used by security professionals for testing.
Electronic vandal	This attacker simply wants to cause as much damage as possible, without any particular target or goal. The motivation might be for fun, or to gain attention or admiration, or stem from some type of social or personal resentment against a person or institution.
Cyberterrorist	This type of attacker tries to disrupt computer systems in an attempt to spread fear and panic. Just as the definition of terrorism is controversial, there is disagreement as to whether or not attacks on computer systems should be considered cyberterrorism if they do not cause physical harm or damage to infrastructure.

ACTIVITY 2-1
Identifying Social Engineering Attacks

Scenario

Develetech's IT department wants to know when they are being attacked and what type of attacks are occurring. As the new security administrator, you will be responsible for determining which events are true social engineering attacks and which are false alarms. The company's upper management is concerned about these false alarms and has tightened security too much in response, and they want to make sure they know the difference between attacks and normal activity. They do not want customers or users to be halted in their tracks when they are performing normal tasks with no malicious intent. They have asked you to analyze a list of recent network interactions and classify them as true social engineering attacks or as false alarms.

1. Social engineering attempt or false alarm? A supposed customer calls the help desk and states that she cannot connect to the e-commerce website to check her order status. She would also like a user name and password. The user gives a valid customer company name, but is not listed as a contact in the customer database. The user does not know the correct company code or customer ID.

   ☑ Social engineering attempt

   ☐ False alarm

2. Social engineering attempt or false alarm? The VP of sales is in the middle of a presentation to a group of key customers and accidentally logs off. She urgently needs to continue with the presentation, but forgets her password. You recognize her voice on the line, but she is supposed to have her boss make the request according to the company password security policy.

   ☐ Social engineering attempt

   ☑ False alarm

3. Social engineering attempt or false alarm? A new accountant was hired and would like to know if he can have the installation source files for the accounting software package, so that he can install it on his computer himself and start work immediately. Last year, someone internal compromised company accounting records, so distribution of the accounting application is tightly controlled. You have received all the proper documentation for the request from his supervisor and there is an available license for the software. However, general IT policies state that the IT department must perform all software installations and upgrades.

   ☐ Social engineering attempt

   ☑ False alarm

4. Social engineering attempt or false alarm? Christine receives an instant message asking for her account name and password. The person sending the message says that the request is from the IT department, because they need to do a backup of Christine's local hard drive.

   ☑ Social engineering attempt

   ☐ False alarm

5. Social engineering attempt or false alarm? Rachel gets an email with an attachment that is named NewVirusDefinitions.vbs. The name in the email is the same as the IT software manager, but the email address is from an account outside the company.

   ☑ Social engineering attempt

   ☐ False alarm

6. Social engineering attempt or false alarm? A user calls the help desk stating that he is a phone technician needing the password to configure the phone and voice-mail system.
   - ☑ Social engineering attempt
   - ☐ False alarm

7. Social engineering attempt or false alarm? A vendor team requests access to the building to fix an urgent problem with a piece of equipment. Although the team has no work order and the security guard was not notified of the visit, the team members are wearing shirts and hats from the preferred vendor.
   - ☑ Social engineering attempt
   - ☐ False alarm

8. Social engineering attempt or false alarm? The CEO of Develetech needs to get access to market research data immediately. You definitely recognize her voice, but a proper request form has not been filled out to modify the permissions. She states that normally she would fill out the form and should not be an exception, but she urgently needs the data.
   - ☐ Social engineering attempt
   - ☑ False alarm

9. Social engineering attempt or false alarm? A purchasing manager is browsing a list of products on a vendor's website when a window opens claiming that software has detected several thousand files on his computer that are infected with viruses. Instructions in the official-looking window indicate the user should click a link to install software that will remove these infections.
   - ☑ Social engineering attempt
   - ☐ False alarm

TOPIC B

Malware

One of the most prevalent threats to computers today is malicious code. As a security professional, or even as a regular computer user, you will likely have experience in dealing with unwanted software infecting your systems. Malware is insidious and difficult to remove, so it can cause a significant amount of damage in many different ways.

Malware is not a monolithic threat, but rather a collection of different methods that can exploit the vulnerabilities in your information security. By identifying the various types of malware and how they operate, you will be better prepared to fight their infection, or better yet, prevent them from infecting your systems in the first place.

Malicious Code Attacks

A *malicious code attack* is a type of software attack where an attacker inserts some type of undesired or unauthorized software, or malware, into a target system. In the past, many malicious code attacks were intended to disrupt or disable an operating system or an application, or force the target system to disrupt or disable other systems. More recent malicious code attacks attempt to remain hidden on the target system, utilizing available resources to the attacker's advantage.

Potential uses of malicious code include launching Denial of Service attacks on other systems; hosting illicit or illegal data; skimming personal or business information for the purposes of identity theft, profit, or extortion; or displaying unsolicited advertisements.

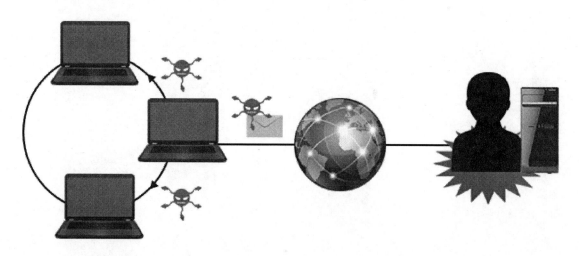

Figure 2–2: A virus spreading to multiple computers is one example of a malicious code attack.

Evidence of a Malicious Code Attack

Malicious code is often combined with social engineering to convince a user that the malware is from a trusted or benign source. Typically, you will see the results of malicious code in corrupted applications, data files, and system files; unsolicited pop-up advertisements; counterfeit virus scan or software update notifications; or reduced system performance or increased network traffic. Any of these could result in malfunctioning applications and operating systems.

Viruses

A *virus* is a piece of code that spreads from one computer to another by attaching itself to other files through a process of self-replication. The code in a virus executes when the file it is attached to is opened. Frequently, viruses are intended to enable further attacks, send data back to the attacker, or even corrupt or destroy data. Because of their self-replicating nature, viruses are difficult to completely remove from a system, and account for billions of dollars of damage every year.

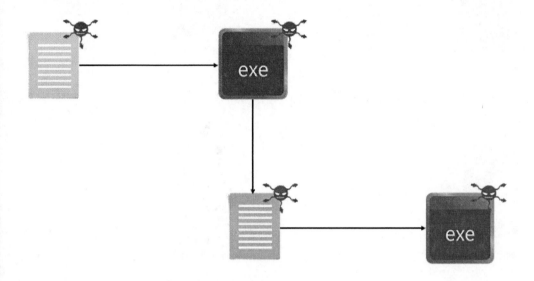

Figure 2-3: A virus replicating itself and attaching to other files across a system.

Worms

In computing, a *worm* is malware that, like a virus, replicates itself across the infected system. However, unlike a virus, it does not attach itself to other programs or files. While viruses tend to interfere with the functions of a specific machine, worms are often intended to interrupt network capabilities. A worm need not carry any sort of malicious payload at all—its primary function is usually just to spread. The act of spreading to enough systems may cripple network bandwidth. Worms that do carry payloads often turn computers into remote zombies that an attacker can use to launch other attacks from.

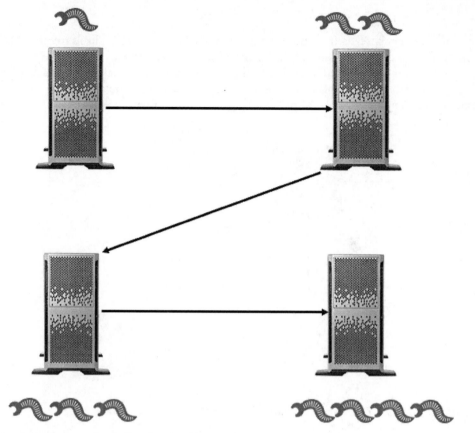

Figure 2–4: A worm replicating itself across servers in a network.

Adware

Adware is software that automatically displays or downloads unsolicited advertisements when it is used. Adware often appears on a user's computer as a browser pop-up. While not all adware is overtly malicious, many adware programs have been associated with spyware and other types of malicious software. Also, it can reduce user productivity by slowing down systems and simply by being an annoyance.

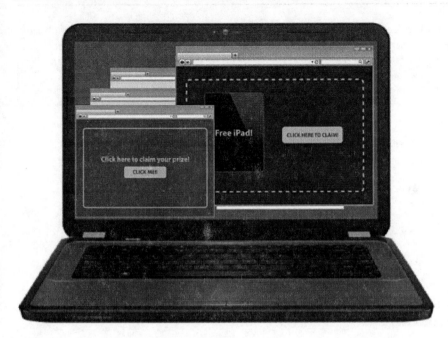

Figure 2-5: Multiple pop-up windows displayed on a computer infected with adware.

Spyware

Spyware is surreptitiously installed malicious software that is intended to track and report the usage of a target system, or collect other data the author wishes to obtain. Data collected can include web browsing history, personal information, banking and other financial information, and user names and passwords. Although it can infect a computer through social engineering tactics, some spyware is included with otherwise legitimate software.

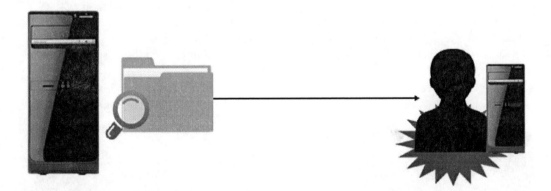

Figure 2-6: An attacker using spyware to read information stored on a target computer.

Note: Adware and spyware are designed to have little to no effect on performance so that they are more difficult to detect. However, victims who are exposed to this type of malware are often infected multiple times, and the effect eventually becomes noticeable.

Trojan Horses

A *Trojan horse*, often simply called a Trojan, is hidden malware that causes damage to a system or gives an attacker a platform for monitoring and/or controlling a system. Unlike viruses, Trojans do not replicate themselves, nor do they attach to other files. Instead, they are often more insidious and remain undetected much more easily. Trojans are usually propagated by social engineering, such as when a user downloads an email attachment that claims to be benign, but is actually malignant.

Note: Trojan horse malware is named after the wooden horse used to trick the forces of Troy in ancient Greek mythology into unwittingly accepting a gift that turned out to be a serious threat.

	To...	☐ troy@apolloartsupplies.example
Send	Cc...	
	Subject	**Speed up your computer with Odysseus!!!**
	Attached	📄 odysseus.exe (3 MB)

Dear Friend,

Tired of slo computer?? Downloiad Odysseus 4 Blazing Speeds!
Waste no time act now!!!1

Regards,
AchaeanSoft Admin

Figure 2-7: An email message meant to trick a user into downloading a Trojan to their computer.

Rootkits

A *rootkit* is code that is intended to take full or partial control of a system at the lowest levels. Rootkits often attempt to hide themselves from monitoring or detection, and modify low-level system files when integrating themselves into a system. Rootkits can be used for non-malicious purposes such as virtualization; however, most rootkit infections install backdoors, spyware, or other malicious code once they have control of the target system.

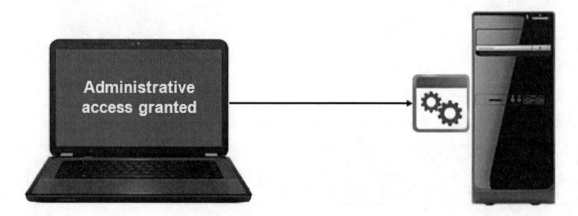

Figure 2-8: An attacker gaining administrative access to a computer infected with a rootkit.

Logic Bombs

A *logic bomb* is a piece of code that sits dormant on a target computer until it is triggered by a specific event, such as a specific date. Once the code is triggered, the logic bomb detonates, and performs whatever actions it was programmed to do. Often, this includes erasing and corrupting data on the target system.

Figure 2-9: A logic bomb set to destroy a computer's data at midnight.

Botnets

A *botnet* is a set of computers that has been infected by a control program called a bot that enables attackers to collectively exploit those computers to mount attacks. Typically, black hats use botnets to coordinate denial of service attacks, send spam email, and mine for personal information or passwords. Users of these infected machines (called *zombies* or *drones*) are often unaware that their computers are being used for nefarious purposes.

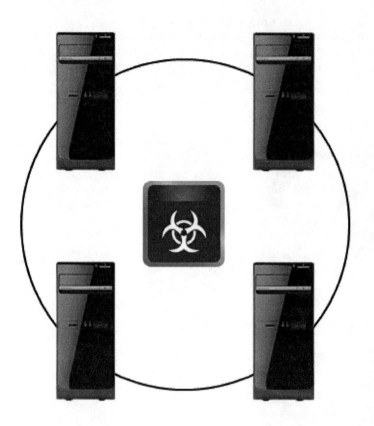

Figure 2-10: A bot that has turned networked computers into zombies.

Ransomware

Ransomware is an increasingly popular variety of malware in which an attacker infects a victim's computer with code that restricts the victim's access to their computer or the data on it. Then, the attacker demands a ransom be paid, usually through an online payment service like PayPal or Green Dot MoneyPak, under threat of keeping the restriction or destroying the information they have locked down. Ransomware is most damaging when it exploits the power of encryption to essentially render data that isn't backed up worthless, which makes victims more likely to pay the ransom to get their files unencrypted. The amount of ransomware has more than doubled from 2012 to 2013 (McAfee® Labs Threats Report: Third Quarter 2013: **http://www.mcafee.com/us/resources/ reports/rp-quarterly-threat-q3-2013.pdf**).

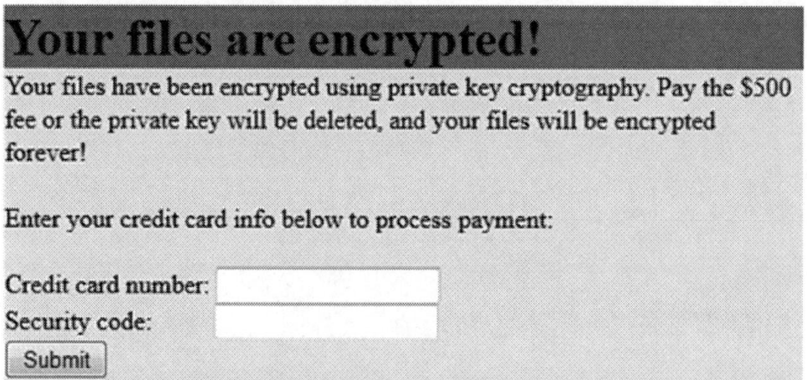

Your files are encrypted!

Your files have been encrypted using private key cryptography. Pay the $500 fee or the private key will be deleted, and your files will be encrypted forever!

Enter your credit card info below to process payment:

Credit card number: _____
Security code: _____

[Submit]

Figure 2-11: An attempt to extort money from a victim by holding their data hostage.

Examples of Ransomware

One example of ransomware is Reveton, which spread in 2012. Once it had infected a computer, Reveton's payload would open windows on the target's computer that claimed the target had committed various computer crimes, such as downloading pirated software. The payload gave the illusion of legitimacy by restricting access to other processes and presenting various law enforcement logos. The attackers demanded extortion money through anonymous paying services in exchange for unlocking the target's computer.

Another, more harmful instance of ransomware is CryptoLocker, which emerged in 2013. Once CryptoLocker infected a system, it would begin encrypting every storage device attached to that system. The malware would then display a message on the target's computer demanding payment in exchange for the private encryption key kept on the attackers' servers. If the ransom was not paid within the time frame, the attackers claimed they would destroy the private key. Because of the strong encryption used, doing this meant that recovering the encrypted data would be impossible with current technology.

Polymorphic Malware

To make them more difficult to detect, attackers began encrypting viruses so that they would infect files with an encrypted copy of themselves. The cryptographic key and a decryption module would be included with the virus and stored in plaintext. The antivirus scanner would then need to detect the virus indirectly through the decryption module. *Polymorphic malware* uses this same virus encryption, only the decryption module is altered each time the virus infects a file. This makes it very difficult for antivirus software to detect an infection that is constantly changing.

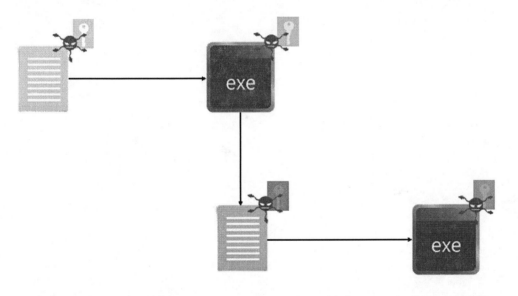

Figure 2–12: A virus changing its decryption module each time it spreads to a new file.

Armored Viruses

The defining quality of *armored viruses* is that they attempt to trick or shield themselves from antivirus software and security professionals. To fool antivirus software, an armored virus is able to obscure its true location in a system and lead the software to believe that it resides elsewhere. This prevents the antivirus software from accurately detecting and removing the infection. Likewise, armored viruses often contain obfuscated code to make it more difficult for security researchers to properly assess and reverse engineer them.

Figure 2–13: An antivirus scanner tricked into believing it has found the true location of a virus.

ACTIVITY 2-2
Identifying Types of Malware

Scenario
As a security professional, one of your responsibilities is to test how resilient the computers you provide to your employees are to malicious software attacks. Your main focus is to determine just what threat different types of malware pose to your employees' data and the computers themselves. In addition, you want to test your own knowledge of malware so that you'll be ready to respond to any such attack when it happens. Consider the following scenarios and identify what kind of malware is infecting your systems.

1. While using your computer, an app window displays on your screen and demands that you pay a fine or be reported to the authorities. You try closing the window, but you're unable to. The other processes on your computer seem to be unavailable, so you try rebooting your machine. When your computer loads, the app window demanding payment pops back up and essentially locks you out of your computer's functions. What type of malware has infected your computer?

   ○ Trojan horse

   ◉ Ransomware

   ○ Adware

   ○ Botnet

2. Checking your email over a period of a week, you notice something unusual: the spam messages that you've been receiving all seem to be trying to sell you something closely related to the websites you happened to visit that day. For example, on Monday you visited a subscription news site, and later that day you noticed a spam email that solicited a subscription to that very news site. On Tuesday, you browsed to an online retailer in order to buy a birthday gift for your friend. The same gift you were looking at showed up in another spam email later that night. What type of malware has infected your computer?

   ○ Adware

   ◉ Spyware

   ○ Ransomware

   ○ Logic bomb

3. You open up your favorite word processing app. As it opens, a window pops up informing you that an important file has just been deleted. You close the word processing app and open up a spreadsheet app. The same thing happens—another file is deleted. The problem continues to spread as you open up several more apps and each time, a file is deleted. What type of malware has infected your system?

   ○ Botnet

   ○ Spyware

   ○ Adware

   ◉ Virus

4. Early in the day, someone claiming to be a coworker sends you an email with an attachment. The sender indicates the attachment is an updated spreadsheet, so you download it. You don't open the file right away, but instead go on to do other work. Not long after, you find that your computer is running unusually slow. Restarting doesn't seem to fix the problem, as your computer slows down so much that any apps you try to use begin locking up and crashing. Realizing that you may have been a victim of social engineering, you delete the supposed spreadsheet from your computer. Doing so eventually stabilizes your machine. What type of malware had infected your computer?

- ● Trojan horse
- ○ Virus
- ○ Botnet
- ○ Spyware

5. What primary characteristic do polymorphic and armored viruses share?

- ○ Smaller file size than typical viruses
- ● Harder to detect than typical viruses
- ○ More destructive than typical viruses
- ○ Spread faster than typical viruses

TOPIC C

Software-Based Threats

You have learned about attacks against the human component of information systems, as well as the danger of malicious code, but there are many other types of security threats that can be aimed directly against the software elements of the system. In this topic, you will identify the types of attacks that target your operating systems and other software.

A software attack against the computers in your organization can severely cripple your company's operations, and part of your job as a security professional is to prevent that. But, as you know, you cannot protect against what you cannot recognize. This topic will help you identify the software attacks that you will need to be on guard against.

Software Attacks

A *software attack* is any attack against software resources, including operating systems, applications, protocols, and files. The goal of a software attack is to disrupt or disable the software running on the target system, or to somehow exploit the target system to gain access to the target system, to other systems, or to a network. Many software attacks are designed to surreptitiously gain control of a computer so that the attacker can use that computer in the future, often for profit or further malicious activity.

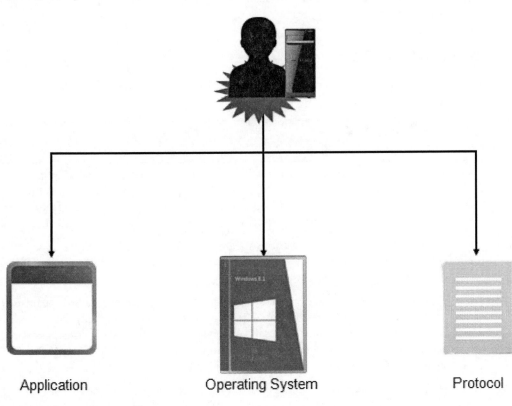

Application   Operating System   Protocol

Figure 2-14: A software attack.

Software Attack Combinations

A software attack might be used by itself or in combination with another type of attack, such as a social engineering attack.

Password Attacks

A *password attack* is any type of attack in which the attacker attempts to obtain and make use of passwords illegitimately. The attacker can guess or steal passwords, or crack encrypted password files. A password attack can show up in audit logs as repeatedly failed logons and then a successful logon, or as several successful logon attempts at unusual times or locations.

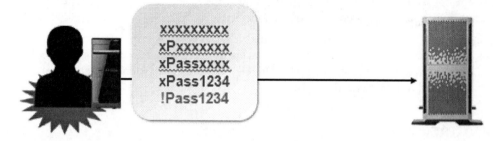

Figure 2-15: A password attack.

Protecting Password Databases

Attackers know the storage locations of encrypted passwords on common systems, such as the Security Accounts Manager (SAM) database on standalone Windows® systems. Password-cracking tools take advantage of known weaknesses in the security of these password databases, so security might need to be increased.

Types of Password Attacks

The following table describes the different types of password attacks that attackers use to crack passwords.

Password Attack Type	Description
Guessing	The simplest type of password attack is making individual, repeated attempts to guess a password by entering different common password values, such as the user's name, spouse's name, or a significant date. Most systems have a feature that will lock out an account after a specified number of incorrect password attempts.
Stealing	Passwords can be stolen by various means, including sniffing network communications, reading handwritten password notes, or observing a user in the act of entering a password.
Dictionary attack	This attack type automates password guessing by comparing passwords against a predetermined list of possible password values, like words in a dictionary. Dictionary attacks are only successful against fairly simple and obvious passwords, because they rely on a dictionary of common words and predictable variations, such as adding a single digit to the end of a word.
Brute force attack	In this attack method, the attacker uses password-cracking software to attempt every possible alphanumeric password combination. Brute force attacks are heavily constrained by time and computing resources, and are therefore most effective at cracking short passwords. However, brute force attacks that are distributed across multiple hardware components, like a cluster of high-end graphics cards, can be very successful at cracking longer passwords.

Password Attack Type	Description
Rainbow tables	These are sets of related plaintext passwords and their hashes. The underlying principle of rainbow tables is to do the central processing unit (CPU)-intensive work of generating hashes in advance, trading time saved during the attack for the disk space to store the tables. Beginning with a base word such as "password" the table then progresses through a large number of possible variations on that root word, such as "passw0rd" or "p@ssw0rd." Rainbow table attacks are executed by comparing the target password hash to the password hashes stored in the tables, then working backward in an attempt to determine the actual password from the known hash.
Hybrid password attack	This attack type utilizes multiple attack methods, including dictionary, rainbow table, and brute force attacks when trying to crack a password.
Birthday attack	This attack type exploits weaknesses in the mathematical algorithms used to generate hashes. This type of attack takes advantage of the probability of different inputs producing the same encrypted outputs, given a large enough set of inputs.
	It is named after the surprising statistical fact that there is a 50 percent chance that two people in a group of 23 will share a birthday.

Password-Cracking Utilities

Commonly available password-cracking utilities include Ophcrack, L0phtCrack, John the Ripper, Cain & Abel, THC Hydra, RainbowCrack, Aircrack, Airsnort, Pwdump, KerbCrack, and Brutus.

Backdoor Attacks

A *backdoor attack* is a type of software attack where an attacker creates a software mechanism called a *backdoor* to gain access to a computer. The backdoor can be a software utility or an illegitimate user account. Typically, a backdoor is delivered through use of a Trojan horse or other malware. Backdoor software typically listens for commands from the attacker on an open port. The backdoor mechanism often survives even after the initial intrusion has been discovered and resolved. Backdoor attacks can be difficult to spot because they may not leave any obvious evidence behind.

Backdoor
Account

Figure 2-16: A backdoor attack.

Takeover Attacks

Backdoor attacks can be the first step in a *takeover attack*, in which an attacker assumes complete control over a system. A takeover attack will manifest itself in the loss of local control over the system under attack. Other attack methods are often used as first steps in a system takeover.

Application Attacks

Application attacks are software attacks that are targeted at web-based and other client-server applications. They can threaten application and web servers, users, other back-end systems, and the application code itself. These attacks can lead to an authentication breach, customer impersonation, information disclosure, *source code* disclosure or tampering, and further network breaches. Application attacks that specifically exploit the trust between a user and a server are called *client-side attacks*.

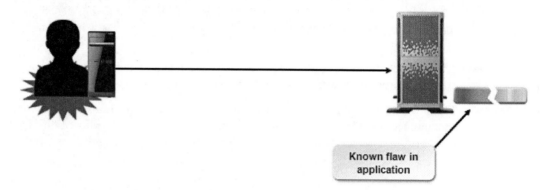

Figure 2–17: An application attack.

Types of Application Attacks

The following table describes the various types of application attacks that systems are vulnerable to.

Application Attack	Description
Cross-site scripting (XSS)	An attack that is directed toward sites with dynamic content. This is done by introducing malicious scripts into a trusted website. Since the website is trusted, the victim's browser grants the script the same permissions as the rest of site, and its malicious code is able to run. Similarly, in a *watering hole attack*, an attacker targets specific groups or organizations, discovers which websites they frequent, and injects malicious code into those sites. Soon after, at least one member of the group or organization is infected, which could compromise the entire group itself.

Application Attack	Description
Command injection attacks	Command injection attacks include several types: • *SQL injection* is an attack that injects a *Structured Query Language (SQL)* query into the input data intended for the server by accessing the client side of the application. The query typically exploits and reads data in the database, modifies data in the database, or executes administrative operations such as shutting down or recovering content off the database. It can also affect the operating system of the SQL server. • *LDAP injection* is an attack that targets web-based applications by fabricating Lightweight Directory Access Protocol (LDAP) statements that typically are created from user input. A system is vulnerable to this attack when the application fails to filter user input properly. • An *XML injection* is an attack that injects corrupted *eXtensible Markup Language (XML)* query data so that an attacker can gain access to the XML data structure and input malicious code or read private data stored on a server. • *Directory traversal* is an attack that allows access to commands, files, and directories that may or may not be connected to the web document root directory. It usually affects the Hypertext Transfer Protocol (HTTP)-based interface.
Zero day exploit	An attack that occurs when the security level of a system is at its lowest, immediately after the discovery of a vulnerability. These attacks are very effective against relatively secure networks because they are difficult to detect even after the attacks are launched.
Cookie manipulation	An attack where an attacker injects a meta tag in an HTTP header, making it possible to modify a *cookie* stored in a browser. This is often done to impersonate a genuine user or authenticate an attacker to gain access to a website fraudulently.
Locally shared object (LSO) attacks	Also called *Flash cookies*, LSOs are data that is stored on a user's computer by websites that use Adobe® Flash Player. A site may be able to track a user's browsing behavior through LSOs, causing a breach of privacy. Even if a user wipes tracking objects from their browser, LSOs may still remain on their system.
Attachment attack	An attack where the attacker can merge malicious software or code into a downloadable file or attachment on a web server so that users download and execute it on client systems.
Malicious add-on	An add-on that is meant to look like a normal add-on, except that when a user installs it, malicious content will be injected to target the security loopholes that are present in a web browser.
Header manipulation	An attack where the attacker manipulates the header information passed between the web servers and clients in HTTP requests. An attacker will either write their own code for this request or go through a free proxy which allows modification to any data request from a browser.
Buffer overflow	An attack in which data goes past the boundary of the destination buffer and begins to corrupt adjacent memory. This causes an app to crash or reboot, and may execute rogue code on a system or result in loss of data.

Application Attack	Description
Integer overflow	An attack in which a computed result is too large to fit in its assigned storage space, which may lead to crashing or data corruption, and may trigger a buffer overflow.
Arbitrary code execution	Also called *remote code execution*, this is an attack that exploits application vulnerabilities by allowing an attacker to execute any command on a victim's machine. An attacker may be able to take complete control over a system with these commands.

ACTIVITY 2–3
Identifying Software Attacks

Scenario

Your IT department wants to know why the performance of some of your computer systems is degrading. In all the cases of poor performance, your IT administrator, Ronald, has already used existing network baseline data to rule out the possibility of this performance degradation being caused by a temporary spike in traffic or insufficient hardware resources. You and Ronald believe your systems are under attack, but now you need to discover the types of attacks so that you can devise an appropriate response.

---

1. Kim, a help desk staffer, gets a phone call from Alex in human resources stating that he cannot log on. Kim looks up the account information for Alex and sees that the account is locked. This is the third time the account has locked this week. Alex insists that he was typing in his password correctly. Kim notices that the account was locked at 6 A.M.; Alex says he was in a meeting at a client's site until 10 A.M. today. This could be a(n):

   ● Password attack.

   ○ Backdoor attack.

   ○ Application attack.

2. Your customer database was recently compromised and much of its data was corrupted. The database administrator, Carly, pulls the log files for you to review. Shortly before the corruption was detected, the log files list various bogus SQL statements being entered into the database. This could be a(n):

   ○ Password attack.

   ○ Backdoor attack.

   ● Application attack.

3. Your file server has been performing sluggishly, and several times a day it is entirely unreachable. You've ruled out traffic spikes and insufficient hardware as the cause, and your antivirus software detects no signs of an infection. You review the usage logs on the server and notice that an administrator account logs in and out remotely several times per day. You've discussed the matter with everyone in IT that is currently authorized to access the file server, and none of them seem to recognize this account. You determine that this unknown administrator account is being used to gain entry into your file server to disrupt its normal operations. This could be a(n):

   ○ Password attack.

   ● Backdoor attack.

   ○ Application attack.

TOPIC D

Network-Based Threats

You reviewed the software-based threats to security. Now you will focus on the different network-based threats to be aware of how they can gain access to and break through network technologies to access information.

The network is the lifeblood of today's business, whether it is your company's local area network (LAN) or your e-commerce connection to the Internet. Most businesses today rely on their networks to be the base of all operations. A network allows people to stay connected to each other in an organized way and allows businesses to access and share information as quickly and securely as possible. A network-based threat can compromise daily business interactions and can be detrimental to keeping information private and secure. This topic will help you identify the network attacks that you will need to be aware of in order to protect your networks.

TCP/IP Basics

Transmission Control Protocol/Internet Protocol (TCP/IP) is the standard network protocol used today, and knowing the basics of TCP/IP is a good start to understanding how network attacks may be launched. TCP/IP is a layered suite of many protocols. By adding header information to the data in a network packet, a protocol at a given layer on the sending host can communicate with the protocol at the corresponding layer at the receiving host.

The logical endpoints of a connection between hosts are called *ports*, and a given port can be open, to allow communication of a certain type, or closed, to prevent it. Each host on a TCP/IP network receives a numeric address as well as a descriptive name. Names are organized hierarchically in domains and mapped to hosts through the Domain Name System (DNS) service.

TCP/IP Layers

The following table describes the layered architecture of TCP/IP in more detail.

Layer	Description	Major Protocols and Utilities
Network Interface/Data Link	Enables the network software to transmit data on the physical network, via the network adapter cards and network media.	Various Ethernet and wireless specifications, not specific to TCP/IP.
Internet	Provides addressing, naming, and routing.	Internet Protocol (IP): Manages numeric host addresses across the Internet.
		Address assignment is typically done automatically through a separate service called Dynamic Host Configuration Protocol (DHCP).
		Internet Control Message Protocol (ICMP): Tests for communication between devices and sends error messages when network function is unavailable.

Layer	Description	Major Protocols and Utilities
Transport	Provides connection and communication services.	Transmission Control Protocol (TCP): A connection-oriented, guaranteed-delivery protocol. This means that it not only sends data, but also waits for acknowledgement (ACK) and fixes errors when possible.
		User Datagram Protocol (UDP): Ensures the consistent transmission of data packets (datagrams) by bypassing error checking, which can cause delays and increased processing requirements.
Application	Provides utilities that enable client applications on an individual system to access the networking software.	Network Basic Input Output System (NetBIOS): A simple, broadcast-based naming service.
		Sockets: A piece of software within an operating system that connects an application with a network protocol, so that the application can request network services from the operating system.
		File Transfer Protocol (FTP): Enables the transfer of files between a user's workstation and a remote host over a TCP network.

IP Port Scanning Attacks

A *port scanning attack* is a type of network attack where a potential attacker scans the computers and devices that are connected to the Internet or other networks to see which TCP and UDP ports are listening and which services on the system are active. Port scans can be easily automated, so almost any system on the Internet will be scanned almost constantly. Some monitoring software can detect port scans, or they might happen without your knowledge.

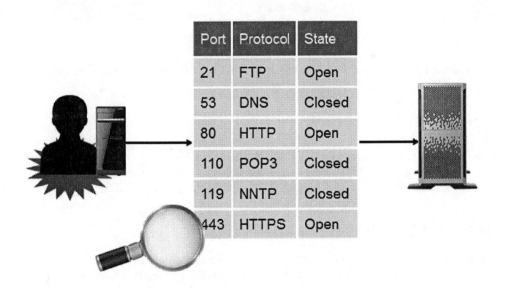

Port	Protocol	State
21	FTP	Open
53	DNS	Closed
80	HTTP	Open
110	POP3	Closed
119	NNTP	Closed
443	HTTPS	Open

Figure 2-18: A port scanning attack. The target system is currently running FTP, HTTP, and HTTPS services.

Port Scanning Utilities

There are many utilities available that potential attackers can use to scan ports on networks, including Nmap, SuperScan, Strobe, and any Telnet client. Many utilities can be downloaded for free from the Internet. Performing port scanning attacks is often the first step an attacker takes to identify live systems and open ports to launch further attacks with other tools.

Xmas Attack

The Xmas Scan is available in popular port scanners such as Nmap. It is mainly used to check which machines are active or reachable, and subsequently what ports are open or responding, so that those machines or ports can be used as an avenue for a follow-up attack. This type of port scanning attack uses an Xmas packet with all the flags turned on in the TCP header of the packet. The name "Xmas" refers to all the flags being on (like lights) and so a packet is lit up like a Christmas tree.

This scan is commonly known as a stealth scan due to its ability to hide the scan in progress, and its ability to pass undetected through some popular firewalls. However, most modern-day intrusion detection systems (IDSs) and some advanced firewalls can detect this type of scan.

Eavesdropping Attacks

An *eavesdropping attack* or *sniffing attack* uses special monitoring software to gain access to private network communications, either to steal the content of the communication itself or to obtain user names and passwords for future software attacks. Attackers can eavesdrop on both wired and wireless network communications. On a wired network, the attacker must have physical access to the network or tap into the network cable. On a wireless network, an attacker needs a device capable of receiving signals from the wireless network. Eavesdropping is very hard to detect, unless you spot an unknown computer leasing an IP address from a DHCP server.

Figure 2-19: An eavesdropping attack in which the malicious user monitors wireless network traffic.

Eavesdropping Utilities

Many utilities are available that will monitor and capture network traffic. Some of these tools can only sniff the traffic that is sent to or received by the computer on which they are installed. Other tools are capable of scaling up to scan very large corporate networks. Examples of these tools include: Wireshark, the Microsoft Network Monitor Capture utility, tcpdump, and dsniff.

Man-in-the-Middle Attacks

A *man-in-the-middle attack* is a form of eavesdropping where the attacker makes an independent connection between two victims (two clients or a client and a server) and relays information between the two victims as if they are directly talking to each other over a closed connection, when in reality the attacker is controlling the information that travels between the two victims. During the process, the attacker can view or steal information to use it fraudulently.

One such scenario is as follows:

1. The attacker intercepts packets from User A that are destined for User B.
2. The attacker modifies the packets to include malicious or fraudulent information.
3. The attacker sends the modified packets to User B disguised as the original sender (User A).

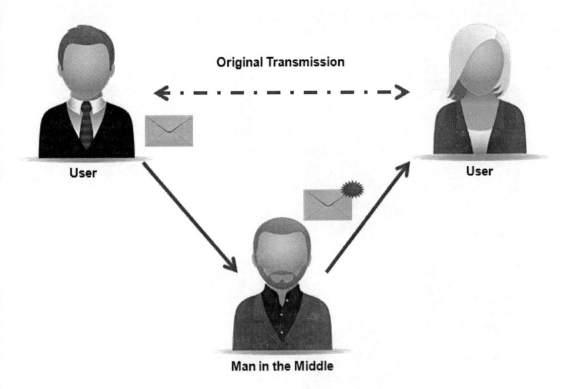

Figure 2-20: A man-in-the-middle attack.

Replay Attacks

A *replay attack* is a network attack where an attacker captures network traffic and stores it for retransmitting at a later time to gain unauthorized access to a specific host or a network. This attack is particularly successful when an attacker captures packets that contain user names, passwords, or other authentication data. In most cases, replay attacks are never discovered.

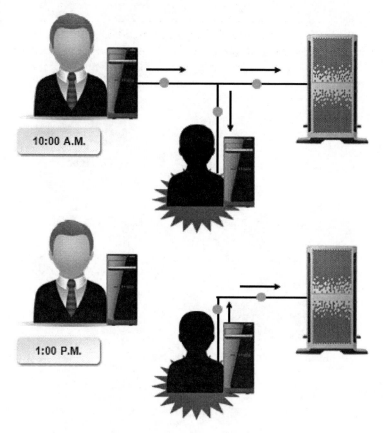

Figure 2–21: A replay attack in which an attacker intercepts a user's transmission, then later repeats that same transmission.

Social Network Attacks

Social network attacks are attacks that are aimed at social networking sites such as Facebook, Twitter, and LinkedIn. As these types of websites have become incredibly popular both for personal and professional use, they have become bigger targets for a variety of threats to security. The following table describes some of the more common attacks launched against social networks and their users.

Social Network Attack	Description
Evil twin attack and *account phishing*	An evil twin attack on a social networking site is an attack where an attacker creates a social network account to impersonate a genuine user. Then, when the friends of that user allow the attacker to become friends with them or join a group, the attacker can gain access to various personal details and even company information if a company has a page on the site. This is often preceded by account phishing, in which an attacker creates an account and joins the friends list of an individual just to try to obtain information about the individual and their circle of friends or colleagues.
Drive-by download	This is a program that is automatically installed on a computer when a user accesses a malicious site, even without clicking a link or giving consent. This often happens when a user searches for a social networking site and selects a site using a fraudulent link. Sometimes a drive-by download may be packaged invisibly together with a program that a user requests to download.

Social Network Attack	Description
Clickjacking	An attack that tricks a user into clicking an unintended link. The attacker uses a combination of visible and invisible HTML frames to fool the user into thinking what they are clicking is what's visible, when in fact the invisible link is layered on top of or beneath the visible frame. This happens when a user is going through a fraudulent networking site or a site that has been hijacked by an attacker.
	For example, someone posts a video on Facebook, and the embedded link redirects to an external site. When you select the **Play** button, you also select the embedded Facebook **Like** option, which posts to your page and possibly to all your friends' pages. Or, perhaps the **Play** button is linked to a malicious download.
Password stealer	A type of software that, when installed on a system, will be able to capture all the passwords and user names entered into the instant messaging application or social network site that it was designed for. This information is sent back to the attacker who can use it for fraudulent purposes.
Spamming	Within social networking, spamming refers to sending unsolicited bulk messages by misusing the electronic messaging services inside the social networking site.

URL Shortening Service

A *URL shortening service* makes it easier to share links on social networking sites by abbreviating the Uniform Resource Locators (URLs). Though they are usually benign, this creates a vulnerability that attackers can exploit because the shortened URL hides the true target of the link. A user may be directed to a fraudulent site that is a source of malware or other threats.

64 on Lean Slides

DoS Attacks

A *Denial of Service (DoS) attack* is a type of network attack in which an attacker attempts to disrupt or disable systems that provide network services by various means, including:

- Flooding a network link with data to consume all available bandwidth.
- Sending data designed to exploit known flaws in an application.
- Sending multiple service requests to consume a system's resources.
- Flooding a user's email inbox with spam messages, causing the genuine messages to get bounced back to the sender.

 Note: Nearly anything can cause a DoS attack if it interrupts or disables a system. For example, pulling a plug from a server will cause a DoS condition.

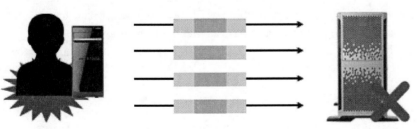

Figure 2-22: A DoS attack in which excess data floods a server, rendering it inoperable.

DoS Targets

The attack can target any service or network device, but is usually mounted against servers or routers, preventing them from responding to legitimate network requests. A DoS attack can also be caused by something as simple as disconnecting a network cable.

DDoS Attacks

A *Distributed Denial of Service (DDoS) attack* is a type of DoS attack that uses multiple computers on disparate networks to launch the attack from many simultaneous sources. The attacker introduces unauthorized software that turns the computer into a zombie/drone that directs the computers to launch the attack.

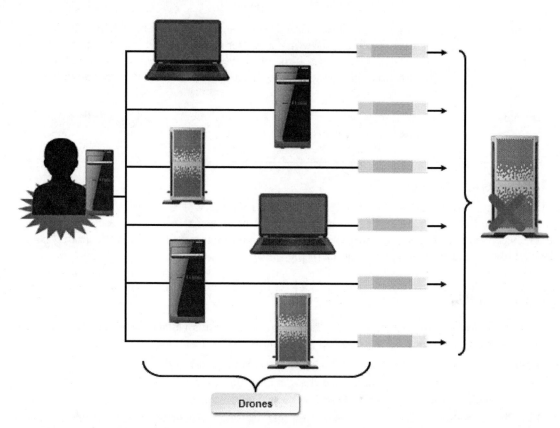

Figure 2–23: A DDoS attack in which drone computers flood a server with data, rendering it inoperable.

Symptoms of DoS and DDoS Attacks

DoS attacks manifest themselves in a variety of ways, including:

- Sudden and overwhelming service requests from hosts outside your network.
- A sudden and unexplained drop in the amount of available Internet bandwidth.
- A sudden and overwhelming drain on a specific resource in a system, causing unusual behavior or freezes.

Types of DoS Attacks

The following table describes some of the different types of DoS and DDoS attacks.

DoS Attack Type	Description
ICMP flood	This attack is based on sending high volumes of ICMP ping packets to a target. Common names for ICMP flood attacks are *Smurf attacks* and *ping floods*. Modern systems and networks are usually well-protected against these types of attacks.
UDP flood	In this attack, the attacker attempts to overwhelm the target system with UDP ping requests. Often the source IP address is spoofed, creating a DoS condition for the spoofed IP.
SYN flood	In this attack, an attacker sends countless requests for a TCP connection (SYN messages) to an FTP server, web server, or any other target system attached to the Internet. The target server then responds to each request with a SYN-ACK message and, in doing so, creates a space in memory that will be used for the TCP session when the remote host (in this case, the attacker) responds with its own SYN-ACK message. However, the attacker has crafted the SYN message (usually through IP spoofing) so that the target server sends its initial SYN-ACK response to a computer that will never reply. So, the target server has reserved memory for numerous TCP connections that will never be completed. Eventually, the target server will stop responding to legitimate requests because its memory resources are flooded with incomplete TCP connections.
Buffer overflow	Many systems and services are vulnerable to a buffer overflow condition, in which too much data is fed into a fixed-length memory buffer, resulting in adjacent areas of memory being overwritten. Attackers can exploit buffer overflow vulnerabilities by deliberately invoking buffer overflow conditions, introducing bad data into memory, thus opening the door for any number of subsequent attack methods or simply causing the system to cease to function or respond. A buffer overflow can also occur when there is an excessive amount of incomplete fragmented traffic on a network. In this case, an attacker may attempt to pass through security systems or IDSs.
Reflected DoS attack	In reflected DoS and DDoS attacks, a forged source IP address is used when sending requests to a large number of computers. This causes those systems to send a reply to the target system, causing a DoS condition.
Permanent DoS attack	Permanent DoS attacks, also called *phlashing*, target the actual hardware of a system in order to prevent the victim from easily recovering from a denial of service. With a successful attack, phlashing forces the victim to repair or replace the hardware that runs the system. Taking advantage of remote administration, the attacker may be able to push corrupted firmware onto the hardware, causing that equipment to brick, or become completely inoperable.

Session Hijacking

A *session hijacking attack* involves exploiting a computer in session to obtain unauthorized access to an organization's network or services. It involves stealing an active session cookie that is used to authenticate a user to a remote server and using that to control the session thereafter. Session hijacking attacks may be used to execute denial of service to either the client's system or the server system, or in some cases, both systems. Attackers may also hijack sessions in order to access sensitive information, like bank accounts or private communications.

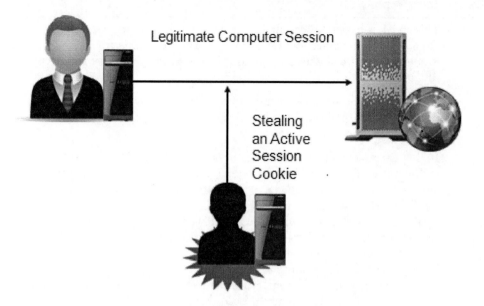

Figure 2–24: An attacker hijacking a user's session over the Internet.

P2P Attacks

Peer-to-peer (P2P) attacks are launched by malware propagating through *P2P* networks. P2P networks typically have a shared command and control architecture, making it harder to detect an attacker. A P2P attack can be used to launch huge DoS attacks. Within a P2P network, personal computers with high-speed connections can be compromised by malware such as viruses and Trojans. An attacker can then control all these compromised computers to launch a DDoS attack.

 Note: Notable P2P programs of the past are Napster, Kazaa, and LimeWire, all of which are now either defunct or no longer P2P. Vuze, µTorrent, and eMule are current P2P clients that enable fast transfers of files between computers and networks.

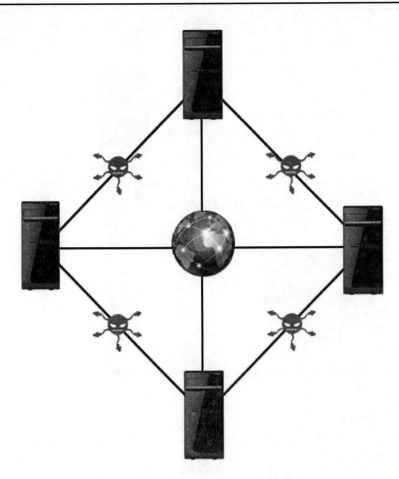

Figure 2-25: A P2P attack in which malware is shared across a network.

ARP Poisoning

Address Resolution Protocol (ARP) is the mechanism by which individual hardware MAC addresses are matched to an IP address on a network. *ARP poisoning*, also known as ARP spoofing, occurs when an attacker with access to the target network redirects an IP address to the MAC address of a computer that is not the intended recipient. At this point, the attacker could choose to capture and alter network traffic before forwarding it to the correct destination, or create a DoS condition by pointing the selected IP address at a non-existent MAC address.

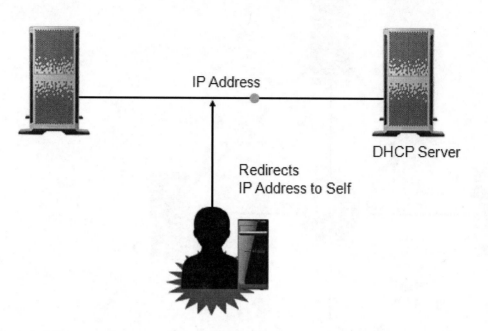

Figure 2-26: An attacker intercepting network traffic by spoofing a machine's IP address.

The Physical Network Address

Switches generally deliver packets based on a unique physical address that is individually assigned to every network adapter board by the adapter's manufacturer. No two network adapters in the world are supposed to have the same physical address. This address is also referred to as the *MAC address* because these addresses operate at the Media Access Control sub-layer of the Data Link layer of the OSI network model.

Transitive Access Attacks

Transitive access is the access given to certain members in an organization to use data on a system without the need for authenticating themselves. The information regarding the list of members that have transitive access is usually saved in a log or host file. If an attacker can access and modify the file, then that will give transitive access to all data and programs to the attacker. Therefore, a *transitive access attack* is an attack that takes advantage of the transitive access given in order to steal or destroy data on a system. This type of attack exploits trust relationships by attacking from the client side of a network.

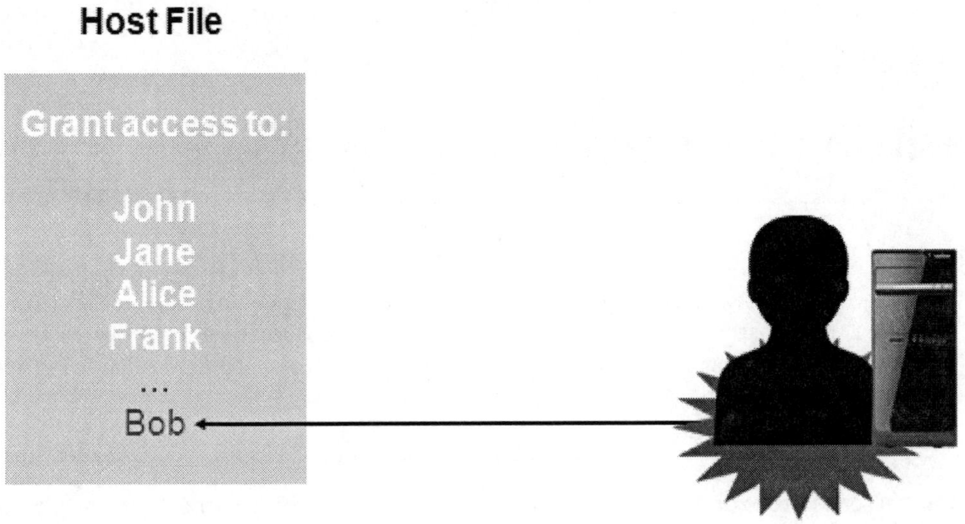

Host File

Figure 2–27: Transitive access attack.

DNS Vulnerabilities

A DNS translates human-readable domain names into their corresponding IP addresses. The following table describes the threats to DNS.

DNS Vulnerability	Description
DNS poisoning	In this technique, an attacker exploits the traditionally open nature of the DNS system to redirect a domain name to an IP address of the attacker's choosing. Once the domain name has been redirected, the attacker can capture data from or serve malware to visitors to the target domain name. A DoS condition could also be created by directing the target domain name to a non-existent IP address.
DNS hijacking	In this technique, an attacker sets up a rogue DNS server. This rogue DNS server responds to legitimate requests with IP addresses for malicious or non-existent websites. In some cases, Internet Service Providers (ISPs) have implemented DNS hijacking to serve advertisements to users who attempt to navigate to non-existent domain names.

Legitimate Use of DNS Spoofing

Some network hardware has DNS spoofing capabilities built in to allow routers to act as proxy DNS servers in the event that designated primary DNS servers are unavailable, which could occur in an Internet connection outage.

ACTIVITY 2–4
Classifying Network–Based Threats

Scenario

You and Ronald, your IT administrator, have been investigating poor performance on the company network. You are certain that your systems are under attack, but now you need to know the types of attacks that are occurring so that you can devise an appropriate response. To determine the exact attack methods, you review incidents.

1. While you are connected to another host on your network, the connection is suddenly dropped. When you review the logs at the other host, it appears as if the connection is still active. This could be a(n):
   - ○ IP spoofing attack.
   - ○ Replay attack.
   - ○ Man-in-the-middle attack.
   - ◉ Session hijacking attack.

2. Your e-commerce web server is getting extremely slow. Customers are calling stating that it is taking a long time to place an order on your site. This could be a(n):
   - ○ DNS poisoning attack.
   - ◉ DoS attack.
   - ○ Eavesdropping attack.
   - ○ ARP poisoning attack.

3. Tina, the network analysis guru in your organization, analyzes a network trace capture file and discovers that packets have been intercepted and retransmitted to both a sender and a receiver during an active session. This could be a(n):
   - ○ IP spoofing attack.
   - ○ Session hijacking attack.
   - ○ Replay attack.
   - ◉ Man-in-the-middle attack.

4. Your intranet webmaster, Tim, has noticed an entry in a log file from an IP address that is within the range of addresses used on your network. But, Tim does not recognize the computer name as valid. Your network administrator, Deb, checks the DHCP server and finds out that the MAC address is not similar to any in their list of MAC addresses in that particular domain. This could be a(n):
   - ◉ ARP poisoning attack.
   - ○ Replay attack.
   - ○ Man-in-the-middle attack.
   - ○ Session hijacking attack.

5. Instead of connecting to your web server IP address, when you enter your website's URL into your browser, it brings you to a site that looks similar to yours but at a completely different IP address. While on this site, your antivirus software alerts you to a possible malware infection. This could be a(n):

- ◉ DNS poisoning/hijacking attack.
- ○ Replay attack.
- ○ ARP poisoning attack.
- ○ Session hijacking attack.

TOPIC E

Wireless Threats and Vulnerabilities

You identified the network-based threats that can affect information systems. Now, you will focus on the wireless threats and vulnerabilities that can cause damage to your internal systems. Wireless networks are everywhere, and protecting devices against wireless vulnerabilities is crucial to protecting sensitive data from unauthorized access.

Wireless networks have quickly become the norm in business today. Most organizations have both a wired and a wireless network for employees to access while on the move within their facilities. Understanding the potential threats and vulnerabilities will allow you to successfully secure the wireless components of an organization's information systems infrastructure.

Wireless Security

Wireless security is any method of securing your wireless LAN network to prevent unauthorized network access and network data theft. You need to ensure that authorized users can connect to the network without any hindrances. Wireless networks are more vulnerable to attacks than any other network system. For one thing, most wireless devices such as laptops, mobile phones, smartphones, and tablets search and connect automatically to the access point offering the best signal, which can be coming from an attacker. Wireless transmissions can also be scanned or sniffed out of the air, with no need to access physical network media. Such attacks can be avoided by using relevant security protocols.

Figure 2–28: A wireless security design.

Rogue Access Points

A *rogue access point* is an unauthorized wireless access point on a corporate or private network. Rogue access points can cause considerable damage to an organization's data. They are not detected easily and can allow private network access to many unauthorized users with the proper devices. A rogue access point can allow man-in-the-middle attacks and access to private information. Organizations should protect themselves from this type of attack by implementing techniques to constantly monitor the system, such as installing an IDS.

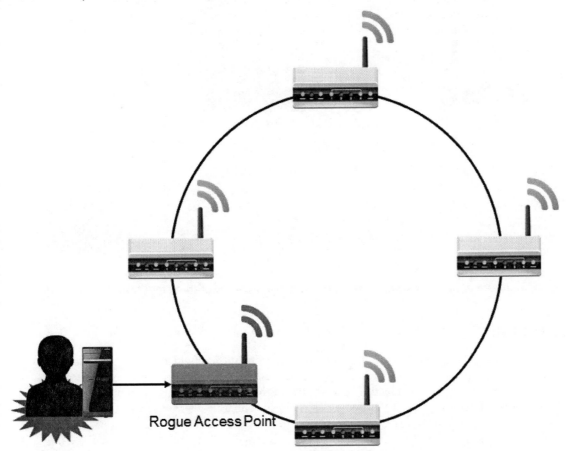

Rogue Access Point

Figure 2–29: A rogue access point that allows an attacker entry into a wireless network.

Evil Twins

Evil twins in the context of wireless networking are access points on a network that fool users into believing they are legitimate. Although they can be installed both in corporate and private networks, typically they are found in public Wi-Fi hotspots where users do not connect transparently and automatically as they do in a corporate network, but rather select available networks from a list. A malicious user can set up such an access point with something as basic as a smartphone with tethering capabilities. Evil twins can be more dangerous than rogue access points because the user thinks that the wireless signal is genuine, making it difficult to differentiate from a valid access point with the same name.

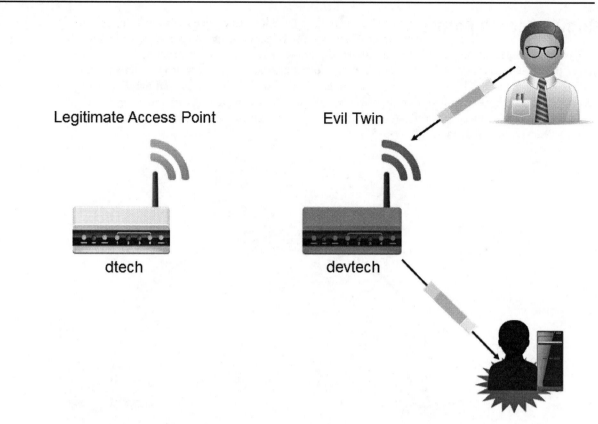

Figure 2–30: An attacker stealing data from a user who connects to an evil twin access point.

Jamming

In wireless networking, *jamming*, also called *interference*, is an attack in which radio waves disrupt 802.11 wireless signals. It usually occurs at home because of various electronic devices, such as microwaves, operating in a bandwidth close to that of the wireless network. When this occurs, it causes the 802.11 signals to wait before transmitting, and the wait can be indefinite at times. Attackers may use a radio transceiver to intercept transmissions and inject jamming packets, disrupting the normal flow of traffic across a network.

Figure 2–31: An attacker interfering with a wireless signal.

Bluejacking

Bluejacking is a method used by attackers to send out unwanted *Bluetooth* signals from smartphones, mobile phones, tablets, and laptops to other Bluetooth-enabled devices. Because Bluetooth has a 30-foot transmission limit, this is a very close-range attack. With the advanced technology available today, attackers can send out unsolicited messages along with images and video. These types of signals can lead to many different types of threats. They can lead to device malfunctions, or even propagate viruses, including Trojan horses. Users should reject anonymous contacts, and should configure their mobile devices to non-discoverable mode.

Figure 2-32: An attacker sending malware to a device via a Bluetooth connection.

Bluesnarfing

Bluesnarfing is a method in which attackers gain access to unauthorized information on a wireless device using a Bluetooth connection within the 30-foot Bluetooth transmission limit. Unlike bluejacking, access to wireless devices such as smartphones, tablets, mobile phones, and laptops by bluesnarfing can lead to the exploitation of private information, including email messages, contact information, calendar entries, images, videos, and any data stored on the device.

Figure 2-33: An attacker stealing a user's sensitive data that is being transmitted over Bluetooth.

Near Field Communication

Near Field Communication (NFC) is a standard of communication between mobile devices like smartphones and tablets in very close proximity, usually when touching or being only a few inches apart from each other. NFC is often used for in-person transactions or data exchange. Despite having a strict physical proximity requirement, NFC is vulnerable to several types of attacks. For example, certain antenna configurations may be able to pick up the RF signals emitted by NFC from several feet away, giving an attacker the ability to eavesdrop from a more comfortable distance. An attacker may also be able to corrupt data as it is being transferred through a method similar to a DoS attack—by flooding the area with an excess of RF signals to interrupt the transfer. If someone loses their NFC device or a thief steals it, and the device has no additional layers of authentication security, then anyone can use the device in a number of malicious ways. Aside from having a shorter range of operation, NFC is more limited than Bluetooth with respect to the amount of data that can be transferred, and communication is more quickly and easily activated.

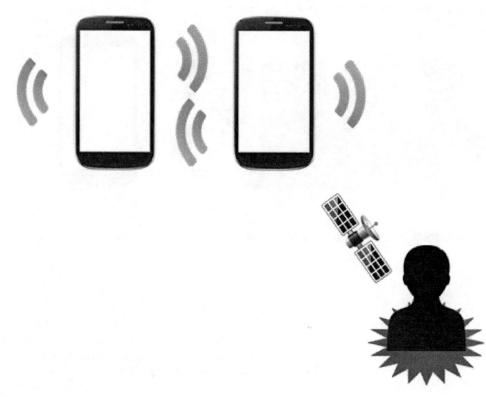

Figure 2-34: An attacker picking up NFC signals from a distance.

War Driving and War Chalking

War driving is the act of searching for instances of wireless networks using wireless tracking devices such as smartphones, tablets, mobile phones, or laptops. It locates wireless access points while traveling, which can be exploited to obtain unauthorized Internet access and potentially steal data. This process can be automated using a GPS device and war driving software.

War chalking is the act of using symbols to mark off a sidewalk or wall to indicate that there is an open wireless network that may be offering Internet access.

Figure 2–35: War driving in a vehicle and a war chalking symbol that indicates a closed wireless network with WEP encryption.

War Driving Tools

There are common tools that can be used for war driving and war chalking:

- NetStumbler
- Kismet
- Aircrack

Note: In the terms war driving and war chalking, "war" stands for wireless access receiver.

IV Attacks

In encryption, an *initialization vector (IV)* is a number added to a key that constantly changes in order to prevent identical text from producing the same exact ciphertext upon encryption. This makes it more difficult for a hacker to decipher encrypted information that gets repeated. An *IV attack* allows the attacker to predict or control the initialization vector in order to bypass this effect. IVs are often compromised if they are constructed with a relatively small bit length. For example, modern systems often have little trouble cracking an IV of 24-bit size.

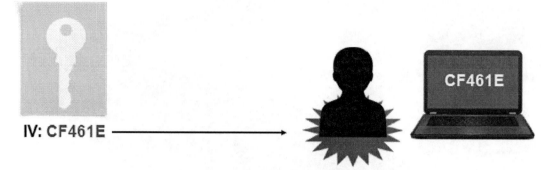

Figure 2-36: An attacker breaking a weak 24-bit (in hexadecimal) IV.

Packet Sniffing

Packet sniffing can be used as an attack on wireless networks where an attacker captures data and registers data flows, which allow the attacker to analyze the data contained in a packet. The attacker can use the data gleaned from this analysis to launch a more effective attack on a network. In its benign form, packet sniffing also helps organizations monitor their own networks against attackers.

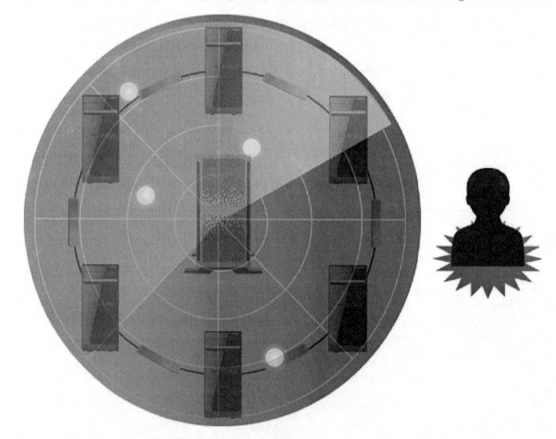

Figure 2-37: An attacker scanning a network's traffic.

Wireless Replay Attacks

With weak or no wireless encryption, an attacker may find it easier to capture packets over a wireless network and replay them in order to manipulate the data stream. Replay attacks can also be used in conjunction with an IV attack to successfully break weak encryption.

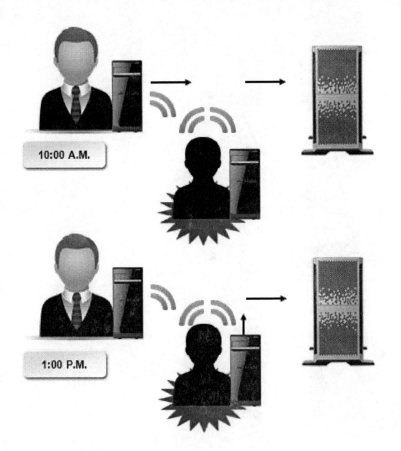

Figure 2-38: A replay attack on a wireless network.

Sinkhole Attacks

Sinkhole attacks take advantage of routing on a wireless network by creating a single node through which all traffic goes. This individual node is able to trick the other nodes into redirecting their traffic. The attacker who controls the sinkhole is potentially able to intercept data packets and slow a network to a crawl. Attackers who exploit routing operations are generally able to do so with powerful wireless transmitters. These transmitters can reach a wide enough area of a network to funnel as much traffic as possible into the sinkhole.

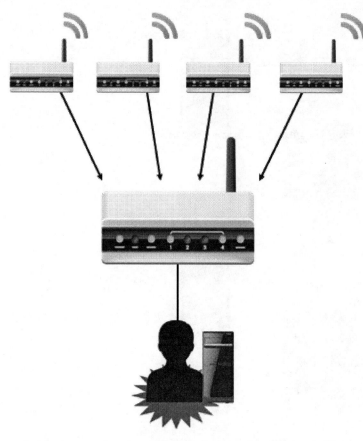

Figure 2–39: An attacker funneling wireless traffic into a single point.

WEP and WPA Attacks

The *Wired Equivalent Privacy (WEP)* algorithm was the earliest algorithm used to secure wireless networks. This method of data encryption was meant to match the security found in wired connections at the time. WEP came in 64-bit, 128-bit, and 256-bit key sizes. However, because it used a stream cipher to encrypt data, WEP relied on an IV to randomize identical strings of text. With a 24-bit IV size, WEP was extremely vulnerable to an IV attack that would be able to predict the IV value. In fact, some freely available software would be able to crack WEP encryption within minutes on standard consumer hardware. Because of this vulnerability, WEP was deprecated in 2004 and should not be used.

WEP was superseded by the much more secure *Wi-Fi Protected Access (WPA)* protocol and its successor, WPA2. Unlike WEP, WPA actually generates a 128-bit key for each individual packet sent, which prevents easy cracking of encrypted information. Although WPA used the same RC4 stream cipher, WPA2 uses the more secure AES block cipher for encryption. Even with this enhanced security, both WPA protocols are vulnerable to attack. In particular, users who secure their WPA wireless networks with weak passwords are susceptible to brute force password cracking attacks. Another potential weakness in WPA allows attackers to inject malicious packets into the wireless data stream.

Currently, WPA2 is considered the most secure wireless encryption protocol and should be used instead of WPA.

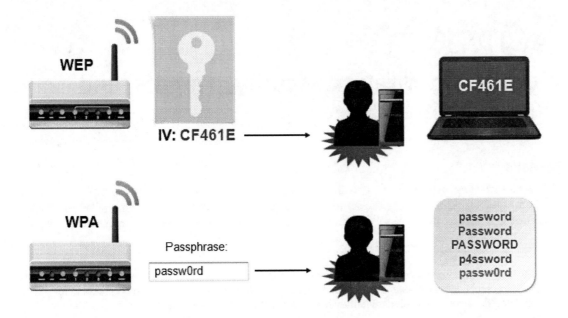

Figure 2-40: An attacker compromising WEP with an IV attack and WPA with a password cracking attack.

WPS Attacks

A serious flaw in both WPA and WPA2 is the *Wi-Fi Protected Setup (WPS)* feature. WPS was intended to strengthen wireless security encryption by adding more methods to authenticate key generation, in case the user chose a weak password. One such method is an 8-digit PIN that is displayed on the physical wireless device and must be entered in order to enroll in the network. However, because of the way that WPS checks each half of the PIN separately, it takes only a few thousand guesses to successfully crack the PIN. This can be done in mere hours.

The WPS feature is on by default on many wireless devices. You should disable it to prevent a potential breach of security, but keep in mind that some devices don't allow it to be properly disabled.

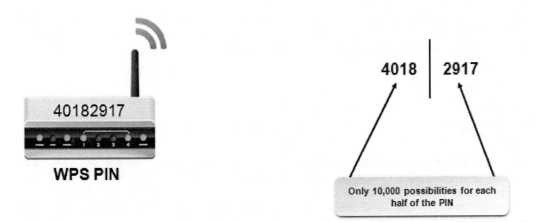

Figure 2-41: A PIN validated by WPS one half at a time, reducing the possible combinations from 100 million to 10 thousand.

ACTIVITY 2-5
Discussing Wireless Security, Threats, and Vulnerabilities

Scenario

You are a security professional for Develetech and your manager has asked you to look into setting up the wireless network. During the setup, you are faced with certain issues which relate to attacks that you have learned about. How well can you identify the types of wireless attacks you are facing?

1. John is given a laptop for official use and is on a business trip. When he arrives at his hotel, he turns on his laptop and finds a wireless access point with the name of the hotel, which he connects to for sending official communications. He may become a victim of which wireless threat?

   ○ Jamming

   ○ War driving

   ○ Bluesnarfing

   ● Evil twins

2. A new administrator in your company is in the process of installing a new wireless device. He is called away to attend an urgent meeting before he can secure the wireless network, and without realizing it, he forgot to switch the device off. A person with a mobile device who is passing the building takes advantage of the open network and hacks the network. Your company may become vulnerable to which type of wireless threat?

   ○ Jamming

   ● War driving

   ○ Bluesnarfing

   ○ Rogue access point

3. Every time Margaret decided to work at home, she would get frustrated with the poor wireless connection. But when she gets to her office, the wireless connection seems normal. What might have been one of the factors affecting Margaret's wireless connection when she worked at home?

   ○ Bluesnarfing

   ● Jamming

   ○ IV attack

   ○ Evil twins

4. Chuck, a sales executive, is attending meetings at a professional conference that is also being attended by representatives of other companies in his field. At the conference, he uses his smartphone with a Bluetooth headset to stay in touch with clients. A few days after the conference, he finds that competitors' sales representatives are getting in touch with his key contacts and influencing them by revealing what he thought was private information from his email and calendar. Chuck is a victim of which wireless threat?

   ○ Packet sniffing

   ○ Bluejacking

   ● Bluesnarfing

   ○ Rogue access point

5. You've tasked Joel, one of your network specialists, with configuring new wireless routers in the building in order to extend the range of your network. Which of the following wireless encryption protocols should you remind Joel to use in order to keep your network secure?

○ WPA

● WPA2 with WPS disabled

○ WPA2 with WPS enabled

○ WEP

TOPIC F

Physical Threats and Vulnerabilities

You have seen how a great number of virtual threats can be very dangerous to an organization. But what about the physical components of your network and your organization's facilities? In this topic, you will identify the types of attacks that are directed against the physical resources in your enterprise.

It is important to keep attackers off your network's computers, but it is also important to keep them from stealing, compromising, or destroying the hardware in which you have invested, or attaching unauthorized hardware to your systems or networks. In order to do that, you need to know about the kinds of attacks that can be mounted against the hardware inside those systems, as well as the vulnerabilities of your organization's overall physical space.

Physical Security

Physical security refers to the implementation and practice of various control mechanisms that are intended to restrict physical access to facilities. In addition, physical security involves increasing or assuring the reliability of certain critical infrastructure elements such as electrical power, data networks, and fire suppression systems. Physical security may be challenged by a wide variety of events or situations, including:

- Facilities intrusions.
- Electrical grid failures.
- Fire.
- Personnel illnesses.
- Data network interruptions.

Physical Security Threats and Vulnerabilities

The following table describes the various areas that physical security threats come from.

Physical Security Threat and Vulnerability	Description
Internal	It is important to always consider what is happening inside an organization, especially when physical security is concerned. For example, disgruntled employees may be a source of physical sabotage of important security-related resources.
External	It is impossible for any organization to fully control external security threats. For example, an external power failure is usually beyond a security specialist's control because most organizations use a local power company as their source of electrical power. However, risks posed by external power failures may be mitigated by implementing devices such as an uninterruptible power supply (UPS) or a generator.
Natural	Although natural threats are easy to overlook, they can pose a significant threat to the physical security of a facility. Buildings and rooms that contain important computing assets should be protected against likely weather-related problems, including tornadoes, hurricanes, snow storms, and floods.

Physical Security Threat and Vulnerability	Description
Man-made	Whether intentional or accidental, people can cause a number of physical threats. For example, a backhoe operator may accidentally dig up fiber optic cables and disable external network access. On the other hand, a disgruntled employee may choose to exact revenge by deliberately cutting fiber optic cables. Man-made threats can be internal or external.

Hardware Attacks

A *hardware attack* is an attack that targets a computer's physical components and peripherals, including its hard disk, motherboard, keyboard, network cabling, or smart card reader. One goal of a hardware attack is the destruction of the hardware itself, or acquisition of sensitive information through theft or other means. A second goal of a hardware attack is to make important data or devices unavailable through theft or vandalism. This second goal is meant to disrupt a company's business or cause embarrassment due to data loss.

BitLocker
Uses AES
128, 256 bit
key

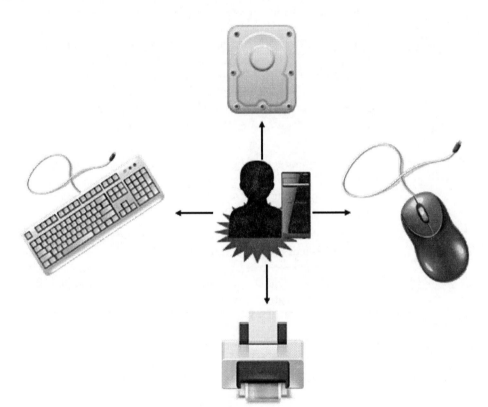

Figure 2-42: Various targets of a hardware attack.

Keylogging Attacks

One type of hardware attack is a technique known as keylogging, which uses software or hardware to capture each keystroke a user types. Keylogging can capture passwords as well as other sensitive data. Keyloggers may also be able to compromise a user's identity if that user is authenticated by a keystroke factor. There are a wide variety of software keyloggers available on the Internet. In addition, hardware such as KeyGhost and KeyGrabber are designed to perform keylogging. One way to mitigate the effects of keylogging is to use a keyboard that encrypts the keystroke signals before they are sent to the system unit. There are also many varieties of keystroke encryption software available.

Environmental Threats and Vulnerabilities

Environmental threats pose system security risks and can be addressed with the specific mitigation techniques described in the following table.

Environmental Threat	Effects and Mitigations
Fire	Fire, whether natural or deliberately set, is a serious environmental security threat because it can destroy hardware and therefore the data contained in it. In addition, it is hazardous to people and systems. You need to ensure that key systems are installed in a fire-resistant facility, and that there are high-quality fire detection and suppression systems on site so that the damage due to fire is reduced.
Hurricanes and tornadoes	Catastrophic weather events such as hurricanes and tornadoes are major security threats due to the magnitude of the damage they can cause to hardware and data. You need to ensure that your information systems are well contained and that your physical structure is built to appropriate codes and standards so that damage due to severe weather is reduced.
Flood	A flood is another major security threat that can cause as much damage as fire can. You should check the history of an area to see if you are in a flood plain before constructing your physical building, and follow appropriate building codes as well as purchase flood insurance. When possible, construct the building so that the lowest floor is above flood level; this saves the systems when flooding does occur. Spatial planning together with protective planning in concurrence with building regulations and functional regulations are precautionary measures that you should look into as well.
Extreme temperature	Extreme temperatures, especially heat, can cause some sensitive hardware components to melt and degrade, resulting in data loss. You can avoid this threat by implementing controls that keep the temperature in your data center within acceptable ranges.
Extreme humidity	Extreme humidity can cause computer components, data storage media, and other devices to rust, deteriorate, and degrade, resulting in data loss. You can avoid this threat by ensuring that there is enough ventilation in your data centers and storage locations, and by using temperature and humidity controls and monitors.

ACTIVITY 2–6
Identifying Physical Threats and Vulnerabilities

Scenario

Your manager, the security administrator in your organization, has asked that you help complete a report for senior management about the possible security risks you face and some suggested solutions. You have been presented with a list of scenarios and have been asked to identify whether the type of attack described in each scenario is a physical security attack.

1. A disgruntled employee removes the UPS on a critical server system and then cuts power to the system, causing costly downtime. This physical threat is a(n): (Select all that apply.)
   - ☐ Internal threat.
   - ☐ External threat.
   - ☐ Man-made threat.
   - ☐ False alarm.

2. A power failure has occurred due to a tree branch falling on a power line outside your facility, and there is no UPS or generator. This physical threat is a(n): (Select all that apply.)
   - ☐ Internal threat.
   - ☐ External threat.
   - ☐ Man-made threat.
   - ☐ False alarm.

3. A backhoe operator on a nearby construction site has accidentally dug up fiber optic cables, thus disabling remote network access. This physical threat is a(n): (Select all that apply.)
   - ☐ Internal threat.
   - ☐ External threat.
   - ☐ Man-made threat.
   - ☐ False alarm.

4. While entering the building through the rear security door, an employee realizes he has left his car keys in his car door lock. He has already swiped his badge to open the door, so he props it open with his briefcase while he returns to his car to retrieve his keys. He has the door in view at all times and no one else enters while the door is propped open. He locks the door behind him once he is in the building. This is a(n): (Select all that apply.)
   - ☐ Internal threat.
   - ☐ External threat.
   - ☐ Man-made threat.
   - ☐ False alarm.

Summary

In this lesson, you identified the main types of security threats you will face: social engineering attacks, malware, software-based attacks, network attacks, wireless attacks, and physical security attacks. Understanding the types of threats you face is an important first step in learning how to protect your network and respond to an intrusion.

What type of attack is of the most concern in your environment?

Which type of attack do you think might be the most difficult to guard against?

Note: Check your LogicalCHOICE Course screen for opportunities to interact with your classmates, peers, and the larger LogicalCHOICE online community about the topics covered in this course or other topics you are interested in. From the Course screen you can also access available resources for a more continuous learning experience.

3 Managing Data, Application, and Host Security

Lesson Time: 3 hours, 30 minutes

Lesson Objectives

In this lesson, you will manage data, application, and host security. You will:

- Manage data security.

- Manage application security.

- Manage device and host security.

- Manage mobile security.

Lesson Introduction

In the previous lesson, you identified common threats and vulnerabilities that can affect people, devices, and networks. Being aware of threats and vulnerabilities is the first step in protecting against them. In this lesson, you will manage data, application, and host security.

Organizations are made up of many different computing devices that use a number of applications and services on a daily basis. As a security professional, it is your job to properly secure all end-user devices, as well as the software and data used on these devices. Security must be applied to all levels of an organization. Without the proper security controls implemented at the level of individual hosts, data storage areas, and applications, all other security controls applied within the organization will be wasted.

TOPIC A

Manage Data Security

In this lesson, you will manage several areas of security that are related to end-user devices. Data security is crucial to keeping a business' proprietary information from being exposed. In this topic, you will implement controls to ensure data security.

A successful business depends on the privacy of its data and client data. Without the proper data-security measures in place, a business cannot guarantee the security of its customers, and this may result in business loss.

Layered Security

An approach to securing systems and their data against attack that incorporates many different avenues of defense is called *layered security*. An effective layered security system implements controls to mitigate each type of threat. Although they can become quite complex and expensive, layered security systems provide optimum protection for organizations that are vulnerable to a wide variety of attack vectors.

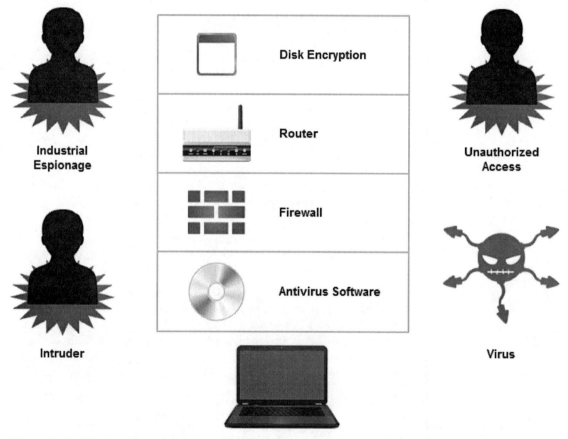

Figure 3-1: A layered approach to security.

Defense in Depth

Defense in depth is a tactic that leverages a layered approach to security, but instead of just focusing on the tools used to protect a system and its data, it is used to plan personnel training, policy adoption, physical protection, and other, more comprehensive security strategies. Since it covers almost every imaginable area of security, defense in depth is an excellent failsafe; if any one element is breached, other secure systems can buy an organization enough time to stop or mitigate the attack.

 Note: Defense in depth comes from the military strategy of delaying an enemy's advance rather than meeting them head on.

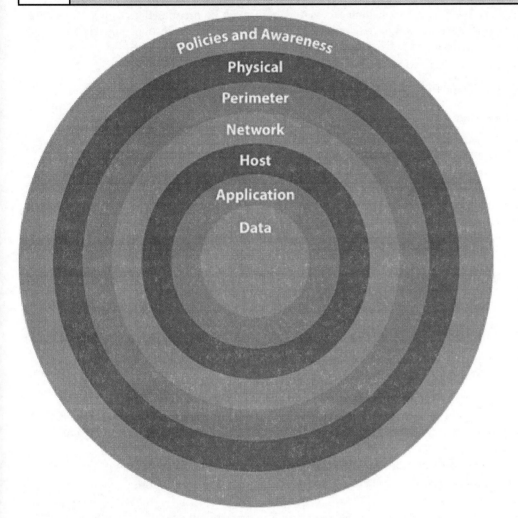

Figure 3-2: Defense in depth.

What Is Data Security?

Data security refers to the security controls and measures taken to keep an organization's data safe and accessible, and to prevent unauthorized access to it. Today's workforce is more mobile than ever before, and the need for enhanced data security is on the rise. Data is now stored and accessed in many locations, so organizations must consider not only the physical access to data storage systems, but also the devices that access them. Data security must be applied at every level of an organization, including:

- The physical environment.
- All devices and systems.
- All mobile devices used for business, especially as the use of smartphones and tablets for business continues to grow.

Data security must be a priority for every business, and it should be incorporated into all security policies.

Data Security Vulnerabilities

Data security vulnerabilities can include the increased use of cloud computing to perform job functions, the lack of restricted physical access to data storage systems, and the lack of user awareness. Any one of these vulnerabilities can lead to unauthorized access to data and data leakage possibilities. *Data leakage* refers to gaining access to data through unintentional user methods such as email and instant messaging, and the use of mobile devices. Data leakage through any of these methods can lead to malicious activity, and possible data loss.

Data Storage Methods

Common data storage methods include:

- Traditional network servers, which include one or more hard disks directly attached to the servers. You might see this configuration referred to as direct-attach storage (DAS).
- Network-attached storage (NAS), which can be a general-purpose computer or an appliance that is specially built to facilitate the storing and serving of files. In most cases, NAS appliances contain multiple hard drives and provide faster data access than traditional file servers, as well as being easier to configure and manage.
- Storage area networks (SANs), which are dedicated networks that provide block-level storage of data.
- Cloud-based storage, which is a service-based data storage system. Data is stored in virtualized pools that are normally hosted by a third party.

Data Encryption Methods

In order to protect data from security vulnerabilities, you should apply a data encryption method that is appropriate to the data level, including:

- Full disk encryption to encrypt an entire disk and all the data stored in it.
- Database encryption to encrypt sensitive data stored in the database. Some organizations may need to comply with regulatory guidelines that require database encryption for specific types of data.
- File encryption to protect individual files that contain private or confidential data.
- Removable media encryption on Secure Digital (SD) cards, CDs, and DVDs, to protect data stored on the media.
- Mobile device encryption to protect any data stored on smartphones or other mobile devices.
- Email encryption to encrypt and protect emails and attachments from being read by unauthorized users. Secure/Multipurpose Internet Mail Extensions (S/MIME), Pretty Good Privacy (PGP), and GNU Privacy Guard (GPG) are utilities that provide this functionality.
- Voice encryption to protect voice communications and data across a network.

Hardware-Based Encryption Devices

In *hardware-based encryption devices*, encryption, decryption, and access control are enforced by a cryptographic module called a *Hardware Security Module (HSM)*. Hardware-based encryption devices do not allow the execution of external programs that attempt to either reset any counters or access their memory. The lockdown in the event of unauthenticated use can also destroy data and encryption keys that are present on a universal serial bus (USB) flash drive or hard drive, based on the level of security enforced in the HSMs.

Hardware-based encryption devices provide benefits such as:

- Preventing storage mapping from the drive to the file system until a user inserts a plug-in smart card into a slot connected to the hard drive.
- Preventing attackers from copying the drive contents without the assigned HSM.

- Providing security controls that are self-governed and not dependent on the operating system; therefore, the hard drive is not affected by malicious code.
- Providing an organization with the proof that each machine is encrypted. In the event of a machine being lost due to a security attack, this will act as an assurance to customers that none of the data has been lost or compromised.

Types of Hardware–Based Encryption Devices

To secure data from unauthorized access, you can use one of several hardware-based encryption devices.

Device	Description
Trusted Platform Module (TPM)	This specification includes the use of *cryptoprocessors* to create a secure computing environment. A TPM can generate cryptographic keys securely and can be used to authenticate hardware, for disk encryption, for digital rights management, or for any other encryption-enabled application. TPM can be used as a basic input/output system (BIOS) security method by using full disk encryption such as BitLocker to secure the operating system's volume.
HSM	A cryptoprocessor device that can be attached to servers and computers to provide digital key security. The modules can provide a number of security functions, including enhancing cryptoprocesses and providing strong authentication services.
USB encryption	Users who store sensitive data on USB devices should take care to protect the devices physically. However, because of their small size and extreme portability, these devices can easily be lost or stolen. USB encryption can be implemented on USB devices to provide an additional way to protect sensitive data stored on the device.
Hard drive encryption	Hard drive encryption is a full disk encryption method used to encrypt and protect data on the entire disk. This type of encryption can be a very effective security measure to protect mobile devices and laptops, which can be misplaced, stolen, or damaged simply because they are moved around.

Data States

Security controls need to protect data no matter what state it is in.

Data State	Description
At rest	Data at rest refers to data in storage, whether in a database, on a disk, or on another storage medium. Data at rest encryption methods include: • PGP Whole Disk Encryption • Microsoft® Windows® BitLocker® disk encryption • OS X® FileVault® • Database encryption for database systems such as MySQL® and Oracle® • TrueCrypt®

Data State	Description
In transit	Data in transit refers to data that is moving across a network, including data for web applications, mobile device apps, and instant messaging. Data is considered to be in transit from when it leaves the storage medium or database until it is saved again or delivered to its destination. There are several encryption methods that protect data in transit, also called *transport encryption*: • HTTPS/Secure Sockets Layer/Transport Layer Security (SSL/TLS) • Wi-Fi Protected Access 2 (WPA2) • Virtual private networks (VPNs) • Internet Protocol Security (IPSec) • Secure Shell (SSH)
In use	Data in use refers to any data that is not at rest and not in transit. This includes data being generated, changed, erased, or viewed at exactly one network node. Protecting data in use is particularly problematic. At most, you can reasonably expect only to mitigate risks associated with data in use. • To protect the swap space, you can use full disk encryption, or you can remove the swap space altogether (if you are not using NVRAM). • Most vulnerabilities stem from the operating system, so hardening the OS can help. • Implement a web proxy at the network border.

Permissions and Access Control Lists

You can use file- and folder-level permissions to designate who can read or change data in a file or folder, but on the enterprise level, it can be impossible to manage millions of individual files and folders.

Access Control Lists (ACLs) enable you to restrict access to resources like files and folders, and they are commonly implemented as Media Access Control (MAC) address filters on wireless routers and access points.

Handling Big Data

Big data refers to data collections that are so large and complex that they are difficult for traditional database tools to manage. Businesses are often prompted to restructure their existing architecture in order to keep up with the demands of big data. This relatively new paradigm presents a challenge to security professionals who must adapt to the massive scope of big data.

There are some general tactics you can leverage to secure big data. Restricting authorized users' visibility will keep them from seeing the data set as a whole and limit them to focusing on only what they need to. Too many users who can see the bigger picture will increase the amount of risk associated with your data. The actual architecture of your data should also be formed with security in mind. Big data that is designed to work only with trusted parties and integrate non-repudiation will benefit.

Data Policies

Corporate security policies such as acceptable use policies (AUPs) deal with protecting data, but some organizations also implement specific data protection policies to clearly define employee responsibilities for protecting personal data that is held by the organization in any form and for any reason.

You might encounter data policies for the following:

- Wiping: Data wiping, sometimes referred to as secure erasing, is a software-based method of overwriting data that permanently destroys all electronic data on a hard drive or other digital media while leaving the storage device operational.
- Disposing: Many organizations have strict policies on disposing of data or storage media to ensure that the data cannot be recovered by unauthorized parties.
- Retention: Organizational data policies often outline what types of data should be retained, as well as how long they should be kept.
- Storage: Organizational data policies can include restrictions on which types of storage devices can be used to hold sensitive data.

Guidelines for Managing Data Security

> **Note:** All Guidelines for this lesson are available as checklists from the **Checklist** tile on the LogicalCHOICE Course screen.

Consider following these guidelines to help manage data security:

- Consider implementing a layered security model that can address numerous threats and vulnerabilities.
- Identify all forms of data storage used by your organization, and select security controls to protect each storage type.
  - Various forms of encryption, as well as permissions and ACLs, can be implemented on practically every type of data storage.
  - For cloud-based storage, examine the provider's security practices and guarantees to ensure that their data-protection measures meet your needs.
- Consider implementing controls to protect data regardless of whether it is in transit, in use, or at rest.
- Consider developing and enforcing data policies that protect data while allowing it to be accessible when needed.

ACTIVITY 3-1
Managing Data Security

Scenario

At Develetech Industries, the Chief Security Officer and Chief Information Officer have developed a staggered plan to implement data encryption on the corporate servers. Your assignment is to install the **BitLocker Drive Encryption** service on Windows Server 2012 R2 and then encrypt the **D:** drive. For this task, the password **!Pass1234** should be used to unlock the encrypted drive, and the recovery key should be saved as a file in the **C:\blkey** folder.

1. Why should Develetech invest in data security?

2. What data encryption method should you implement when you need to send data for Develetech's annual earnings report as an attachment in an email from your mobile device to the board of directors?
   - ○ Database encryption
   - ○ Email encryption
   - ○ Mobile device encryption
   - ○ Full disk encryption

3. How can data leakage affect the organization, and how could it be prevented?

4. Install the **BitLocker Drive Encryption** service on the Windows Server 2012 R2 computer.
   a) If the **Server Manager** window isn't displayed, select its icon on the Desktop taskbar.

b) In the **Server Manager** window, in the **Configure this server** section, select **Add roles and features**.

WELCOME TO SERVER MANAGER

QUICK START

1 Configure this local server

2 Add roles and features

3 Add other servers to manage

WHAT'S NEW

4 Create a server group

LEARN MORE

c) On the **Before you begin** page, select **Next**.
d) On the **Select installation type** page, verify that the **Role-based or feature-based** radio button is selected and select **Next**.
e) On the **Select destination server** page, verify that your server is selected and select **Next**.
f) On the **Select server roles** page, select **Next**.
g) On the **Select features** page, check **BitLocker Drive Encryption**.
h) In the **Add Roles and Features** dialog box, select **Add Features**.
i) Select **Next**.
j) Check **Restart the destination server automatically if required**.
k) In the **Add Roles and Features** message box, select **Yes**.
l) Select **Install**.
   Windows Server 2012 restarts.
m) Log back in.
n) In the **Add Roles and Features Wizard**, select **Close**.

> **Note:** There may be a delay before the wizard reappears.

5. Configure **BitLocker Drive Encryption** on the **D:** drive, with the password **!Pass1234** being the unlock mechanism, and the recovery key saved in the **C:\blkey** folder.

   a) Open **File Explorer**, and select **BACKUP (D:)**.

b) Right-click **BACKUP (D:)**, and select **Turn on BitLocker**.

c) On the **Choose how you want to unlock this drive** page, check **Use a password to unlock this drive**.
d) In the **Enter your password** text box, type *!Pass1234* and in the **Reenter your password** text box, type *!Pass1234* again.
e) Select **Next**.
f) On the **How do you want to back up your recovery key** page, select **Save to a file**.
g) In the **Save BitLocker recovery key as** dialog box, select **Local Disk (C:)**, and then select **New folder**.
h) Type *blkey* and then press **Enter**.
i) Double-click **blkey** to open the folder, and select **Save**.

j) In the **BitLocker Drive Encryption** message box, select **Yes**.

In a production environment, you would most likely also save the recovery key onto a removable drive.
k) Select **Next**.
l) On the **Choose how much of your drive to encrypt** page, verify that **Encrypt used disk space only** is selected and then select **Next**.

m) Select **Start encrypting**.

BitLocker Drive Encryption ✕

Encrypting...

Drive D: 9.7% Completed

Close

Manage BitLocker

n) If you see the message that encryption is complete, select **Close**.

o) Examine the **File Explorer** window.

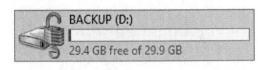

BACKUP (D:)

29.4 GB free of 29.9 GB

The drive icon for **D:** now shows a lock on it.

p) Close File Explorer, and minimize Server Manager.

TOPIC B

Manage Application Security

In the previous topic, you managed data security. Now, you will focus on the applications that use the data. Insecure applications can easily undermine the hardening efforts on the systems and network level if their security flaws are exploited. In this topic, you will manage application security.

Applications run on nearly every system in an organization, and are increasingly being delivered to those systems over the web. Insecure web-based applications can be vulnerable to a wide range of attacks, leaving your business at great risk. Employee or customer data could be stolen or damaged, or Denial of Service (DoS) conditions could be created. If your organization creates applications, unchecked vulnerabilities could result in dissatisfied customers and lost business. Even if you, personally, are not responsible for the application development functions in your organization, knowing some of the ways in which applications can be secured and how to mitigate threats can make you a more effective security professional.

What Is Application Security?

Application security ensures that the proper development, deployment, and maintenance of software is in place to protect applications from threats and vulnerabilities. Application security is applied in every phase of the software development process and should be incorporated into the initial design of all applications. With threats and attacks to applications on the rise, attackers will attempt to access and steal sensitive information through any vulnerability that exists in an application.

Patch Management

Patch management is the practice of monitoring for, obtaining, evaluating, testing, and deploying software patches and updates. As the number of computer systems in use has grown over recent years, so has the volume of vulnerabilities and corresponding patches and updates intended to address those vulnerabilities. So, the task of managing and applying them can be very time-consuming and inefficient without an organized patch management system. In typical patch management, software updates are evaluated for their applicability to an environment and then tested in a safe way on non-production systems. Finally, an organized plan for rolling out a valid patch across the organization is executed.

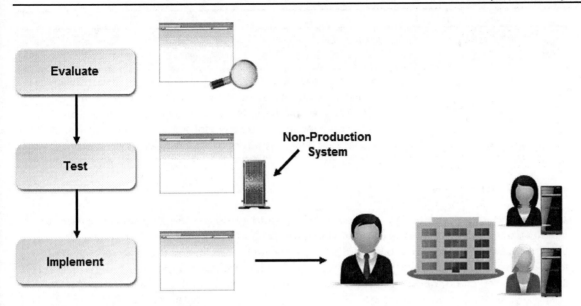

Figure 3-3: A system for patch management.

Many organizations have taken to creating official patch management policies that define the who, what, where, when, why, and how of patch management for that organization.

A patch management program might include:

- An individual responsible for subscribing to and reviewing vendor and security patches and updating newsletters.
- A review and triage of the updates into urgent, important, and non-critical categories.
- An offline patch-test environment where urgent and important patches can be installed and tested for functionality and impact.
- Immediate administrative push delivery of approved urgent patches.
- Weekly administrative push delivery of approved important patches.
- A periodic evaluation phase and pull rollout for non-critical patches.

Application Security Methods

Several common application security methods are implemented to prevent and treat possible security threats and attacks.

Application Security Method	Description
Configuration baseline	An application configuration baseline is created at many points during the application development life cycle. A baseline is composed of the minimum security requirements needed for an application to be complete. Organizations should determine a security baseline at the start of application development and track changes to make updates as needed. The baseline is also helpful when updates and changes are proposed.
Application hardening	This is the process used to configure a default application to prevent security threats and vulnerabilities. Each type of application will have its own configurations and methods used to increase security.

Application Security Method	Description
Patch management	Utilize a patch management system for your third-party software to ensure that every application is running with the latest security requirements and updates issued by manufacturers. Organizations should have an application patch management system in place to ensure that all patches are analyzed and installed as necessary.

Input Validation

Input validation involves ensuring that the data entered into a field or variable in an application is within acceptable bounds for the object that will receive the data. Input data should be within the size constraints of the memory location that will store it, be formatted in the expected way, and make sense in the context for which it will be used. If a given piece of input data cannot meet these standards, it should be considered invalid and should not be processed.

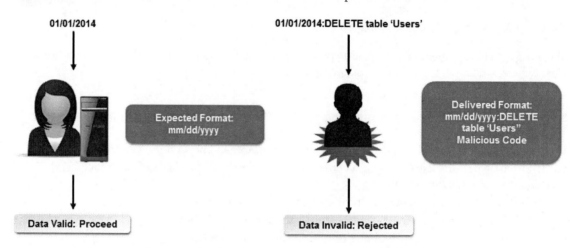

Figure 3–4: Input validation thwarting an attacker.

For example, say an input field on a web page asks for a date. An unvalidated input could allow an attacker to submit a chunk of text that is actually malicious code intended to exploit a vulnerability in the server or operating system software. Proper input validation would check to see if the submitted value is in the expected format (for example, mm/dd/yyyy for a date input). If the format is not correct, validation fails and the value is not recorded.

Input Validation Vulnerabilities

Input validation vulnerabilities can occur in any type of software. Websites and web-based applications are tempting targets for attackers to use input validation attacks on because they are often developed by inexperienced coders, or put together in a hurry, with little thought to application or data security. All input fields from any source should be validated before processing.

Command Injection

Command injection, which is when an attacker sends additional commands to an application through an unchecked input field, is one way to exploit input validation vulnerabilities. For example, an attacker may use a Structured Query Language (SQL) injection attack to send extra SQL commands to a database through a web form or Uniform Resource Locator (URL). When the commands are successfully executed, that attacker could gain the ability to access, change, or delete data in the target database.

Client–Side and Server–Side Validation

Data that you enter into an application can be validated at the client side or at the server side, or at both:

- Client-side validation involves performing all input validation and error recovery from within the browser by using JavaScript, Asynchronous JavaScript and XML (AJAX), VBScript, or HTML 5 attributes.
- Server-side validation involves performing all input validations and error recovery at the server by using a scripting language such as Perl, PHP, or ASP.

Client-side validation is generally thought to provide an enhanced user experience, because when faulty data is entered, the user receives immediate feedback as he or she is completing the form or otherwise entering the data. On the other hand, server-side validation is generally recognized as being essential to providing application-level security. Users can easily bypass client-side validation, and JavaScript can be disabled in the browser, but when validation occurs at the server, the end user cannot evade your security efforts.

It is often recommended that you employ a combination of client-side and server-side validation to provide feedback to the average users and to protect your server and data against the malicious users.

Error and Exception Handling

Error and exception handling is a strategy organizations use to design and develop security measures that are targeted at possible errors in an application. This type of development strategy is used to prevent attackers from gathering and using sensitive data that may be presented in an error message when the application fails under normal working conditions. For example, in some cases when an attacker enters a user name and password, he or she may get an error message back stating that the password does not match the registered user name. In this case, the attacker now knows a valid user name and can attempt to use that information to learn the valid password.

Valid User Name

Incorrect Password

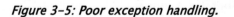

Attacker

Message:

Incorrect password

Figure 3–5: Poor exception handling.

XSS

In a *cross-site scripting (XSS) attack*, the attacker takes advantage of scripting and input validation vulnerabilities in an interactive website to attack legitimate users in two different ways. In a *stored attack*, the attacker injects malicious code or links into a website's forums, databases, or other data. When a user views the stored malicious code, or clicks a malicious link, an attack is perpetrated against the user.

In a *reflected attack*, the attacker poses as a legitimate user and sends information to a web server in the form of a page request or form submission. This information is in fact an attack, and when the web server responds to the request, the attack is directed at the targeted user or users. In this way, the attack is reflected off the server to users.

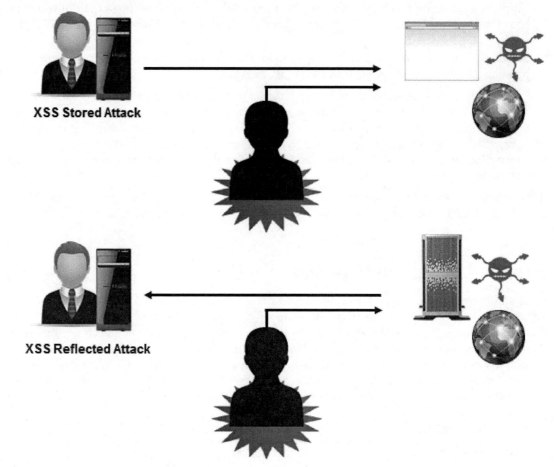

XSS Stored Attack

XSS Reflected Attack

Figure 3-6: Stored and reflected XSS attacks.

XSRF

In a *cross-site request forgery (XSRF) attack*, an attacker takes advantage of the trust established between an authorized user of a website and the website itself. This type of attack exploits a web browser's trust in a user's unexpired browser cookies. Websites that are at the most risk are those that perform functions based on input from trusted authenticated users who authenticate automatically using a saved browser cookie stored on their machines. The attacker takes advantage of the saved authentication data stored inside the cookie to gain access to a web browser's sensitive data.

This functionality is found on most web pages and is allowed when a user logs in to access account information. If, when logging in, the user selects the **Remember Me** option, then a cookie is saved and accessed the next time they visit that web page.

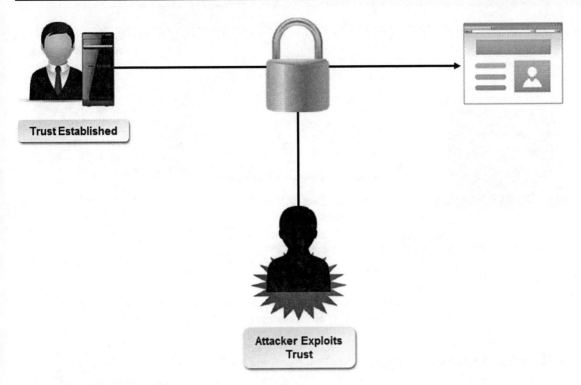

Figure 3-7: An XSRF attack.

Cross-Site Attack Prevention Methods

To protect systems from XSS and XSRF attacks, you must verify that the proper security controls and development guidelines are implemented in applications you develop and run or that you purchase from third parties:

- Do not allow Hypertext Markup Language (HTML) formatting in form fields.
- Use input validation on all fields, strings, variables, and cookies.
- Limit the expiration time for cookies, and do not unnecessarily store data in cookies.
- Encrypt data communications between clients and servers.
- Inform end users to not use the **Remember Me** option when authenticating on websites.

Fuzzing

Fuzzing is a testing method used to identify vulnerabilities and weaknesses in applications by sending the application a range of random or unusual input data and noting any failures and crashes that result. Fuzzing is used to identify potential security issues and areas that may be vulnerable to attacks within an application. This type of testing is usually performed in the final phases of the application development process. Organizations may consider this type of testing on any application that transmits sensitive data and performs online transactions.

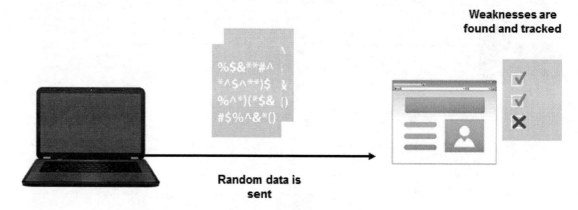

Figure 3-8: Testing input vulnerabilities in a web app.

Fuzzing Tools

There are various pre-built fuzzing tools available to help generate the fuzzy input data for testing procedures. Some of the best known include SPIKE Proxy and Peach Fuzzer™ Framework.

Web Browser Security

Because many applications are implemented through web browser interfaces, it is very important to ensure proper security within individual web browser installations. Specific security features will vary depending on the browser, but most browsers offer some common features. Popular web browsers include Microsoft® Internet Explorer®, Mozilla® Firefox®, Apple® Safari®, and Google Chrome™.

Security Feature	Description
Pop-up blocker	In most browsers, the pop-up blocking feature is enabled by default to prevent websites from displaying pop-up windows without user authorization. It can be configured to specify sites that are allowed to open pop-up windows.
Parental controls	Most browsers will have some sort of parental controls to manage Internet access. For example, Mozilla Firefox works with the built-in Windows® parental controls.
Automated updating	Most browsers can be configured to automatically check for updates and request the user to install them.
Encryption	Support for current strong encryption standards includes SSL2, SSL3, and TLS.
Proxy support	Many popular browsers support proxy mechanisms, including Hypertext Transfer Protocol (HTTP), Hypertext Transfer Protocol Secure (HTTPS), File Transfer Protocol (FTP), Socket Secure (SOCKS), Gopher, and Rapid Spanning Tree Protocol (RSTP).
Web content	All browsers provide options to enable or disable JavaScript, with options for some specific features.

Security Feature	Description
Advanced security	Most browsers have options provided to remove: • Cookies • Web cache • Download and browsing history • Saved form and search history • Offline website data • Saved passwords • Authenticated sessions

Note: For additional information, check out the LearnTO **Configure Security Settings in Google Chrome** presentation from the **LearnTO** tile on the LogicalCHOICE Course screen.

Note: For additional information, check out the LearnTO **Configure Security Settings in Mozilla Firefox** presentation from the **LearnTO** tile on the LogicalCHOICE Course screen.

Guidelines for Establishing Web Browser Security

There are some general security guidelines that can be implemented to ensure web browser security:

• Harden the host machine or device.
• Install all the latest software versions and patches.
• Configure the security settings built in to the software.
• Disable scripting when appropriate.
• Disable auto-complete and password saving features.
• Install anti-malware software.

ACTIVITY 3-2
Configuring a Web Browser

Data Files

C:\093022Data\Managing Data, Application, and Host Security\IESecurity.rtf

Scenario

You are the security administrator for Develetech Industries, and you need to make sure your new Windows Server 2012 R2 computers with Microsoft Internet Explorer are secure. In the past, the company's IT department has had problems with users storing passwords in their Internet browsers. They have also had problems with users visiting sites that contain inappropriate content, and users have also downloaded unauthorized programs to their computers. Before connecting the new Windows Server 2012 R2 computers to your network, you need to make sure that the browser is configured properly to minimize the likelihood of attacks.

The IT department has designed a security deployment plan for all new systems, including the new Windows Server 2012 R2 computers with Internet Explorer, and documented it as IESecurity.rtf. Before the IT department deploys the browser to all users, this security configuration needs to be set up manually on a test system to verify that clients will still have the appropriate level of web access.

1. Review the security specifications in the IESecurity.rtf file.
   a) Open **C:\093022Data\Managing Data, Application, and Host Security\IESecurity.rtf**.
   b) The file opens in WordPad. Review the security specifications in the document and close WordPad.

2. Verify that Internet Explorer Advanced Security Configuration is installed.
   a) Start Internet Explorer.
   b) Verify that the **Internet Explorer Enhanced Security Configuration is enabled** screen appears as the default home page.
   c) Select the **Effects of Internet Explorer Enhanced Security Configuration** link.
   d) Review the specifications, and select the **Home** button to return to the home page.

3. Configure Internet Explorer with the appropriate zone level for the Internet zone.

a) Select **Tools→Internet options**.

b) In the **Internet Options** dialog box, select the **Security** tab.
c) With the **Internet** zone selected, select **Custom level**.
d) In the **Security Settings - Internet Zone** dialog box, scroll down to the **ActiveX controls and plug-ins** section.
e) Verify that **Allow Scriptlets** and **Automatic prompting for ActiveX controls** are disabled.
f) Press **End** to scroll down to the end of the list.
g) Verify that the **Scripting of Java applets** is disabled and the **Logon** is set to **Prompt for user name and password**.
h) From the **Reset to** drop-down list, verify that **High (default)** is selected.

i) Select **OK**.

4. Block insecure cookies.
   a) Select the **Privacy** tab.

b) Move the **Settings** slider to **High** to block insecure cookies from the Internet zone.

```
┌──────────────────────────────────────────────────────────┐
│                  Internet Options              [ ? ] [ X ] │
├──────────────────────────────────────────────────────────┤
│  General │ Security │ Privacy │ Content │ Connections │ Programs │ Advanced │
│ ┌────────────────────────────────────────────────────────┐ │
│ │ Settings                                                 │ │
│ │ Select a setting for the Internet zone.                  │ │
│ │                                                          │ │
│ │          High                                            │ │
│ │          - Blocks all cookies from websites that do not  │ │
│ │          have a compact privacy policy                   │ │
│ │          - Blocks cookies that save information that can  │ │
│ │          be used to contact you without your explicit    │ │
│ │          consent                                         │ │
│ │                                                          │ │
│ │  [ Sites ] [ Import ] [ Advanced ] [ Default ]           │ │
│ └────────────────────────────────────────────────────────┘ │
│  Location                                                  │
│  ☐ Never allow websites to request your      [ Clear Sites ] │
│    physical location                                       │
│  Pop-up Blocker                                            │
│  ☑ Turn on Pop-up Blocker                    [ Settings ]   │
│  InPrivate                                                 │
│  ☑ Disable toolbars and extensions when InPrivate Browsing starts │
│                                                            │
│                          [ OK ]  [ Cancel ]  [ Apply ]     │
└──────────────────────────────────────────────────────────┘
```

c) Select **Apply**.

5. Configure the appropriate websites to allow use of cookies.
   a) Select **Sites**.
   b) In the **Address of website** text box, type *fcc.gov* and select **Allow**.
   c) In the **Address of website** text box, type *microsoft.com* and select **Allow**.

Managed websites:

Domain	Setting
fcc.gov	Always Allow
microsoft.com	Always Allow

d) Select **OK** twice.

6. Enable the Content Advisor in Internet Explorer 11.
   a) On the Desktop, right-click the **Start** button and select **Command Prompt**.

b) In the **Administrator: Command Prompt** window, type *gpedit.msc* and then press **Enter** to open the Local Group Policy Editor.

c) Expand **User Configuration→Administrative Templates→Windows Components→Internet Explorer→Internet Control Panel** and select **Content Page**.

d) In the right pane, double-click **Show Content Advisor on Internet Options**.

e) In the **Show Content Advisor on Internet Options** dialog box, select **Enabled**, and then select **OK**.

f) Close the Local Group Policy Editor and the command prompt.

7. Set the appropriate Content Advisor rating levels.

a) In Internet Explorer, select **Tools→Internet options**.

b) Select the **Content** tab.

c) In the **Content Advisor** section, select **Enable**.

> **Note:** If **Content Advisor** doesn't appear, restart Internet Explorer.

d) In the **Content Advisor** dialog box, on the **Ratings** page, in the **Select a category to view the rating levels** list, scroll down and select **Language**.

e) Adjust the rating slider to **Limited**.

```
┌─────────────────────────────────────────────────────────┐
│                   Content Advisor              [  X  ]    │
├─────────────────────────────────────────────────────────┤
│  ┌──────────┬───────────────┬─────────┬──────────┐       │
│  │ Ratings  │ Approved Sites │ General │ Advanced │       │
│  └──────────┴───────────────┴─────────┴──────────┘       │
│                                                           │
│  Select a category to view the rating levels:             │
│  ┌──────────────────────────────────────────────┐ ▲      │
│  │ 🔍 Depiction of gambling                        │        │
│  │ 🔍 Depiction of tobacco use                     │        │
│  │ 🔍 Depiction of weapon use                      │ ▤      │
│  │ 🔍 Incitement/depiction of discrimination or harm│       │
│  │ 🔍 Language                                      │        │
│  │ 🔍 Nudity                                        │ ▼      │
│  └──────────────────────────────────────────────┘        │
│                                                           │
│  Adjust the slider to specify what users are allowed to see:│
│                                                           │
│  ├─────────────────■──────────────────────────────┤       │
│                                                           │
│                        Limited                            │
│  ┌─ Description ──────────────────────────────────┐      │
│  │ No abusive or vulgar terms in any context. Profanity,│  │
│  │ swearing, or mild expletives only in artistic, medical,│ │
│  │ educational, sports or news context              │      │
│  │                                                  │      │
│  │ To view the Internet page for this rating service,│ ┌────────┐ │
│  │ click More Info.                                 │ │More Info│ │
│  └──────────────────────────────────────────────┘ └────────┘ │
│                                                           │
│               ┌──────┐  ┌────────┐  ┌───────┐            │
│               │  OK  │  │ Cancel │  │ Apply │            │
│               └──────┘  └────────┘  └───────┘            │
└─────────────────────────────────────────────────────────┘
```

f) Scroll down to the end of the list.

g) Set the rating level for the **Violence** category to **Limited**.

h) Select **OK**.

i) In the **Create Supervisor Password** dialog box, in the **Password** text box, type *!Pass1234* and press **Tab**. In the **Confirm password** text box, type *!Pass1234*

j) In the **Hint** text box, type *same as Administrator*

k) Select **OK**.

l) In the **Content Advisor** message box, select **OK**, then select **OK** again to close the **Internet Options** dialog box.

m) Navigate to **google.com** to select **OK** in the **Security Alert** message box.

n) Verify that you are being blocked from viewing the website, indicating that **Content Advisor** is enabled. Select **Cancel**.

8. Configure the appropriate forms settings.

   a) Open the **Internet Options** dialog box.

   b) On the **Content** tab, in the **AutoComplete** section, select **Settings**.

c) In the **AutoComplete Settings** dialog box, in the **Use AutoComplete for** section, uncheck the **User names and passwords on forms** check box.

d) Select **OK**.

e) On the **General** tab, in the **Browsing history** section, select **Delete**.

f) In the **Delete Browsing History** dialog box, check the **Passwords** check box and select **Delete**.

Internet Explorer has finished deleting the selected browsing history.

9. Close and reopen Internet Explorer to apply the changes.

10. Test connectivity to unrated sites.

a) Navigate to any website, and verify that the **Content Advisor** information box is displayed.

b) Select **Cancel**.

11. Turn off **Content Advisor** to avoid issues later.

a) Open the **Internet Options** dialog box.

b) Select the **Content** tab.

c) In the **Content Advisor** section, select **Disable**.

d) In the **Supervisor Password Required** dialog box, in the **Password** text box, type *!Pass1234* and select **OK**.

e) Select **OK** to confirm your change.

f) Select **OK** to close the **Internet Options** dialog box.

g) Close Internet Explorer.

NoSQL Databases

For many years, the relational database management system (RDBMS) was the prevailing model for database management, but with the advent of cloud computing and other technological advancements, an alternative model is emerging. A *NoSQL database* is a database that provides data storage and retrieval in a non-relational manner. Instead of using tables and relationships between tables, NoSQL databases use a variety of other models to organize and group data:

- Key-value stores are the most basic type of NoSQL database. Each item in the database is stored as an attribute name, or key, along with the associated value.
- Document stores contain documents that have standard encoding such as XML, and that are assigned a key for key-value type lookups. Document stores also provide ways to search for and retrieve documents based on their contents.
- Graph stores contain information about networks, such as social connections.
- Column stores contain information from very large datasets that store columns of data together, as opposed to the more traditional row-based storage.

NoSQL databases are well suited to storing data from web applications because they easily store the session information that enables web developers to manage session information for any user who visits a website. They also support the creation and maintenance of a global user profile store, which can be used to authenticate access to websites and applications. Many organizations are using NoSQL databases to support agile applications, as well as big data projects such as banking applications and document storage.

Database Security

For relational databases, security measures include:

- Role-based security configuration parameters.
- Encrypted communications.
- Access control for rows and fields.
- User-level permissions for stored procedures.

For NoSQL databases, it's important to recognize the potential security weaknesses that need to be addressed if you plan to implement a NoSQL database. As you evaluate the various NoSQL offerings, consider the following:

- Are there weaknesses inherent in the authentication mechanism? Some NoSQL databases do not require password credentials for the database itself.
- Are there weaknesses in the authorization scheme? Some NoSQL databases are configured so that all users that are created have read-only access to the entire database.
- Is there data encryption, or is data stored and sent in cleartext?

To counteract these potential vulnerabilities, you might need to make sure that developers who create applications that access NoSQL databases are incorporating security controls in the applications themselves.

Guidelines for Managing Application Security

Follow these guidelines for managing application security:

- Consider establishing security configuration baselines for applications that are used throughout the organization. Periodically review applications to ensure that the security baselines are being met.
- Identify ways to harden applications—especially web browsers—and implement whatever measures are needed to maximize the security of the applications used by your organization.
- Implement a patch management system for applications.
- For applications that require user input, implement input validation controls.

- For client-server applications, consider implementing a combination of client-side validation and server-side validation.
- For applications developed in-house, implement error and exception handling.
- Implement methods to protect against XSS and XSRF attacks.
- Implement measures to protect relational and NoSQL databases and the applications that rely on their data.

ACTIVITY 3–3
Managing Application Security

Scenario

At Develetech, you've met with your IT team about several new projects that are in the works. The company recently launched a new customer website and is facing a security issue that you need to address. In addition, the IT team is in the process of developing a mobile app, and you've been tasked with performing a security evaluation. By managing the security of the applications that you and your customers use every day, you will help keep software-related threats at bay.

1. Develetech has a new public-facing website that includes forums for customers to discuss the company's products and any technical issues they may be having. You've received reports that several forum users had their accounts hijacked. These hijacked accounts started spamming the forums, which led to them being banned. In your investigation, you noticed that all of the users that were impersonated had either commented on or simply visited a specific forum thread. In this thread, a user invoked an HTML script in their comment. This could be a(n):

   ○ XSRF attack.

   ○ Stored XSS attack.

   ○ Reflected XSS attack.

   ○ Fuzzing test.

2. The IT department's engineering team is currently developing a mobile app that gives customers another interface for accessing Develetech's online store. You are one of the app's beta testers and are looking for any security vulnerabilities. During your test, you select a product that is on sale and the app crashes. As it crashes, a message pops up that reveals information about what kind of database the app was attempting to connect to and how the data is supposed to be referenced. You determine that this is information that an attacker can easily use to their advantage. This is an example of:

   ○ Insufficient input validation.

   ○ Poor database management.

   ○ Insufficient XSS and XSRF prevention.

   ○ Poor error/exception handling.

3. Using this mobile app, customers will be able to log in with individual accounts. When customers create an account with the app, they enter personal information into a standard registration form. To prevent an attacker from injecting malicious code into the account database, you should implement which of the following security techniques in your app? (Select all that apply.)

   ○ Patch management

   ○ Client-side input validation

   ○ Server-side input validation

   ○ Error/exception handling

4. In evaluating the mobile app, your IT team has decided to migrate the existing SQL database to a NoSQL database to greater facilitate the web app experience for customers. What security concerns do you need to remind your team of for this transition?

TOPIC C

Manage Device and Host Security

In the previous topics, you managed data and application security. You also need to make sure that the devices and hosts using the data and applications are also secure. In this topic, you will manage device and host security.

To properly protect an organization's assets as a whole, you must be able to secure its networks, devices, and end user systems. Most viruses today start from an individual machine first, then spread to other devices through a network. In order to prevent this type of infiltration, you must be able to establish necessary security measures on all the devices within an organization.

Hardening

Hardening is a general term for any security technique in which the default configuration of a system is altered in an attempt to close vulnerabilities and generally protect the system against attacks. Typically, hardening is implemented to conform with the security requirements in a defined security policy. Many different hardening techniques can be employed, depending on the type of system and the desired level of security. When hardening a system, it is important to keep in mind its intended use, because hardening a system can also restrict the system's access and capabilities. The need for hardening must be balanced against the access requirements and usability in a particular situation.

Figure 3–9: A hardened server.

Operating System Security

Each type of operating system has unique vulnerabilities that present opportunities for would-be attackers. Systems from different vendors have different weaknesses, as do client and server systems. As soon as a vulnerability is identified, vendors will try to correct it while, at the same time, attackers will try to exploit it. There can never be a single comprehensive list of vulnerabilities for each operating system, so security professionals must stay up-to-date with the system security information posted on vendor websites and in other security references.

Operating System Security Settings

General operating system security settings include:

- Managing services running on the operating system.
- Configuring the operating system's built-in firewall.
- Configuring Internet security options.
- Managing all automatic updates and patches for software and services.
- Enabling necessary auditing and logging functions when applicable.

TCB

The *Trusted Computing Base (TCB)* is a hardware, firmware, and software component of a computer system that is responsible for ensuring that the security policy is implemented and the system is secure. This means that the security properties of an entire system could be jeopardized should defects occur inside the TCB. The TCB is implemented in the hardware through processor rings or privileges, in the firmware through driver and resource protection, and in the operating system's isolation of resources and services from applications, which is referred to as a *Trusted Operating System (TOS)*.

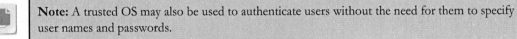 **Note:** A trusted OS may also be used to authenticate users without the need for them to specify user names and passwords.

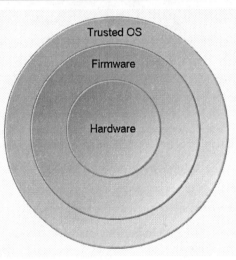

Figure 3-10: TCB.

Security Baselines

A *security baseline* is a collection of security and configuration settings that are to be applied to a particular host in the enterprise. The host software baseline is a benchmark against which you can compare other hosts in your network. When creating a baseline for a particular computer, the settings you decide to include will depend on its operating system and its function in your organization and should include manufacturer recommendations.

Because each baseline configuration is specific to a particular type of system, you will have separate baselines defined for desktop clients, file and print servers, Domain Name System (DNS)/BIND servers, application servers, directory services servers, and other types of systems. You will also have different baselines for all those same types of systems, depending on the operating system in use.

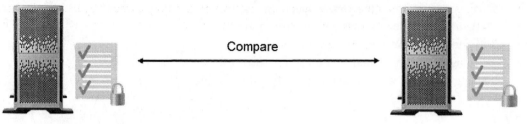

Figure 3–11: Comparing security baselines.

When establishing a security baseline for your host(s), you may find it helpful to make use of the many software tools that are available. Tools are available to scan for and detect a very wide range of vulnerabilities ranging from port scanners to password analyzers to tools that scan for specific hard-to-detect vulnerabilities. For Unix-based systems, check to see if your software vendor provides any analysis tools that you could make use of, as they will likely make the analysis process far easier. Two such tools for Unix are Nessus® and Nmap. When dealing with Microsoft-based systems, tools such as the Microsoft Baseline Security Analyzer (MBSA) and the Security Configuration Wizard (SCW) are good places to start.

Software Updates

Software manufacturers regularly issue different types of system updates that can include security-related changes to the software.

Update Type	Description
Patch	A small unit of supplemental code meant to address either a security problem or a functionality flaw in a software package or operating system.
Hotfix	A patch that is often issued on an emergency basis to address a specific security flaw.
Rollup	A collection of previously issued patches and hotfixes, usually meant to be applied to one component of a system, such as the web browser or a particular service.
Service Pack	A larger compilation of system updates that can include functionality enhancements, new features, and typically all patches, updates, and hotfixes issued up to the point of the Service Pack's release.

Application Blacklisting and Whitelisting

Application blacklisting is the practice of preventing the execution of programs that an organization has deemed to be undesirable, whether due to security issues or for any other reason. To implement blacklisting, you would list the applications that should be denied system access, and then prevent them from being installed or run on the target system. Blacklisting is used in many antivirus and antispam utilities, as well as in intrusion detection systems (IDSs) and intrusion prevention systems (IPSs).

Conversely, in *application whitelisting*, you would maintain a list of approved applications, and only those applications would be permitted to be installed or run on the target system. Whitelisting is a good example of the principle of implicit deny.

Both blacklisting and whitelisting have benefits and drawbacks:

* Blacklisting does enable you to prevent specific applications from running on a system. The downside is that it blocks only those applications that have been identified as undesirable, so new applications might be granted access even though they pose a security risk.

- Whitelisting provides a more thorough solution than blacklisting, particularly in regard to new applications that might contain vulnerabilities, but the administrative overhead required to create and maintain a whitelist can be prohibitive.

Logging

In computing terms, *logging* is using an operating system or application to record data about activity on a computer. The resulting *log* files are usually stored as text files in known locations. The level of detail available in log files can vary from showing only significant errors to the recording of every keystroke, mouse movement, and network packet. Use care when enabling logging features—detailed logging, or even simple logging on a high-volume system, can rapidly consume a large amount of storage space. Reviewing the activity recorded in log files can be difficult due to the variations in formatting and detail, but is worthwhile because the review may reveal a great deal about a suspected attack. Log files themselves can be the target of an attack; therefore, for security purposes, it is recommended that you restrict access to and back up important logs.

Log files are stored   **Log files are generated from the system**

Figure 3-12: A server generating and storing log files.

Auditing

Computer *security auditing* is the process of performing an organized technical assessment of the security strengths and weaknesses of a system. Computer security audits can include reviewing log files—either manually or via software—testing the strength of passwords, scanning the network for open ports or rogue servers and workstations, reviewing user and group permissions, and reviewing the physical security related to the system or systems in question.

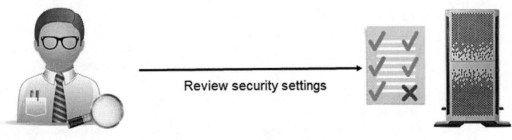

Review security settings

Figure 3-13: A security professional performing an audit.

Anti-malware Software

Anti-malware software is protective software that scans individual computers and entire enterprise networks for known viruses, Trojans, worms, and other malicious programs. Some programs attempt to scan for unknown harmful software. It is advisable to install anti-malware software on all computers and keep it updated according to your organization's patch management policy.

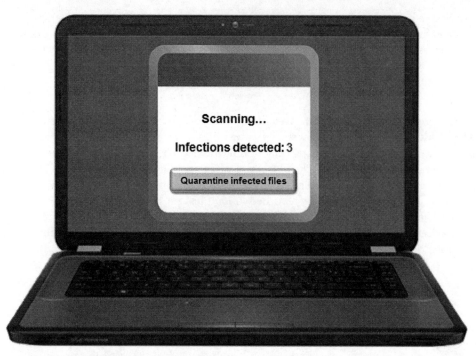

Figure 3-14: Anti-malware software that has detected several infected files.

Types of Anti-malware Software

Many types of anti-malware software are commonly used to protect systems from specific threats and attacks.

Type	Description
Antivirus software	An application that scans files for executable code that matches specific patterns known to be common to viruses. Antivirus software also monitors systems for activity that is associated with viruses, such as accessing the boot sector. Antivirus software should be deployed on various network systems as well as on individual computers, and the signature database and program updates should be downloaded and installed on a regular basis as well as whenever a new threat is active.
Anti-spam	Spam detection has become an important task for end users. There are many different ways end users can protect themselves against spammers. Detection can include an anti-spam filtering program that will detect specific words that are commonly used in spam messages. The message may be rejected once the words are found. This can cause issues if the detection system rejects legitimate messages that may contain one of the keywords. Other detection methods are used to block Internet Protocol (IP) addresses of known spammers or to pose an email address that is not in use or is too old to collect spam. These methods can help reduce the number of spam messages in your inbox. Some examples of anti-spam software include SPAMfighter, iHateSpam, Cloudmark for Microsoft® Outlook®, and BullGuard™ Internet Security Suite.
Anti-spyware	This software is specifically designed to protect systems against spyware attacks. Some antivirus software packages include protection against adware and spyware, but in most cases it is necessary to maintain anti-spyware protection in addition to antivirus protection. Some examples of anti-spyware include Webroot® Spy Sweeper and STOPzilla AntiMalware.

Type	Description
Pop-up blockers	Malicious software can be attached to *pop-up* ads or other pop-up content on websites. (Pop-ups are windows or frames that load and appear automatically when a user connects to a particular web page.) Pop-up blockers prevent pop-ups from sites that are unknown or untrusted, and prevent the transfer of unwanted code to the local system. Most Internet browsers include some type of pop-up blocking feature.
Host-based firewalls	This is software that is installed on a single system to specifically guard against networking attacks. The software is configured to monitor incoming and outgoing network packets in order to control and prevent unauthorized access.

Windows Firewall Configuration

Windows Firewall is a software-based firewall that is included with all current Windows operating system client and server versions. You can configure the firewall by using the Windows Firewall program in **Control Panel**, or through **Group Policy** settings, although most versions of Windows will provide a wizard. You can use the Windows Firewall with Advanced Security console to monitor the rules that control the flow of information to and from the system, specify new rules, modify existing rules, or delete rules. For more information, see the Windows Firewall entries in the Help and Support Center, and the Windows Firewall Technical Reference on the Microsoft TechNet website.

Types of Firewall Rules

There are three types of firewall rules that you can set using the Windows Firewall with Advanced Security console:

* Inbound rules: These rules define the action to be performed by the firewall on the data that enters the system from another system.
* Outbound rules: These rules define the action to be performed by the firewall on the data that flows out of the system.
* Connection security rules: These rules define the type of authentication that is needed to allow communication between the systems.

For more information about the Windows Firewall with Advanced Security console, refer to the Overview of Windows Firewall with Advanced Security at **http://technet.microsoft.com/en-us/library/dd448535(WS.10).aspx**.

Virtualization Security Techniques

The overall security of a system that is hosting a virtualization environment is crucial to ensuring the security of the network and devices connected to it. There are a number of security techniques available to properly secure a virtual host machine.

Security Technique	Description
Patch management	A patch management system must be in place to ensure that all relevant patches are installed. This is especially important for any patches released that apply to the virtualization software itself. Virtual environments need to be checked for patch compatibility before a patch can be applied. Also, careful analysis must be done to determine when and if general operating system patches should also be installed on the host. In some cases, these patches can threaten the security of the virtualization environment.

Security Technique	Description
Least privilege	The concept of least privilege should be applied when determining access control assignments to any virtual environment. Access to all environments must be monitored on a regular basis to prevent unauthorized access.
Logging	User activities in the virtual environment should be logged and reviewed to check for irregular activity and any possible security breaches.
Design	Applying good security measures to all virtualization environments starts with a good design. By planning carefully and determining what security controls should be used on each component of the virtual environment, you can prevent many security-related issues once the virtualization environment is launched.
Snapshots	Consistently capturing snapshots, or the state a virtual environment is in at a certain point in time, will provide you with a quick and easy way to recover the entire environment should it be compromised or degrade in performance.
Host availability	Also called *host elasticity*, the availability of a virtual host is dependent on its ability to adapt to various system changes. Unavailable hosts that provide security functionality may leave your system vulnerable to an attack.
Sandboxing	Sandboxing is the practice of isolating an environment from a larger system in order to guarantee that the environment runs in a controlled, secure fashion. Virtual environments are often used as sandboxes to test potentially malicious code from untrusted sources, or to test new network functionality before it is applied to a live environment.

Hardware Security Controls

Because security is most often breached at the end user level, hardware security controls can be applied to help prevent security issues:

* Proper logoff and shutdown procedures must be enforced for all systems when not in use.
* Wireless communication devices must be approved by the IT department and installed properly.
* Mobile devices, such as laptops, mobile phones, and smartphones, must be properly stored and secured in a cabinet or safe when not in use.
* Cable locks should be installed and used on all end user hardware components.
* Strong password policies should be enforced on all end user devices.

Non-standard Hosts

As organizations grow and technological advancements are incorporated into their computing environments, it's inevitable that the duties of a security professional will become increasingly complex. There are many non-standard hosts that you might encounter, each of which could be considered to be *static environments*, which are operating systems and other computing environments that are not updated or changed, either by design or due to other circumstances such as age.

Non-standard Host Type	Description
Supervisory control and data acquisition (SCADA) systems	A type of industrial control system that monitors and controls industrial processes such as manufacturing and fabrication; infrastructure processes such as power transmission and distribution; and facility processes such as energy consumption and HVAC systems.
Embedded-software systems	Some hosts, such as game consoles, printers, Smart TVs, and motor vehicles include software that is not meant to be updated or is not normally updated by an IT department.
Mainframe computers	Highly stable and reliable computers that are used for mission-critical applications and bulk data processing. Often employing virtualization, modern mainframes can run multiple operating systems and provide large amounts of data throughput.
Some mobile devices	Mobile devices such as smartphones and tablets may be considered non-standard hosts if their Android or iOS versions are old enough to no longer be supported by the manufacturer.

Security Controls for Non-standard Hosts

Due to the wide variety of non-standard hosts and static environments, there are a corresponding number of security controls that you might want or need to apply to those hosts, including:

- Layered security, including network segmentation and application firewalls, to isolate at-risk systems from the remainder of the network environment.
- Manual updates on an ad hoc basis for older versions of Android and iOS.
- Firmware version control for SCADA and embedded systems.
- Wrappers, which are software that contains other data or software, such as legacy code. Wrappers enable the contained data or software to operate in newer environments.
- Controlling redundancy (the provision of multiple identical instances of a system for fault tolerance) and diversity (the provision of multiple different implementations of the same specification to minimize common vulnerabilities).

Strong Passwords

A *strong password* is a password that meets the complexity requirements that are set by a system administrator and documented in a security policy or password policy. Strong passwords increase the security of systems that use password-based authentication by protecting against password guessing and brute force password attacks.

Password complexity requirements should meet the security needs of an individual organization, and can specify:

- The minimum length of the password.
- Required characters, such as a combination of letters, numbers, and symbols.
- Forbidden character strings, such as the user account name or dictionary words.

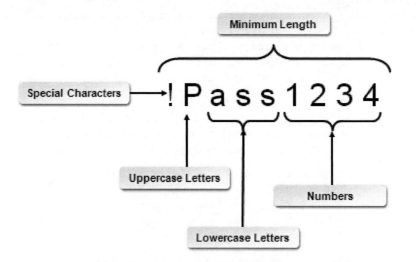

Figure 3-15: The elements of a strong password.

> **Note:** For additional information, check out the LearnTO **Create a Strong Password** presentation from the **LearnTO** tile on the LogicalCHOICE Course screen.

Guidelines for Establishing Device and Host Security

In order to establish device and host security, you must implement security measures that protect the devices themselves from attack, and that prevent unauthorized access to your network, while ensuring that legitimate users continue to have the appropriate level of connectivity between internal and external networks.

Device Security Guidelines

Follow these guidelines for establishing device security:

- For software-based systems, harden the base operating system to close security holes in running services.
- For hardware-based systems, install the latest firmware updates to address known security issues.
- Implement your hardware and software manufacturers' security recommendations.
- Implement strict access control and use strong, robust passwords so that unauthorized persons cannot access and reconfigure the systems.
- Secure router configuration files to keep configuration details secret.
- Configure appropriate ingress and egress filters to help prevent IP spoofing and DoS attacks.
- Disable IP source routing to prevent attackers from gaining information about the internal network.
- Implement a routing protocol that supports authentication, such as Routing Information Protocol (RIP) version 2 (RIPv2), Enhanced Interior Gateway Routing Protocol (EIGRP), or Open Shortest Path First (OSPF), to enable a greater level of security and authentication and to help prevent unauthorized changes to routing tables.
- Protect routers, virtual local area networks (VLANs), Network Address Translation (NAT) devices, and other internetworking devices with properly configured firewalls.
- To protect against Address Resolution Protocol (ARP) poisoning, verify that all routers are configured properly and are set up with notifications and appropriate monitoring software.
- Implement NAT to hide the true IP scheme of your network.
- Close unused well-known Transmission Control Protocol (TCP) and User Datagram Protocol (UDP) ports.
- Place appropriate servers in a demilitarized zone (DMZ).

- Disable IP directed broadcasts on routers.
- Protect all internetwork devices and network media from unauthorized physical access to prevent wiretapping, vandalism, and theft.
- Test the functionality of systems after hardening to make sure that required services and resources are accessible to legitimate users.
- Document your changes.

Host Security Guidelines

Follow these guidelines to establish host security:

- Require strong passwords to protect against password-cracking utilities, to keep passwords secure, and to protect password databases.
- Implement your hardware and software manufacturers' security recommendations.
- Implement antivirus, anti-spyware, and anti-adware software to protect against malicious code.
- Disable unnecessary services to prevent attackers from exploiting them.
- Restrict access permissions so that only those users who absolutely need access are allowed into the system.
- Implement security policies to control, limit, or restrict user interaction with the system.
- Physically secure mission-critical servers and devices by installing them in locked rooms to which only trusted administrators have access.
- Plan backup strategies to protect sensitive data and provide methods to restore the data in the event of data loss or corruption. Backup media should be stored offsite. Backups help ensure business continuity in the event of an attack.
- Test the functionality of systems after hardening to make sure that required services and resources are accessible to legitimate users.
- Utilize scanning and auditing tools to detect potential vulnerabilities in your systems.
- Identify non-standard hosts and what measures can and need to be taken to protect them against vulnerabilities.
- Document your changes.

 Access the Checklist tile on your LogicalCHOICE course screen for reference information and job aids on How to Define Windows Firewall Rules.

ACTIVITY 3-4
Implementing Auditing

Scenario

As the security administrator for Develetech, you have been asked to configure your domain controllers to detect any unauthorized logon attempts. Failed logon attempts will be recorded and readily viewable for auditing purposes. Implementing this type of policy can alert you to repeated password cracking attempts, which may prompt you to take measures to prevent a system breach.

1. Enable the auditing of all failed account logon events on your domain controllers.

   a) In the **Server Manager** window, in the menu bar at the top right, select **Tools→Group Policy Management**.

   b) If necessary, in the console tree, expand your domain object.

   c) If necessary, expand **Domain Controllers** and select **Default Domain Controllers Policy**.

   - Group Policy Management
     - Forest: domain100.internal
       - Domains
         - domain100.internal
           - Default Domain Policy
           - My Policy
           - Domain Controllers
             - Default Domain Controllers Policy

   d) If necessary, in the **Group Policy Management Console** message box, select **OK**.

   e) From the menu bar, select **Action→Edit**.

f)   In the console tree, under **Computer Configuration**, expand **Policies→Windows Settings→Security Settings→Local Policies**.

> **Default Domain Controllers Policy [SERVER100.DOMA**
> ⊿ 💻 Computer Configuration
>   ⊿ 📋 Policies
>   ▷ 📄 Software Settings
>   ⊿ 📄 Windows Settings
>   ▷ 📄 Name Resolution Policy
>   📄 Scripts (Startup/Shutdown)
>   ⊿ 🔒 Security Settings
>   ▷ 📄 Account Policies
>   ⊿ 📄 Local Policies
>   ▷ 📄 Audit Policy
>   ▷ 📄 User Rights Assignment
>   ▷ 📄 Security Options

 Note: It may take a few moments for **Security Settings** to expand.

g)   Under **Local Policies**, select **Audit Policy**.

h)   In the details pane, double-click **Audit account logon events**.

i)   In the **Audit account logon events Properties** dialog box, on the **Security Policy Setting** tab, check the **Define these policy settings** check box, verify that the **Success** check box is checked, and check the **Failure** check box to enable auditing of failed logon attempts.

> Security Policy Setting | Explain
>
>   Audit account logon events
>
> ☑ Define these policy settings
>
>   Audit these attempts:
>
>   ☑ Success
>
>   ☑ Failure

j)   Select **OK**.

k) Verify that the **Policy Setting** for the **Audit account logon events** policy is changed to **Success, Failure**.

Policy ▲	Policy Setting
Audit account logon events	Success, Failure
Audit account management	Not Defined
Audit directory service access	Not Defined
Audit logon events	Not Defined
Audit object access	Not Defined
Audit policy change	Not Defined
Audit privilege use	Not Defined
Audit process tracking	Not Defined
Audit system events	Not Defined

2. Force a Group Policy update.
   a) On the Desktop, right-click the **Start** button and select **Command Prompt**.
   b) At the prompt, enter *gpupdate /force*
   c) Verify that the computer policy update has completed successfully, and close the **Administrator: Command Prompt** window.
   d) Close the **Group Policy Management Editor** and **Group Policy Management** windows.

3. Generate auditing entries in the security log.
   a) Right-click the **Start** button and select **Shut down or sign out→Sign out**.
   b) Attempt to log back on as **Administrator** with an incorrect password.
   c) Select **OK**, and in the **Password** text box, enter *!Pass1234*

4. Verify that your auditing changes obtain the desired results.
   a) In **Server Manager**, select **Tools→Event Viewer**.
   b) In the console tree, expand **Windows Logs** and select the **Security** log.

c) In the **Actions** pane, in the **Security** section, select **Filter Current Log**.

Actions

Security ▲

Open Saved Log...

Create Custom View...

Import Custom View...

Clear Log...

Filter Current Log...

Properties

Find...

Save All Events As...

Attach a Task To this Log...

View ▶

Refresh

Help ▶

d) In the **Filter Current Log** dialog box, in the **Keywords** drop-down list, check the **Audit Failure** check box and select **OK**.

e) The latest filtered event with **Logon** in the **Task Category** column represents your failed logon attempt. Double-click the log entry to review its content.

General | Details

An account failed to log on.

Subject:
    Security ID: SYSTEM
    Account Name: SERVER100$
    Account Domain: DOMAIN100
    Logon ID: 0x3E7

Log Name:	Security		
Source:	Microsoft Windows security	Logged:	2/12/2014 11:13:26 AM
Event ID:	4625	Task Category:	Logon
Level:	Information	Keywords:	Audit Failure
User:	N/A	Computer:	Server100.domain100.internal
OpCode:	Info		
More Information:	Event Log Online Help		

f) Close the log file.

g) Close the **Event Viewer** window.

ACTIVITY 3-5
Hardening a Server

Data Files

C:\093022Data\Managing Data, Application, and Host Security\MBSASetup-x64-EN.msi

C:\093022Data\Managing Data, Application, and Host Security\Windows-KB890830-x64-V5.9.exe

 Note: Microsoft updates some of their security tools on a regular basis. The versions of the tools this activity was written to may not be the same versions you are using. If this is the case, the screenshots and object names may be different than what you see in your environment.

Scenario

As Develetech's security administrator, one of your primary responsibilities is to make sure all network computers are secured in accordance with the organization's security policy. Based on this policy, a recent audit has revealed that there is a machine that needs some additional security features installed.

You must configure security parameters that include:

- Running the Microsoft Baseline Security Analyzer (MBSA) to scan for system vulnerabilities.
- Scanning for and removing any malware by using the Malicious Software Removal Tool.
- Running the **Security Configuration Wizard** to perform all suggested security configuration settings.

---

1. Install the MBSA.
    a) Open File Explorer and navigate to **C:\093022Data\Managing Data, Application, and Host Security**.
    b) Double-click the **MBSASetup-x64-EN** file.
    c) In the **MBSA Setup** wizard, select **Next**.
    d) On the **License Agreement** page, select **I accept the license agreement** and select **Next**.
    e) On the **Destination Folder** page, select **Next** to accept the default folder.
    f) On the **Start Installation** page, select **Install**.
    g) In the **MBSA Setup** message box, select **OK**.

2. Use the MBSA to scan your system to establish baseline security values.
    a) On the Desktop, double-click the **Microsoft Baseline Security Analyzer 2.3** shortcut to open it.

Microsoft
Baseline S...

    b) In the **Microsoft Baseline Security Analyzer 2.3** window, in the **Check computers for common security misconfigurations** section, select the **Scan a computer** link.

 Scan a computer
Check a computer using its name or IP Address.

c) Verify that your computer name appears in the **Computer name** drop-down list, and uncheck the **Check for SQL administrative vulnerabilities** and **Check for security updates** check boxes.

Options:

☑ Check for Windows administrative vulnerabilities

☑ Check for weak passwords

☑ Check for IIS administrative vulnerabilities

☐ Check for SQL administrative vulnerabilities

☐ Check for security updates

▨ Configure computers for Microsoft Update and scanning prerequisites

▨ Advanced Update Services options:

◯ Scan using assigned Windows Server Update Services(WSUS) servers only

◯ Scan using Microsoft Update only

◯ Scan using offline catalog only

d) Select **Start Scan**.

e) Review the scan results and select any **What was scanned** or **How to correct this** links to view the security recommendations reported by MBSA.

f) After you have reviewed the report, close the **Microsoft Baseline Security Analyzer 2.3** window.

3. Run the Malicious Software Removal Tool.

a) In File Explorer, if necessary, navigate to **C:\093022Data\Managing Data, Application, and Host Security**.

b) Double-click the **Windows-KB890830-x64-V5.9** file.

c) In the **Microsoft Windows Malicious Software Removal Tool** wizard, select **Next**.

d) On the **Scan type** page, verify that **Quick scan** is selected and select **Next**.

> **Note:** Even a quick scan will take a few moments.

e) When the scan completes, select the **View detailed results of the scan** link and verify that none of the malware listed has infected your server.

Microsoft Safety Scanner	X

This tool helps remove the following malicious software. For information on specific malicious software, click an entry.

Malware	Scan results
DOS/Alureon	Not infected
DOS/Bancos	Not infected
DOS/Ramnit	Not infected
DOS/Sinowal	Not infected
Java/Bancos	Not infected
Win32/Afcore	Not infected
Win32/Alcan	Not infected
Win32/Alemod	Not infected
Win32/Allaple	Not infected
Win32/Alureon	Not infected
Win32/Antinny	Not infected
Win32/Atak	Not infected
Win32/Babonock	Not infected
Win32/Badtrans	Not infected
Win32/Bafruz	Not infected
Win32/Bagle	Not infected
Win32/Baglezip	Not infected

OK

f) In the **Microsoft Safety Scanner** dialog box, select **OK**.

g) Select **Finish** and close File Explorer.

4. **According to general system hardening guidelines, what additional software should you install to combat malware on all systems?**

○ Security Configuration Wizard

○ Antivirus software

○ A firewall

○ Database software

5. Use the **Security Configuration Wizard** to configure services settings.

a) In **Server Manager**, select **Tools→Security Configuration Wizard**.

b) On the **Welcome to the Security Configuration Wizard** page, select **Next**.

c) On the **Configuration Action** page, verify that the **Create a new security policy** option is selected and select **Next**.

Select the action you want to perform:

◉ Create a new security policy
○ Edit an existing security policy
○ Apply an existing security policy
○ Rollback the last applied security policy

d) Verify that your server name appears in the **Server** text box and select **Next**.
e) After the wizard builds the security configuration database, select **Next** twice.
f) On the **Select Server Roles** page, scroll down to review the roles for which you can use the **Security Configuration Wizard** to harden your server. The **Security Configuration Wizard** uses this list to determine which services to leave running on your server. Select **Next**.
g) On the **Select Client Features** page, scroll down to review the client features list. The **Security Configuration Wizard** also uses this list to determine which services it should leave running on your server. Select **Next**.
h) On the **Select Administration and Other Options** page, scroll down to review the installed options. Select **Next**.
i) On the **Select Additional Services** page, select **Next**.
j) On the **Handling Unspecified Services** page, verify that **Do not change the startup mode of the service** is selected. You can use this page to configure the **Security Configuration Wizard** to automatically disable any services not specified within the wizard. Select **Next**.
k) On the **Confirm Service Changes** page, review the changes the **Security Configuration Wizard** proposes to your server's services. As you can see, the **Security Configuration Wizard** disables all services it identifies as unnecessary for the roles your server will now perform. Select **Next**.

6. Skip the options for securing network communications and for configuring registry settings.
   a) On the **Network Security** page, check the **Skip this section** check box and select **Next**.
   b) On the **Registry Settings** page, check the **Skip this section** check box and select **Next**.

7. Use the **Security Configuration Wizard** to configure **Audit Policy** settings.
   a) On the **Audit Policy** page, verify that the **Skip this section** check box is unchecked and select **Next**.
   b) Review the **System Audit Policy** page. By default, the **Security Configuration Wizard** enables auditing of successful activity on your server. Select **Next**.
   c) Review the **Audit Policy Summary** page. This page summarizes the changes the **Security Configuration Wizard** will make. Scroll down to verify them and select **Next**.

8. Save the security policy generated by the **Security Configuration Wizard**.
   a) On the **Save Security Policy** page, select **Next**.
   b) On the **Security Policy File Name** page, in the **Security policy file name** text box, at the end of the current path, type *DtechSCW1*

Security policy file name (a '.xml' file extension will be appended if not provided):

C:\Windows\security\msscw\Policies\DtechSCW1   Browse...

c) In the **Description** field, type *Services and auditing as recommended by SCW.*
d) Select **Next** and then select **Apply now**.
e) Select **Next** to apply the policy.

> Note: This process might take a few minutes.

f) Once the application is complete, select **Next**.

g) Select **Finish**.

TOPIC D

Manage Mobile Security

Earlier in this lesson, you identified the general importance of securing data on all devices, including mobile devices. Mobile security goes beyond basic data security, however. Today, mobile devices are used everywhere and are deployed by many companies for employees' business use. In this topic, you will manage mobile security.

Mobile devices are everywhere today. Organizations deploy mobile devices to their employees to use for work-related purposes and will most likely include mobile security measures in their security policies. With this in mind, it is important to understand the most common devices used today and what threats and vulnerabilities apply. As a security professional, it is also your job to understand what techniques are used to secure mobile devices and how they prevent unauthorized access to mobile devices and sensitive data.

Mobile Device Types

A mobile device is a small handheld computing device. There are a number of common mobile devices used for work purposes today:

- Smartphones: Examples include Apple® iPhones®, BlackBerry® devices, Windows Phone® devices, and Android™ phones.
- Wi-Fi enabled devices: Examples include Apple® iPads®, the Apple® iPod touch®, and Android-based tablets such as the Barnes & Noble NOOK Color™.

Mobile Device Vulnerabilities

Modern mobile phones have the ability to transfer voice data, emails, photos, and videos, and can access the Internet. Some may have remote network access. With these functions, users can assume all the same threats related to desktop computers and laptops will apply. For example, viruses and spam can infect mobile devices as they would desktop and wireless devices by email or downloaded programs. If a mobile device is lost or stolen, it is an inconvenience to the user who lost access to the information, but attackers can hack into the device as they would a desktop or laptop computer.

Mobile Device Security Controls

Organizational security policies should implement and enforce mobile security controls on all mobile devices used for business. There are a number of controls used to provide mobile device security.

Security Control	Description
Use device management	To help more easily and efficiently implement various mobile controls, you should set up a mobile device management system. The practice of managing mobile devices attached to a network is typically centralized through special-purpose servers that push updates and send administrative commands to those mobile devices.
Enable screen lock	The screen lock option on all mobile devices should be enabled with strict requirements on when the device will be locked. Once the device is locked, it can only be accessed by entering the code that the user has set up.

Security Control	Description
Require a strong password	A strong password should be set up by the user to access the device once it has been turned on. Password requirements will be different for every organization and should be documented in the organization's security policy.
Configure device encryption	When possible, all mobile devices should be configured to use data encryption to protect company-specific data that may be stored and accessed on the device.
Require remote wipe/ sanitization/lockout	*Data wiping* is a method used to remove any sensitive data from a mobile device and permanently delete it.
	Data sanitization is the method used to repeatedly delete and overwrite any traces or bits of sensitive data that may remain on the device after data wiping has been done.
	Lockout is a method of restricting access to sensitive data on a device without deleting it from memory. However, a skilled attacker may be able to bypass a lockout and capture sensitive data, especially if it is unencrypted.
	Remote options are available, so you can perform these functions remotely in case the phone is lost or stolen. Wipe, sanitization, and lockout guidelines and requirements should be included in the security policies for companies that use mobile devices.
Enable global positioning system (GPS) tracking	GPS tracking service functionality is available on a number of mobile devices and can be added in most cases when required for business reasons. This feature is used as a security measure to protect mobile devices that may be lost or stolen.
Enforce access control	Like other computing platforms, mobile devices should be regulated in terms of who can access what. Implementing authentication and authorization when employees use mobile devices will uphold the principle of least privilege. This can encompass data shared on a network, or it can even extend to restricting access to the mobile hardware itself.
Enforce application control	Setting restrictions on what apps a user can access may prevent employees from unwittingly using insecure software on their mobile devices. Depending on your needs, you may whitelist a set of apps that you deem safe, while blocking the rest. Alternatively, you may draft a blacklist of apps you know to be off limits.
Use asset tracking and inventory control	Keeping track of the mobile devices that you provide your users is vital to establishing a certain security standard that an organization must abide. Take consistent inventory of any mobile devices provisioned to employees to ensure that every single one is accounted for. Likewise, there are many ways you can track devices in real time, such as through GPS or QR codes.
Limit removable storage capabilities	Because removable storage like SD cards further detaches information from the user and device, your employees need to exercise caution. You should mandate that easily lost and often-shared removable storage components do not contain sensitive information, especially in plaintext. Major mobile operating systems limit the exposure certain apps and their internally stored data have to other apps and processes on a device, but removable storage is usually not afforded that same protection.

Security Control	Description
Implement *storage segmentation*	Mobile device proliferation goes hand-in-hand with the rise of cloud storage technologies, so be prepared to assess how best to manage data storage in your organization. Consider dividing data storage along certain lines (e.g., cloud vs. local) based on your security needs. When you segment the data storage in your network, you give yourself a greater level of access control over mobile devices and their users.
Disable unused features	Every feature has the potential to be another point of vulnerability in a mobile system, so it's good practice to disable any features that don't serve a purpose in your organization. For example, Google account syncing on a corporate-provisioned Android phone may be unnecessary.

Note: For additional information, check out the LearnTO **Secure a Mobile Device** presentation from the **LearnTO** tile on the LogicalCHOICE Course screen.

Mobile Application Security Controls

Beyond the day-to-day user operation of mobile devices, you may be tasked with securing app development for mobile devices. Creating in-house apps may greatly benefit your employees and increase their productivity, but there are certain pitfalls that you must avoid. The following table lists some of the major controls for developing a secure mobile app.

Security Control	Description
Encryption and key management	Like any other device or system, encryption is one of the most important controls when it comes to data security. Because mobile devices are more likely to be lost or stolen, keeping the data they contain secure is especially vital. This is why you should develop your app to use strong encryption protocols when it deals with the transfer or storage of sensitive data.
	Similarly, the keys involved in cryptography need to be managed to ensure that they are exchanged and stored properly. If they are not, the data your app's users work with can be easily stolen by attackers. Various key protocols like Diffie-Hellman and Public Key Infrastructure (PKI) can be implemented in your mobile app.
Credential management	Just like cryptographic keys, the credentials that your users enter into your app need to have some mechanism to keep them secure from an attack. This could be anything from enforcing password complexity requirements to using SSL/TLS encryption for credentials transmitted over the web.
Authentication and *transitive trust*	There are various approaches to user authentication you may include in your app, including basic HTTP authentication or authentication provided by OS-specific *application programming interfaces (APIs)*. Another method is transitive trust, which allows a trust relationship to extend beyond its original form. For example, if Alex trusts Beth, and Beth trusts Cindy, then Alex will trust Cindy. Keep in mind that this method of trust, because it is so extensible, can be exploited with the same extensibility.

Security Control	Description
Restrict *geo-tagging*	Geo-tagging is the process of actively adding geographical identification metadata to an app or its data. Unless you restrict geo-tagging in your app, your users will be easily located and the security of the data they work with may be compromised.
Application whitelisting	Mobile apps often communicate and share processes with other apps on a device. Like controlling access to apps on a user's device, you should restrict what apps your own app communicates with. Keeping a whitelist of acceptable apps will ensure that your app is not compromised by insecure software that is out of your control.

BYOD Controls

Bring your own device (BYOD) is an emerging phenomenon in the office workplace. Since mobile devices are now so integral to every day life, it is inevitable that employees will bring their own to supplement the devices provided to them by their employers. Unsurprisingly, this practice introduces a whole host of security issues and legal concerns into a corporate environment. Since an employee's personal property is out of the employer's control, it is difficult to account for every risk, threat, and vulnerability involved with these devices. Some companies have elected to outright ban BYOD to prevent such security incidents; however, for a number of reasons, this isn't always feasible.

The following table lists various controls you can implement to mitigate the security issues introduced by BYOD.

Security Control	Description
Corporate policies and acceptable use policies	One of the first things you should do to meet BYOD head on is to draft a corporate policy for how BYOD is treated in your organization. You might mandate that BYOD isn't tolerated at all, or you might include information on how your security team will respond to BYOD-related incidents.
	Likewise, you should draft an acceptable use policy that your employees need to be aware of and follow. You should clearly outline what types of devices are allowed and how they are or are not allowed to be used. This policy depends on explicit user acceptance to be effective, so be sure that everyone within your organization is compliant.
On-boarding and *off-boarding* employees	New employees should be acclimated to the acceptable use policies as quickly as possible, as you won't necessarily know right away that they have brought their own device to use at work. Likewise, employees who are leaving the organization should be prevented from taking any sensitive data or access with them. This can be difficult without some prior control mechanism in place.

Security Control	Description
Decide on data ownership and support ownership	Although an employee's personal devices are their own property, the lines between ownership are often blurred when it comes to your company's data. You need to come up with a clear boundary that defines what the employee owns versus what the company owns. That way, an employee who is allowed to access and administrate company secrets on their personal device cannot claim ownership of said secrets.
	Another question to ask yourself is: who should offer support for BYODs? A company that provisions its own hardware and software should be able to provide help desk support, but what about the great variety of mobile devices that employees may bring in to the office? Consider that, if you don't provide adequate support, any security vulnerabilities that exist in employees' personal devices may affect your network.
Patch management and antivirus management	Depending on the operating system and its software, some mobile devices can be easily patched. However, others may be more difficult to patch, which could leave them vulnerable. Consider implementing a patch management system to mitigate the threat of outdated hardware and software.
	Likewise, many mobile devices lack antivirus software. To prevent your network from infection, you may want to encourage users to download antivirus apps onto their personal devices.
Consider architecture and infrastructure needs	As more and more devices are added to your corporate network, you may need to expand and update your infrastructure. Otherwise, your current office setup may be inadequate to serve a large number of mobile devices. If your network architecture isn't focused enough on wireless, that will need to change in order to accommodate BYOD. As you've seen, wireless networking will likely introduce new challenges to your organization's security.
Forensics	As BYODs become more prevalent, so too will their relevance to security investigations you conduct. This may present a challenge when you consider all of the different operating systems and hardware that you may need to perform forensics on. Your knowledge of forensic procedures and tools needs to be current, not just with a limited set of specifications, but encompassing a wide variety of devices.
Privacy	Employees may be concerned that their privacy is at risk by being exposed to the corporate network, especially if that network is shared by many people. You should reassure your employees by providing them with the tools and knowhow to keep their private information and device usage secure.
Control for on-board camera, microphone, and video use	It's very easy to secretively take pictures, record video, or capture audio with mobile devices. For many organizations, this is already a concern. With personal devices in play, it becomes much more difficult to stop this from happening. You may need to re-evaluate the openness of certain rooms and systems in order to control for this threat.

Guidelines for Managing Mobile Security

Follow these guidelines to manage mobile security:

* Familiarize yourself with the different types of mobile devices and operating systems.
* Implement a centralized mechanism for managing devices on your network.
* Enforce screen lock, password input, and other device access features.
* Disable unnecessary features.
* Have a plan for remotely wiping our locking out data in case of theft.
* Enable device-wide encryption, if available.
* Apply some form of access and application control on all devices.
* Manage how data is stored and how data storage should be restricted.
* Keep track of devices and take inventory.
* Consider your employees' BYOD needs.
* Draft rules and regulations that employees must agree to for mobile use, along with general corporate policies.
* Acclimate new employees to these protocols and have a plan for off-boarding former employees.
* Consider the legal issues of BYOD: data ownership, privacy concerns, and how much of their device usage you can control.
* Adjust your system architecture and infrastructure as needed.
* When developing apps, enforce proper encryption and key management protocols.
* Select the proper authentication methods and credential management systems to keep users secure.
* Restrict what your app communicates with and how.

ACTIVITY 3-6
Managing Mobile Security

Before You Begin

If you have a mobile device and are able to demonstrate its security features, get it out now.

Scenario

Your CEO at Develetech has noticed an influx of mobile device usage in the workplace. She asks you how this will impact the company's security, and what you can do to meet any challenges that arise. In this evolving work environment, you will begin to consider what new security concerns need addressing and how it will be best to address them.

1. What are some of the security concerns you have about the common mobile devices you use or support?

2. Develetech policy requires that you ensure your smartphone is secured from unauthorized access in case it is lost or stolen. To prevent someone from accessing data on the device immediately after it has been turned on, what security control should be used?
   - ○ GPS tracking
   - ○ Device encryption
   - ○ Screen lock
   - ○ Sanitization

3. An employee's car was recently broken into, and the thief stole a company tablet that held a great deal of sensitive data. You've already taken the precaution of securing plenty of backups of that data. What should you do to be absolutely certain that the data doesn't fall into the wrong hands?
   - ○ Remotely lock out access.
   - ○ Remotely wipe and sanitize the device.
   - ○ Encrypt the device.
   - ○ Enable GPS to track the device.

4. You begin noticing that, more and more often, employees at Develetech are using their own personal devices to get work done in the office. To address this new challenge to security, you decide to draft an acceptable use policy that employees must agree to. What sort of protocols and controls should you include in this policy to address the BYOD phenomenon in your organization?

5. Develetech is developing a mobile app for internal use only. This app needs to provide a great deal of security, as it will work with sensitive company data. What security controls should you instruct your engineers to implement in the design of the app?

6. Pair up with a partner who has a different mobile device and examine the security features on that mobile device. Use the main menu to open the security settings.

7. Look at the specific security settings for each device such as the screen lock feature, device encryption options, and GPS tracking features. Compare the available settings on each device.

Summary

In this lesson, you managed the security of data, applications, and hosts. These components are vital to an organization's operations, and must be secured properly in order to control access. The skills and information in this lesson should help you to implement the right controls at the data, application, and host levels.

What experience have you had securing data, applications, or hosts for your organization?

Have you ever dealt with mobile security issues for your organization? Are there any security controls that would have prevented these issues?

Note: Check your LogicalCHOICE Course screen for opportunities to interact with your classmates, peers, and the larger LogicalCHOICE online community about the topics covered in this course or other topics you are interested in. From the Course screen you can also access available resources for a more continuous learning experience.

4 Implementing Network Security

Lesson Time: 4 hours, 30 minutes

Lesson Objectives

In this lesson, you will implement network security. You will:

- Configure security parameters on network devices and technologies.

- Identify network design elements and components.

- Implement network protocols.

- Apply secure network administration principles.

- Secure wireless traffic.

Lesson Introduction

Now that you have reviewed all the threats and vulnerabilities that can cause damage to your organization, as well as defended against attacks directed at your data and applications, it is time to focus on the components that contribute to network security. Understanding network components and knowing how to properly secure an organization's network is one of the most important steps in becoming a successful Security+® certified professional.

Securing your networks against intruders is not that different from securing your own home. You can secure the perimeter of your home by locking the doors and installing alarm systems, but if intruders get past those, they will have access to everything. So, you cannot just secure from the outside in; you need to secure from the inside out, by doing things like locking up your valuables in a home safe. Securing your internal network and components accomplishes the same goal; it prevents intruders who get in from stealing your valuable hardware, software, and data.

TOPIC A

Configure Security Parameters on Network Devices and Technologies

In this topic, you will configure security parameters on the network devices and technologies that you, as a security professional, will likely use. You cannot fully secure a network without first understanding the devices and technologies that make the network function.

To fully understand how network security principles are applied and managed, you must first understand how the network devices and technologies operate. This is the key to successfully securing a network's components and operations. As a Security+ professional, you may have to not only secure the network as a whole, but also manage security settings for specific devices that are used within a network.

Network Components

The following table describes several common components that make up a network.

Network Component	Description
Device	Any piece of hardware such as a computer, server, printer, or smartphone.
Media	Connects devices to the network and carries the data between devices.
Network adapter	Hardware that translates the data between the network and a device.
Network operating system	Software that controls network traffic and access to network resources.
Protocol	Software that controls network communications using a set of rules.

Network Devices

Different types of internetwork devices provide different levels of connectivity and security between network interconnections and network segments. The following table lists common network devices.

Device	Description
Router	A device that connects multiple networks that use the same protocol. Routers can examine the protocol-based addressing information in the network packets and determine the most efficient path for data to take. They can also filter network traffic based on other criteria. Most routers will not forward broadcast network traffic.
Switch	A device that has multiple network ports and combines multiple physical network segments into a single logical network. It controls network traffic on the logical network by creating dedicated, or "switched," connections that contain only the two hosts involved in a transmission. Standard switches generally forward broadcasts to all ports on the switch, but will send individual packets to the specific destination host based on the unique physical address assigned to each network adapter. Some switches can perform routing functions based on protocol addresses.

Device	Description
Proxy server	A system that can isolate internal networks from the Internet by downloading and storing Internet files on behalf of internal clients. It intercepts requests for web-based or other external resources that come from internal clients, and, if it does not have the data in its cache, generates a completely new request packet using itself as the source. In addition to providing security, the data cache can also improve client response time and reduce Internet traffic by providing frequently used pages to clients from a local source. A proxy server can also include Network Address Translation (NAT) and firewall functionality.
Firewall	Any software or hardware device that protects a system or network by blocking unwanted network traffic. Firewalls generally are configured to stop suspicious or unsolicited incoming traffic, but permit most types of outgoing traffic. The types of traffic blocked or permitted through a firewall are configured using predefined rule sets. Information about the incoming or outgoing connections can be saved to a log, and used for network monitoring or hardening purposes. There are three common types of firewalls: • *Host or personal firewalls* are installed on a single computer and are used to secure most home computers. • *Network-based firewalls* are dedicated hardware/software combinations that protect all the computers on a network behind the firewall. • *Web application-based firewalls* are specifically deployed to secure an organization's web-based applications and transactions from attackers.
Load balancer	A network device that performs load balancing as its primary function. *Load balancing* is the practice of spreading out the work among the devices in a network. By sharing the work, more resources are available and data is processed faster. By balancing the workload between devices, all the devices in the network perform more efficiently. Often, a dedicated program or hardware device is used to provide the balancing service.
All-in-one security appliance	A single network security device that is used to perform a number of security functions to secure a network. Most devices will contain firewall, intrusion prevention, load balancing, filtering, and reporting functionalities.

Multifunction Network Devices

A *multifunction network device* is any piece of network hardware that is meant to perform more than one networking task without having to be reconfigured. An excellent example of a multifunction network device is a combination switch, router, Dynamic Host Configuration Protocol (DHCP) server, and firewall that is installed in many small office or home networks. In larger corporate networks, multifunction devices are available in a wide variety of configurations, including switch and router, or router and load balancer configurations.

Application Aware Devices

An *application aware device* is a network device that manages the information of any applications that interface with it. This information includes the state of applications and the resources they require, in order to more efficiently designate resources across a network. Examples of application aware devices include firewalls, intrusion detection systems, intrusion prevention systems, and proxies.

Router Discovery Protocols

The following table describes router discovery protocols, the language that routers use to communicate with each other.

Protocol	Description
Routing Information Protocol (RIP)	This is a simple distance-vector protocol that is easy to configure, works well inside simple autonomous systems, and is best deployed in small networks with only a few routers in an environment that does not change much. Most equipment that supports RIP costs less than equipment that supports more complicated routing protocols.
RIPv2	RIPv2 enhances RIP by supporting the following features: • Next Hop Addressing: Includes Internet Protocol (IP) address information in routing tables for every router in a given path to avoid sending packets through extra routers. • Authentication: Enables password authentication and the use of a key to authenticate routing information to a router. • Subnet mask: Supports more subnets and hosts on an internetwork by supporting Variable Length Subnet Masks (VLSMs) and including length information in routing information. • Multicast packet: Decreases the workload of non–RIPv2 hosts by communicating only with RIPv2 routers. RIPv2 packets use 224.0.0.9 as their IP multicast address.
Interior Gateway Routing Protocol (IGRP)	This is a distance-vector routing protocol developed by Cisco as an improvement over RIP and RIPv2. It was designated as a protocol best deployed on interior routers within an autonomous system (AS).
Enhanced Interior Gateway Routing Protocol (EIGRP)	This is a proprietary routing protocol developed by Cisco and is considered a hybrid protocol. It includes features that support VLSM and classful and classless subnet masks. Additional updates reduce convergence times and improve network stability during changes.

Network Analysis Tools

The following table describes some of the analysis tools used within a network that function as security measures.

Network Technology	Description
Sniffer	A device or program that monitors network communications on the network wire or across a wireless network and captures data. A sniffer can be used to gather information passed through a network, or to selectively record specific types of transactions based on devices, protocols, or applications used.
Spam filters	Programs used to read and reject incoming messages that contain target words and phrases used in known spam messages.
Protocol analyzer	Also known as a *network analyzer*, this is a type of diagnostic software that can examine and display data packets that are being transmitted over a network. Protocol analyzers can gather all the information passed through a network, or selectively record certain types of transactions based on various filtering mechanisms. On a wired network, it is possible to gather information on all or just part of the network. On a wireless network, traffic can be captured on one wireless channel at a time.

IDS

An *intrusion detection system (IDS)* is a detection control system that scans, audits, and monitors the security infrastructure for signs of attacks in progress. IDS software can also analyze data and alert security administrators to potential infrastructure problems. An IDS can comprise a variety of hardware sensors, intrusion detection software, and IDS management software. Each implementation is unique, and depends on an organization's security needs and the components chosen. For example, an IDS can be set up to use host-based detection, where it monitors a computer system for unexpected behavior or drastic changes to the system's state.

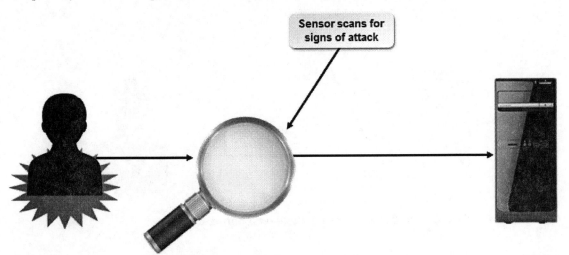

Figure 4-1: An IDS scanning for signs of an intrusion.

NIDS

A *network intrusion detection system (NIDS)* is a type of IDS that primarily uses passive hardware sensors to monitor traffic on a specific segment of the network. It cannot analyze encrypted packets because it has no method for decrypting the data. It can sniff traffic and send alerts about anomalies or concerns. One particular use for an NIDS is rogue machine detection. A *rogue machine* is any unknown or unrecognized device that is connected to a network, often with malicious intent. By using various techniques to scan for suspicious behavior, an NIDS can spot a rogue machine.

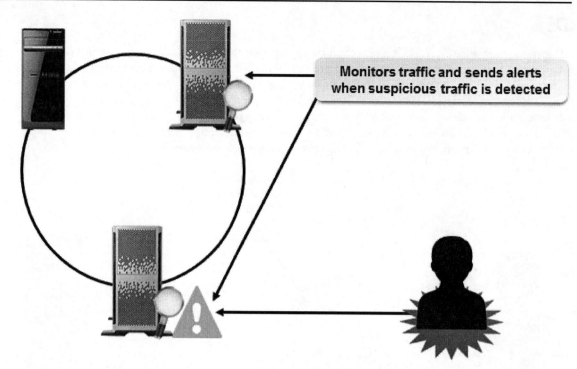

Figure 4-2: A NIDS scanning for suspicious activity on a network.

WIDS

A *wireless IDS (WIDS)* is a type of NIDS that scans the radio frequency spectrum for possible threats to the wireless network, primarily rogue access points. A WIDS usually compares the Media Access Control (MAC) address of a device that acts as an access point to known addresses, and if it doesn't find a match, it gives out an alert. However, MAC address spoofing can complicate the efficacy of a WIDS.

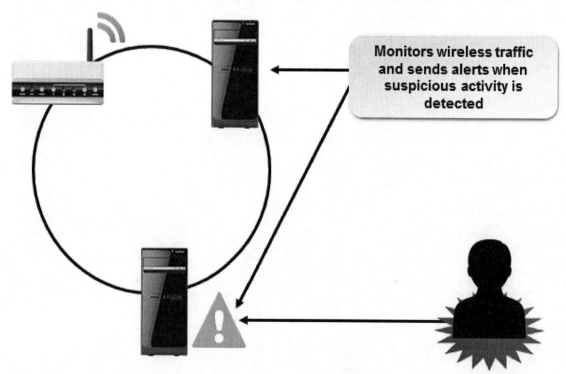

Figure 4-3: A wireless IDS.

IPS

An *intrusion prevention system (IPS)* has the monitoring capability of an IDS, but actively works to block any detected threats. This allows an IPS to take the extra steps necessary to prevent an intrusion into a system.

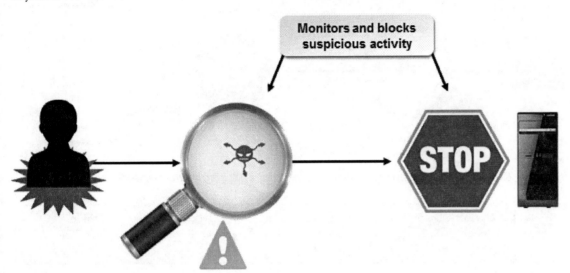

Figure 4-4: An IPS blocking an intrusion attempt.

NIPS

A *network intrusion prevention system (NIPS)* monitors suspicious network and system traffic and reacts in real time to block it. Blocking may involve dropping unwanted data packets or resetting the connection. One advantage of using the NIPS is that it can regulate traffic according to specific content, because it examines packets as they travel through the IPS. This is in contrast to the way a firewall behaves, which blocks IP addresses or entire ports.

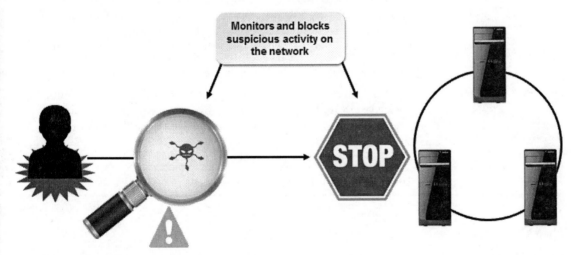

Figure 4-5: A NIPS blocking suspicious activity on a network.

WIPS

A *wireless IPS (WIPS)* is a type of NIPS that scans the radio frequency spectrum for possible threats to the wireless network, primarily rogue access points, and can actively block this malicious traffic. Like a NIPS, a WIPS can drop undesired packets in real time as they come in through the network.

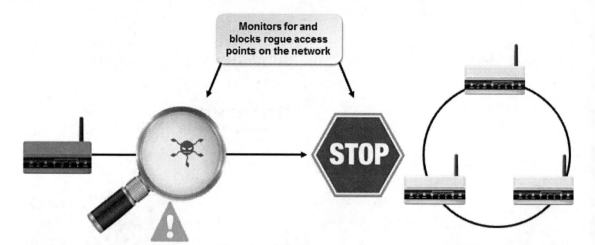

Figure 4-6: A WIPS blocking a rogue access point from attaching to the network.

Note: For additional information, check out the LearnTO **Decide Between Intrusion Detection and Prevention** presentation from the **LearnTO** tile on the LogicalCHOICE Course screen.

Types of Network Monitoring Systems

The following table describes the various methods you can use to monitor your network.

Monitoring System	Description
Behavior-based monitoring	This system detects changes in normal operating data sequences and identifies abnormal sequences. When behavior-based systems are installed, they have no performance baseline or acceptable traffic pattern defined. Initially, these systems will report all traffic as a threat. Over time, however, they learn which traffic is allowed and which is not with the assistance of an administrator.
Signature-based monitoring	This solution uses a predefined set of rules provided by a software vendor to identify traffic that is unacceptable.
Anomaly-based monitoring	This system uses a database of unacceptable traffic patterns identified by analyzing traffic flows. Anomaly-based systems are dynamic and create a performance baseline of acceptable traffic flows during their implementation process.
Heuristic monitoring	This system is set up using known best practices and characteristics in order to identify and fix issues within the network.

VPNs

A *virtual private network (VPN)* is a private network that is configured by tunneling through a public network, such as the Internet. VPNs provide secure connections between endpoints, such as routers, clients, or servers, by using tunneling to encapsulate and encrypt data. Special *VPN protocols* are required to provide the VPN tunneling, security, and data encryption services.

Figure 4-7: Using a VPN to tunnel through the Internet and access a private server.

> **Note:** For additional information, check out the LearnTO **Differentiate Among VPN Tunneling Protocols** presentation from the **LearnTO** tile on the LogicalCHOICE Course screen.

VPN Concentrator

A *VPN concentrator* is a single device that incorporates advanced encryption and authentication methods in order to handle a large number of VPN tunnels. It is geared specifically toward secure remote access or site-to-site VPNs. VPN concentrators provide high performance, high availability, and impressive scalability.

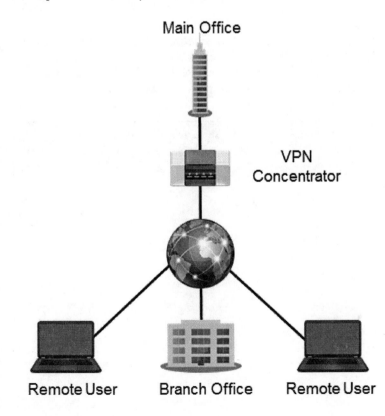

Figure 4-8: A VPN concentrator.

Web Security Gateways

A *web security gateway* is a utility used primarily to intentionally block internal Internet access to a predefined list of websites or categories of websites. The utility is configured by administrators to deny access to a specified list of Uniform Resource Locators (URLs). This type of software can also be used for tracking and reporting a business' Internet usage and activity. Web security gateways can provide a number of functions, including *URL filtering*, which is based on blacklist settings; malware inspection, which is used to identify infected packets; and content inspection, which is used to scan the contents of a packet for abnormalities.

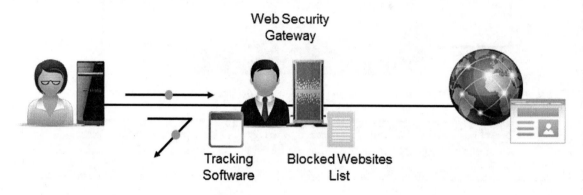

Figure 4–9: A web security gateway tracking a user's Internet usage and denying them access to a specific website.

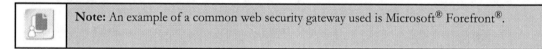

Note: An example of a common web security gateway used is Microsoft® Forefront®.

Blacklists

Blacklists contain addresses that are automatically blocked. URL filtering functions use the entries in a blacklist to allow or deny access to a particular website. Some organizations may use a whitelist or greylist, depending on their access control specifications. When a URL is specified on a whitelist, access is allowed, and when a URL is specified on a greylist, temporary access is granted.

 Access the Checklist tile on your LogicalCHOICE course screen for reference information and job aids on How to Configure Security Parameters on Network Devices and Technologies.

ACTIVITY 4-1
Configuring Firewall Parameters

Before You Begin

You are logged on to your Windows Server 2012 R2 server as **Administrator**. You will work with a partner in this activity.

Scenario

You are the security administrator for a business called Develetech Industries, which manufactures home electronics. Develetech, looking to expand their industry presence, added a new office to accommodate their increasing workforce. The IT staff at this new office are hard at work getting a domain set up and functional for their employees, and you've been tasked with making sure the domain is a secure one. You'll team up with your IT coworkers to ensure that the domain is configured with proper security parameters.

In a meeting with your team, you decided that it would be best to begin by configuring a solution fundamental to all secure networks: a firewall. First, you'll turn on your firewall's logging feature to detail connections that successfully pass through it. This may provide valuable reference information in the future should any malicious activity breach the firewall. After that, you'll disable your firewall's default behavior of allowing Point-to-Point Tunneling Protocol (PPTP) traffic through. Compared to other forms of VPN tunneling, PPTP is insecure, and you want to be certain that no such connections can be made into the domain. Configuring these basic firewall parameters is a good starting point to securing a network.

1. Configure firewall logging.
    a) In **Server Manager**, select **Tools→Windows Firewall with Advanced Security**.

b) In the **Windows Firewall with Advanced Security** window, in the middle pane, select the **Windows Firewall Properties** link.

Overview

Domain Profile is Active

- ✓ Windows Firewall is on.
- ⊘ Inbound connections that do not match a rule are blocked.
- ✓ Outbound connections that do not match a rule are allowed.

Private Profile

- ✓ Windows Firewall is on.
- ⊘ Inbound connections that do not match a rule are blocked.
- ✓ Outbound connections that do not match a rule are allowed.

Public Profile

- ✓ Windows Firewall is on.
- ⊘ Inbound connections that do not match a rule are blocked.
- ✓ Outbound connections that do not match a rule are allowed.

➡ Windows Firewall Properties

Getting Started

> **Note:** You may also select **Properties** from the **Actions** pane on the right.

c) In the **Windows Firewall with Advanced Security** dialog box, in the **Logging** section, select the **Customize** button.

d) In the **Customize Logging Settings for the Domain Profile** dialog box, in the **Name** text box, verify that the log file will be saved to **%systemroot%\system32\LogFiles\Firewall** as **pfirewall.log**.

e) From the **Log successful connections** drop-down list, select **Yes**.

f) Select **OK** twice.

2. Test an inbound connection to the server.

a) On the Desktop taskbar, right-click the **Start** button and select **Command Prompt**.

b) In the command prompt, enter *ping server##*, where *##* is your partner's student number.

c) Wait for the pinging to finish, then close the command prompt.

3. Verify that the inbound connection made it through the firewall and was logged.

a) From the Desktop taskbar, open File Explorer.

b) Navigate to **C:\Windows\System32\LogFiles\Firewall**.

c) Double-click **pfirewall** to open the log file in Notepad.

d) In Notepad, select **Edit→Find**.

e) In the **Find what** text box, type *icmp* and select **Find Next** three times.

f) Verify that the firewall has logged a successful ICMP connection from your partner's IP address.

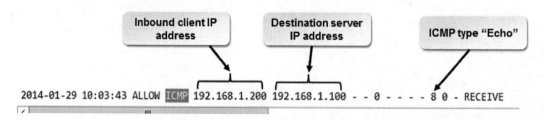

g) Close Notepad and File Explorer.

4. Block a connection protocol on the firewall.

    a) In the **Windows Firewall with Advanced Security** window, in the left pane, select **Inbound Rules**.

    b) In the **Inbound Rules** list, scroll down and right-click **Routing and Remote Access (PPTP-In)**, then select **Properties**.

    c) In the **Routing and Remote Access (PPTP-In) Properties** dialog box, in the **General** section, uncheck the **Enabled** check box.

    d) In the **Action** section, select **Block the connection**.

    e) Select **OK**.

    f) In the **Inbound Rules** list, verify that the **PPTP-In** rule is disabled.

        Routing and Remote Access (PPTP-In)

    g) Close the **Windows Firewall with Advanced Security** window.

ACTIVITY 4–2
Configuring a Network Intrusion Detection System

Data Files

C:\093022Data\Implementing Network Security\Snort_2_9_6_0_Installer.exe

C:\093022Data\Implementing Network Security\WinPcap_4_1_3.exe

C:\093022Data\Implementing Network Security\develetechrules.txt

Before You Begin

You will be working with a partner in this activity.

Scenario

Although a firewall is a good place to start when assessing network traffic, you and your team at Develetech realize the need for more concentrated methods of detecting malicious behavior. You suggest installing an intrusion detection system on the network to alert the team to any suspicious activity. One widely used application that can function as a NIDS is Snort.

There are many different connection protocols and parameters that qualify as suspicious, and you will eventually need to draft and apply them to the NIDS, but for now, you'll focus on setting the system up and testing out its basic ability to detect network intrusions. Your team has already written a simple configuration file to use with Snort that will detect all ICMP traffic sent from any internal IP address to your domain controller with a custom alert message. These predefined rules will be the only thing Snort detects. Configuring and testing a NIDS is a fundamental task in securing your network from attack, and will prepare you for more advanced implementations in the future.

1. Install Snort on the server.
    a) Open File Explorer and navigate to **C:\093022Data\Implementing Network Security**.
    b) Double-click **Snort_2_9_6_0_Installer**.
    c) In the **Snort 2.9.6.0 Setup** window, select **I Agree**.
    d) On the **Choose Components** page of the installation wizard, select **Next**.
    e) On the **Choose Install Location** page, select **Next** to accept the default **Destination Folder**.
    f) When installation completes, select **Close**.
    g) In the **Snort 2.9.6.0 Setup** message box, select **OK** to acknowledge that WinPcap needs be to installed.

2. Install the WinPcap driver.
    a) In File Explorer, double-click **WinPcap_4_1_3**.
    b) In the **WinPcap 4.1.3 Setup** installation wizard, on the **Welcome to the WinPcap 4.1.3 Setup Wizard** page, select **Next**.
    c) On the **License Agreement** page, select **I Agree**.
    d) On the **Installation options** page, leave the **Automatically start the WinPcap driver at boot time** check box checked, and select **Install**.
    e) When installation completes, select **Finish**.

 Note: The WinPcap driver provides packet capturing functionality and is a requirement for many Windows-based security tools.

3. Place the custom intrusion rules file into the **rules** directory.

    a) In File Explorer, copy the **develetechrules** text file.

    b) Navigate to **C:\Snort\rules** and paste the text file.

    c) Close File Explorer.

4. Use Snort to find your local network adapter **Index** number.

    a) Right-click the **Start** button and select **Command Prompt**.

    b) At the prompt, enter *cd C:\Snort\bin* to change to the Snort directory.

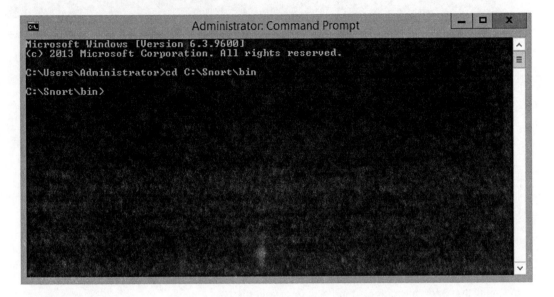

    c) Enter *snort -W*

    d) Verify that two adapters are listed. Under the **Index** column, note the number associated with your local network adapter.

5. Run Snort in intrusion detection mode.

a) At the prompt, enter *snort -A console -i# -c C:\Snort\rules\develetechrules.txt -l C:\Snort\log* where **#** is your local network adapter's **Index** number that you noted in the previous step.

Snort runs in IDS mode using your custom configuration file and outputting to a log file. Any alerts will be sent directly to the command console.

6. Test Snort's intrusion detection capabilities.

   a) Open a command prompt.
   b) At the prompt, enter *ping server##*, where *##* is your partner's student number.
   c) Verify that Snort has detected the ping from your partner.

   d) Close the command prompts on both machines.

TOPIC B

Network Design Elements and Components

Now that you have learned what devices and technologies make up a network's architecture, you can move on to the security design elements and components of a network. The design elements and components of a network are just as important as the devices and technologies used to set up that network. In this topic, you will identify the network design elements and components of a successful network.

Many factors can go into properly setting up and securing a network from common threats and vulnerabilities, but understanding how the design elements and components work within that network enables you to easily manage and make the necessary security-related adjustments.

NAC

Network Access Control (NAC) is a general term for the collected protocols, policies, and hardware that govern access on device network interconnections. NAC provides an additional security layer that scans systems for conformance and allows or quarantines updates to meet policy standards. Security professionals will deploy a NAC policy according to an organization's needs based on three main elements: authentication method, endpoint vulnerability assessment, and network security enforcement. Once the NAC policy is determined, security professionals must determine where NAC will be deployed within their network structure.

> **Note:** Network Access Protection (NAP) is the Microsoft implementation of NAC.

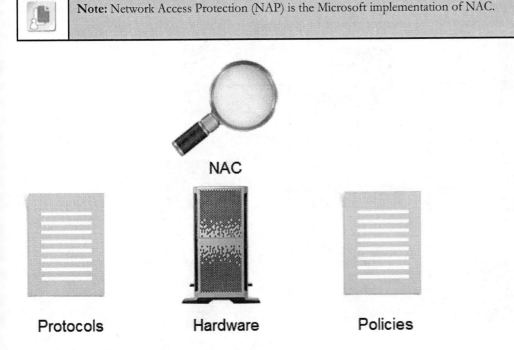

Protocols   Hardware   Policies

Figure 4-10: NAC protocols, hardware, and policies.

DMZs

A *demilitarized zone (DMZ)* is a small section of a private network that is located between two firewalls and made available for public access. A DMZ enables external clients to access data on private systems, such as web servers, without compromising the security of the internal network as a whole. The external firewall enables public clients to access the service; the internal firewall prevents them from connecting to protected internal hosts.

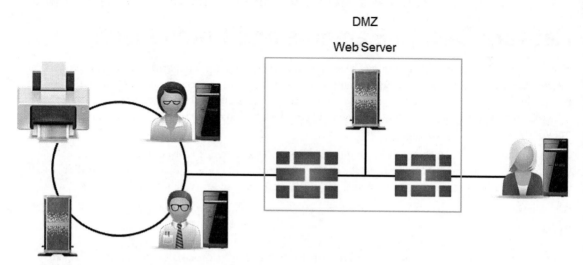

Figure 4–11: A user connecting to a web server behind a DMZ.

VLANs

A *virtual local area network (VLAN)* is a point-to-point logical network that is created by grouping selected hosts together, regardless of their physical location. A VLAN uses a switch or router that controls the groups of hosts that receive network broadcasts. VLANs can provide network security by enabling administrators to segment groups of hosts within the larger physical network.

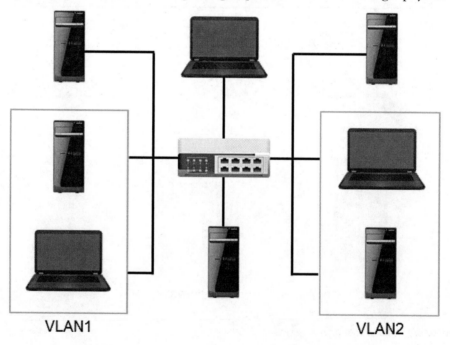

Figure 4–12: A switch segmenting hosts on a VLAN.

VLAN Vulnerabilities

Improperly configured VLAN devices and associated switches give attackers the opportunity to redirect packets from one VLAN to another (through VLAN hopping) and to capture those packets and the data they contain.

Some VLAN switch configurations can also be open to other attacks such as Denial of Service (DoS), traffic flooding, and MAC address spoofing. Being aware of these types of attacks and correctly configuring a VLAN implementation can eliminate these types of attacks.

Subnetting

Subnetting is a network design element that is used to divide a large network into smaller logical networks. Each node is configured with an IP address and a subnet address in order to segment a network into subnetworks and to create a routing structure. By creating logical groupings of network devices based on an addressing scheme, data flow and security measures can be managed more easily on a smaller scale than on a large network.

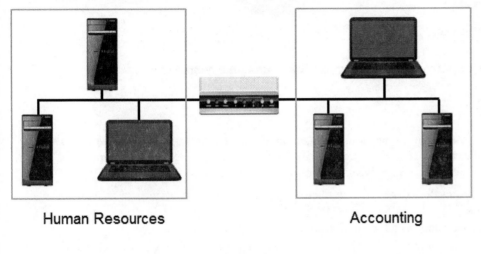

Human Resources   Accounting

Network

Figure 4-13: A subnet that divides a network based on different departments in a company.

NAT

Network Address Translation (NAT) is a simple form of Internet security that conceals internal addressing schemes from the public Internet. A router is configured with a single public IP address on its external interface and a private, non-routable address on its internal interface. A NAT service translates between the two addressing schemes. Packets sent to the Internet from internal hosts all appear as if they came from a single IP address, preventing external hosts from identifying and connecting directly to internal systems.

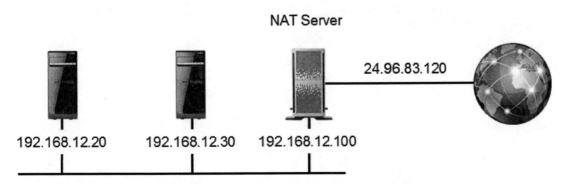

Figure 4-14: A NAT server translating internal IP addresses to an external IP address for Internet communication.

Remote Access

Remote access is the ability to connect to network systems and services from an offsite or remote location. Remote access methods enable authorized users to access and use systems and services through a secure Internet connection. Remote access is often most secure when users are able to connect through a VPN.

Offsite Employee

Figure 4–15: An employee accessing company data through a remote connection.

Telephony

Telephony provides voice communications through devices over a distance. Modern networks are designed to handle more than just the traditional networking components and, in some cases, may also be expected to carry converged data. Common telephony components include:

• Voice over Internet Protocol (VoIP) implementations, in which voice traffic is transmitted over the IP network.
• Private branch exchange implementations.
• *Computer telephony integration (CTI),* which incorporates telephone, email, web, and computing infrastructures.

Virtualization

Virtualization technology separates computing software from the hardware it runs on via an additional software layer. This enables a great deal of additional flexibility and increases hardware utilization by running multiple operating systems on a single computer, each thinking it is the only system present. In addition, virtualization allows hardware resources in an organization to be pooled and leveraged as part of a virtual infrastructure, increasing available processing and storage capacity. Virtualization has many uses in the modern IT environment:

• Running multiple operating systems on one computer, reducing hardware requirements.
• Separating software applications within a single operating system to prevent conflicts.
• Increasing utilization of processing and storage resources throughout the organization by creating a virtual infrastructure.

Figure 4–16: Running multiple operating systems on one computer.

Cloud Computing

Cloud computing is a method of computing that involves real-time communication over large networks to provide the resources, software, data, and media needs of a user, business, or organization. This method of computing usually relies on the Internet to provide computing capabilities that a single machine cannot. "The cloud" refers to the resources that are available on the particular network. This could include business websites, consumer websites, storage services, IT-related services, file editing applications, and social networking websites. The main idea behind cloud computing is that you can access and manage your data and applications from any computer anywhere in the world, while the storage method and location are hidden.

Figure 4-17: A user accessing various resources from a cloud computing architecture over the Internet.

Cloud Computing Deployment Models

Cloud computing technologies can be deployed using four basic methods. The following table describes those methods.

Deployment	Description
Private	Private cloud services are usually distributed by a single company or other business entity over a private network. The hosting may be done internally, or it may be done offsite. With private cloud computing, organizations can exercise greater control over the privacy and security of their services. This type of delivery method is geared more toward banking and governmental services that require strict access control in their operations.
Public	Public cloud computing is done over the Internet by organizations that offer their services to general consumers. With this model, businesses are able to offer subscriptions or pay-as-you-go financing, while at the same time providing lower-tier services free of charge. Because public cloud computing relies on the Internet, security is always a concern.
Community	When multiple organizations share ownership of a cloud service, they are deployed as a community cloud. This is usually done in order to pool resources for a common concern, like standardization and security policies.
Hybrid	Hybrid cloud computing combines two or more of the deployment methods into one entity. The advantage to this approach is best realized in organizations that depend on internal cloud services in their operation, but also offer computing services to the general public.

Cloud Computing Service Types

Described in the following table are the three main services that cloud computing provides to users.

Service	Description
Software	*Software as a Service (SaaS)* refers to using the cloud to provide applications to users. This service eliminates the need for users to have the software installed on their computers and for organizations to purchase and maintain software versions. Examples include Microsoft® Office 365™, Salesforce®, and Gmail™.
Platform	*Platform as a Service (PaaS)* refers to using the cloud to provide virtual systems, such as operating systems, to customers. Examples include Oracle® Database, Microsoft Windows Azure™ SQL Database, and Google App Engine™.
Infrastructure	*Infrastructure as a Service (IaaS)* refers to using the cloud to provide access to any or all infrastructure needs a client may have. This can include data centers, servers, or any networking devices needed. IaaS can guarantee quality of service (QoS) for clients. Examples include Amazon® Elastic Compute Cloud®, Microsoft Windows Azure Virtual Machines, and OpenStack™.

Note: Some of service types overlap, and some organizations offer suites that encompass more than one service type.

ACTIVITY 4–3
Examining Network Design Components

Scenario

You've been tasked with establishing a security baseline for Develetech's network. Before you begin, you need to reacquaint yourself with some of the fundamental elements of networking in order to consider how to protect your company's technological infrastructure.

1. In what situation might you want to install a DMZ on your network?

2. What is the role of NAT on a network?

3. Which telephony technology allows telephone, email, fax, web, and computer actions to be integrated to work together?
   - ○ PBX
   - ○ VoIP
   - ○ CTI
   - ○ DMZ

4. Develetech is in the testing phase of a new accounting application and needs to verify its functionality on various operating systems before deploying it to customers, but is dealing with hardware availability issues. What network design component would you suggest in this scenario?

5. The CEO of Develetech proposes establishing cloud computing technology to centralize the services and software that employees use every day. However, he stipulates that security is a priority due to the sensitive and confidential nature of the data that the company deals with. You also know that resources are unlikely to be shared with any competitors. What cloud computing deployment model do you suggest to him?
   - ○ Hybrid
   - ○ Community
   - ○ Private
   - ○ Public

TOPIC C

Implement Networking Protocols and Services

As you continue to explore the realm of network security, you will need to understand how networking protocols are used within a network. In this topic, you will implement common networking protocols.

You may be able to successfully design and set up a network, but it will not function without the proper protocols applied. There are a number of different protocols designed to operate within different types of networks. Depending on the type of network you are securing, you may come across a number of different protocols, and it is your job to implement them properly in your network.

The OSI Model

The *Open Systems Interconnection (OSI) model* is a way to abstract how a network is structured based on how it communicates with other elements in the network, similar to the Transmission Control Protocol/Internet Protocol (TCP/IP) model. These elements are divided into seven discrete layers with a specific order. The order determines the hierarchy of interaction between the layers—a layer supports the layer above it, while at the same time it is supported by the layer below it. The main purpose of the OSI model is to encourage seamless and consistent communication between different types of network products and services.

The following table describes the seven layers of the OSI model, in order from the first layer to the seventh.

Number	Layer	Description	Major Protocols and Utilities
1	Physical	Defines connections between devices and physical transmission media.	Specifications of physical connection components like cabling and wiring, as well as basic network devices like hubs, repeaters, switches, and adapters.
2	Data link	Provides a link between two directly connected nodes, as well as detecting and fixing errors in the physical layer.	Point-to-Point Protocol (PPP): A connection protocol that provides encryption, authentication, and compression between nodes. G.hn: A standard that defines telephony networking over power lines and coaxial cables.
3	Network	Provides the protocols for transferring data from one node to another in a system with multiple nodes with unique addresses (a network).	Internet Protocol (IP): Manages numeric host addresses across the Internet. Internet Control Message Protocol (ICMP): Tests for communication between devices and sends error messages when network function is unavailable. Routing Information Protocol (RIP): Prevents loops in routing by limiting the number of intermediary devices between a source and its destination.

Number	Layer	Description	Major Protocols and Utilities
4	Transport	Controls the reliability of data transmission between nodes on a network for the benefit of the higher layers.	Transmission Control Protocol (TCP): A connection-oriented, guaranteed-delivery protocol. This means that it not only sends data, but also waits for acknowledgement (ACK) and fixes errors when possible.
			User Datagram Protocol (UDP): Ensures the consistent transmission of data packets (datagrams) by bypassing error checking, which can cause delays and increased processing requirements.
			Stream Control Transmission Protocol (SCTP): Combines the features of TCP and UDP into one protocol.
5	Session	Controls the connections between computers through checkpointing so that connections, when terminated, may be recovered.	Network File System (NFS): Allows clients to access files on a network as if they were accessing local storage.
			Socket Secure (SOCKS): Routes data packets on a network through a proxy server and includes authentication.
6	Presentation	Transforms data into a format that can be understood by the programs in the application layer above it.	Independent Computing Architecture (ICA): Specifies the transmission of data between client and application server.
7	Application	Allows client interaction with software by identifying resource and communication requirements.	Hypertext Transfer Protocol (HTTP): Allows the exchange of information across the World Wide Web.
			File Transfer Protocol (FTP): Enables the transfer of files between a user's workstation and a remote host over a TCP network.
			Domain Name System (DNS): Translates human-intelligible domain names into their corresponding IP addresses.

OSI Model and Security

As a security professional, understanding the layers of the OSI model makes it easier for you to identify threats and their targets, as well as how these threats will impact your network. Additionally, securing your network by layers is a useful strategy in securing your network entirely, as the layers are designed to integrate with each other. If the most fundamental layer (physical) fails, then the rest are likely to fail as well. Likewise, if an attack hits a poorly secured application layer, then the secured bottom layers will be unable to rectify the situation above.

TCP/IP

The following table describes the basic protocols that make up the Internet protocol suite.

Internet Protocol	Description
Transmission Control Protocol/Internet Protocol (TCP/IP)	This is a non-proprietary, routable network protocol suite that enables computers to communicate over all types of networks. TCP/IP is the native protocol of the Internet and is required for Internet connectivity.
IP version 4 (IPv4)	This is an Internet standard that uses a 32-bit number assigned to a computer on a TCP/IP network. Some of the bits in the address represent the network segment; the other bits represent the computer, or node, itself. For readability, the 32-bit IPv4 address is usually separated by dots into four 8-bit octets, 10101100.00010000.11110000.00000001, and each octet is converted to a single decimal value. Each decimal number can range from 0 to 255, but the first number cannot be 0. In addition, all four numbers in a host address cannot be 0 (0.0.0.0) or 255 (255.255.255.255).
IP version 6 (IPv6)	This is an Internet standard that increases the available pool of IP addresses by implementing a 128-bit binary address space. IPv6 also includes new efficiency features, such as simplified address headers, hierarchical addressing, support for time-sensitive network traffic, and a new structure for unicast addressing. IPv6 addresses are usually separated by colons into eight groups of four hexadecimal digits: 2001:0db8:85a3:0000:0000:8a2e:0370:7334. While all eight groups must have four digits, leading zeros can be omitted, such as 2001:db8:85a3:0:0:8a2e:370:7334, and groups of consecutive zeros can be replaced with two colons, such as 2001:db8:85a3::8a2e:370:7334. IPv6 is not compatible with IPv4, so now it is narrowly deployed on a limited number of test and production networks. Full adoption of the IPv6 standard will require a general conversion of IP routers to support interoperability. IPv6 uses an Institute of Electrical and Electronics Engineers (IEEE) standard called Extended Unique Identifier (EUI). A host computer implemented with EUI-64 can assign itself a 64-bit IPv6 interface identifier automatically.
Dynamic Host Configuration Protocol (DHCP)	This is a protocol used to automatically assign IP addressing information to IP network computers. Except for a few systems that have manually assigned static IP addresses, most IP systems obtain addressing information dynamically from a central DHCP server or a router configured to provide DHCP functions. Therefore, a DHCP service is a critical component of an IP implementation in most corporate environments.

The IEEE

The Institute of Electrical and Electronics Engineers (IEEE) is an organization dedicated to advancing theory and technology in the electrical sciences. The standards wing of IEEE issues standards in areas such as electronic communications, circuitry, computer engineering, electromagnetics, and nuclear science. See **www.ieee.org** for more information.

APIPA

. Automatic Private IP Addressing (APIPA) is a Microsoft® Windows® service that enables DHCP client computers to initialize TCP/IP when DHCP is unavailable. With APIPA, DHCP clients can get IP addresses when the DHCP servers malfunction or when the computer does not have connectivity. APIPA self-allocates addresses randomly from a small range of 169.254.0.1 to 169.254.255.254

Simple TCP/IP Services

Simple TCP/IP Services is a Microsoft implementation that supports several TCP/IP services such as Character Generator, Daytime, Discard, and Quote of the Day. For more information on the Simple TCP/IP Services, visit **http://technet.microsoft.com/en-us/library/cc725973.aspx**.

DNS

The *Domain Name System (DNS)* is the primary name resolution service on the Internet and private IP networks. DNS is a hierarchal system of databases that map computer names to their associated IP addresses. DNS servers store, maintain, and update databases and respond to DNS client name resolution requests to translate human-intelligible host names to IP addresses. The DNS servers on the Internet work together to provide global name resolution for all Internet hosts.

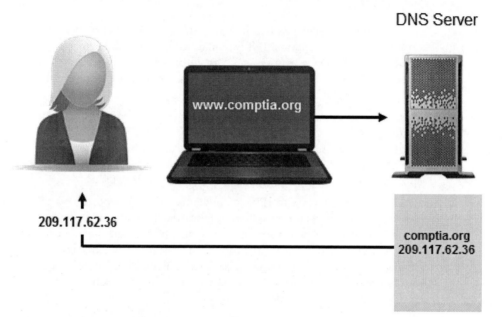

Figure 4-18: A DNS server translating a domain name to its IP address.

DNS Security Measures

In any corporate network, the DNS is the most likely target that is attacked first. There are several applications available in the IT market that help secure a DNS. Some of the measures that can be taken to secure a DNS are:

- Placing the DNS server in the DMZ and within the firewall perimeter.
- Setting firewall rules to block incoming non-essential services requests.
- Exposing only essential ports.
- Strengthening DHCP filtering.
- Preventing buffer overflows.
- Using Secure Sockets Layer (SSL).
- Keeping the DNS updated regularly. Operating system vendors issue security patches to update the DNS.
- Backing up the DNS and saving the backups in different geographical locations.

HTTP

Hypertext Transfer Protocol (HTTP) is the TCP/IP protocol that enables clients to connect to and interact with websites. It is responsible for transferring the data on web pages between systems.

HTTP defines how messages are formatted and transmitted, as well as what actions web servers and the client's browser should take in response to different commands.

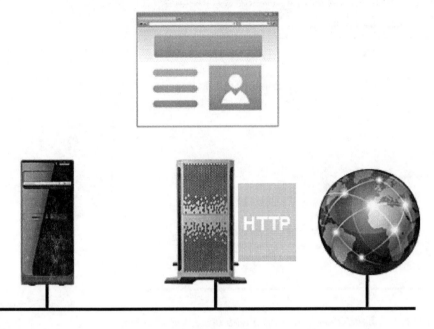

Web Client   **Web Server**

Figure 4-19: HTTP translating a client request to access Internet resources using a web browser.

Web Server Security

Hackers primarily try to break into the web servers of organizations. The moment the security of web servers is breached, the hacker gets direct access to all the sensitive data stored on the web servers. Securing web servers remains one of the toughest challenges security administrators face. To effectively secure web servers, you should:

- Remove unnecessary services running in the background. Most often, services such as remote registry services, print server service, and RAS, which are not required for web servers, run in the background.
- Avoid remote access to web servers. Administrators should try to log on locally.
- Store web applications, website logs that contain user information, and other related files on another, secured, drive.
- Install security patches regularly.
- Delete or disable unused user accounts.
- Use the appropriate security tools. There are several useful security tools available to secure web servers.
- Use port scanners to scan the web servers regularly.

SSL/TLS

Secure Sockets Layer (SSL) and *Transport Layer Security (TLS)* are security protocols that combine digital certificates for authentication with public key data encryption. Both protocols protect sensitive communication from eavesdropping and tampering by using a secure, encrypted, and authenticated channel over a TCP/IP connection. SSL/TLS is a server-driven process; any web client that supports SSL or TLS, including all current web browsers, can connect securely to an SSL- or TLS-enabled server.

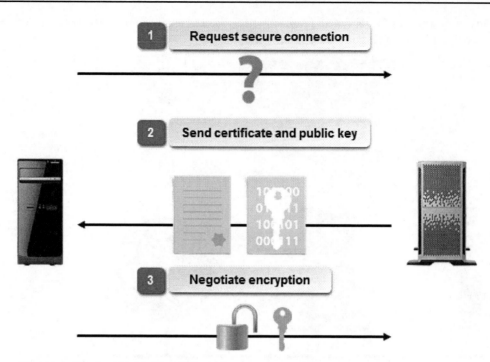

Figure 4-20: An SSL/TLS handshake securing a web browsing session.

TLS vs. SSL

Although often used in conjunction with one another, SSL is a predecessor of TLS. The latest versions of TLS are more secure than SSL, but very few websites currently implement them.

HTTPS

Hypertext Transfer Protocol Secure (HTTPS) is a secure version of HTTP that supports web commerce by providing a secure connection between a web browser and a server. HTTPS uses SSL/TLS to encrypt data. Virtually all web browsers and servers today support HTTPS. An SSL- or TLS-enabled web address begins with the protocol identifier **https://**.

 Note: HTTPS is also referred to as HTTP over SSL/TLS.

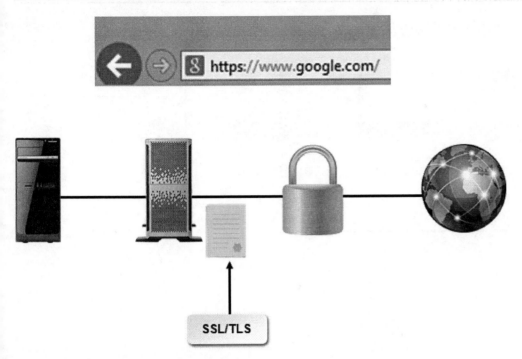

Figure 4–21: A website using an HTTPS connection.

SSH

Secure Shell (SSH) is a protocol used for secure remote login and secure transfer of data. SSH consists of a server and a client. Most SSH clients also implement login terminal-emulation software to open secure terminal sessions on remote servers. To ensure security, the entire SSH session, including authentication, is encrypted using a variety of encryption methods. SSH is the preferred protocol for working with File Transfer Protocol (FTP) and is used primarily on Linux and Unix systems to access shell accounts. Microsoft Windows does not offer native support for SSH, but it can be implemented by using a third-party tool.

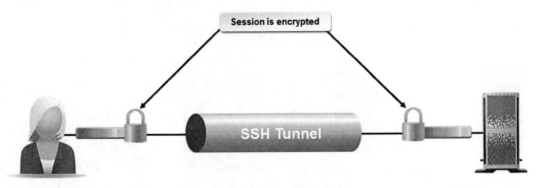

Figure 4–22: Using an SSH tunnel to remotely access a web server.

SNMP

Simple Network Management Protocol (SNMP) is a service used to collect information from network devices for diagnostic and maintenance purposes. SNMP includes two components: management systems, and agent software, which is installed on network devices such as servers, routers, and printers. The agents send information to an SNMP manager. The SNMP manager can then notify an administrator of problems, run a corrective program or script, store the information for later review, or ask the agent about a specific network device.

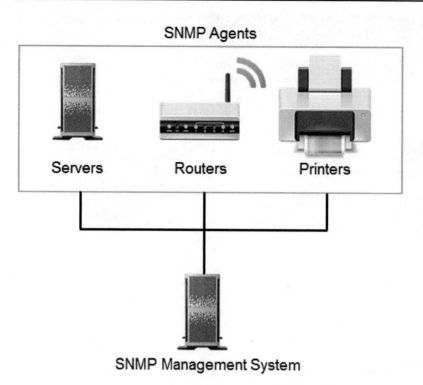

Figure 4–23: An SNMP management system receiving information from its agents.

ICMP

Internet Control Message Protocol (ICMP) is an IP network service that reports on connections between two hosts. It is often used for simple functions, such as the `ping` command that checks for a response from a particular target host. Attackers can use redirected ICMP packets in two ways: to flood a router and cause a DoS attack by consuming resources (Smurf attack), and to reconfigure routing tables by using forged packets.

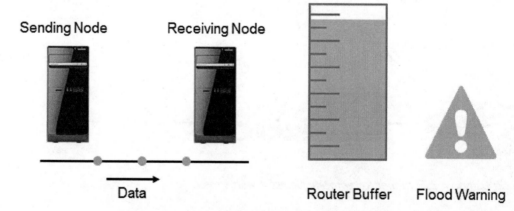

Figure 4–24: A Smurf attack flooding nodes on a network using ICMP.

IPSec

Internet Protocol Security (IPSec) is a set of open, non-proprietary standards that you can use to secure data as it travels across the network or the Internet. IPSec uses an array of protocols and services to provide data authenticity and integrity, anti-replay protection, non-repudiation, and protection against eavesdropping and sniffing. Unlike SSL/TLS and SSH, IPSec operates at the Internet layer of the TCP/IP model, so the protocol is not application dependent.

Figure 4-25: IPSec policy securing a connection between two computers.

IPSec System Support

Many operating systems support IPSec, including Windows Server 2012 and 2008, Microsoft Windows XP and later, Linux, Unix, and Sun Solaris. Internetworking devices, such as most routers, also support IPSec. While IPSec is an industry standard, it is implemented differently in each operating system and device.

IPSec Policies

An IPSec policy is a set of security configuration settings that define how an IPSec-enabled system will respond to IP network traffic. The policy determines the security level and other characteristics for an IPSec connection. Each computer that uses IPSec must have an assigned policy. Policies work in pairs; each of the endpoints in a network communication must have an IPSec policy with at least one matching security method in order for the communication to succeed. Some default IPSec policies include secure server, server, client, IP filters, filter action, authentication method, tunnel setting, and connection type.

iSCSI

The *Internet Small Computer System Interface (iSCSI)* is a protocol implementing links between data storage networks using IP. This protocol is designed to extend across wide area networks without needing any new infrastructure. Users can enter commands and remotely manage data servers from great distances, and iSCSI can centralize data storage so that the information is not bound to individual servers. As iSCSI does not inherently provide encryption during transmission, an attacker can monitor these transmissions, alter data, or corrupt it. Protocols like IPSec may be able to mitigate this vulnerability, but at the cost of performance.

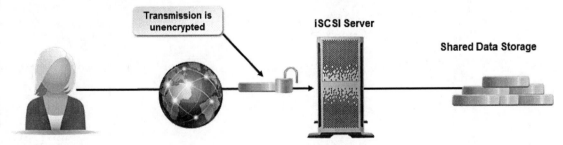

Figure 4-26: A client connecting to iSCSI storage facilities over the Internet.

Fibre Channel

Like iSCSI, *Fibre Channel* is a protocol designed to link data storage across a network and provide remote access over large distances. However, Fibre Channel requires installing special-purpose cabling in place of existing infrastructure. This makes Fibre Channel a more expensive option, but one that typically affords greater performance and reliability. Implementing security controls like encryption and authentication is difficult on Fiber Channel, which may leave data vulnerable to session hijacking and man-in-the-middle attacks.

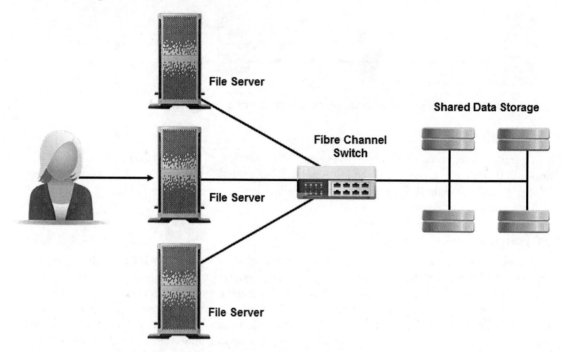

Figure 4–27: Accessing data storage through Fibre Channel.

FCoE

Fibre Channel over Ethernet (FCoE) allows traditional Fibre Channel protocols to use high-speed Ethernet networks to transmit and store data. This protocol decreases the infrastructure cost of cabling, as well as lowering the amount of physical hardware devices like network interface cards and switches that are required. Likewise, power and cooling costs may be reduced. FCoE is subject to much of the same security pitfalls as traditional Fibre Channel, and should not be considered a viable alternative as far as security is concerned.

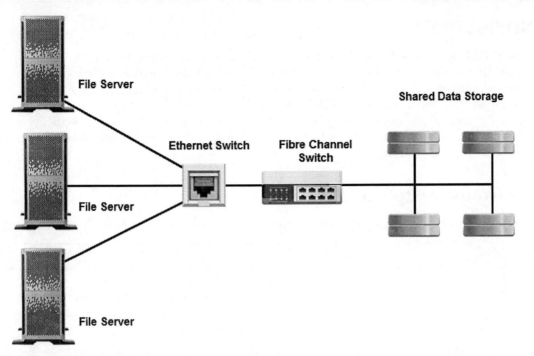

Figure 4-28: Fibre Channel implemented over Ethernet.

Telnet

Telnet is a network protocol that allows a client to initiate remote command access to a host over TCP/IP. The client runs a Telnet program that can establish a connection with a remote server, granting the client a virtual terminal into the server. Most modern operating systems include support for Telnet, which makes it an ideal protocol for remoting into machines running different operating systems. However, use of Telnet today is discouraged, as it introduces major security vulnerabilities. The Telnet protocol is not encrypted, so packets can be easily analyzed and attackers can eavesdrop on credential input. Man-in-the-middle attacks are also relatively easy, as Telnet does not require any sort of authentication between client and host. This has led to networking professionals abandoning Telnet for more secure remote access protocols like SSH.

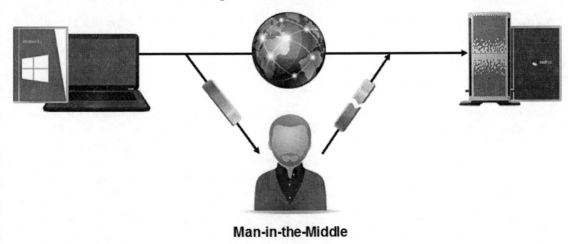

Man-in-the-Middle

Figure 4-29: A Windows client using Telnet to remote into a Linux server, as a man-in-the-middle attack occurs.

NetBIOS

Network Basic Input Output System (NetBIOS) is an interface that allows applications to properly communicate over different computers in a network. NetBIOS has three basic functions: communication over sessions, connectionless communication using datagrams, and name registration. Attackers can exploit NetBIOS by obtaining information about a system, including registered name, IP addresses, and operating system/applications used. To harden NetBIOS against an attack, you should implement strong password policies, limit root access on a network share, and disable null session capability.

File Transfer Protocols

The following table describes the protocols that are used to support file transfers within a network.

Protocol	Description
File Transfer Protocol (FTP)	This protocol enables the transfer of files between a user's workstation and a remote host. With FTP, a user can access the directory structure on a remote host, change directories, search and rename files and directories, and download and upload files.
Simple File Transfer Protocol (SFTP)	This protocol was an early unsecured file transfer protocol that has since been declared obsolete.
Trivial File Transfer Protocol (TFTP)	This is a very limited protocol used primarily as an automated process of configuring boot files between machines. Because it offers almost no security, this protocol is used primarily on local networks instead of on the Internet.
FTP over SSH	Also called *Secure FTP*, FTP over SSH is a secure version of FTP that uses an SSH tunnel as an encryption method to transfer, access, and manage files. Secure FTP is used primarily on Windows systems.
Secure Copy Protocol (SCP)	This protocol uses SSH to securely transfer computer files between a local and a remote host, or between two remote hosts. SCP can also be implemented as a command-line utility that uses either SCP or SFTP to perform secure copying. SCP is used primarily on Unix systems.
File Transfer Protocol Secure (FTPS)	This protocol, also known as *FTP-SSL*, combines the use of FTP with additional support for SSL/TLS.

Ports and Port Ranges

In networks, a port is the endpoint of a logical connection. Client computers connect to specific server programs through a designated port. All ports are assigned a number in a range from 0 to 65,535. The Internet Assigned Numbers Authority (IANA) separates port numbers into three blocks: well-known ports, which are preassigned to system processes by IANA; registered ports, which are available to user processes and are listed as a convenience by IANA; and dynamic ports, which are assigned by a client operating system as needed when there is a request for service.

 Note: IANA manages the registration of well-known ports, and also lists registered ports as a convenience. For a complete list of TCP and UDP ports, see the IANA website at **www.iana.org/assignments/port-numbers**.

TCP and UDP ports are assigned in one of three ranges listed in the following table. Hackers will target commonly used, well-known ports for attack, but may scan for open registered or dynamic ports as well.

Range	Numbers	Description
Well-known ports	0 to 1,023	Specific port numbers are most vulnerable to attack.
Registered ports	1,024 to 49,151	Too system-specific for direct target by attackers, but they might scan for open ports in this range.
Dynamic or private ports	49,152 to 65,535	Constantly changing; cannot be targeted by number, but attackers might scan for open ports in this range.

Common Default Network Ports

This table lists some of the most common network port numbers.

Port Number	Service
21	FTP (File Transfer Protocol)
22	SSH (Secure Shell)
25	SMTP (Simple Mail Transfer Protocol)
53	DNS (Domain Name System)
80	HTTP (Hypertext Transfer Protocol)
110	POP3 (Post Office Protocol)
139	NetBIOS Session Service
143	IMAP (Internet Message Access Protocol)
443	HTTPS (Hypertext Transfer Protocol Secure)
3389	RDP (Remote Desktop Protocol)

Access the Checklist tile on your LogicalCHOICE course screen for reference information and job aids on How to Implement Networking Protocols and Services.

ACTIVITY 4-4
Installing an IIS Web Server

Data Files

C:\093022Data\Implementing Network Security\Register.htm

C:\093022Data\Implementing Network Security\dac10001.gif

Before You Begin

You will work with a partner in this activity.

Scenario

You are the security administrator of a state university in the United States. The university is expected to start a web portal where students can enroll themselves. Before hosting the site live, the IT team has planned to test the functionality on a test server. You have been assigned to create a web server for the test team and to set up a default web page. You also need to establish file transfer services for students and faculty in your offline learning programs to exchange large files quickly and efficiently.

1. Verify that the Windows Remote Management service is running.
   a) In **Server Manager**, select **Tools→Services**.
   b) In the **Services** window, scroll down and double-click **Windows Remote Management (WS-Management)**.
   c) In the dialog box, verify that the **Service status** is **Running**. If the service is stopped, from the **Startup type** drop-down list, select **Automatic**. Select **Start**.

   > **Note:** The Web Server role requires this service to be running in order to install.

   d) Select **OK** to close the dialog box and then close the **Services** window.

2. Install and configure **Web Server (IIS)**.
   a) In **Server Manager**, select **Add roles and features**.
   b) On the **Before you begin** page, select **Next**.
   c) On the **Select installation type** page, verify that the **Role-based or feature-based** radio button is selected, and select **Next**.
   d) On the **Select destination server** page, verify that your server is selected, and select **Next**.
   e) On the **Select server roles** page, scroll down and expand **Web Server (IIS)**.

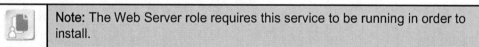

   f) Check the **FTP Server** check box.
   g) Expand **Web Server→Security** and check all of the check boxes.
   h) Select **Next**, then on the **Select features** page, select **Next** again.

i) Review the web server services and check the **Restart the destination server automatically if required** check box.

j) In the **Add Roles and Features Wizard** message box, select **Yes**.

k) Select **Install**.

l) Once the installation has completed, select **Close**.

3. Enable IIS logging on the default website.

   a) From the **Server Manager** window, select **Tools→Internet Information Services (IIS) Manager**.

   b) In the **Connections** pane, expand your server object.

   c) In the **Internet Information Services (IIS) Manager** message box, check the **Do not show this message** check box and select **No**.

   d) Expand **Sites**.

   e) Select **Default Web Site**.

   f) In the **Default Web Site Home** pane, double-click **Logging**.

Logging

   g) In the **Logging** pane, scroll down to the **Log File Rollover** section and verify that IIS logging is enabled and will create a new log file daily.

4. Enable the appropriate file permissions and execution settings on the default public website.

   a) In the **Connections** pane, select **Default Web Site**.

   b) In the **Default Web Site Home** pane, select **Directory Browsing**.

Directory
Browsing

 Caution: Make sure that you select **Directory Browsing** once, rather than double-clicking it.

c) In the **Actions** pane on the right, select **Edit Permissions**.

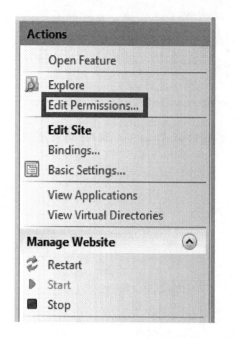

d) In the **wwwroot Properties** dialog box, select the **Security** tab.
e) In the **Group or user names** list, scroll down and select **Users (DOMAIN##\Users)**, where **##** is the same unique number assigned to your computer name.

f) Verify that users have **Read & execute**, **List folder contents**, and **Read** permissions to the local website files.

g) Close the **wwwroot Properties** dialog box.
h) In the **Default Web Site Home** pane, double-click **Authentication**.
i) In the **Authentication** pane, select **Anonymous Authentication**.
j) In the **Actions** pane, select **Disable**.
k) In the **Authentication** pane, select **Windows Authentication**.
l) In the **Actions** pane, select **Enable**.

5. Set up the default website.
   a) Using File Explorer, navigate to the **C:\093022Data\Implementing Network Security** folder.
   b) Copy the files **Register** and **dac10001**.

> **Note:** These are .htm and .gif files, respectively.

   c) Navigate to the **C:\inetpub\wwwroot** folder.
   d) Paste the **Register** and **dac10001** files in the **wwwroot** folder.
   e) Rename **Register** as *Default*
   f) Close File Explorer.

6. Verify the authentication credentials of the website.
   a) From the Desktop taskbar, select the **Internet Explorer** icon.

b) In the Internet Explorer **Address** bar, type *http://server##* and then press **Enter**.

> **Note:** Remember to replace *##* with the unique number assigned to you.

c) Verify that you have to enter authentication credentials in order to view the website.
d) In the **Windows Security** dialog box, in the **User name** text box, type *Administrator*
e) Press **Tab**.
f) In the **Password** text box, type *!Pass1234* and press **Enter**.
g) If necessary, make Internet Explorer the active window.
h) Verify that you have successfully connected to the enrollment website.
i) Close Internet Explorer.

7. Set up the FTP connection.
   a) Return to the **Internet Information Services (IIS) Manager** window.
   b) In the **Contents** pane, right-click **Sites** and select **Add FTP Site**.
   c) In the **Add FTP Site** dialog box, on the **Site Information** page, in the **FTP site name** text box, type *Default FTP Site*
   d) In the **Physical path** text box, type *C:\inetpub\ftproot* as the path.
   e) Select **Next**.
   f) On the **Binding and SSL Settings** page, in the **SSL** section, select **No SSL**. Select **Next**.
   g) On the **Authentication and Authorization Information** page, in the **Authentication** section, check the **Basic** check box and select **Finish**.

h) In the **Connections** pane, select **Default FTP Site**, and in the **Default FTP Site Home** pane, double-click **FTP Authorization Rules**.
   i) In the **Actions** pane, select the **Add Allow Rule** link.
   j) Verify that all users are allowed access to the FTP site. In the **Permissions** section, check the **Read** check box and select **OK**.
   k) Close the **Internet Information Services (IIS) Manager** window.

8. Verify the FTP connection to your partner's server.
   a) From the Desktop taskbar, right-click the **Start** button and select **Command Prompt**.
   b) In the command line, enter *ftp server##*, where *##* is your partner's student number.
   c) When the system prompts you to enter a user name, enter *Administrator*
   d) When the system prompts you to enter the password, enter *!Pass1234*

> **Caution:** Be careful when inputting the password, as the characters will not appear for you to check.

e) Verify that you are logged in.

```
Microsoft Windows [Version 6.3.9600]
(c) 2013 Microsoft Corporation. All rights reserved.

C:\Windows\system32>ftp server100
Connected to Server100.domain100.internal.
220 Microsoft FTP Service
User (Server100.domain100.internal:(none)): Administrator
331 Password required
Password:
230 User logged in.
ftp>
```

f) Enter *close* to log out of the FTP session, then close the **Command Prompt** window.

ACTIVITY 4-5
Securing Network Traffic Using IPSec

Before You Begin

You will work with a partner in this activity.

Scenario

As the security administrator for Develetech, you want to be sure you successfully implement Windows IPSec policies and management tools to support your ever-growing security policies.

Much of Develetech's manufacturing is done in sites throughout the world that are in different domains. The company is actively looking for new hires to add to their expanding international teams. It is your responsibility to set up computers in each site, so that potential new employees can fill out background check applications and send them to a security officer for review. You want to transfer the applicants' data securely between the computers in different domains by using IPSec. Because you do not have Kerberos-based authentication in your workgroup, or a certificate authority (CA) available at the various manufacturing sites, IPSec security will be based on the use of pre-shared keys. For your implementation of IPSec, you will use a pre-shared key of **key123**.

1. Create a custom Microsoft Management Console (MMC) containing **IP Security Policy Management** and **IP Security Monitor**.
   a) Switch to your Windows Server 2012 R2 machine.
   b) Open the **Search Charm**, and in the search box, type *mmc*
   c) From the list of results, select **mmc**.
   d) Maximize the **Console1 - [Console Root]** window.
   e) Select **File→Add/Remove Snap-in**.
   f) In the **Available snap-ins** list, scroll down and select **IP Security Monitor**, then select **Add**.
   g) Select **IP Security Policy Management** and select **Add**.
   h) In the **Select Computer or Domain** dialog box, select **The Active Directory domain of which this computer is a member** and select **Finish**.

   > ⦿ The Active Directory domain of which this computer is a member

   i) Select **OK** to close the **Add or Remove Snap-ins** dialog box.
   j) Select **File→Save As**.
   k) Type *IPSec Management* as the file name.
   l) Select **Save** to save the console to the default location.

2. Modify the appropriate IPSec policy for your computer to use a pre-shared key of **key123**.
   a) In the console tree pane of the **IPSec Management** console window, select **IP Security Policies on Active Directory**, and double-click the **Secure Server (Require Security)** policy.
   b) In the **Secure Server (Require Security) Properties** dialog box, in the **IP Filter List**, verify that the **All IP Traffic** filter is selected and select **Edit**.
   c) In the **Edit Rule Properties** dialog box, select the **Authentication Methods** tab.
   d) In the **Authentication method preference order** section, select **Add**.
   e) In the **New Authentication Method Properties** dialog box, select **Use this string (preshared key)**.

Caution: Enter the key exactly as it appears here. IPSec is case-sensitive.

f) In the **Use this string (preshared key)** text box, type *key123*

⦿ Use this string (preshared key):

key123

g) Select **OK**.
h) In the **Authentication method preference order** list, verify that **Preshared Key** is selected and select **Move up**.
i) Verify that **Preshared Key** is now first in the list. Select **OK**.

IP Filter List	Filter Action	Authentication...	Tu
☑ All IP Traffic	Require Security	Preshared Key...	No
☑ All ICMP Traffic	Permit	<None>	No
☑ <Dynamic>	Default response (ea...	Kerberos	<N

j) In the **Secure Server (Require Security) Properties** dialog box, select **OK**.

3. Assign the policy to your domain.
   a) From the Desktop taskbar, select the **Server Manager** icon to return to it.
   b) Select **Tools→Group Policy Management**.
   c) In the **Group Policy Management** window, in the console tree, select **Default Domain Policy**.
   d) In the **Group Policy Management Console** dialog box, select **OK**.
   e) Select **Action→Edit**.

f) In the **Group Policy Management Editor** window, in the console tree under **Computer Configuration**, expand **Policies→Windows Settings→Security Settings**, and select **IP Security Policies on Active Directory (DOMAIN##.INTERNAL)**, where ## is your domain number.

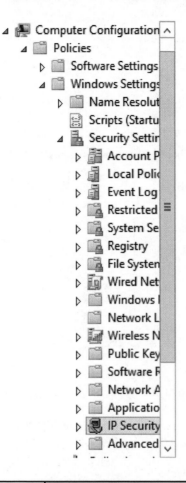

 Note: It may take a moment for the security settings to expand.

g) In the right pane, select the **Secure Server (Require Security)** policy and select **Action→Assign**.

h) Verify that the **Policy Assigned** value for the **Secure Server (Require Security)** policy is **Yes**.

Client (Respond Only)	Communicate normally (...	No
Secure Server (Requi...	For all IP traffic, always re...	Yes
Server (Request Sec...	For all IP traffic, always re...	No

Note: After you assign the policy, you need to wait for your partner before proceeding to the next step.

4. Make sure the IPSec Policy Agent service starts automatically.

a) From the **Server Manager** window, select **Tools→Services**.

b) In the **Services** window, scroll down and double-click **IPsec Policy Agent**.

c) If necessary, from the **Startup type** drop-down list, select **Automatic**.

Startup type:	Automatic ⌄
	Automatic (Delayed Start)
	Automatic
	Manual
	Disabled
Service status:	Running

d) If necessary, select **Apply**, then select **Start**.

e) Select **OK** and then close the **Services** window.

5. Verify that you have the **Secure Server (Require Security)** policy active in your domain.

   a) From the Desktop taskbar, select **IPSec Management - [Console Root\IP Security Policies on Active Directory]**.

   b) In the tree pane of the **IPSec Management** console window, expand **IP Security Monitor** and expand your server object.

   c) If necessary, select the server object and select **Action→Reconnect**.

   d) Verify that your computer object appears with a green upward-pointing arrow.

   ⊿ 🖥 IP Security Monitor
      ⊿ 🔒 SERVER100
           📁 Active Policy
         ▷ 📁 Main Mode
         ▷ 📁 Quick Mode
   ▷ 🖥 IP Security Policies on Activ

   e) In the tree pane, select **Active Policy**.

   f) Verify that the **Policy Name** shows **Secure Server (Require Security)**, indicating that the policy is active in your domain. This may take a few moments.

Item	Description
✕ Policy Name	Secure Server (Require Security)

6. Test the connection to your partner's server.

   a) Open the **Search Charm**.

   b) Type **\\Server##**, where **##** is your partner's student number, and press **Enter**.
   File Explorer opens to your partner's computer.

   c) Close File Explorer.

   d) In the **IPSec Management** window, in the tree pane, expand **Main Mode**.

   e) Select the **Security Associations** folder.

   f) In the middle pane, verify that your partner's IP address is listed in the **Peer** column, and then in the tree pane, expand **Quick Mode**.

   g) Select the **Statistics** folder, and observe the data sent back and forth with your partner's computer.

   h) Select **File→Save** and then close the **IPSec Management** window.

7. To prevent connection problems with other classroom hosts, unassign the IPSec policy.

   a) From the taskbar, select **Group Policy Management Editor** and verify that **IP Security Policies on Active Directory (DOMAIN##.INTERNAL)** is selected.

   b) Select the **Secure Server (Require Security)** policy and select **Action→Un-assign**.

   c) Close all open windows except **Server Manager**.

TOPIC D

Apply Secure Network Administration Principles

In the previous topics, you covered the networking components, devices, and protocols. With this experience, you are prepared to apply the security administration principles used to govern network security. In this topic, you will apply the various administration principles that relate to network security.

It is important to understand what makes up a network, and how it is designed, but it is just as important to understand the principles applied to managing the network's day-to-day operations and security. How a network is managed can not only affect its security, but it can also affect its availability to the users who need to access it. With the proper security administration principles applied, a business can ensure that systems and applications are available to the users who rely on them.

Rule-Based Management

Rule-based management is the use of operational rules or restrictions to govern the security of an organization's infrastructure. Typically, rules are incorporated into organizational policies that get disseminated throughout an organization.

Example

A company that uses a security policy to determine how employees can access the Internet and other network resources is an example of a rule-based management approach.

Network Administration Security Methods

There are many methods that an organization can use to secure the networking infrastructure.

Security Method	Description
Flood guard	This is a tool used by network administrators and security professionals to protect resources from flooding attacks, such as Distributed Denial of Service (DDoS) attacks. Flood guards can be implemented at the enterprise level and are designed to protect an organization's entire network. The tool includes detectors that are distributed throughout a network at points that are susceptible to DDoS attacks. The detectors will react when an attack occurs and will apply appropriate mitigation techniques. As a security professional, you may need to advise organizations if and when they need to consider a flood guard installation.
Loop protection	Network loops can occur when one or more pathways exist between the endpoints in a network and packets get forwarded over and over again. This can be of concern in complex networks with many networking devices and can cause flooding issues within the network. Security professionals must assess and determine what loop protection methods are needed, such as applying proper router configurations and verifying that proper manufacturer configurations are also applied.

Security Method	Description
Port security	Properly securing ports on a network includes: • Disabling unnecessary services. • Closing ports that are by default open or have limited functionality. • Regularly applying the appropriate patches. • Hiding responses from ports that indicate their status and allow access to pre-configured connections only.
Secure router configuration	Ensuring that all routers on the network are properly secured will protect your network from attacks and can also prevent routing loops, which are caused by a routing algorithm error that creates a looping pattern.
MAC limiting	MAC limiting is the technique of defining how many different MAC addresses may connect to a network device like a router. When the preset limit is exceeded, the device may trigger a warning, disable new MAC learning, or shut down completely, depending on how it is configured.
MAC filtering	MAC filtering is the technique of allowing or denying devices with certain MAC addresses to connect to a network. This may be in the form of a whitelist in which only the MAC addresses specified are granted access, or a blacklist in which certain MAC addresses are explicitly blocked.
Network separation	Splitting your network into two or more logically separated networks helps separate critical network functions from lower-priority functions so that security can be managed on a critical versus non-critical basis. It can also prevent intruders from getting to other systems, and helps enforce access control efforts.
VLAN management	VLAN configurations can be very complicated. With proper management procedures in place, security measures can be implemented and managed quickly. Most organizations will keep track of VLAN configurations using diagrams and documentation.
Implicit deny	Use the principle of implicit deny so that the firewall blocks any traffic it does not recognize.
Log analysis	Regular monitoring and analysis of security logs helps detect any unauthorized intrusion attempts on the network. It is also wise to regularly review logs and assess any data leaks and insider threats that may be present.

Unified Threat Management

Unified threat management (UTM) refers to a system that centralizes various security techniques—firewall, anti-malware, network intrusion prevention, URL filtering, content inspection, malware inspection, etc.—into a single appliance. In addition, UTM security appliances usually include a single console from which a security administrator can monitor and manage various defense settings. UTM was created in response to a number of difficulties that administrators face in deploying discrete security systems; namely, managing several complex platforms as well as meeting the significant cost requirements. UTM systems help to simplify the security process by being tied to only one vendor and requiring only a single, streamlined application to function. This makes management of your organization's security easier, as you no longer need to be familiar with or know the quirks of each individual security implementation.

Nevertheless, UTM has its downsides. When defense is unified under a single system, this creates the potential for a single point of failure that could affect an entire network. Discrete security systems, if they fail, might only compromise that particular avenue of attack. Additionally, UTM systems can struggle with latency issues if they are subject to too much network activity.

Figure 4–30: Unified threat management combining the functionality of various security techniques into one device.

Guidelines for Applying Network Security Administration Principles

> **Note:** All Guidelines for this lesson are available as checklists from the **Checklist** tile on the LogicalCHOICE Course screen.

Almost all security administrators are faced with the challenge of securing their networks to prevent attacks from external and internal sources. In order to do this efficiently, every organization facing this issue should have a well-defined network security administration model. This model should contain best practices and guidelines that any new security administrator can follow as he or she takes up the responsibility of securing the network. To apply network security administration principles, you should:

- Manage the network devices such as firewalls, routers, switches, load balancers, proxies, and other all-in-one appliances to ensure that configurations conform with your security policies.
- Maintain documentation about all current server configurations.
- Establish and document baselines that suit your organization.
- Set up strong Access Control Lists (ACLs) in sensitive resources on your network, and use the principle of implicit deny to ensure that unauthorized users and groups cannot inadvertently access information when they do not have specific rights to do so.
- Update antivirus software regularly. If possible, this task should be automated.
- Configure the required network services only. Configuring too many network services creates additional exploit points.
- Disable unused interfaces and unused application service ports.
- Have a good backup strategy and disaster recovery plan (DRP) in place.
- Apply security updates and patches regularly.

- Ensure that sensitive data is well encrypted.
- Regularly check event logs for unusual activities.
- Monitor network activities on a regular basis.

ACTIVITY 4-6
Securing a Windows Server 2012 R2 Router

Before You Begin

You will work with a partner in this activity. The two peer routers will represent the two routers in the DMZ.

Scenario

As the security administrator for Develetech, you have the task of ensuring that the routers at the company's headquarters are secure. In the past, the company had problems with attackers accessing services and data that they were not supposed to have access to through the routers. Before connecting the new Windows Server 2012 routers behind a firewall on your network, you want to make sure that your routers are hardened to minimize the likelihood of attacks, especially DDoS and spoofing attacks from external users. After you configure the routers, your team will test the connections from laptops to make sure the security is not too restrictive.

To prevent users from accessing restricted information and to prevent attackers from getting data, Develetech's IT department has decided to create a DMZ by implementing two software-based routers using the Windows Server 2012 Routing and Remote Access Servers. These routers will be installed behind the existing hardware-based firewall, which has already been hardened. To help ensure security on these software-based routers, they will run RIPv2 and will communicate with each other securely through RIP peer security. The company also wants to implement packet filters to drop incoming external packets with internal private IP addresses as the source addresses to prevent attackers from spoofing internal IP addresses on the private subnet.

---

1. Install RIPv2 for IP, using the Local Area Connection as the RIP interface.
   a) From the **Server Manager** window, select **Tools→Routing and Remote Access**.
   b) Expand your server object and then expand **IPv4**.
   c) Select the **General** object, and select **Action→New Routing Protocol**.

New Interface...
New Routing Protocol...
Show TCP/IP Information...
Show Multicast Forwarding Table...
Show Multicast Statistics...
Refresh
Export List...
Properties
Help

   d) In the **New Routing Protocol** dialog box, in the **Routing protocols** list, select **RIP Version 2 for Internet Protocol** and select **OK**.
   e) Under **IPv4**, select the **RIP** object and select **Action→New Interface**.
   f) In the **Interfaces** list, verify that **Local Area Connection** is selected and select **OK** twice.

2. Modify the RIP's security properties with the appropriate peer router settings.

    a) In the tree pane, if necessary, select the **RIP** object and select **Action→Properties**.

    b) In the **RIP Properties** dialog box, select the **Security** tab.

    c) Select **Accept announcements from listed routers only**.

    d) In the **Router IP address** text box, type your partner's IP address.

    e) Select **Add**.

    f) Select **OK**.

3. Verify filtering on the external router interface.

    a) In the **Routing and Remote Access** window, under **IPv4**, select **General**.

    b) In the right pane, select **Loopback Adapter**.

    c) Select **Action→Properties**.

    d) On the **General** tab, select **Inbound Filters**.

    e) Select **New**.

    f) Check the **Source network** check box.

    g) Under **Source network**, in the **IP address** text box, type *192.168.0.0*

h) In the **Subnet mask** text box, type *255.255.0.0*

```
┌─────────────────────────────────────────────────────────┐
│                     Add IP Filter              │ ? │ X │ │
├─────────────────────────────────────────────────────────┤
│                                                         │
│  ☑ Source network                                       │
│                                                         │
│     IP address:       │ 192 . 168 .  0  .  0 │          │
│                                                         │
│     Subnet mask:      │ 255 . 255 .  0  .  0 │          │
│                                                         │
│  ☐ Destination network                                  │
│                                                         │
│     IP address:       │     .     .     .    │          │
│                                                         │
│     Subnet mask:      │     .     .     .    │          │
│                                                         │
│  Protocol:            │ Any                    ▼ │      │
│                                                         │
│                                                         │
│                                                         │
│                            ┌────────┐   ┌────────┐      │
│                            │   OK   │   │ Cancel │      │
│                            └────────┘   └────────┘      │
└─────────────────────────────────────────────────────────┘
```

i) Select **OK**.

j) Under **Filter action**, select **Receive all packets except those that meet the criteria below** and select **OK**.

Inbound Filters

These filters control which packets are forwarded or processed by this network.

Filter action:

(•) Receive all packets except those that meet the criteria below

( ) Drop all packets except those that meet the criteria below

Filters:

Source Address	Source Network Mask	Destination Address	Destination Mask
192.168.0.0	255.255.0.0	Any	Any
Any	Any	Any	255.255.255.255
Any	Any	Any	255.255.255.255
Any	Any	Any	255.255.255.255
Any	Any	Any	255.255.255.255
Any	Any	Any	255.255.255.255
Any	Any	Any	255.255.255.255

[New...] [Edit...] [Delete]

[OK] [Cancel]

---

k) Select **OK**.

4. Verify the connection.

   a) If necessary, under **IPv4**, select **General**.

   b) In the right pane, scroll to the right, and under the **Incoming bytes** and **Outgoing bytes** sections, verify that data packets are received and sent.

   c) In the tree in the left pane, select **RIP**.

   d) In the right pane, under the **Responses sent** and **Responses received** sections, verify that responses are sent and received.

    Note: If no responses appear, right-click **RIP** and select **Refresh**. You may need to do this several times.

   e) Close the **Routing and Remote Access** window.

ACTIVITY 4-7
Securing a File Server

Scenario

Your next task as Develetech's security administrator is to make sure your file servers are secure. As the security administrator, you will implement the following system-wide security measures:

- Disable any unnecessary services that may pose a security risk.
- Securely share the **ITData** folder on each server. Only members of the Administrators group and individually designated users should be able to access this folder. John Greg, a junior member of the IT team and a non-Administrator, frequently needs to consult and edit the documents in the folder.
- Enable encryption on the **ITData** folder using Windows Encrypting File System (EFS).

---

1. Verify that unnecessary services are turned off.
   a) From the **Server Manager** window, select **Tools→Services**.
   b) In the **Services** window, in the right pane, scroll down and double-click **Print Spooler**.
   c) If necessary, in the **Print Spooler Properties (Local Computer)** dialog box, from the **Startup type** drop-down list, select **Disabled** and select **Stop**.
   d) Select **OK**.
   e) In the **Services** window, in the right pane, scroll down and double-click **Remote Procedure Call (RPC) Locator**.
   f) If necessary, in the **Remote Procedure Call (RPC) Locator Properties (Local Computer)** dialog box, from the **Startup type** drop-down list, select **Disabled** and select **Stop**.
   g) Select **OK**.
   h) Close the **Services** window.

2. Verify that the **STORAGE** drive is formatted as NTFS.
   a) Open File Explorer, right-click the **STORAGE (S:)** drive, and select **Properties**.
   b) Verify that the file system is NTFS. Select **OK** to close the **STORAGE (S:) Properties** dialog box.

    Note: The EFS feature requires a volume to be in the NTFS format before files or folders can be encrypted on it.

3. Share the **S:\ITData** folder with John Greg.
   a) Double-click the **STORAGE (S:)** drive to open it.
   b) Right-click the **ITData** folder and select **Properties**.

c) Select the **Sharing** tab and select **Share**.

```
┌─────────────────────────────────────────────┬───┐
│             ITData Properties               │ X │
├─────────────────────────────────────────────┴───┤
│ General │ Sharing │ Security │ Previous Versions │ Customize │
│                                                  │
│  ┌─ Network File and Folder Sharing ──────────┐  │
│  │                                            │  │
│  │    📁    ITData                            │  │
│  │         Not Shared                         │  │
│  │                                            │  │
│  │   Network Path:                            │  │
│  │   Not Shared                               │  │
│  │                                            │  │
│  │    ┌──────────┐                            │  │
│  │    │ Share... │                            │  │
│  │    └──────────┘                            │  │
│  └────────────────────────────────────────────┘  │
│                                                  │
│  ┌─ Advanced Sharing ─────────────────────────┐  │
│  │  Set custom permissions, create multiple    │  │
│  │  shares, and set other advanced sharing     │  │
│  │  options.                                   │  │
│  │                                            │  │
│  │    ┌────────────────────┐                  │  │
│  │    │ 🛡 Advanced Sharing... │               │  │
│  │    └────────────────────┘                  │  │
│  └────────────────────────────────────────────┘  │
└──────────────────────────────────────────────────┘
```

d) In the **File Sharing** window, select the drop-down list, then select **Find people**.

```
┌──────────────────────────────────────────┬───┐
│                                          │ ∨ │
├──────────────────────────────────────────┴───┤
│ Everyone                                      │
│ Find people...                                │
│ 👤 Administrator                    Read/Write │
└───────────────────────────────────────────────┘
```

e) In the **Enter the object names to select** field, type *John* and then select **Check Names**.
   User John E. Greg automatically populates the object names text box.

f) Select **OK**, and then in the **Permission Level** drop-down list for **John E. Greg**, select **Read/Write**.

g) Select **Share** to share the folder.

h) In the **File Sharing** window, verify that your folder is shared. Select **Done**.

```
┌──────────────────────────────────────────────────────────────┐
│                                                              │
│   Your folder is shared.                                     │
│                                                              │
│   You can e-mail someone links to these shared items, or     │
│   copy and paste the links into another program.             │
│                                                              │
│   ┌─ Individual Items ──────────────────────────────────┐ ∧ │
│   │                                                      │   │
│   │    📁   ITData                                       │   │
│   │        \\SERVER100\ITData                            │   │
│   │                                                      │   │
│   └──────────────────────────────────────────────────────┘   │
│                                                              │
└──────────────────────────────────────────────────────────────┘
```

i) In the **ITData Properties** dialog box, select **Advanced Sharing** to display the **Advanced Sharing** dialog box.

j) In the **Advanced Sharing** dialog box, select **Permissions**.

k) In the **Permissions for ITData** dialog box, select **Add**.

l) Type *John* and select the **Check Names** button.

m) Select **OK**.

n) In the **Permissions for John E. Greg** section, check the **Allow** check box for **Full Control** and select **OK**.

o) Select **OK** to close the **Advanced Sharing** window.

4. Encrypt the **S:\ITData** folder.

a) In the **ITData Properties** dialog box, on the **General** tab, select **Advanced**.

b) In the **Advanced Attributes** dialog box, check the **Encrypt contents to secure data** check box.

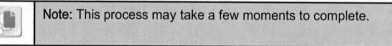

c) Select **OK** to close the **Advanced Attributes** dialog box.

d) Select **Apply** to encrypt the folder.

e) In the **Confirm Attribute Changes** dialog box, select **OK**.

f) When the encryption application completes, select **OK** to close the **ITData Properties** dialog box.

Note: This process may take a few moments to complete.

g) Verify that the encryption is applied by selecting outside the folder.
The folder name has changed to a green color, indicating that it is encrypted.

Name
ITData

h) Close File Explorer.

5. EFS encrypts files and folders on an individual basis, whereas BitLocker encrypts an entire drive. In what situation(s) might you use EFS instead of BitLocker?

TOPIC E

Secure Wireless Traffic

In the previous topics, you applied the devices, components, protocols, and security administration principles used in network security, and now you will secure the wireless components of a network. Wireless networking is common in all local area network (LAN) environments, and wireless devices and protocols pose their own security challenges. In this topic, you will secure traffic over wireless LAN connections.

Wireless networking has become a standard in most networks because of the mobility it gives to network users and the simplicity of connecting components to a LAN. However, that very simplicity creates security problems, because any attacker with physical access and a laptop with a wireless network adapter can attach to your wireless LAN, and once an attacker is on your network, you're vulnerable. If you know the right security procedures, you can provide the convenience of wireless connections to your users without compromising network security.

Wireless Networks

Wireless networks are, fundamentally, networks that do not rely solely on physical cabling in a network infrastructure. Instead, data in a wireless network is transmitted through low-frequency radio waves in the invisible electromagnetic spectrum. The signals emitted with these waves can cover small or large distances, and they can effectively pass through physical objects like walls in order to reach their destination. The advantages of wireless networking include the ease of portability, saving on the costly expense of cabling, and physical space not being as much of an obstacle. This makes wireless communication a powerful tool used in cell phone networks, home networks, enterprise networks, and the Internet.

Nevertheless, the wide and oftentimes unrestrained propagation of wireless signals has led to the need for new security policies dealing specifically with wireless networking.

Wireless Antenna Types

Wireless networking signals can be amplified using a variety of different antenna types. The two main categories of antennas are directional and omni-directional. Directional antennas transmit signals to a specific point. As a result, they typically have a large *gain* or the reliable connection range and power of a signal measured in decibels, and they are less susceptible to interference than omni-directional antennas. Omni-directional antennas send and receive radio waves from all directions, usually as the main distribution source of a wireless signal. These antennas are common on wireless routers and mobile wireless adapters, as these devices require providing or receiving service in all possible directions. The coverage provided by omni-directional antennas limits their gain.

The following table describes the different types of directional and omni-directional antennas.

Antenna Category	Antenna Type	Description
Omni-directional	Rubber duck	A rubber duck or rubber ducky is a small omnidirectional antenna that is usually sealed in a rubber jacket. As is typical of omni-directional antennas, rubber ducks have little gain. However, because of their small size, they are ideal for mobility and are often used in walkie-talkies or other two-way radios, as well as short range wireless networking.

Antenna Category	Antenna Type	Description
	Ceiling dome	As the name suggests, this omni-directional antenna is installed in ceilings and is commonly used to cover rooms in a building with a wireless signal.
Directional	Yagi	A directional antenna used primarily in radio, but also employed in long distance wireless networking to extend the range of hotspots.
	Parabolic	A very precise directional antenna, used often in satellite dishes, that has a significant amount of gain. Because they are so precise, it is somewhat more difficult to establish a connection with a parabolic antenna.
	Backfire	A small directional antenna that looks similar to a parabolic dish, but with less gain. Backfire antennas are used in wireless networks to efficiently target a specific physical area without overextending coverage.
	"Cantenna"	This is a homemade directional antenna that can extend wireless networks or help to discover them. As the name suggests, cantennas typically involve placing a metal can over another antenna, such as a satellite dish, in an attempt to increase its gain.

802.11 Standards

There are various 802.11 standards that you may encounter in networking implementations in your role as a security professional. Each of the approved standards in the 802.11 family has different characteristics, described in the following table.

Wireless Protocol	Description
802.11	A family of specifications developed by the IEEE for wireless LAN communications between wireless devices or between wireless devices and a base station. The standard is supported by various working groups, known collectively as 802.11x. It specifies wireless data transfer rates of up to 2 megabits per second (Mbps) in the 2.4 gigahertz (GHz) frequency band.
802.11a	The approved specification for a fast, secure, but relatively expensive wireless protocol. 802.11a supports speeds up to 54 Mbps in the 5 GHz frequency band. Unfortunately, that speed has a limited range of only 60 feet, which, depending on how you arrange your access points, could severely limit user mobility.
802.11b	The first specification to be called Wi-Fi, 802.11b is the least expensive wireless network protocol. 802.11b provides for an 11 Mbps transfer rate in the 2.4 GHz frequency. (Some vendors, such as D-Link, have increased the rate on their devices to 22 Mbps.) 802.11b has a range up to 1,000 feet in an open area and a range of 200 to 400 feet in an enclosed space (where walls might hamper the signal). It is backward compatible with 802.11, but is not interoperable with 802.11a.
802.11g	The specification for wireless data throughput at the rate of up to 54 Mbps in the 2.4 GHz band. It is compatible with 802.11b and may operate at a much faster speed.
802.11n	A recent specification for wireless data throughput. The specification increased speeds dramatically, with data throughput up to 600 Mbps in the 2.4 GHz or 5 GHz ranges.

Wireless Protocol	Description
802.11ac	A specification that improves on 802.11n by adding wider channels in the 5 GHz band to increase data throughput to a total of 1300 Mbps.

Wireless Security Protocols

The following table describes security protocols often used in wireless networking.

Security Protocol	Description
Wired Equivalent Privacy (WEP)	Provides 64-bit, 128-bit, and 256-bit encryption using the Rivest Cipher 4 (RC4) algorithm for wireless communication that uses the 802.11a and 802.11b protocols. WEP is considered a security hazard and has been deprecated because it relied on an initialization vector (IV) to randomize identical strings of text. With a 24-bit IV size, WEP was extremely vulnerable to an IV attack that would be able to predict the IV value.
Wireless Transport Layer Security (WTLS)	The security layer of the Wireless Application Protocol (WAP) that uses public key cryptography for mutual authentication and data encryption. In most cases, WTLS is meant to provide secure WAP communications, but if it is improperly configured or implemented, it can expose wireless devices to attacks that include email forgery and sniffing data that has been sent in plaintext.
802.1x	An IEEE standard used to provide a port-based authentication mechanism over a LAN or wireless LAN. For wireless communications, 802.1x uses the 802.11a and 802.11b protocols. 802.1x also uses the Extensible Authentication Protocol (EAP) to provide user authentication against a directory service.
Wi-Fi Protected Access (WPA/WPA2)	The security protocol introduced to address some of the shortcomings in WEP. WPA was introduced during the development of the 802.11i IEEE standard, and WPA2 implemented all the mandatory components of the standard. It provides for dynamic reassignment of keys to prevent the key-attack vulnerabilities of WEP: • WPA provides improved data encryption through the *Temporal Key Integrity Protocol (TKIP)*, which is a security protocol created by the IEEE 802.11i task group to replace WEP. It is combined with the existing WEP encryption to provide a 128-bit encryption key that fixes the key length issues of WEP. • In addition to TKIP, WPA2 adds Advanced Encryption Standard (AES) cipher-based *Counter Mode with Cipher Block Chaining Message Authentication Code Protocol (CCMP)* encryption for even greater security and to replace TKIP. It provides a 128-bit encryption key. • Both standards have been extended to include several types of user authentication through EAP, which is considered poor in WEP. WEP regulates access to a wireless network based on a computer's hardware-specific MAC address, which is relatively easy to figure out, steal, and use (that is, sniff and spoof). EAP is built on a more secure public key encryption system to ensure that only authorized network users can access the network.

Security Protocol	Description
EAP	A framework that allows clients and servers to authenticate with each other using one of a variety of plug-ins. Because EAP does not specify which authentication method should be used, it enables the choice of a wide range of current authentication methods, and allows for the implementation of future authentication methods. EAP is often utilized in wireless networks and can also be used in wired implementations. Two common EAP implementations are: • *Protected Extensible Authentication Protocol (PEAP),* which is an open standard developed by a coalition made up of Cisco Systems, Microsoft, and RSA Security. • *Lightweight Extensible Authentication Protocol (LEAP),* which is Cisco Systems' proprietary EAP implementation.

WAP

Wireless Application Protocol (WAP) is a protocol designed to transmit data such as web pages, email, and newsgroup postings to and from wireless devices such as mobile phones, smartphones, and handheld computers over very long distances, and display the data on small screens in a web-like interface.

WAP uses the proprietary Wireless Markup Language (WML) rather than native Hypertext Markup Language (HTML). WAP has five layers: Wireless Application Environment, Wireless Session Protocol, Wireless Transport Protocol, WTLS, and the Wireless Datagram Protocol. The WAP standard was developed by companies such as Ericsson, Motorola, and Nokia. The standard is currently maintained by the Open Mobile Alliance (OMA), on the web at **www.openmobilealliance.org**.

VPNs and Open Wireless

Open wireless networks are a major security risk when accessed directly. Because they are insecure, attackers can perform any number of attacks on the network, as well as compromise each individual user's communications. This is why, when forced to use open wireless, you should tunnel through using a VPN, if feasible. VPNs provide authentication techniques and encrypt your data in transit over the Internet, even when using an insecure wireless hotspot. However, VPNs will not provide an adequate level of defense if they don't use secure tunneling protocols. For example, PPTP is vulnerable to man-in-the-middle attacks; instead, you should use the more secure IPSec protocol when tunneling with a VPN.

Figure 4–31: A VPN tunnel through an insecure wireless hotspot.

Wireless Security Methods

The following table describes a number of security methods you can use to ensure that your wireless network is secure from unauthorized access.

Security Method	Countermeasures
Configuration	• Secure your wireless router or access point administration interface. • Change default administrator passwords (and user names). • Disable remote administration. • Secure/disable the reset switch/function. • Change the default SNMP parameter. • Change the default channel. • Regularly upgrade the Wi-Fi router firmware to ensure that you have the latest security patches and critical fixes. • Implement MAC filtering.
Service Set Identifier (SSID)	• Don't broadcast your SSID. • Change the default SSID broadcast.
Encryption	• Enable WPA2 encryption instead of WEP. • Change the default encryption keys. • Avoid using pre-shared keys (PSK).
Network	• Assign static IP addresses to devices. • Use the Remote Authentication Dial-In User Service Plus (RADIUS+) network directory authentication where feasible. • Use a VPN. • Perform periodic rogue wireless access point scans. • Perform periodic security assessments.
Antenna placement and power level configuration	• Reduce your wireless LAN transmitter power. • Position the router or access point safely. The radio frequency range of each access point should not extend beyond the physical boundaries of the organization's facilities. • Adjust the power level controls on routers and access points as needed to help minimize power consumption within the wireless network. It can be difficult to manage the power of wireless to reduce the power used, while providing the right level of power to operate the network.
Client	• Do not auto-connect to open Wi-Fi networks. • Enable firewalls on each computer and the router.

Captive Portals

A *captive portal* is a technique that requires a client attempting to connect to the Internet to authenticate through a web page. Unless the client opens a browser and completes the necessary steps on the web page, their packets are intercepted and they will be unable to properly use the Internet. Captive portals are commonly used by Wi-Fi hotspots, especially free and/or public ones, in order to get the user to agree to an acceptable use policy before they begin using the service. Captive portals may also be used to authenticate users by requiring them to log in with the proper credentials, preventing unauthorized users from joining the network.

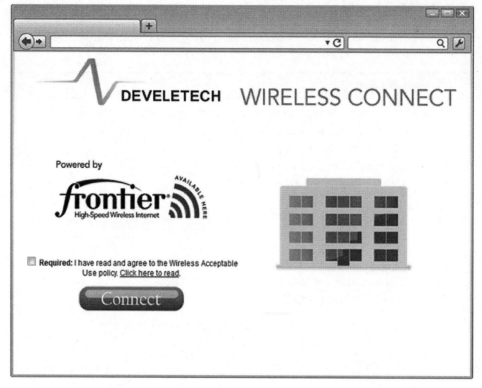

Figure 4-32: A captive portal requiring the user to accept a policy before they can use the Wi-Fi hotspot.

Site Surveys

In a general sense, a *site survey* is the collection of information on a location, including access routes, potential obstacles, and best positioning of materials, for the purpose of constructing something in the best possible way. Wireless networks may go through a site survey phase in order to ascertain exactly how to design the network with respect to the hardware's location. Successful site surveys lead to networks and their users having quality coverage and bandwidth, while at the same time being conscious of security protocols and requirements. This is generally accomplished by modeling the proposed environment using specialized tools that collect RF signal data. For example, the frequencies emitted by wireless access points might be hindered by walls in a building, while at the same time traveling farther in open air. You, as a security-minded administrator, might determine that positioning access points where walls limit signals actually prevents those past the walls—beyond the designated area—from attempting to use the access point. In doing this, you uphold your company's protocols that stipulate not to extend a wireless network beyond a specified physical range.

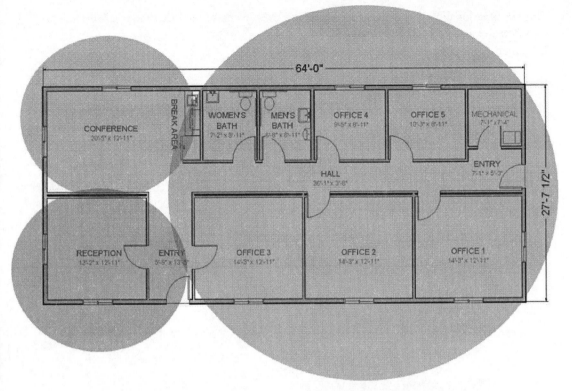

Figure 4-33: A site survey determining where a wireless network should extend to in an office building and where it should not.

Guidelines for Securing Wireless Traffic

When you secure wireless traffic, you must prevent unauthorized network access and the theft of network data while ensuring that authorized users can connect to the network. Some steps you might take to secure wireless traffic include:

- Keep sensitive data private. Do not include any data on a wireless device, such as a smartphone, that you are not willing to lose if the device is lost or stolen.
- Install antivirus software if it is available for your wireless devices.
- Update the software on wireless devices and routers to provide additional functionality as well as to close security holes in wireless devices, such as:
  - Prevent bluejacking and bluesnarfing attacks by disabling the discovery setting on Bluetooth connections.
  - Set Bluetooth connections to hidden.
- Use a VPN with a strong tunneling protocol like IPSec if you're connecting to an insecure open wireless network.
- Conduct a site survey to determine the best possible ways to position your wireless infrastructure with respect to security.
- Implement a security protocol.
- Implement appropriate authentication and access control, such as RADIUS to prevent authentication attacks, including war driving.
- Implement an IDS on the wireless network for monitoring network activity to protect against rogue access point attacks and data emanation.
- Don't rely solely on MAC filtering and disabling SSID broadcasts.
- Implement a captive portal requiring login credentials to protect against unauthorized users accessing your Wi-Fi hotspot.
- Implement your hardware and software manufacturers' security recommendations.

- Test the functionality of systems after hardening them to make sure that required services and resources are accessible to legitimate users.
- Document your changes.

ACTIVITY 4–8
Securing Wireless Traffic

Scenario

You have been assigned the task of tightening security for the sales department of Develetech Industries. Many of the employees in this department are mobile users, and they need to connect to the company network and the Internet through devices like laptops and smartphones. Running Ethernet cables to the former is often impractical, and the latter can only connect wirelessly. However, the department manager is concerned that attackers may try to steal client information. He says that employees often run applications and transfer customer data and sales information across the network. It is your responsibility to make sure that the routers employees must connect to are configured to prevent unauthorized access.

You'll start by turning off the insecure Wi-Fi Protection Setup (WPS) feature and defining a unique SSID that employees will recognize and trust. Then, you'll use WPA2 to encrypt wireless traffic with a passphrase that only employees are told. To ensure that no one except administrators can alter these important settings, you'll change the default router administration password. In addition, you'll block any insecure connection attempts to the administration portal. Lastly, you'll save all of your configuration settings as a local backup. With this configuration in place, your wireless users will be much less susceptible to the many dangers of Wi-Fi networking.

---

1. Connect to the wireless router's configuration interface.
    a) From the Desktop taskbar, select **Internet Explorer**.
    b) In the **Address** bar, enter *http://ui.linksys.com*
    c) From the list of routers, select the **E1200** link.
    d) Select the **2.0.04/** link.
    e) In the **Internet Explorer** message box, select **Add**.
    f) In the **Trusted sites** dialog box, select **Add** to add the site to the **Trusted sites** zone. Select **Close**.
    g) In the **Warning** message box, check the **Do not show me this again** check box and select **OK**.

 Note: This website emulates a common router configuration interface. When working with a real device, you will typically connect to **http://192.168.1.1** and be prompted to enter a user name and password. For a list of default user names and passwords by router, navigate to **http:// www.routerpasswords.com**.

2. Turn off WPS and set an SSID for your wireless network.
    a) On the menu bar at the top of the page, select the **Wireless** tab.

Setup						Linksys E1200	E1200
	Setup	Wireless	Security	Access Policy	Applications & Gaming	Administration	Status
	Basic Setup	IPv6 Setup	DDNS	MAC Address Clone	Advanced Routing		

    b) In the **Wi-Fi Protected Setup™** section, select **Manual**.

c) In the **Network Name (SSID)** text box, double-click and type *dtech*

d) Select **Save Settings**, then in the **Message from webpage** message box, select **OK**.

e) Select **Save Settings** again, then select **Continue**.

3. Set WPA2 encryption with a passphrase.

a) Under the **Wireless** tab on the menu bar, select the **Wireless Security** link.

b) From the **Security Mode** drop-down list, select **WPA2 Personal**.

c) In the **Passphrase** text box, type *!Pass1234*

d) Select **Save Settings**, then select **Continue**.

4. Configure the router's administration settings.

a) On the menu bar, select the **Administration** tab.

b) In the **Router Password** text box, double-click and type *P@ssw0rd*

c) In the **Re-Enter to Confirm** text box, type the same password.

d) In the **Local Management Access** section, uncheck the **HTTP** check box and check the **HTTPS** check box.

e) In the **Local Management Access** section, for the **Access via Wireless** option, select **Disabled**.

f) In the **Remote Management Access** section, verify that **Remote Management** is disabled.

Management		
Router Access	Router Password:	••••••••
	Re-Enter to Confirm:	••••••••
Local Management Access	Access via:	☐ HTTP ☑ HTTPS
	Access via Wireless:	○ Enabled ◉ Disabled
Remote Management Access	Remote Management:	○ Enabled ◉ Disabled

g) At the bottom of the web page, select **Save Settings**.

h) On the **Your settings have been successfully saved** page, select **Continue**.

5. Save a backup of the router configuration.

a) In the **Back Up and Restore** section near the bottom of the page, select **Back Up Configuration**.

Back Up and Restore	Back Up Configuration	Restore Configuration

b) In the Internet Explorer file download message box, select the **Save** down arrow, then select **Save as**.

c) In the **File name** text box, type *routerconfig1* and select **Save**.

d) Verify that the configuration file was downloaded successfully.

e) Close Internet Explorer.

Summary

In this lesson, you identified the many different components that play a role in securing a network against threats and vulnerabilities. You also successfully applied security protocols and administrative policies to strengthen the defense of your network without compromising its availability to legitimate users. Having a good, basic network security understanding will enable you to evaluate an organization's security infrastructure as well as to provide valuable advice on network security management.

Were there any network security components you were familiar with? What experience do you have with them?

Do you have any experience with securing a wireless network? If so, then what security measures have you applied?

Note: Check your LogicalCHOICE Course screen for opportunities to interact with your classmates, peers, and the larger LogicalCHOICE online community about the topics covered in this course or other topics you are interested in. From the Course screen you can also access available resources for a more continuous learning experience.

5 | Implementing Access Control, Authentication, and Account Management

Lesson Time: 2 hours, 15 minutes

Lesson Objectives

In this lesson, you will implement access control, authentication, and account management security measures. You will:

- Implement access control and common authentication services.

- Implement account management security controls.

Lesson Introduction

In previous lessons, you examined data security, application security, host and device security, and network security. User access control, authentication, and user account management form the next logical steps in ensuring the security of an organization. In this lesson, you will identify how access control methods, authentication services, and account management security measures and best practices are applied to protect the identity of users within a system.

The way users access and log in to systems can be like a doorway into an organization's applications, data, and services. Because of this, it is crucial to apply appropriate access control and authentication services to your information systems infrastructure. You are also responsible for securing the identity of the individuals accessing systems and services within the organization. To adopt the right security posture, you will need to be able to implement access control, authentication services, and account management controls properly.

TOPIC A

Access Control and Authentication Services

Access control and authentication are among the primary factors in computer security. Although access control and authentication always have the same goal, there are many different approaches to accomplishing both. In this topic, you will discuss some of the primary authentication services and access control mechanisms used today.

Strong authentication and access control are the first lines of defense in the battle to secure network resources. But applying access control and authentication is not a single process; there are many different methods and mechanisms, some of which can even be combined into more complex schemes. As a network professional, you will need to be familiar with the major access control and authentication services used today so you can implement and support the ones that are appropriate for your environment.

Directory Services

A *directory service* is a network service that stores identity information about all the objects in a particular network, including users, groups, servers, clients, printers, and network services. The directory also provides user access control to directory objects and network resources. Directory services can also be used to centralize security and to control access to individual network resources.

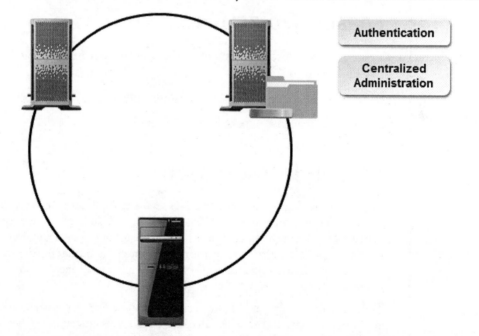

Figure 5-1: A directory service that centralizes administration and authentication in a network.

Directory Schema

The structure of the directory is controlled by a *schema* that defines rules for how objects are created and what their characteristics can be. Most schemas are extensible, so they can be modified to support the specific needs of an organization.

LDAP

The *Lightweight Directory Access Protocol (LDAP)* is a directory access protocol that runs over Transmission Control Protocol/Internet Protocol (TCP/IP) networks. LDAP clients authenticate to the LDAP service, and the service's schema defines the tasks that clients can and cannot perform while accessing a directory database, the form the directory query must take, and how the directory server will respond. The LDAP schema is extensible, which means you can make changes or add on to it.

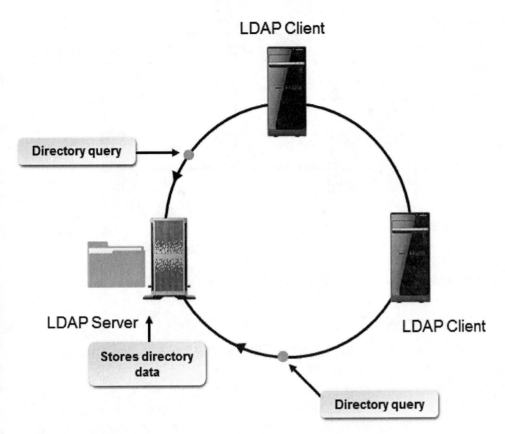

LDAP Client

Directory query

LDAP Server

Stores directory data

LDAP Client

Directory query

Figure 5–2: LDAP clients sending directory queries to an LDAP server.

Directory Management Tools

Most directory services implementations ship with some management tools of their own. In addition, there are a wide variety of third-party LDAP browsing and administration tools available from both open- and closed-source vendors.

While a plaintext editor might be useful in troubleshooting situations, graphical user interface (GUI) utilities are generally easier to work with. In addition to preconfigured tools, you can create scripts that use LDAP to automate routine directory maintenance tasks, such as adding large numbers of users or groups, and checking for blank passwords or disabled or obsolete user accounts.

LDAPS

Secure LDAP (LDAPS) is a method of implementing LDAP using Secure Sockets Layer/Transport Layer Security (SSL/TLS) encryption protocols to prevent eavesdropping and man-in-the-middle attacks. LDAPS forces both client and server to establish a secure connection before any transmissions can occur, and if the secure connection is interrupted or dropped, LDAP likewise closes. The server implementing LDAPS requires a signed certificate issued by a certificate authority, and the client must accept and install the certificate on their machine.

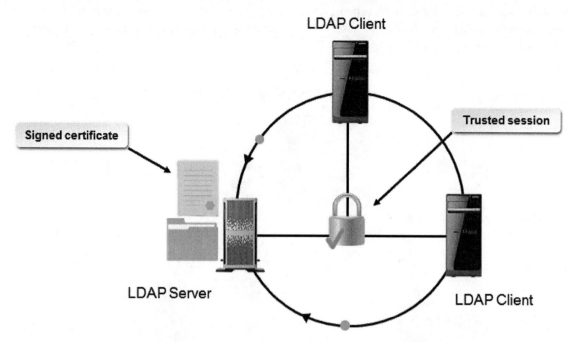

Figure 5–3: LDAP clients communicating with an LDAP server over SSL/TLS.

Common Directory Services

There are a variety of robust directory services available, both paid and free, open and closed source. The following table describes the most common ones.

Directory Service	Description
Microsoft® *Active Directory®*	A directory service that holds information about all network objects for a single domain or multiple domains. Active Directory allows administrators to centrally manage and control access to resources using Access Control Lists (ACLs). It allows users to find resources anywhere on the network. Active Directory also has a schema that controls how accounts are created and what attributes an administrator may assign to them. Active Directory Application Mode (ADAM) is a lightweight version of Active Directory.
Sun Java™ System Directory Server	This is the latest version of Sun Microsystems' Directory Server. It was formerly known as Sun ONE Directory Server and iPlanet Directory Server. Sun Java System Directory Server is built with 64-bit technology and marketed toward large installations that require reliable scaling. The software is free, and paid support is available from Sun.
OpenDS	An open-source directory server that runs on Linux, Unix, Microsoft® Windows®, and Mac OS X®. OpenDS is written by Sun in Java. It supports LDAPv3 and Directory Service Markup Language version 2 (DSMLv2).
OpenLDAP	A free, open-source LDAP implementation with distributions available for most operating systems.
Open Directory	Apple's customized implementation of OpenLDAP that is part of the Server app for Mac OS X. Open Directory is somewhat compatible with both Active Directory and Novell's eDirectory™ and integrates both the LDAP and Kerberos standards.

Directory Service Vulnerabilities

Each directory service has its own vulnerabilities; however, like any other server or service, there are some common vulnerability areas to be aware of:

- All categories of network-based attacks, including:
  - Denial of Service (DoS)/Distributed Denial of Service (DDoS) attacks.
  - Unencrypted transmission of data.
  - Man-in-the-middle attacks.
  - Packet sniffing/capture attacks.
- Buffer overflow attacks.
- Security of user and administrator accounts and passwords.

Backing Up Active Directory

Before you harden Active Directory, you should back it up in case anything goes wrong. You back up Active Directory by backing up the computer's system state data within the Windows Backup utility. In addition to Active Directory, backing up the computer's System State Data also backs up the following components:

- Registry
- COM+ Class Registration database
- Boot and system files
- Certificate Services database (if you have installed Certificate Services on the server)
- The SYSVOL folder (if the server is a domain controller)
- The IIS Metabase (if you have installed IIS)

> **Access the Checklist tile on your LogicalCHOICE course screen for reference information and job aids on How to Back Up Active Directory.**

ACTIVITY 5-1
Backing Up Active Directory

Before You Begin

A partition labeled **BACKUP (D:)** already exists for backing up sensitive server data.

Scenario

As Develetech's security administrator, your boss has asked you to make sure that Active Directory is secure. You want to make sure that you have a current backup of Active Directory in case you encounter any problems. This will ensure that all users and computers registered on the domain will not be lost in the event of hardware failure, user carelessness, or malicious behavior. You have a **D** drive on your server that you'll save the backup to.

1. Verify that **Active Directory Users and Computers** displays the components you will be backing up.
   a) In **Server Manager**, select **Tools→Active Directory Users and Computers**.
   b) In the **Active Directory Users and Computers** window, if necessary, expand the domain object.
   c) Select **Users**.

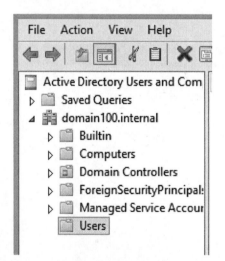

   d) Verify that there are various user and group objects such as **Administrator**, **Guest**, and **Domain Admins**. In the console tree, select **Domain Controllers**.

e) Verify that your server appears in the list of domain controllers. Close **Active Directory Users and Computers**.

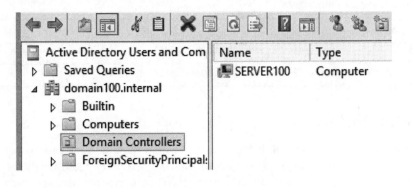

2. Back up your domain controller's system state data.

a) In **Server Manager**, select **Tools→Windows Server Backup**.

b) If necessary, from the left pane, select **Local Backup**.

c) In the **Actions** pane on the right side, select **Backup Once**.

d) In the **Backup Once Wizard**, on the **Backup Options** page, verify that **Different options** is selected and select **Next**.

> Create a backup now using:
>
> ○ Scheduled backup options
>
>   Choose this option if you have created a scheduled backup and want to use the same settings for this backup.
>
> ◉ Different options
>
>   Choose this option if you have not created a scheduled backup or to specify a location or items for this backup that are different from the scheduled backup.
>
> To continue, click Next.

e) On the **Select Backup Configuration** page, select **Custom** and then select **Next**.

f) On the **Select Items for Backup** page, select **Add Items**.

g) Check the **System state** check box and select **OK**.

> ☐ Bare metal recovery
> ☑ System state
> ☐ EFI System Partition
> ☐ Local disk (C:)
> ☐ BACKUP (D:)
> ☐ STORAGE (S:)
> ☐ Recovery

h) On the **Select Items for Backup** page, select **Next**.

i) On the **Specify Destination Type** page, verify that the **Local drives** option is selected and select **Next**.

j) On the **Select Backup Destination** page, verify that **BACKUP (D:)** is the backup destination and select **Next**.

k) On the **Confirmation** page, select **Backup**.

The **Backup Progress** page displays a progress bar. After a few moments, the backup operation will begin enumerating the **System state** files.

l)   Select the **Close** button to close the wizard.

> **Note:** The backup operation will continue to run in the background even after you close the wizard. You may proceed, as this will take a while to complete.

m) Close the **wbadmin - [Windows Server Backup (Local)\Local Backup]** window.

Remote Access Methods

With today's mobile workforce, there are several different methods that organizations can use to provide remote employees and customers with access to their network resources. Companies that require privacy may connect to a gateway remote access server (RAS) that provides access control services to all or part of the internal network. Also, an intermediate network—such as the Internet —can provide remote access from a remote system or a wireless device to a private network. Especially in this case, care must be taken to secure transmissions as they pass over the public network.

Tunneling

Tunneling is a data-transport technique that can be used to provide remote access in which a data packet is encrypted and encapsulated in another data packet in order to conceal the information of the packet inside. This enables data from one network to travel through another network. The tunnel can provide additional security by hiding user-encrypted data from the carrier network. Tunneling is typically employed as a security measure in VPN connections.

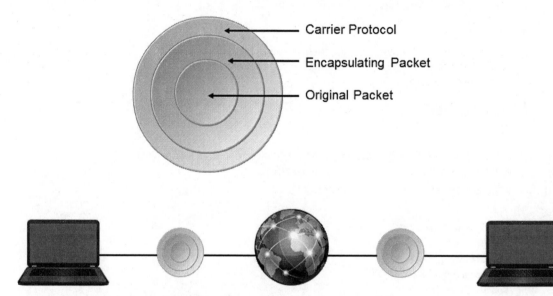

Figure 5–4: Data tunneling through the Internet.

Remote Access Protocols

The following table describes the common protocols used to provide remote access to networks.

Protocol	Description
Point-to-Point Protocol (PPP)	This is a legacy Internet standard for sending IP datagram packets over serial point-to-point links. Its most common use is for dial-up Internet access. It can be used in synchronous and asynchronous connections. Point-to-Point Protocol over Ethernet (PPPoE) and Point-to-Point Protocol over ATM (PPPoA) are more recent PPP implementations used by many Digital Subscriber Line (DSL) broadband Internet connections. PPP can dynamically configure and test remote network connections, and is often used by clients to connect to networks and the Internet. It also provides encryption for passwords, paving the way for secure authentication of remote users.
Point-to-Point Tunneling Protocol (PPTP)	This is a Microsoft VPN Layer 2 protocol that increases the security of PPP by providing tunneling and data encryption for PPP packets. It uses the same authentication types as PPP, and is a common VPN method among older Windows clients. PPTP encapsulates any type of network protocol and transports it over IP networks. However, because it has serious vulnerabilities, PPTP is no longer recommended by Microsoft.
Layer Two Tunneling Protocol (L2TP)	This is an Internet-standard protocol combination of PPTP and Layer 2 Forwarding (L2F) that enables the tunneling of PPP sessions across a variety of network protocols, such as IP, Frame Relay, or Asynchronous Transfer Mode (ATM). L2TP was specifically designed to provide tunneling and security interoperability for client-to-gateway and gateway-to-gateway connections. L2TP does not provide any encryption on its own and L2TP tunnels appear as IP packets, so L2TP employs IP Security (IPSec) Transport Mode for authentication, integrity, and confidentiality.
Secure Socket Tunneling Protocol (SSTP)	This protocol uses the Hypertext Transfer Protocol over Secure Sockets Layer (HTTP over SSL) protocol and encapsulates an IP packet with a PPP header and then with an SSTP header. The IP packet, PPP header, and SSTP header are encrypted by the SSL session. An IP header containing the destination addresses is then added to the packet. It is supported in all current Windows operating systems.

Note: L2TP has wide vendor support because it addresses the IPSec shortcomings of client-to-gateway and gateway-to-gateway connections.

HOTP

HMAC-based one-time password (HOTP) is an algorithm that generates *one-time passwords (OTPs)* using a hash-based authentication code (HMAC) to ensure the authenticity of a message. One-time passwords are meant to replace insecure static passwords as an additional factor of authentication. As the name suggests, the OTP is valid only for that one particular session; after that, it will no longer be of use in access or authentication. This is a particularly strong defense against an attacker who is able to discover someone else's credentials, as the attacker will be unable to make use of them after the user is finished with their session. OTPs are also an alternative to authentication methods that require installing specific software on each machine that is used to access a system. OTPs based on HMAC provide greater interoperability across software and hardware platforms, as well as being freely available as an open-source standard. Most major mobile operating systems, including Android®, iOS, and Windows Phone®, offer HMAC tokens for use in authentication.

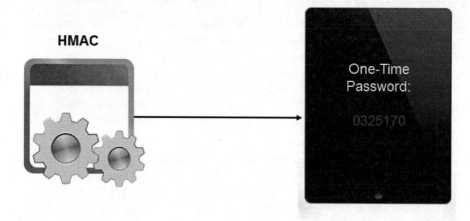

Figure 5–5: An HMAC providing a one-time password for use in authentication.

TOTP

Timed HMAC-based one-time password (TOTP) improves upon the HOTP algorithm by introducing a time-based factor to the one-time password authentication. HOTP and other one-time passwords have a weakness that allows an attacker to take advantage of the password if it is never used. The temporary password is only invalidated after it is successfully used to authenticate, but if it never is, then it could stay active indefinitely. If an attacker gains access to a password that isn't used, then they could easily compromise a system that relies on OTP. The TOTP algorithm addresses this security flaw by generating and invalidating new passwords in specific increments of time, such as 60 seconds. If the attacker gains access to the generated password and is unable to use it to authenticate within 60 seconds, they will fail to penetrate the system's defense. It is unlikely that an attacker will be able to carry out the necessary steps in that short window of time, so time-based OTPs are a very useful defense against authentication abuse.

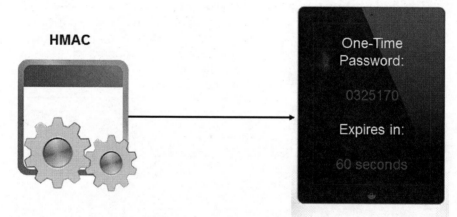

Figure 5–6: A one-time password that will expire shortly.

PAP

Password Authentication Protocol (PAP) is an authentication protocol that sends user IDs and passwords as plaintext. It is generally used when a remote client is connecting to a non-Windows server that does not support strong password encryption. When the server receives a user ID and password pair, it compares them to its local list of credentials. If a match is found, the server accepts the credentials and allows the remote client to access resources. If no match is found, the connection is terminated. Because it lacks encryption, PAP is extremely vulnerable and has been largely phased out as a legacy protocol.

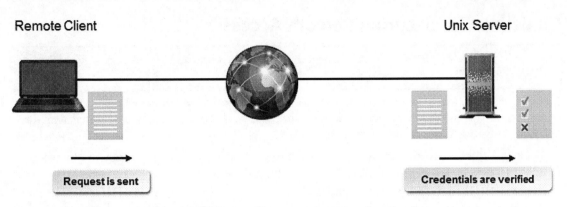

Remote Client

Unix Server

Request is sent

Credentials are verified

Figure 5-7: A server matching credentials it receives to those in its database.

CHAP

Challenge Handshake Authentication Protocol (CHAP) is an encrypted authentication protocol that is often used to provide access control for remote access servers. CHAP was developed so that passwords would not have to be sent in plaintext. It is generally used to connect to non-Microsoft servers. CHAP uses a combination of Message Digest 5 (MD5) hashing and a challenge-response mechanism, and it accomplishes authentication without ever sending passwords over the network. It can accept connections from any authentication method except for certain unencrypted schemes. For these reasons, CHAP is a more secure protocol than PAP. However, CHAP is also considered a legacy protocol, particularly because the MD5 hash algorithm is no longer suitably secure.

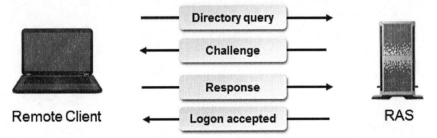

| Directory query |
| Challenge |
| Response |
| Logon accepted |

Remote Client

RAS

Figure 5-8: The CHAP handshake procedure validating user authenticity.

The CHAP Process

The following table describes each step of the CHAP handshake process.

Step	Description
Step 1	The remote client requests a connection to the RAS.
Step 2	The remote server sends a challenge sequence, which is usually a random value.
Step 3	The remote client uses its password as an encryption key to encrypt the challenge sequence and sends the modified sequence to the server.
Step 4	The server encrypts the original challenge sequence with the password stored in its local credentials list and compares the results with the modified sequence received from the client: • If the two sequences do not match, the server closes the connection. • If the two sequences match, the server allows the client to access resources.

Guidelines for Securing Remote Access

> **Note:** All Guidelines for this lesson are available as checklists from the **Checklist** tile on the LogicalCHOICE Course screen.

Remote access is a useful and often necessary tool in a modern information technology environment. Use the following guidelines to ensure that your users can connect remotely with an adequate layer of security to protect your systems:

- Set up a VPN for offsite employees to connect to your internal network through the Internet.
- Use secure tunneling protocols like L2TP with IPSec in your VPN.
- Avoid insecure tunneling protocols like PPTP.
- For those employees who access highly sensitive data, implement one-time password authentication.
- Implement time-based OTPs to mitigate the threat of a session being hijacked.
- Avoid using PAP and CHAP and other outdated remote access protocols that fail to provide adequate protection.

ACTIVITY 5-2
Securing a Remote Access Server

Before You Begin

The Windows Server 2012 R2 server computer has a physical local area network (LAN) adapter and also a virtual Microsoft Loopback Adapter to simulate the presence of an external connection object.

Scenario

One of the next tasks as Develetech's security administrator is to make sure your remote access servers are secure. In the past, the company has had problems with attackers accessing services and data that they were not supposed to have access to through VPN connections. You will now provide VPN services through new Windows Server 2012 R2 RRAS servers, which you will secure before connecting to the network. Develetech's IT department will install the new VPN RRAS server in the demilitarized zone (DMZ). The DMZ has already been secured. Also, the Active Directory team has already created a remote access security policy to determine who will have VPN access to RRAS servers in your domain.

You need to configure the VPN server with system-wide security settings that include:

- Permitting only L2TP clients with IPSec encryption to connect.
- Blocking insecure PPTP packets from external networks.

---

1. Enable and configure security on the remote access server.
   a) In **Server Manager**, select **Tools→Security Configuration Wizard**.
   b) In the **Security Configuration Wizard**, on the **Welcome to the Security Configuration Wizard** page, select **Next**.
   c) Verify that **Create a new security policy** is selected and select **Next**.

   > Select the action you want to perform:
   >
   > ◉ Create a new security policy
   > ○ Edit an existing security policy
   > ○ Apply an existing security policy
   > ○ Rollback the last applied security policy

   d) Select **Next** to accept the server name.
   e) When the processing is complete, select **Next** twice.

f) On the **Select Server Roles** page, scroll down and verify that the **Remote access/VPN server** check box is checked and select **Next**.

View: | Installed roles ∨

Select the server roles that the selected server performs:

☐ ▷ Password Synchronization
☐ ▷ Print Server
☑ ▷ Remote access/VPN server
☐ ▷ Remote COM+
☑ ▷ Remote SCW Configuration and Analysis

g) On the **Select Client Features** page, select **Next**.
h) On the **Select Administration and Other Options** page, select **Next**.
i) On the **Select Additional Services** page, select **Next**.
j) On the **Handling Unspecified Services** page, verify that **Do not change the startup mode of the service** is selected, and select **Next**.

This security policy might be applied to servers with services not specified by the policy. When an unspecified service is found, perform the following action:

◉ Do not change the startup mode of the service

○ Disable the service

k) On the **Confirm Service Changes** page, select **Next**.
l) On the **Network Security** page, select **Next**.
m) Scroll down, and uncheck the **Routing and Remote Access (PPTP-In)** and **Routing and Remote Access (PPTP-Out)** check boxes.

☐ ▷ Routing and Remote Access (PPTP-In)
☐ ▷ Routing and Remote Access (PPTP-Out)

n) Select **Routing and Remote Access (L2TP-In)** and select **Edit**.
o) In the **Edit Rule (Routing and Remote Access (L2TP-In))** dialog box, in the **Action** section, select **Allow only secure connections** and check the **Require encryption** check box.
p) Select **OK** and then select **Next**.
q) On the **Registry Settings** page, check the **Skip this section** check box and select **Next**.
r) On the **Audit Policy** page, check the **Skip this section** check box and select **Next**.
s) On the **Save Security Policy** page, select **Next**.
t) On the **Security Policy File Name** page, in the **Security policy file name** text box, at the end of the path, type *RA Security*
u) In the **Description** text box, type *Configure Remote Access* and select **Next**.
v) On the **Apply Security Policy** page, select **Apply now** and select **Next**.
w) When the process is complete, select **Next**, then select **Finish**.

2. Start the RRAS server.

a) In **Server Manager**, select **Tools→Routing and Remote Access**.

b) Select your server object and select **Action→All Tasks→Start**.

File	Action	View	Help

Configure and Enable Routing and Remote Access

Disable Routing and Remote Access

Enable DirectAccess...

All Tasks ▶ | Start

Stop

Delete | Pause

Refresh | Resume

Properties | Restart

Help

Static Routes

c) In the **Routing and Remote Access** message box, select **Yes** to re-enable the service and start the server.

d) After the server arrow turns green, close the **Routing and Remote Access** window.

PGP

Pretty Good Privacy (PGP) is a publicly available email security and authentication utility that uses a variation of public key cryptography to encrypt emails: the sender encrypts the contents of the email message and then encrypts the key that was used to encrypt the contents. The encrypted key is sent with the email, and the receiver decrypts the key and then uses the key to decrypt the contents. PGP also uses public key cryptography to digitally sign emails to authenticate the sender and the contents.

GPG

GNU Privacy Guard (GPG) is a free, open-source version of PGP that provides equivalent encryption and authentication services. GPG is compliant with current PGP services and meets the latest standards issued by the Internet Engineering Task Force (IETF).

RADIUS

Remote Authentication Dial-In User Service (RADIUS) is an Internet standard protocol that provides centralized remote access authentication, authorization, and auditing services. When a network contains several remote access servers, you can configure one of the servers to be a RADIUS server, and all of the other servers as RADIUS clients. The RADIUS clients will pass all authentication requests to the RADIUS server for verification. User configuration, remote access policies, and usage logging can be centralized on the RADIUS server. In this configuration, the remote access server is generically known as the *Network Access Server (NAS)*.

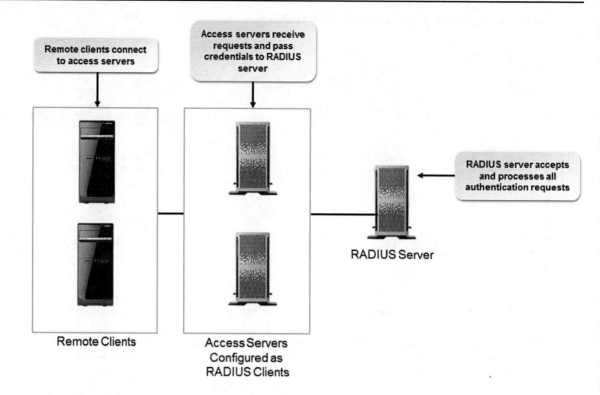

Figure 5–9: A RADIUS server authenticating remote client requests.

Diameter

Diameter is an authentication protocol that improves upon RADIUS by strengthening some of its weaknesses. The name "Diameter" comes from the claim that Diameter is twice as good as RADIUS. Diameter is a stronger protocol in many ways but is not as widespread in its implementation due to the lack of products using it.

NPS

Network Policy Server (NPS) is a Microsoft Server 2012 implementation of a RADIUS server. It helps in administrating VPNs and wireless networks. NPS was known as Internet Authentication Service (IAS) in Windows Server 2003.

TACACS

The *Terminal Access Controller Access Control System (TACACS)* and *TACACS Plus (TACACS+)* protocols provide centralized authentication and authorization services for remote users. TACACS+ also supports multi-factor authentication. TACACS+ is considered more secure and more scalable than RADIUS because it accepts login requests and authenticates the access credentials of the user. TACACS+ includes process-wide encryption for authentication, whereas RADIUS encrypts only passwords. The original TACACS and another extension developed by Cisco, *XTACACS*, have been effectively replaced by the more secure TACACS+.

Kerberos

Kerberos is an authentication service that is based on a time-sensitive ticket-granting system. It was developed by the Massachusetts Institute of Technology (MIT) to use a single sign-on (SSO) method where the user enters access credentials that are then passed to the authentication server, which contains an access list and allowed access credentials. Kerberos can be used to manage access control to many different services using one centralized authentication server.

The Kerberos Process

In the Kerberos process:

1. A user logs on to the domain.
2. The user requests a ticket granting ticket (TGT) from the authenticating server.
3. The authenticating server responds with a time-stamped TGT.
4. The user presents the TGT back to the authenticating server and requests a service ticket to access a specific resource.
5. The authenticating server responds with a service ticket.
6. The user presents the service ticket to the resource.
7. The resource authenticates the user and allows access.

SAML

Security Assertion Markup Language (SAML) is a data format based on XML that is used to exchange authentication information between a service, an identity provider, and the requesting client. SAML coordinates the various identity assertions between these three sources. Using XML as a framework, SAML defines security request information in markup language. This request information contains details such as when a request was issued, what resource is being requested, and any conditions that need to be met. One overarching purpose of SAML is to provide an efficient way of implementing web-based single sign-on authentication across many different protocols.

> Access the Checklist tile on your LogicalCHOICE course screen for reference information and job aids on How to Set Up Remote Access Authentication.

ACTIVITY 5-3
Setting Up Remote Access Authentication

Scenario

As part of your remote access implementation, the senior network administrator at Develetech favors implementing an NPS with RADIUS authentication so that the administrators can obtain detailed authentication information and use a single remote access policy for all RRAS servers. She also recommends configuring the policy to automatically disconnect users if their connections are idle for 15 minutes. Taking these steps will ensure that remote access authentication is consistent and the VPN is less vulnerable to man-in-the-middle attacks on inactive sessions.

 Note: In this case, the NPS and RRAS servers are the same computer. In a production environment, however, you would typically use at least one NPS server separate from the RRAS servers.

1. Set up the NPS with RADIUS authentication.
   a) In **Server Manager**, select **Tools→Network Policy Server**.
   b) In the **Network Policy Server** window, select **RADIUS Clients and Servers**.
   c) In the right pane, select **Configure RADIUS Clients**.
   d) Select **Action→New**.
   e) In the **New RADIUS Client** dialog box, in the **Friendly name** text box, type the name of your server.

   > Friendly name:
   > Server100

   f) In the **Address (IP or DNS)** text box, type your server's static IP address.

   g) In the **Shared Secret** section, in the **Shared secret** and **Confirm shared secret** text boxes, type **!Pass1234** and select **OK**.

   h) Minimize the **Network Policy Server** window.

2. Configure your RRAS server to use RADIUS for authentication.
   a) Open **Routing and Remote Access**.
   b) In the **Routing and Remote Access** window, select your server and select **Action→Properties**.
   c) In the **SERVER## (local) Properties** dialog box, select the **Security** tab.
   d) From the **Authentication provider** drop-down list, select **RADIUS Authentication**.
   e) Select **Configure** to display the **RADIUS Authentication** dialog box. You use this dialog box to define the name of the NPS server.
   f) In the **RADIUS Authentication** dialog box, select **Add**.
   g) In the **Add RADIUS Server** dialog box, in the **Server name** text box, type the name of your server to match the friendly name (**Server##**), and select **Change**.
   h) In the **Change Secret** dialog box, in the **New secret** and **Confirm new secret** text boxes, type **!Pass1234** and select **OK**.
   i) In the **Add RADIUS Server** dialog box, select **OK**.
   j) In the **RADIUS Authentication** dialog box, select **OK**.
   k) In the **SERVER## (local) Properties** dialog box, select **OK**.

    Note: This may take a few moments.

l)   If necessary, select **OK** to confirm the server restart. Otherwise, select **Action→All Tasks→Restart** to manually restart the server.

3. Configure the NPS and RRAS servers to report all successful and failed authentication attempts using accounting.

a)   On the Desktop taskbar, select **Network Policy Server**.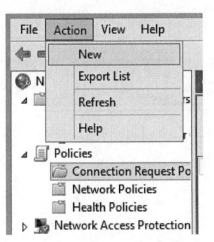

b)   In the **Network Policy Server** window, select **NPS (Local)** and select **Action→Properties**.

c)   In the **Network Policy Server (Local) Properties** dialog box, verify that the **Rejected authentication requests** and **Successful authentication requests** check boxes are checked and select **OK**.

d)   On the Desktop taskbar, select **Routing and Remote Access**.

e)   In the **Routing and Remote Access** window, verify that your server is selected and select **Action→Properties**.

f)   In the **SERVER## (local) Properties** window, select the **Security** tab.

g)   From the **Accounting provider** drop-down list, select **RADIUS Accounting** and select **Configure**.

h)   In the **RADIUS Accounting** dialog box, select **Add**.

i)   In the **Add RADIUS Server** dialog box, in the **Server name** text box, type the name of your server.

j)   Select **Change**.

k)   In the **Change Secret** dialog box, in the **New secret** and **Confirm new secret** text boxes, type *! Pass1234* and select **OK**.

l)   Select **OK** three times.

m) In the **Routing and Remote Access** window, if necessary, select your server object.

n)   Select **Action→All Tasks→Restart** to manually restart the server.
     RRAS will now report successful and failed user authentication attempts to the NPS server.

o)   Close the **Routing and Remote Access** window.

> **Note:** By default, NPS stores the accounting information it receives in the **C:\Windows\System32\LogFiles\laslog** file.

4. Create a policy to automatically disconnect idle VPN connections after 15 minutes.

a)   In the **Network Policy Server** window, expand **Policies**.

b)   Select **Connection Request Policies** and select **Action→New**.

c)   In the **New Connection Request Policy** wizard, in the **Policy name** text box, type *Disconnect Idle Connections*

d)   From the **Type of network access server** drop-down list, select **Remote Access Server(VPN-Dial up)** and select **Next**.

e)   On the **Specify Conditions** page, select **Add**.

f)   In the **Select condition** dialog box, scroll down to the bottom of the list and select **NAS Port Type**.

g)   In the **Select condition** dialog box, select **Add**.

h) In the **NAS Port Type** dialog box, in the **Common dial-up and VPN tunnel types** list, check the **Virtual (VPN)** check box, and select **OK**.

Specify the access media types required to match this policy.

Common dial-up and VPN tunnel types

- [ ] Async (Modem)
- [ ] ISDN Sync
- [ ] Sync (T1 Line)
- [x] Virtual (VPN)

Common 802.1X connection tunnel types

- [ ] Ethernet
- [ ] FDDI

i) Select **Next**.

j) On the **Specify Connection Request Forwarding** page, verify that **Authenticate requests on this server** is selected and select **Next**.

⦿ Authenticate requests on this server

◯ Forward requests to the following remote RADIUS server group for authentication:

k) On the **Specify Authentication Methods** page, select **Next**.

l) On the **Configure Settings** page, in the **RADIUS Attributes** section, select **Standard**.

m) Select **Add**.

n) In the **Add Standard RADIUS Attribute** dialog box, in the **Attributes** list, scroll down and select **Session-Timeout**.

o) Select **Add**.

p) In the **Attribute Information** dialog box, in the **Attribute value** text box, type *15* and select **OK**.

q) Select **Close**.

r) Select **Next** and then select **Finish**.

 Note: This may take a few moments.

s) Close the **Network Policy Server** window.

 Note: Because the VPN has been configured on a virtual adapter, the policy cannot be tested.

TOPIC B

Implement Account Management Security Controls

In the previous topic, you implemented the various access control and authentication services used to manage access to systems and hardware. Account management security controls are similar in that they control how accounts are managed within an organization. In this topic, you will implement account management security controls.

A single organization can contain a number of different account types that are assigned to its employees. With this in mind, you need to be able to apply proper controls that will guard against unauthorized access to user and group account information. As a security professional, it is your job to know what controls should be implemented and what policies should be enforced to effectively manage account security.

Identity Management

Identity management is an area of information security that is used to identify individuals within a computer system or network. Identities are created with specific characteristics and information specific to each individual or resource in a system. When pertaining to security, restrictions and access controls are assigned using an individual's identity within a system, network, or organization. Security professionals need to apply proper security controls to protect the identities of all individuals within a system and to prevent *identity theft* by unauthorized users.

One aspect of identity management is the protection of personally identifiable information (PII), which is covered later in the course.

Account Management

Account management is a common term used to refer to the processes, functions, and policies used to effectively manage user accounts within an organization. Account management job functions should follow the appropriate processes and security guidelines documented in an organizational security policy or account management policy. User accounts allow or deny access to an organization's information systems and resources; therefore, with the proper controls in place, organizations can properly manage accounts.

Account Privileges

Account privileges are permissions granted to users that allow them to perform various actions such as creating, deleting, and editing files, and also accessing systems and services on the network. Privileges can be assigned by user or by group. *User assigned privileges* are unique to each system user and can be configured to meet the needs of a specific job function or task. *Group based privileges* are assigned to an entire group of users within an organization. Each user within the group will have the same permissions applied. This can be very effective for large organizations with many users where privileges can be assigned at a departmental level. It is a universal best practice to assign privileges by group. User and group privileges should be well-documented in an organization's account policy. A user who has unique user assigned privileges and who is also a member of a group will be granted both sets of privileges.

Account Policy

An *account policy* is a document that includes an organization's requirements for account creation, account monitoring, and account removal. Policies can include user-specific guidelines or group management guidelines. User account policies will vary and can be customized to meet the needs of the business. As a security professional, you will need to research and analyze your organization's policy needs based on business requirements. Some common policy statements include:

- Who can approve account creation.
- Who is allowed to use a resource.
- Whether or not users can share accounts or have multiple accounts.
- When and how an account should be disabled or modified after a user access review.
- When to enforce general account prohibition.
- What rules should be enforced for password history, password strength, and password reuse.

Multiple Accounts

Multiple user accounts occur when one individual has several accounts for a system or resource. Accounts may differ depending on the level of access applied, such as a user level account versus an administrator account. It is common within an organization for an individual user to have more than one account for a number of systems. There are issues related to assigning and managing multiple accounts, such as:

- Lack of user awareness of the various accounts.
- Assigning the right level of data access and permissions to the appropriate accounts.
- Managing the privileges, permissions, and data replication for each individual's accounts.

A common use case for multiple accounts is for system administrators who have a user level account with typical user privileges for daily work such as preparing documents, using the Internet, and sending email, and an administrator-level account for use only to perform system procedures such as managing users or configuring servers. A user in this situation typically prefers to be able to use the same environment configuration, such as Windows desktop settings, document history, and web browser favorites lists, when switching between accounts. The management challenge is to enable the user to be able to access the elevated privileges of the administrative account when needed, without losing all the other environment settings that support productivity.

Shared Accounts

Shared accounts are accessed by more than one user or resource, and unlike traditional unshared accounts, they are not associated with any one individual. Shared accounts are typically associated with a specific role or purpose that many users can share for a variety of reasons:

- Anonymous and guest accounts function as a way for visitors to access a system.
- Temporary accounts are useful for employees or contractors who work for a company inconsistently.
- Administrative accounts allow multiple authorized professionals access to higher privileges.
- Batch process accounts allow for easily automating many different types of tasks.

Shared accounts are an inherent security risk. Since many different people will use one account, it is extremely difficult—and often impossible—to hold specific individuals accountable in case of a breach. Likewise, the users themselves may recognize this and become careless with security, something they might avoid if they were logged in to their own personal accounts. The other major risk involves password changes to an account. Since frequent password changing is a common policy, organizations will need to ensure that everyone who has access to an account knows when the password will change, and what that new password will be. This necessitates distributing passwords to a large group of people, which itself poses a significant challenge to security. If you decide that shared accounts are worth the risk, make sure to be discreet in how you choose who has access, what privileges those accounts will have, and how you will perform successful security audits.

Account Federation

Account federation is the practice of linking a single account and its characteristics across many different account management systems. SSO is a subset of account federation that specifically works with authentication, whereas account federation encompasses all of the policies and protocols that contribute to an identity. This provides a centralized account management structure that eliminates the need for superfluous account information. Federated accounts not only relieve some of the strain on the host, but users find that streamlining a single account for multiple use cases is much more practical and efficient than needing many different accounts. However, this also creates a single point of compromise for a user's identity. If the federated account's credentials are stolen, then an attacker can use that account in all of its different functions.

> **Note:** Google accounts and Microsoft accounts are examples of account federation.

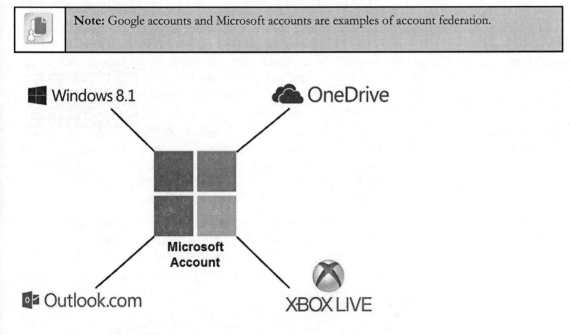

Figure 5-10: A Microsoft account can be used across many different systems.

Account Management Security Controls

To maintain and enforce the security needs of an organization, strict account management security controls should be implemented and enforced. The following table describes some of these controls.

Security Control	Description
User ID and password requirements	User IDs and passwords should be implemented and managed with a number of strict guidelines: • User IDs and passwords should be required to access all data systems and services within a network or when accessing services on the Internet. • Unique user IDs should be required and documented for each system user. • Strong, complex passwords should be required and documented for every system user, along with the character length requirements. • Password and user account recovery procedures should be documented and followed by all administrators. • Passwords should change often, and reusing the same passwords should not be allowed.
Account access restrictions	Account access guidelines should be documented for each type of account used within an organization. For example, user account and group account privileges, and systems access information should be documented. The concept of least privilege should be used when granting or denying access.
Account management guidelines	Account management can include a number of different tasks. The most common security guidelines include account creation, disablement, lockout, and expiration. Security guidelines should include organizational procedures for each account action and what specific conditions must be present to allow for an account change or deletion.
Multiple account guidelines	There can be many issues revolving around multiple user accounts. Users may have access to many different systems, or have more than one user account for an individual system. When managing multiple accounts: • Ensure proper documentation of all accounts assigned to an individual, including privileges, permissions, and data access rights assigned to each type of account. • Verify that user accounts are assigned properly, and that each individual has only the necessary accounts assigned to perform his or her job. • Verify that the proper level of access is assigned to each account.
Continuous monitoring	Account management should be considered an ongoing practice with regard to security. Monitoring various events like successful and failed logon attempts, escalation of rights and privileges, and assigning new users and groups, will help you zero in on any account abuse.

Credential Management

Credential managers were created to help users and organizations more easily store and organize account user names and passwords. These applications typically store credentials in an encrypted database on the local machine. From there, an authenticated user can retrieve the proper credentials for the relevant system. This is particularly helpful for users with multiple accounts across many systems, and because credential managers may be used to automatically fill in forms with user names and passwords, they can defend against keystroke-logging malware.

However, credential managers are only as strong as the passwords they store. Simple or easily guessed passwords will provide an attacker with an easy way to access an account, no matter how securely that password is stored. Furthermore, if the credential manager encrypts the database of passwords by generating a key from a master password, then an attacker who discovers the master password will compromise the entire credential database. Credential managers that use multi-factor authentication are more secure in case of such attacks.

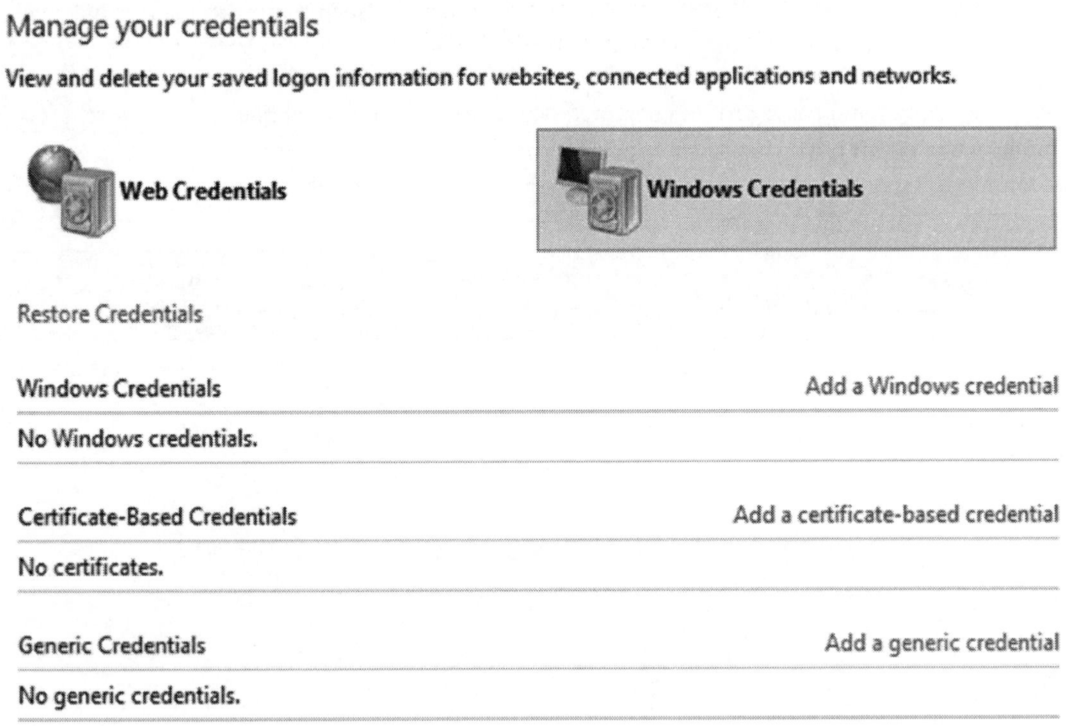

Manage your credentials

View and delete your saved logon information for websites, connected applications and networks.

Web Credentials   Windows Credentials

Restore Credentials

Windows Credentials   Add a Windows credential

No Windows credentials.

Certificate-Based Credentials   Add a certificate-based credential

No certificates.

Generic Credentials   Add a generic credential

No generic credentials.

Figure 5-11: The Windows Credential Manager that stores encrypted passwords in a database.

Note: Examples of credential management software include cross-platform apps LastPass, KeePass, and 1Password; Apple's Keychain for iOS and OS X; and Credential Manager for Windows.

Group Policy

The Group Policy service in Windows systems provides several different methods for managing account security across a domain. Examples include:

- Enforcing account password properties like length, complexity, and age.
- Enforcing account lockout thresholds and durations.
- Storing account passwords using reversible encryption.
- Enforcing Kerberos logon restrictions and ticket lifetimes.
- Auditing account management events.
- Assigning specific rights and controls to individual or group accounts.

Guidelines for Implementing Account Management Security Controls

With proper account management security controls in place, you can ensure that the identity and logon information for all individuals within an organization is fully protected from unauthorized access or theft. Use the following guidelines when managing account security:

- Implement the principle of least privilege when assigning user and group account access.
- Ensure that an account policy exists and includes all account policy guidelines.

- Verify that account request and approval procedures exist and are enforced.
- Verify that account modification procedures exist and are enforced.
- Verify that strong user name and password guidelines exist and are documented.
- Verify that account usage guidelines exist and are documented, such as how to manage inactive accounts.
- Limit the use of multiple and shared accounts to protect them from abuse.
- Store user names and passwords in encrypted databases with credential management software.
- Implement a group policy for wider access control.
- Continuously monitor account events such as logons and privilege escalation.

Access the Checklist tile on your LogicalCHOICE course screen for reference information and job aids on How to Implement Account Management Security Controls.

ACTIVITY 5-4
Implementing Account Management Security Controls

Scenario

Without proper security controls, any network is vulnerable to threats and attacks. As a security administrator at Develetech, you cannot risk the sensitive information stored on the network being stolen. As it is organizational policy to enforce certain account management security controls, you will make sure new users are not careless in the credentials that they use to access this sensitive information. You and your team have determined that, for optimum account security, user passwords must be restricted in the following ways:

- Users cannot change their passwords to previously used passwords until after a certain number of unique ones.
- Passwords must be a certain length and of a certain complexity to prevent cracking attempts.
- Too many login attempts with incorrect passwords will lock an account for a short period of time, preventing anyone from signing in under that account.

You will then test this new policy. Implementing account management controls such as password requirements are essential to securing identity in a system.

---

1. Create and link a new Group Policy Object.
   a) In **Server Manager**, select **Tools→Group Policy Management**.
   b) In the console tree, under **Domains**, select your **domain##.internal** object and select **Action→Create a GPO in this domain, and Link it here**.

🖳 File	Action	View	Window	Help
⬅ ➡		Create a GPO in this domain, and Link it here...		
🖳 Grou		Link an Existing GPO...		
⊿ 🛆 F		Block Inheritance		

   c) In the **New GPO** dialog box, in the **Name** text box, type *My Policy*
   d) Select **OK**.

> **Note:** It may take a few moments for your computer to create the policy.

2. Enforce password history in the new policy.
   a) Under your domain object in the console tree, right-click **My Policy** and select **Edit**. The **Group Policy Management Editor** window opens.
   b) In the console tree, under **Computer Configuration**, expand **Policies→Windows Settings→Security Settings→Account Policies**, and then select **Password Policy**.

> **Note:** It may take a few moments for **Security Settings** to expand.

   c) In the right pane, double-click **Enforce password history**.
   d) Check the **Define this policy setting** check box.

e) In the **passwords remembered** text box, double-click and type *24*

Enforce password history

☑ Define this policy setting

Keep password history for:

| 24 | ▲▼ | passwords remembered |

f) Select **OK**.

3. Set a minimum password length and complexity.
   a) In the right pane, double-click **Minimum password length**.
   b) Check the **Define this policy setting** check box.
   c) In the **characters** text box, double-click and type *7*

Minimum password length

☑ Define this policy setting

Password must be at least:

| 7 | ▲▼ | characters |

d) Select **OK**.
   e) Double-click **Password must meet complexity requirements**.
   f) Check the **Define this policy setting** check box and select the **Enabled** option.
   g) Select **OK**.

4. Change the account lockout duration.
   a) In the expanded console tree, select **Account Lockout Policy**.
   b) In the right pane, double-click **Account lockout duration**.
   c) Check the **Define this policy setting** check box.
   d) In the **minutes** text box, double-click and type *15*

Account lockout duration

☑ Define this policy setting

Account is locked out for:

| 15 | ▲▼ | minutes |

e) Select **Apply**.
   f) In the **Suggested Value Changes** dialog box, select **OK** to accept the suggested changes.
   g) Select **OK** to close the **Account lockout duration Properties** dialog box.
   h) Open a command prompt.

    i) Enter *gpupdate /force*

```
C:\Users\Administrator>gpupdate /force
Updating policy...

Computer Policy update has completed successfully.
User Policy update has completed successfully.
```

    j) When the policy is finished updating, close the command prompt.

5. Test the policy.
    a) In **Server Manager**, select **Tools→Active Directory Users and Computers**.
    b) In the **Active Directory Users and Computers** window, from the console tree, select **Users**.
    c) Select **Action→New→User**.
    d) In the **New Object - User** dialog box, provide the following information:
       • **First name:** *Chris*
       • **Initials:** *A*
       • **Last name:** *Wilkins*
       • **User logon name:** *ChrisW*

Create in:	domain100.internal/Users

First name:	Chris	Initials:	A
Last name:	Wilkins		
Full name:	Chris A. Wilkins		

User logon name:

ChrisW	@domain100.internal ∨

User logon name (pre-Windows 2000):

DOMAIN100\	ChrisW

    e) Select **Next**.
    f) In the **Password** and **Confirm password** text boxes, type *chris1*
    g) Select **Next**.
    h) Select **Finish**.
    i) Verify that the user password does not meet the policy requirements (at least seven characters and sufficiently complex), confirming that the policy is active. Select **OK**.
    j) Select **Back**.
    k) In the **Password** and **Confirm password** text boxes, type *!Pass1234*
    l) Select **Next**.
    m) Select **Finish**.
       The password meets the requirements and is accepted.
    n) Close all open windows except for **Server Manager**.

Summary

In this lesson, you identified how access control, authentication, and account management methods and services are used within organizations. Managing how users access resources is key to not only protecting unauthorized access to systems, but also to protecting the identity of users connecting to systems. Implementing the proper services and security controls can help ensure that the organization as a whole is protected from attacks.

What experience do you have with access control? What types of access control services are you familiar with?

What account management security controls have you come across in your current job role? Do you think they are sufficient in properly protecting employees' personal information?

Note: Check your LogicalCHOICE Course screen for opportunities to interact with your classmates, peers, and the larger LogicalCHOICE online community about the topics covered in this course or other topics you are interested in. From the Course screen you can also access available resources for a more continuous learning experience.

6 | Managing Certificates

Lesson Time: 3 hours

Lesson Objectives

In this lesson, you will manage digital certificates. You will:

- Install a CA hierarchy.

- Enroll certificates for entities.

- Secure network traffic using certificates.

- Renew certificates.

- Back up and restore certificates and private keys.

- Revoke certificates.

Lesson Introduction

In the previous lesson, you applied access control, authentication, and account management to protect the identity of users within a system. Once that is in place, you can begin installing certificate authorities to provide secure network communications between services and clients on your network. In this lesson, you will manage certificate-based security.

Certificates enable users, servers, clients, and applications to prove their identities and validate their communications across almost any network connection. As a security professional, you should be able to manage all the phases of the certificate process, from installation or enrollment to revocation, to ensure certificates are available and used properly.

TOPIC A

Install a CA Hierarchy

You can implement certificate-based security either by obtaining certificates from a public Certificate Authority (CA) or by establishing your own CA. If you plan to use your own CA servers to issue certificates on your network, then the first step in the process of setting up public key security is installing the CA servers. In this topic, you will install CA servers into a CA hierarchy.

You can trust a certificate only if you can trust the CA that issued it, and you can trust that CA only if you can trust the CA above it in the chain. The entire certificate security system will fail if the basic CA hierarchy is not properly established and authorized. If your job as a security professional requires you to implement a CA design by installing CAs, you can use the skills in this topic to make sure it is done properly.

Digital Certificates

A *digital certificate* is an electronic document that associates credentials with a public key. Both users and devices can hold certificates. The certificate validates the certificate holder's identity and is also a way to distribute the holder's public key. A server called a *Certificate Authority (CA)* issues certificates and the associated public/private key pairs.

User with Certificate   Device with Certificate

Figure 6-1: A device and a user with their own digital certificates.

Certificate Authentication

When a user authenticates using a certificate, the user presents a digital certificate in place of a user name and password. A user is authenticated if the certificate is validated by a CA.

Certificate authentication is therefore the process of identifying end users in a transaction that involves a series of steps to be carried out before the user's identity is confirmed. These can include initiating a secure transaction, such as a client requesting access to a secure site. The secure site presents its digital certificate to the client, enclosing its public key and verified digital signature. The client browser validates the signature against its cache of trusted and acknowledged certificates, comparing it to a library of CAs.

Once the digital signature is accepted, certificate authentication is successful. If the issuing CA does not match one in the library of CAs, then certificate authentication is unsuccessful and the user obtains a notification that the digital certificate supplied is invalid.

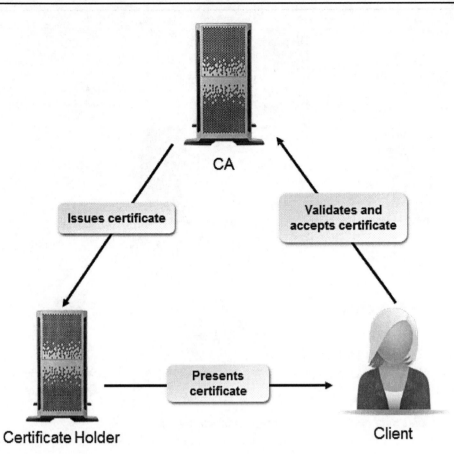

Figure 6–2: The process of certificate authentication.

PKI

A *Public Key Infrastructure (PKI)* is a system that is composed of a CA, certificates, software, services, and other cryptographic components, for the purpose of enabling authenticity and validation of data and entities. The PKI can be implemented in various hierarchical structures and can be publicly available or maintained privately by an organization. A PKI can be used to secure transactions over the Internet.

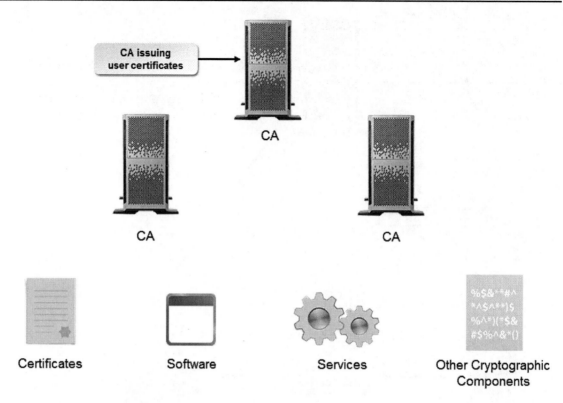

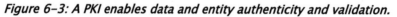

Figure 6–3: A PKI enables data and entity authenticity and validation.

PKI Components

A PKI contains several components:

- Digital certificates, to verify the identity of entities.
- One or more CAs, to issue digital certificates to computers, users, or applications.
- A *Registration Authority (RA)*, responsible for verifying users' identities and approving or denying requests for digital certificates.
- A *certificate repository database*, to store the digital certificates.
- A *certificate management system*, to provide software tools to perform the day-to-day functions of the PKI.
- A *certificate signing request (CSR)*, a message sent to a CA in which a resource applies for a certificate.

PKCS

Public Key Cryptography Standards (PKCS) is the most common CSR format, developed by a consortium of vendors to send information over the Internet in a secure manner using a PKI. Important PKCS standards include:

- *PKCS #7—Cryptographic Message Syntax Standard*: A PKCS that describes the general syntax used for cryptographic data, such as digital signatures.
- *PKCS #10—Certification Request Syntax Standard*: A PKCS that describes the syntax used to request certification of a public key and other information.

For more information on PKCS, visit **http://www.emc.com/emc-plus/rsa-labs/standards-initiatives/public-key-cryptography-standards.htm**.

CA Hierarchies (Trust Models)

A *CA hierarchy* or *trust model* is a single CA or group of CAs that work together to issue digital certificates. Each CA in the hierarchy has a parent-child relationship with the CA directly above it. A CA hierarchy provides a way for multiple CAs to distribute the certificate workload and provide certificate services more efficiently. If a CA is compromised, only those certificates issued by that particular CA and its children are invalid. The remaining CAs in the hierarchy will continue to function.

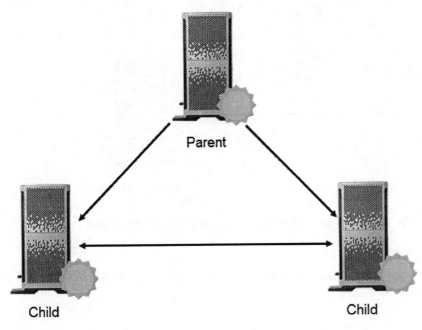

Figure 6-4: A parent-child trust model of CAs.

The Root CA

The *root CA* is the topmost CA in the hierarchy and, consequently, the most trusted authority. The root CA issues and self-signs the first certificate in the hierarchy. The root CA must be secured, because if it is compromised, all other certificates become invalid.

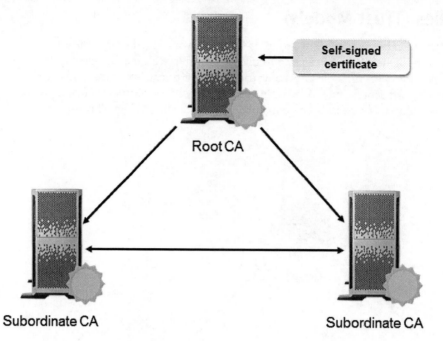

Figure 6–5: The root CA self-signs the certificates it sends down the hierarchy.

Microsoft® CA Terminology

If a Microsoft® CA is integrated with Active Directory®, it is called an enterprise CA; if not, it is considered a standalone CA.

Public and Private Roots

Root CAs can be designated as either public or private:

- A *private root CA* is created by a company for use primarily within the company itself. The root can be set up and configured in-house or contracted to a third-party vendor.
- A *public root CA* is created by a third-party or commercial vendor for general access by the public.

Private Root CA

Public Root CA

Figure 6–6: Public and private root CAs.

Commercial CAs

VeriSign® is a well-known provider of public certificate services, along with Comodo™, GlobalSign®, and Entrust®.

Subordinate CAs

Subordinate CAs are any CAs below the root in the hierarchy. Subordinate CAs issue certificates and provide day-to-day management of the certificates, including renewal, suspension, and revocation.

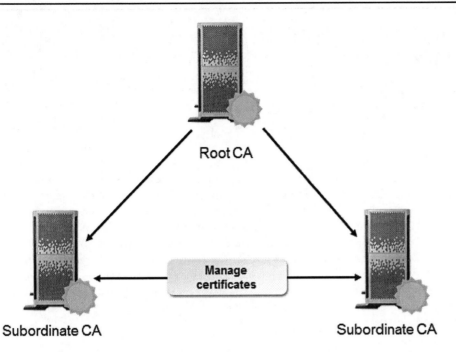

Figure 6-7: The subordinate CAs issue and manage certificates.

Offline Root CAs

To provide the most secure environment possible for the root CA, companies will often set up the root CA and then take it offline, allowing the subordinate CAs to issue all certificates. The root CA remains offline and is not patched again once it is taken offline. All updates are installed physically on all subordinate CAs. This strategy ensures that the root CA is not accessible by anyone on the network and thus, it is much less likely to be compromised.

CA Hierarchy Design Options

The design of your CA hierarchy will depend on your organization's business and security requirements. The following table describes how CA hierarchies are implemented in different company profiles.

Company Profile	CA Hierarchy Implementation
Thousands of employees worldwide	The subordinate CAs are designated by geographic location to balance the number of issued certificates among the individual CAs.
Individuals need to access specific applications only	The subordinate CAs are designated by function or department so the individual CAs serve groups of people with specific resource needs.
Tight security allows individuals to have differing levels of access to the same resources	The subordinate CAs are designated by the security required to obtain a certificate. Some CAs may be set up to issue a certificate with a network ID and password; other CAs may require a person to present a valid driver's license.

 Access the Checklist tile on your **LogicalCHOICE** course screen for reference information and job aids on How to Install a CA Hierarchy.

ACTIVITY 6-1
Installing a CA

Scenario

As the security administrator for a state university, one of your job functions is to make sure the CA hierarchy designed by the IT department is implemented correctly. To prevent users from receiving unapproved certificates and accessing information that they are not supposed to, and also to prevent attackers from getting data, the university has decided to implement a new secure CA using Windows Server 2012 R2 CAs. The IT design team has created and documented a CA implementation plan that calls for installing a root CA for the entire university. Along with installing the CA, you will install the Web Enrollment feature so that you may perform various tasks on the CA using a web browser. The Windows Server 2012 R2 systems on which you will install Certificate Services have already been hardened to minimize the likelihood of attacks against the operating system itself from external users.

---

1. Verify that the Windows Remote Management service is running.
   a) In **Server Manager**, select **Tools→Services**.
   b) In the **Services** window, scroll down and double-click **Windows Remote Management (WS-Management)**.
   c) In the dialog box, verify that the **Service status** is **Running**. If the service is stopped, from the **Startup type** drop-down list, select **Automatic**. Select **Start**.
   d) Select **OK** to close the dialog box, and then close the **Services** window.

   > **Note:** The Certificate Services role requires this service to be running in order to install.

2. Install Active Directory Certificate Services on the server.
   a) In **Server Manager**, in the **Configure this local server** section, select **Add roles and features**.
   b) In the **Add Roles and Features Wizard**, on the **Before you begin** page, select **Next**.
   c) On the **Select installation type** page, verify that the **Role-based or feature-based installation** radio button is selected and select **Next**.
   d) On the **Select destination server** page, verify that your server is selected and select **Next**.
   e) On the **Select server roles** page, in the **Roles** section, check the **Active Directory Certificate Services** check box.
   f) In the **Add Roles and Features Wizard** dialog box that pops up, select **Add Features**.
   g) Select **Next**, then on the **Select features** page, select **Next** again.
   h) On the **Active Directory Certificate Services** page, select **Next**.
   i) On the **Select role services** page, check the **Certification Authority Web Enrollment** check box.
   j) In the **Add Roles and Features Wizard** dialog box that pops up, select **Add Features**.
   k) Select **Next**, then on the **Confirm installation selections** page, check the **Restart the destination server automatically if required** check box and select **Yes**.

l) Select **Install**. When installation completes, select the **Configure Active Directory Certificate Services on the destination server** link.

3. Configure Active Directory Certificate Services.
   a) In the **AD CS Configuration** wizard, on the **Credentials** page, select **Next**.
   b) On the **Role Services** page, check the **Certification Authority** and **Certification Authority Web Enrollment** check boxes, then select **Next**.
   c) On the **Setup Type** page, select the **Standalone CA** option. Select **Next**.

> Enterprise certification authorities (CAs) can use Active Directory Domain Services (AD DS) to simplify the management of certificates. Standalone CAs do not use AD DS to issue or manage certificates.
>
> ○ Enterprise CA
>
> Enterprise CAs must be domain members and are typically online to issue certificates or certificate policies.
>
> ◉ Standalone CA
>
> Standalone CAs can be members or a workgroup or domain. Standalone CAs do not require AD DS and can be used without a network connection (offline).

   d) On the **CA Type** page, with the **Root CA** option selected, select **Next**.
   e) On the **Private Key** page, with the **Create a new private key** option selected, select **Next**.
   f) On the **Cryptography for CA** page, select **Next** to accept the default values.
   g) On the **CA Name** page, in the **Common name for this CA** text box, double-click and type *UniversityCA##* as the common name for the CA. Select **Next**.
   h) On the **Validity Period** page, select **Next** to accept the default validity period for the certificate.
   i) On the **CA Database** page, select **Next** to accept the default storage location for the CA database and log.
   j) On the **Confirmation** page, select **Configure**.
   k) After configuration completes, on the **Results** page, select **Close**.
   l) Close the **Add Roles and Features Wizard**.

4. Verify that Active Directory Certificate Services was configured properly.
   a) In **Server Manager**, select **Tools→Certification Authority**.
   b) In the **certsrv - [Certification Authority (Local)]** window, in the left pane, select your CA object (**UniversityCA##**) and select **Action→Properties**.

c) In the **UniversityCA## Properties** dialog box, in the **Certification authority (CA)** section, verify that the **Name** appears as you configured it during installation. Select **View Certificate**.

d) Verify that the certificate will expire in five years. Select **OK** to close the **Certificate** dialog box.

e) Select **OK** to close the **UniversityCA## Properties** dialog box, and leave the **certsrv** window open.

ACTIVITY 6-2
Securing a Windows Server 2012 R2 CA

Scenario

In the past, the university has had problems with unauthorized users being granted certificates. One of the next tasks as the university's security administrator is to make sure the CA server is secured so that only faculty members (along with server administrators) have Read and Enroll permissions to both the User Certificate and Web Server Certificate Templates. You have installed new Windows Server 2012 R2 CAs in your domain so that you have the ability to configure the CA server to restrict authenticated user access to certificate templates. You will start by creating the Faculty group. Then, using Public Key Services, you will restrict the aforementioned certificate templates so that members of this group are the only non-administrators that may read or enroll these templates. Restricting access to certificate templates will help prevent certificates from being issued to unauthorized users.

 Note: In the classroom, your CA is actually installed as a standalone CA. You will still be able to perform the required permissions configurations in Active Directory.

1. Create an Active Directory group containing all the faculty user accounts.
   a) In **Server Manager**, select **Tools→Active Directory Users and Computers**.
   b) In the **Active Directory Users and Computers** window, if necessary, expand your **domain##.internal** object and select the **Users** folder.
   c) Select **Action→New→Group**.
   d) In the **New Object - Group** dialog box, in the **Group name** text box, type *Faculty*
   e) In the **Group scope** section, select the **Domain local** option.
   f) Verify that in the **Group type** section, the **Security** option is selected.
   g) In the **New Object - Group** dialog box, select **OK**.

2. Create a new **Faculty User** account and add it to the **Faculty** group.
   a) Select **Action→New→User**.
   b) In the **New Object - User** dialog box, in the **First name** text box, type *Faculty* and press **Tab** twice.
   c) In the **Last name** text box, type *User*
   d) Verify that **Faculty User** is displayed as the full user name.

e) Press **Tab** twice, and in the **User logon name** text box, type *facultyuser*

New Object - User

Create in: domain100.internal/Users

First name:	Faculty	Initials:	

Last name: User

Full name: Faculty User

User logon name:

facultyuser	@domain100.internal ▾

User logon name (pre-Windows 2000):

DOMAIN100\	facultyuser

[< Back] [Next >] [Cancel]

---

f) Select **Next**.

g) In the **Password** text box, type *!Pass1234* as the password, and press **Tab**.

h) In the **Confirm password** text box, type *!Pass1234* to confirm the password.

i) Uncheck the **User must change password at next logon** check box.

j) Check the **User cannot change password** check box and select **Next**.

k) Select **Finish**.

l) In the right pane, select the **Faculty User** account.

🖳 Enterprise R...	Security Group...	Members of this group ...
🖳 Faculty	Security Group...	
👤 Faculty User	User	
🖳 Group Polic...	Security Group...	Members in this group c...

m) Select **Action→Add to a group**.

n) In the **Select Groups** dialog box, in the **Enter the object names to select** text box, type *Faculty* and select **Check Names**, and then select **OK**.

o) In the **Active Directory Domain Services** message box, select **OK**.

p) Close the **Active Directory Users and Computers** window.

3. Use Active Directory to grant the **Faculty** group **Read** and **Enroll** permissions to the **User** template.

a) In **Server Manager**, select **Tools→Active Directory Sites and Services**.

b) Select **View→Show Services Node**.

Add/Remove Columns...	
Large Icons	
Small Icons	
List	
● Detail	
Show Services Node	
Customize...	

c) Expand **Services** and **Public Key Services**, and select **Certificate Templates**.

- Active Directory Sites and Servic
  - ▷ Sites
  - ▲ Services
    - ▷ AuthN Policy Configurat
    - ▷ Claims Configuration
    - ▷ Group Key Distribution S
    - ▷ Microsoft SPP
    - ▷ MsmqServices
    - ▷ NetServices
    - ▲ Public Key Services
      - ▷ AIA
      - ▷ CDP
      - Certificate Templates
      - ▷ Certification Authorit
      - ▷ Enrollment Services
      - ▷ KRA

d) In the templates list, scroll down and double-click **User**.
e) In the **User Properties** dialog box, select the **Security** tab.

f) With **Authenticated Users** selected, verify that the **Allow** box for **Read** is checked.

```
┌────────────────────────────────────────────────────────────┐
│              User Properties              [ ? ]  [ X ]       │
├────────────────────────────────────────────────────────────┤
│  General   │ Request Handling │ Subject Name │ Extensions   │
│     Security      │      Object      │    Attribute Editor   │
│                                                              │
│  Group or user names:                                        │
│  ┌────────────────────────────────────────────────────┐    │
│  │ ▓▓ Authenticated Users                              │    │
│  │ 🔱 Domain Admins (DOMAIN100\Domain Admins)          │    │
│  │ 🔱 Domain Users (DOMAIN100\Domain Users)            │    │
│  │ 🔱 Enterprise Admins (DOMAIN100\Enterprise Admins)  │    │
│  │                                                      │    │
│  └────────────────────────────────────────────────────┘    │
│                                  [  Add...  ] [  Remove  ]   │
│                                                              │
│  Permissions for Authenticated Users   Allow      Deny       │
│  ┌────────────────────────────────────────────────────┐    │
│  │  Full Control                         ☐          ☐  │    │
│  │  Read                                 ☑          ☐  │    │
│  │  Write                                ☐          ☐  │    │
│  │  Enroll                               ☐          ☐  │    │
│  │                                                      │    │
│  └────────────────────────────────────────────────────┘    │
│  For special permissions or advanced settings, click        │
│  Advanced.                             [    Advanced    ]    │
│                                                              │
│    [  OK  ]   [  Cancel  ]   [  Apply  ]   [  Help  ]        │
└────────────────────────────────────────────────────────────┘
```

> **Note:** It may take a few moments for the **Group or user names** list to finish loading.

g) Select **Add**.

h) In the **Select Users, Computers, Service Accounts, or Groups** dialog box, in the **Enter the object names to select** text box, type *Faculty* and select **Check Names**.

i) In the **Multiple Names Found** dialog box, verify that the **Faculty** group is selected and select **OK** twice.

j) In the **User Properties** dialog box, with the **Faculty** group selected, verify that the **Allow** box for **Read** is checked. Check the **Allow** box for **Enroll** and select **OK**.

4. Use Active Directory Public Key Services to configure the appropriate faculty permission on the **WebServer** template.

   a) In the templates list, double-click **WebServer**.

   b) In the **WebServer Properties** dialog box, select the **Security** tab.

   c) With **Authenticated Users** selected, verify that the **Allow** box for **Read** is checked.

   d) Select **Add**.

   e) In the **Select Users, Computers, Service Accounts, or Groups** dialog box, in the **Enter the object names to select** text box, type *Faculty* and select **OK**.

f) In the **Multiple Names Found** dialog box, verify that the **Faculty** group is selected and select **OK**.

g) In the **WebServer Properties** dialog box, with the **Faculty** group selected, verify that the **Allow** box for **Read** is checked. Check the **Allow** box for **Enroll** and select **OK**.

h) Close the **Active Directory Sites and Services** window.

TOPIC B

Enroll Certificates

Using certificates is a process that has several stages. The first stage is enrolling and installing certificates for the entities (such as users, devices, and services) that need them. In this topic, you will enroll certificates for various entities that require them.

A CA by itself does not do you any good. You have to get the certificates enrolled properly for the appropriate entities in order to implement certificate-based security. If a user, server, or client machine does not have the right certificate, there is nothing you can do to secure communications to or from that entity. The skills you will learn in this topic will help you request and install the proper certificates for each security situation.

The Certificate Enrollment Process

Users and other entities obtain certificates from the CA through the certificate enrollment process.

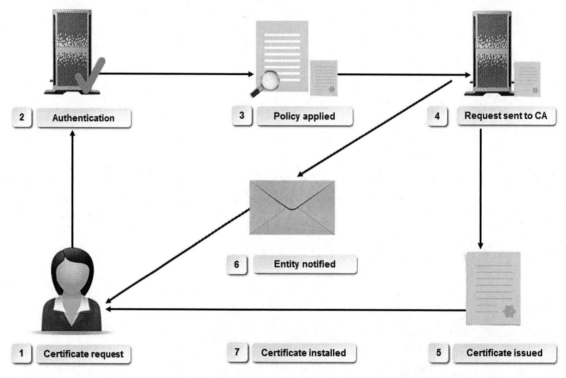

Figure 6–8: The certificate enrollment process.

The following table describes each enrollment step.

Enrollment Step	Explanation
1. Entity requests certificate	An entity follows the procedure (for example, filling out an online form) to obtain a certificate.
2. RA authenticates entity	Authentication is determined by the certificate policy requirements (for example, a network user ID and password, driver's license, or other unique identifier).
3. Policy applied to request	The RA applies the certificate policy that pertains to the particular CA that will issue the certificate.

Enrollment Step	Explanation
4. Request sent to CA	If the identity of the entity is authenticated successfully and the policy requirements are met, the RA sends the certificate request on to the CA.
5. CA issues certificate	The CA creates the certificate and puts it in the repository.
6. Entity notified	The CA notifies the entity that the certificate is available, and the certificate is delivered.
7. Certificate installed	Once the certificate is obtained, it can be installed using the appropriate tool.

The Certificate Life Cycle

There are several main phases in the certificate life cycle.

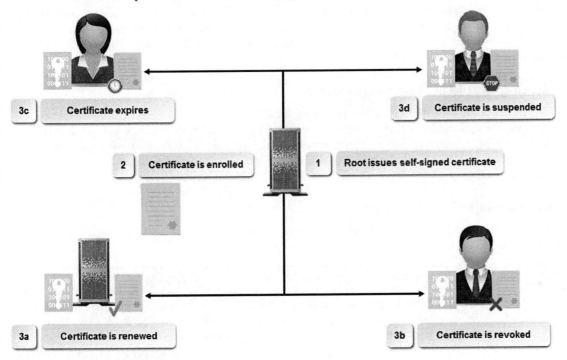

Figure 6-9: The certificate life cycle.

The following table describes each life cycle phase.

Certificate Life Cycle Phase	Description
1. Issuance	The life cycle begins when the root CA has issued its self-signed key pair. The root CA then begins issuing certificates to other CAs and end users.
2. Enrollment	Users and other entities obtain certificates from the CA through certificate enrollment.
3a. Renewal	Certificates can be renewed more than once depending on the certificate policy parameters.
3b. Revocation	Certificates can be revoked before their expiration date, which renders them permanently invalid. Certificates can be revoked for a variety of reasons, including misuse, loss, or compromise.

Certificate Life Cycle Phase	Description
3c. Expiration	Certificates expire after a given length of time, which is established in the certificate policy and configured in the issuing CA. The expiration parameter is part of the certificate data. If the root CA's certificate expires, the entire CA becomes inactive.
3d. Suspension	Some CAs support temporary suspension of certificates, in addition to permanent revocation.

Certificate Life Cycle Management

As a general rule, the longer the life cycle is, the less administrative overhead is involved. This could pose a higher security risk, however, because a longer life cycle also gives attackers more time to break the cryptography of the key pair or otherwise compromise the system. Also, with a shortened lifetime, new developments in cryptography could allow you to have entities renew certificates that are more secure. The actual life cycle of your certificates will be based on your business requirements and security needs.

Balancing Certificate Life Cycle Needs

Although it would seem that a long key pair combined with a very complex algorithm would provide the longest life cycle and less administrative overhead, this combination can increase the time it takes to encrypt and decrypt data on the network. A long life cycle also allows attackers more time to break the code. You must balance the needs for security and accessibility when you design your certificate hierarchy.

Certificate Life Cycle Factors

The following table shows the most common factors that affect a certificate's life cycle, although this is not an exhaustive list.

Factor	Variables	Implications
Length of the private key	What length key is appropriate? 56 bit, 128 bit, 256 bit, 1024 bit, or 2048 bit?	The longer the key, the more data bits there are to work with. Long keys require more resources (more central processing unit [CPU] cycles or memory, more computers, more time, and so on) to break. Attackers may not think it is worth the effort.
Strength of the cryptography used	How complex will the algorithm be? Will it be created by a programmer or developed by algorithm software?	The more complex the mathematical functions are that are used in the algorithm, the harder it is for an attacker to decrypt. But it means that the time taken to generate the keys will also be higher.
Physical security of the CA and private key	Where is the CA kept? Is it in a locked area or just protected by a password? Who has access to it?	Higher physical security is essential for longer life cycles. All the policies in the world will not protect a private key if it is not physically secure. Keep in mind that physical security may be expensive.

Factor	Variables	Implications
Security of issued certificates and their private keys	Where is the private key stored? On a smart card? On the desktop? Is a password required?	The more secure the user's private keys are, the better they are for the security of the overall system. Conversely, users can forget passwords or lose smart cards, and that means more work for administrators.
Risk of attack	Is your CA offline or online? Is your root CA within your company or handled by a third-party company? What type of business are you in? Does your company have an intranet?	Your CA may be secure, but an attacker can use another access point that is not as secure on your network to gain access to the CA.
User trust	Who is using the issued certificates? External or internal users?	You can generally trust internal users (employees on the corporate network) more than external users (individuals accessing through the Internet).
Administrative involvement	Long life cycles require less administrative work. Short life cycles require more administrative work.	Although a long life cycle requires less administrative work (renewals, revocations, and so on), it also gives attackers more time to gain access. This makes it important for administrators to keep track of certificate issues.

 Access the Checklist tile on your LogicalCHOICE course screen for reference information and job aids on How to Enroll Certificates.

ACTIVITY 6-3
Enrolling Certificates

Scenario

Now that your CA server is functional, one of the next tasks as the university's security administrator is to enroll certificates for entities that require them. The university, located in the fictional city and state of Greene City, Richland, maintains a web-based student registration system. Internet Information Services (IIS) has already been hardened on your CAs and all university web servers. One of the first implementations of using certificates will be to make sure the data being transferred is secure on the student registration web servers. Before you can enable the secure web communications, you will need to enroll a certificate for the web server.

 Note: The focus of this activity is on enrolling a certificate for a website, not using the certificate to enable secure web communications.

1. Create a file-based request for a new web server certificate from your CA.

   a) In **Server Manager**, select **Tools→Internet Information Services (IIS) Manager**.

   b) Maximize the **Internet Information Services (IIS) Manager** window.

   c) In the left pane, select your web server object.

   d) In the **SERVER## Home** pane, in the **IIS** section, double-click **Server Certificates**.

   e) In the **Actions** pane, select the **Create Certificate Request** link.

   f) In the **Request Certificate** wizard, on the **Distinguished Name Properties** page, in the **Common name** text box, type *Server##*

   g) In the **Organization** text box, type *Registrar* and press **Tab**. In the **Organizational unit** text box, type *University* and press **Tab**.

   h) In the **City/locality** text box, type *Greene City* and press **Tab**. In the **State/province** text box, type *Richland*

   Specify the required information for the certificate. State/province and City/locality must be specified as official names and they cannot contain abbreviations.

Common name:	Server100
Organization:	Registrar
Organizational unit:	University
City/locality:	Greene City
State/province:	Richland
Country/region:	US

   i) Select **Next** to move to the next page of the wizard.

   j) On the **Cryptographic Service Provider Properties** page, select **Next** to accept the default **Cryptographic service provider** and **Bit length** settings.

k) For the file name, type *C:\Certreq.txt* and select **Finish** to generate and save the request file.

Specify a file name for the certificate request:

C:\Certreq.txt [...]

---

2. Submit the request to your CA server.

   a) Open File Explorer and double-click the **C:** drive.
   b) Double-click the **Certreq** file.
      The file opens in Notepad.
   c) Select **Edit→Select All** and then select **Edit→Copy**.
   d) Close the **Notepad** and **Local Disk (C:)** windows.
   e) From the taskbar, select **Internet Explorer**.
   f) In the **Address** bar, enter *http://server##/certsrv*, where *##* is your student number.
   g) In the **Internet Explorer** message box, select **Add** to add the certificate server to the **Trusted sites** zone.
   h) In the **Trusted sites** dialog box, select **Add** to add the certificate server to the **Trusted sites** zone. Select **Close**.
   i) On the **Welcome** web page, in the **Select a task** section, select the **Request a certificate** link.
   j) On the **Request a Certificate** web page, select the **advanced certificate request** link.
   k) On the **Advanced Certificate Request** web page, select the **Submit a certificate request by using a base-64-encoded CMC or PKCS #10 file, or submit a renewal request by using a base-64-encoded PKCS #7 file** link.
   l) On the **Submit a Certificate Request or Renewal Request** web page, right-click in the **Saved Request** text box and select **Paste**.

Saved Request:

Base-64-encoded certificate request (CMC or PKCS #10 or PKCS #7):

```
GmonhLTyVWcAnpvylfkwDQYJKoZIhvcNAQEFBQAD
feb0+zdIPHKM6NxOivhcDYEwl6nd3Ci+vns/nhcQ
MuiVWrM8EKrCSBfbJCBsrxICEMmmM9k4R7QBL/Ov
XOvgH1SxT3V36A0rtTdf8D0=
-----END NEW CERTIFICATE REQUEST-----
```

Additional Attributes:

Attributes:

[   ]

[Submit >]

---

   m) Select the **Submit** button.
   n) On the **Certificate Pending** web page, in the upper-right corner, select the **Home** link.

o) Minimize Internet Explorer.

3. Issue the requested server certificate.

a) From the taskbar, switch to the **certsrv** window.

b) In the **certsrv** window, in the console tree, expand your certificate server and select the **Pending Requests** folder.

c) In the right pane, scroll to the right and verify that the certificate listed has a **Request Common Name** of **Server##**.

d) Select the certificate, then select **Action→All Tasks→Issue**.

e) Select the **Issued Certificates** folder.

f) Verify that the newly issued certificate appears in the details pane, and minimize the **certsrv** window.

4. Download the newly issued certificate as a file.

a) From the taskbar, select the **Internet Explorer** icon to maximize it.

b) Select the **View the status of a pending certificate request** link.

c) Select the **Saved-Request Certificate** link.

d) On the **Certificate Issued** web page, select the **Download certificate** link.

e) In the file download message box at the bottom, select the **Save** drop-down arrow, then select **Save as**.

f) In the **Save As** dialog box, in the **File name** text box, type *C:\Webcert.cer* and then select **Save**.

5. Install and verify the certificate.

a) In the file download message box at the bottom, select **Open**.

b) In the **Certificate** dialog box, select **Install Certificate**.

```
┌──────────────────────────────────────────────────────────┐
│ ▣            Certificate                         [ X ]    │
├──────────────────────────────────────────────────────────┤
│ ┌────────┬──────────────────────────────┐                │
│ │General │ Details │ Certification Path  │                │
│ ├────────┴──────────────────────────────────────────────┐│
│ │                                                        ││
│ │  ▣   Certificate Information                            ││
│ │ ────────────────────────────────────────────────────  ││
│ │  This certificate is intended for the following        ││
│ │  purpose(s):                                            ││
│ │     • Ensures the identity of a remote computer         ││
│ │                                                        ││
│ │ ────────────────────────────────────────────────────  ││
│ │    Issued to:  Server100                                ││
│ │                                                        ││
│ │    Issued by:  UniversityCA100                          ││
│ │                                                        ││
│ │    Valid from  2/5/2014  to  2/5/2015                   ││
│ │                                                        ││
│ │            [Install Certificate...]  [Issuer Statement]││
│ └────────────────────────────────────────────────────────┘│
│                                          [    OK    ]     │
└──────────────────────────────────────────────────────────┘
```

c) In the **Certificate Import Wizard**, on the **Welcome to the Certificate Import Wizard** page, select **Next**.

d) On the **Certificate Store** page, select **Next** to allow Windows to automatically select the store location based on the file certificate type.

 Note: Computer certificates include a fully qualified domain name (FQDN) to identify a domain that is wholly unique with respect to all other domains on the Internet. For classroom testing purposes, your domain does not need to be this unique, so the certificate is placed in the **User** store.

e) On the **Completing the Certificate Import Wizard** page, select **Finish** to complete the wizard steps.

f) In the **Certificate Import Wizard** message box, select **OK**.

 Note: You may need to wait a few moments for the certificate to install before the message box appears.

g) In the **Certificate** dialog box, select **OK** to close it.

h) Close Internet Explorer.

i) In the **Internet Information Services (IIS) Manager** window, select your server object, and in the **IIS** section, double-click **Server Certificates**.

j) In the **Actions** pane, select the **Complete Certificate Request** link.

k) In the **Complete Certificate Request** dialog box, in the **File name containing the certification authority's response** text box, type *C:\Webcert.cer*

l) In the **Friendly name** text box, type *WebCert* and select **OK**.

File name containing the certification authority's response:

C:\Webcert.cer

...

Friendly name:

WebCert

m) Verify that the certificate is displayed in the list of server certificates.

 Server Certificates

Use this feature to request and manage certificates that the Web server can use with websites configured for SSL.

Filter:	Go ▾ Show All	Group by: No Grouping ▾	
Name ▲	Issued To	Issued By	Expiration Date
	UniversityCA100	UniversityCA100	2/4/2019 10:39:00 ...
WebCert	Server100	UniversityCA100	2/5/2015 10:22:21 ...

n) Close all open windows except **Server Manager**.

TOPIC C

Secure Network Traffic by Using Certificates

Once an entity has a certificate enrolled, you can use the certificate to secure network traffic flowing to and from that entity. Setting up the security is the next step in the process, so, in this topic, you will use certificates to secure network communications.

The end result of all your PKI planning, installation, and configuration is a mechanism for securing network communications. As you know by now, unsecured network communication is open to a variety of attacks, including eavesdropping. Attackers can use simple tools to steal data as it travels across the network and, most importantly, capture user names and passwords to get into your most sensitive systems. If you secure data using certificates, you will have another method for keeping attackers out of the critical components in your network.

The SSL Enrollment Process

You can use certificates to implement Secure Sockets Layer (SSL). The process has several steps, as explained in the following table.

SSL Enrollment Step	Explanation
1. Request	The client requests a session with the server.
2. Response	The server responds by sending its digital certificate and public key to the client.
3. Negotiation	The server and client then negotiate an encryption level.
4. Encryption	Once they agree on an encryption level, the client generates a session key, encrypts it, and sends it with the public key from the server.
5. Communication	The session key then becomes the key used in the conversation.

> Access the Checklist tile on your LogicalCHOICE course screen for reference information and job aids on How to Secure Network Traffic by Using Certificates.

ACTIVITY 6-4
Securing Network Traffic with Certificates

Before You Begin

A certificate has been installed on the web server. There is a home page for a student registration website on the server at the URL **http://server##**.

Scenario

Now that you have obtained and installed the required certificate, your next task as the university's security administrator is to enable secure communications on the student registration website, which the university's webmaster has created on the web server. You need to ensure that the enrollment data being transferred to and from the registration website is secured. To achieve this, you'll bind the WebCert certificate to the enrollment site and require SSL for any connections.

1. Verify that you can connect to the student registration website.

    a) Open Internet Explorer.

    b) In the **Address** bar, type *http://server##*, where *##* is your student number, and press **Enter**.

    c) In the **Windows Security** dialog box, in the **User name** text box, type *Administrator* and press **Tab**. Type *!Pass1234* as the password and select **OK**.

    d) Verify that you can see the home page of the online enrollment system, and then close Internet Explorer.

2. Bind the WebCert certificate to the **Default Web Site** object.

    a) Open Internet Information Services (IIS) Manager, and with your server object expanded, expand **Sites**, and then select the **Default Web Site** object.

    b) In the **Actions** pane, select **Bindings**.

    c) In the **Site Bindings** dialog box, click **Add**.

    d) In the **Add Site Binding** dialog box, from the **Type** drop-down list, select the **https** option.

    e) From the **SSL certificate** drop-down list, select the **WebCert** certificate.

f) Select **OK**.

Type	Host Name	Port	IP Address	Binding Informa...
http		80	*	
https		443	*	

Site Bindings — Add... | Edit... | Remove | Browse | Close

g) In the **Site Bindings** dialog box, select **Close**.

3. Enable the appropriate secure communications method and encryption level for the student registration website.

a) On the **Default Web Site Home** page, in the **IIS** section, double-click the **SSL Settings** option.

SSL Settings

b) On the **SSL Settings** page, check the **Require SSL** check box.
c) In the **Actions** pane, select **Apply**.
d) Verify that a message appears indicating that the change was successful.

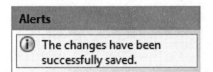

Alerts
ⓘ The changes have been successfully saved.

e) Minimize the **Internet Information Services (IIS) Manager** window.

4. Test insecure communication with the student enrollment website.

a) Open Internet Explorer.
b) In the **Address** bar, enter *http://server##*

c) Verify that you receive **HTTP Error 403.4 – Forbidden**.

HTTP Error 403.4 – Forbidden

The page you are trying to access is secured with Secure Sockets Layer (SSL).

Most likely causes:
- Secure Sockets Layer (SSL) is enabled for the URL requested.
- The page request was made over HTTP, but the server requires the request from a secure channel that uses HTTPS.

Things you can try:
- Browse to the URL over a secure channel by using the "https:" prefix instead of "http:".
- If the Web site does not have an SSL certificate or should not require HTTPS, disable the setting.
- Verify the SSL Settings in IIS Manager by connecting to the server, site, application or page and opening the SSL Settings feature.
- Verify the configuration/system.webserver/security/access@sslFlags attribute at the server, site, application, or page level.

---

5. **Why did the connection fail?**
   - ○ Because the server now requires secure communications.
   - ○ Because you typed an invalid URL.
   - ○ Because you did not log on.
   - ○ Because the certificate has expired.

6. **How can you connect successfully?**
   - ○ By using the SFTP protocol.
   - ○ By using the HTTPS protocol.
   - ○ By using a certificate to authenticate the user.
   - ○ By logging on as a different user.

7. Test secure communication with the student enrollment website.
   a) In the **Address** bar, enter *https://server##*
   b) In the **Security Alert** message box, select **OK** to acknowledge that you are making a secure connection.
   c) Log on as **Administrator** with a password of *!Pass1234* and select **OK**.
   d) Verify that you are able to connect to the enrollment site.

   e) Next to the **Address** bar, select the **Security report** icon. 🔒
      The message "Website Identification" appears.
   f) Select the **View certificates** link.
   g) Verify that the name on the certificate matches the name of the site, indicating that this is the web server certificate you issued for this server.
   h) Select **OK** to close the certificate.
   i) Close Internet Explorer.

TOPIC D

Renew Certificates

After you initially configure certificate-based security, the remainder of your certificate management tasks have to do with maintaining the certificates over the rest of their life cycle. Because certificates are temporary and can expire, your first concern will be renewing existing certificates at the appropriate intervals. In this topic, you will renew certificates.

Certificate Renewal

Just like a driver's license, certificates are designed to expire at regular intervals. If a driver's license was good indefinitely, society would have no way to verify over time that the driver was still qualified to drive. And if certificates did not expire, an entity on the network could use one indefinitely even if its job role or function had changed. So that drivers can keep their licenses past the expiration period, most motor vehicle departments have a renewal process in place that does not interrupt a driver's right to be on the road. It is the same way with certificates. You should renew certificates appropriately so that you do not have any interruptions in your security services.

> Access the Checklist tile on your LogicalCHOICE course screen for reference information and job aids on How to Renew Certificates.

ACTIVITY 6-5
Renewing a CA Certificate

Scenario

Your root CA certificate is nearing its expiration. To maintain the integrity of your CA hierarchy, you need to renew the certificate.

1. Renew the root CA certificate at the root CA server.
   a) Open Certification Authority, select your CA object, and select **Action→All Tasks→Renew CA Certificate**.
   b) In the **Install CA Certificate** dialog box, select **Yes** to stop **Active Directory Certificate Services**.

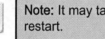

Install CA Certificate	x
Active Directory Certificate Services cannot be running during this operation. Do you want to stop Active Directory Certificate Services now?	
	Yes No

   c) In the **Renew CA Certificate** dialog box, verify that **Yes** is selected and select **OK** to renew the certificate and generate a new key pair.

   > **Note:** It may take a few moments for Active Directory Certificate Services to restart.

2. Verify the certificate renewal.
   a) With your CA object selected, select **Action→Properties**.

b) With **Certificate #1** selected, select **View Certificate**.

```
┌─ Certification authority (CA) ─────────────────────────────┐
│                                                            │
│   Name:          UniversityCA100                           │
│                                                            │
│   CA certificates:                                         │
│   ┌──────────────────────────────────────────────────┐    │
│   │ Certificate #0                                     │    │
│   │ Certificate #1                                     │    │
│   │                                                    │    │
│   │                                                    │    │
│   │                                                    │    │
│   │                                                    │    │
│   │                                                    │    │
│   │                                                    │    │
│   └──────────────────────────────────────────────────┘    │
│                              ┌───────────────────────┐     │
│                              │   View Certificate     │     │
│                              └───────────────────────┘     │
└────────────────────────────────────────────────────────────┘
```

c) Verify that the renewed certificate will expire five years from the current date. In the **Certificate** dialog box, select **OK** to close the certificate.

d) In the **UniversityCA## Properties** dialog box, select **OK** to close it.

ACTIVITY 6-6
Renewing a Web Server Certificate

Scenario
Your web server's certificate is about to expire. You must renew it immediately so that it can continue to support secure communications over SSL.

1. Renew the web server's certificate.
   a) From the taskbar, select **Internet Information Services (IIS) Manager**. In the **Internet Information Services (IIS) Manager** window, select your server object.
   b) On the **SERVER## Home** page, in the **IIS** section, double-click **Server Certificates**.
   c) On the **Server Certificates** page, select the **WebCert** certificate.
   d) In the **Actions** pane, select **Renew**.
   e) In the **Renew an Existing Certificate** wizard, select the **Create a renewal certificate request** option and select **Next**.
   f) On the **Specify save as file name** page, in the **Specify a file name for the certificate renewal request** text box, type *C:\Certrenewal.txt* to name the certificate renewal request file and its location. Select **Finish**.

   > Specify the file name for the certificate request. This information can be sent to a certification authority for signing.
   >
   > Specify a file name for the certificate renewal request:
   >
   > | C:\Certrenewal.txt | ... |

2. Submit the request to your CA server.
   a) Open File Explorer and double-click the **C:** drive.
   b) Double-click the **Certrenewal** file.
      The file opens in Notepad.
   c) Select **Edit→Select All** and then select **Edit→Copy**.
   d) Close the **Notepad** and **Local Disk (C:)** windows.
   e) Open Internet Explorer.
   f) In the **Address** bar, enter *https://server##/certsrv*, where *##* is your student number.
   g) In the **Security Alert** dialog box, select **OK**.
   h) If necessary, add the site to the trusted sites zone.
   i) Select the **Request a certificate** link.
   j) Select the **advanced certificate request** link.
   k) Select the **Submit a certificate request by using a base-64-encoded CMC or PKCS #10 file, or submit a renewal request by using a base-64-encoded PKCS #7 file** link.
   l) Right-click the **Saved Request** text box and select **Paste**.
   m) Select **Submit**.
   n) On the **Certificate Pending** web page, select the **Home** link.

3. Issue the requested renewal of the web server certificate.
   a) From the taskbar, open the **certsrv** window, and in the right pane, double-click the **Pending Requests** folder.

    b) Scroll to the right and select the pending request with a **Request Common Name** of **Server##** and select **Action→All Tasks→Issue**.

    c) Select the **Issued Certificates** folder.

    d) Verify that the renewed certificate appears in the details pane, at the bottom of the list. The **Request ID**, **Certificate Effective Date**, and **Issued Common Name** should align with the certificate you just issued.

    e) Minimize the **certsrv** window.

4. Download the newly issued certificate as a file.

    a) In Internet Explorer, select the **View the status of a pending certificate request** link.

    b) Select the **Saved-Request Certificate** link.

    c) If necessary, in the **Web Access Confirmation** message box, select **Yes**.

    d) On the **Certificate Issued** web page, select **Download certificate**.

    e) In the file download message box at the bottom, select the **Save** drop-down arrow, then select **Save as**.

    f) In the **Save As** dialog box, in the **File name** text box, type *C:\Webcertrenew.cer* and select **Save**.

5. Install and verify the certificate.

    a) In the file download message box at the bottom, select **Open**.

    b) In the **Certificate** dialog box, select **Install Certificate**.

    c) In the **Certificate Import Wizard**, on the **Welcome to the Certificate Import Wizard** page, select **Next**.

    d) On the **Certificate Store** page, select **Next** to allow Windows to automatically select the store location based on the file certificate type.

    e) On the **Completing the Certificate Import Wizard** page, select **Finish** to complete the wizard steps.

    f) In the **Certificate Import Wizard** message box, select **OK**.

    g) In the **Certificate** dialog box, select **OK** to close it.

    h) Close Internet Explorer.

    i) In the **Internet Information Services (IIS) Manager** window, on the **Server Certificates** page, in the **Actions** pane, select **Complete Certificate Request**.

    j) In the **Complete Certificate Request** dialog box, in the **File name containing the certification authority's response** text box, type *C:\Webcertrenew.cer* as the file name.

    k) In the **Friendly name** text box, type *WebCertRenew* and select **OK**.

Complete a previously created certificate request by retrieving the file that contains the certificate authority's response.

File name containing the certification authority's response:

| C:\Webcertrenew.cer | ... |

Friendly name:

| WebCertRenew |

---

    l) Verify that the certificate is displayed in the list of server certificates.

    m) Minimize the **Internet Information Services (IIS) Manager** window.

TOPIC E

Back Up and Restore Certificates and Private Keys

Previously, you renewed your CA server's certificate to keep it from expiring. However, there are other, more major issues that can arise. Certificates and their associated private keys may be lost or destroyed, so you'll need some way to recover them. In this topic, you will learn methods to back up certificates and keys so that you can restore them if they are lost or compromised.

Without keys, public key security simply cannot function. Due to their necessity, keys should be safeguarded closely. However, despite the best precautions, keys are occasionally damaged or lost. You need to have backup procedures for certificates and keys so that you can restore them when needed.

Private Key Protection Methods

Private keys are crucial to the security of a CA hierarchy and must be protected from loss, theft, or compromise. To secure a private key:

*   Back it up to removable media and store the media securely.
*   Delete it from insecure media.
*   Require a password to restore the private key.
*   Never share a key.
*   Never transmit a key on the network or across the Internet after it is issued.
*   Consider using key escrow to store a private key with trusted third parties.

Key Escrow

Key escrow, an alternative to key backups, can be used to store private keys securely, while allowing one or more trusted third parties access to the keys under predefined conditions. The third party is called the *key escrow agent*. For example, in certain situations, a government agency might require private keys to be placed in escrow with the agency. Commercial CAs can also act as escrow agents on a contract basis for organizations that do not want to back up and manage their own private keys.

M of N Control

In a key escrow scheme, there are only a certain number of agents or trustees that have the authority to recover a key. To prevent a single authorized agent from recovering a key, the *M of N scheme* is commonly used. The M of N scheme is a mathematical control that takes into account the total number of key recovery agents (N) along with the number of agents required to perform a key recovery (M). If the number of agents attempting to recover a key does not meet or exceed M, then the key will not be recovered. The exact values of M and N will vary with the implementation.

Private Key Restoration Methods

In the event that a private key is lost or damaged, you must restore the key from a backup or from escrow before you can recover any encrypted data.

*   If you are using key escrow, the key is divided among escrow agents. The agents can use the parts to reconstruct the lost key or decrypt the information directly.
*   If the key has been backed up to removable media, it can be restored from the backup location.

The EFS Recovery Agent

The *Encrypting File System (EFS)* uses Microsoft Windows NTFS-based public key encryption. Windows Server 2012 R2 automatically creates encryption certificates and public keys based on a user's credentials; or, you can use Windows Server 2012 R2's Active Directory Certificate Services (AD CS) to distribute certificates and keys.

File encryption keys, which are used to encrypt the files, are stored by the public key. The files are then accessible only by using the file owner's private key. The file encryption keys are then stored in the Windows operating system kernel and are never copied to the paging file, thus providing another level of security. This, however, will not protect against damage to the operating system or server itself.

The problem you can encounter with encryption is how to recover encrypted files in the event the user account under which files were encrypted no longer exists. For example, this problem can occur if you delete a user account after the user leaves your organization. Windows Server 2012 R2 enables you to define an EFS *recovery agent*. A recovery agent is an individual who has the necessary credentials to recover files that were encrypted by another user. By default, Windows Server 2012 R2 designates the domain administrator as an EFS recovery agent.

Key Archival and Recovery

You can also use AD CS to archive private keys in the protected CA database, which enables the private keys to be recovered. Key recovery does not recover encrypted data or messages, but it does enable a user or administrator to recover keys that can subsequently be used for data recovery (or data decryption).

Private Key Replacement

If a private key is lost, you might wish to replace the key entirely after you recover any encrypted data:

1. First, recover the private key.
2. Decrypt any encrypted data.
3. Destroy the original private key.
4. Obtain a new key pair.
5. Finally, re-encrypt the data using the new private key.

Access the Checklist tile on your LogicalCHOICE course screen for reference information and job aids on How to Back Up and Restore Certificates and Private Keys.

ACTIVITY 6-7
Backing Up a Certificate and Private Key

Scenario

The university has decided to secure email communications through the use of individual email certificates for all students and staff members. The security design team has developed recommendations for the strength of the email certificates. The team has also developed recommendations for maintaining backup copies of the email certificates and their associated private keys to guard against loss or compromise of the certificates. As the security administrator, your job is to support enrollment for email certificates and to maintain backups of each issued certificate. You will need an email certificate enrolled and backed up for your own personal Administrator user account.

1. Request a certificate for email protection for the Administrator user.
   a) Open Internet Explorer.
   b) Connect to **https://server##/certsrv**, where **##** is your student number.
   c) In the **Security Alert** message box, select **OK** to acknowledge that you are making a secure connection.
   d) Select the **Request a certificate** link.
   e) Select the **advanced certificate request** link.
   f) Select the **Create and submit a request to this CA** link.
   g) In the **Web Access Confirmation** dialog box, select **Yes** to verify the certificate request.
   h) Type *Administrator* as the **Name** and *administrator@domain##.internal* as the **E-Mail**.
   i) From the **Type of Certificate Needed** drop-down list, select **E-Mail Protection Certificate**.
   j) In the **Key Options** section, in the **Key Size** text box, verify that the key size is **1024**.
   k) Check the **Mark keys as exportable** check box.

   Type of Certificate Needed:

   [E-Mail Protection Certificate ▾]

   Key Options:

   ◉ Create new key set   ○ Use existing key set

   CSP: [Microsoft Enhanced RSA and AES Cryptographic Provider ▾]

   Key Usage: ○ Exchange   ○ Signature   ◉ Both

   Key Size: [1024] Min: 384 (common key sizes: 512 1024 2048 4096 8192 16384)
   Max:16384

   ◉ Automatic key container name   ○ User specified key container name

   ☑ Mark keys as exportable

   ☐ Enable strong private key protection

   l) Scroll down and select **Submit**.
   m) On the **Certificate Pending** web page, select the **Home** link.

2. Issue the pending user certificate.
   a) From the taskbar, select **certsrv**.
   b) In the **certsrv** window, select the **Pending Requests** folder.

    c) Scroll to the right to confirm that the **Request Common Name** for the certificate is **Administrator**. Select the pending request and select **Action→All Tasks→Issue**.

3. Install the new email certificate for the Administrator user.

    a) From the taskbar, select **Internet Explorer**.

    b) In Internet Explorer, select the **View the status of a pending certificate request** link.

    c) Select the **E-Mail Protection Certificate** link.

    d) In the **Web Access Confirmation** dialog box, select **Yes**.

    e) Select **Install this certificate**.

    f) Verify that the message "Your new certificate has been successfully installed" is displayed, and close Internet Explorer.

4. Create a Certificates MMC console for the Administrator user.

    a) Open the **Search Charm** and type *mmc*

    b) Select **mmc**.

    c) Maximize the **Console1 - [Console Root]** window.

    d) Select **File→Add/Remove Snap-in**.

    e) From the **Available snap-ins** list on the left, select **Certificates** and select **Add**.

    f) In the **Certificates snap-in** dialog box, verify that **My user account** is selected and select **Finish**.

    g) Select **OK**.

    h) Select **File→Save As**.

    i) In the **Save As** dialog box, in the **File name** text box, type *Certificates.msc* and select **Save**.

5. Export the certificate and its private key to a backup drive.

    a) In the **Certificates** console, expand **Certificates - Current User**.

b) Expand the **Personal** folder and select the **Certificates** folder.

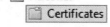

    Console Root

       ⊿ 🖳 Certificates - Current User

          ⊿ 📁 Personal

             📁 Certificates

c) Select the certificate with an intended purpose of **Secure Email**.

Issued To ▲	Issued By	Expiration Date	Intended Purposes
🔐 Administrator	UniversityCA01	2/20/2015	Secure Email

d) Select **Action→All Tasks→Export**.
e) In the **Certificate Export Wizard**, on the **Welcome to the Certificate Export Wizard** page, select **Next**.
f) Select **Yes, export the private key**, and select **Next**.

Export Private Key
    You can choose to export the private key with the certificate.

    Private keys are password protected. If you want to export the private key with the certificate, you must type a password on a later page.

    Do you want to export the private key with the certificate?

      ◉ Yes, export the private key

      ○ No, do not export the private key

g) On the **Export File Format** page, select **Next** to accept the default file format and include all certificates in the certification path if possible.
h) On the **Security** page, check the **Password** check box, and in the **Password** and **Confirm password** text boxes, type *!Pass1234* and select **Next**.
i) In the **File name** text box, type *S:\mailcert* and select **Next**.
j) Select **Finish**.
k) Select **OK** to close the message box.

6. Verify that the certificate was exported.
   a) Open File Explorer.
   b) Double-click the **S:** drive.
   c) Verify that the **mailcert** file appears, and close the File Explorer window.

ACTIVITY 6-8
Restoring a Certificate and Private Key

Before You Begin

There is a backup copy of the Administrator user's email certificate and private key on a secondary drive. There is a Certificates MMC console for the Administrator user.

Scenario

A staff member's email certificate and private key were accidentally deleted. Fortunately, you have followed the procedures in your security policy document and maintain backup copies of all user certificates and private keys. You can use these backups to restore the certificate and private key and correct the user's problem.

1. Create a key-compromise situation by deleting the Administrator user's email certificate.
   a) In the **Certificates** console, with the **Secure Email** certificate selected, select **Action→Delete**.
   b) In the **Certificates** dialog box, select **Yes** to confirm the deletion.

2. Restore the certificate and private key from the backup.
   a) In the **Certificates** console, in the **Personal** folder, verify that the **Certificates** folder is selected and select **Action→All Tasks→Import**.

   b) In the **Certificate Import Wizard**, on the **Welcome to the Certificate Import Wizard** page, select **Next**.
   c) On the **File to Import** page, in the **File name** text box, type *S:\mailcert.pfx* and select **Next**.
   d) On the **Private key protection** page, type *!Pass1234* as the password.
   e) Check the **Mark this key as exportable. This will allow you to back up or transport your keys at a later time** check box. Select **Next**.
   f) On the **Certificate Store** page, select **Next** to place the certificate in the **Personal** store.
   g) On the **Completing the Certificate Import Wizard** page, select **Finish**.
   h) In the message box, select **OK**.

i) Verify that the restored certificate appears in the **Certificates** folder in the **Personal** store. Close the **Certificates** window and select **Yes** when prompted to save console settings.

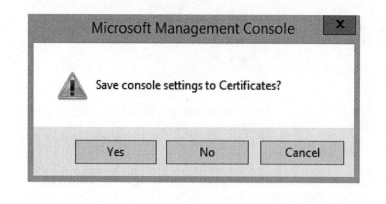

TOPIC F

Revoke Certificates

You have performed certificate renewal, which is necessary when you want a security entity to be able to continue using a certificate past its original expiration period. You might sometimes encounter the opposite case, when you want a security entity to stop using a certificate for a specified period of time. To do that, you must revoke the certificate, which will be covered in this topic.

Remember that certificates are sort of like driver's licenses; although they are only good for a limited period, most people can simply renew theirs to keep it valid past the original expiration date. But sometimes, a driver loses the right to drive. In the same way, sometimes a security principal no longer needs a certificate or should no longer be able to authenticate with a certificate. Just like the driver's license, the certificate has to be revoked to prevent its further use.

Certificate Revocation

Certificates can be revoked before expiration for one of several reasons:

- The certificate owner's private key has been compromised or lost.
- The certificate was obtained by fraudulent means.
- The certificate holder is no longer trusted. This can occur in normal circumstances, such as when an employee leaves a company, or it can be due to a system intrusion, such as when a subordinate CA is attacked.

Compromised CA

One example of a CA that is no longer trusted is the former certificate authority called DigiNotar. In 2011, the Dutch government revealed that DigiNotar was hacked, and that the hackers granted at least 500 fraudulent certificates for agencies such as the CIA and England's MI6. The Dutch government then took action to shut down the compromised CA, and many of its certificates were revoked.

The CRL

A *Certificate Revocation List (CRL)* is a list of certificates that were revoked before the expiration date. Each CA has its own CRL that can be accessed through the directory services of the network operating system or a website. The CRL generally contains the requester's name, the request ID number, the reason why the certificate was revoked, and other pertinent information.

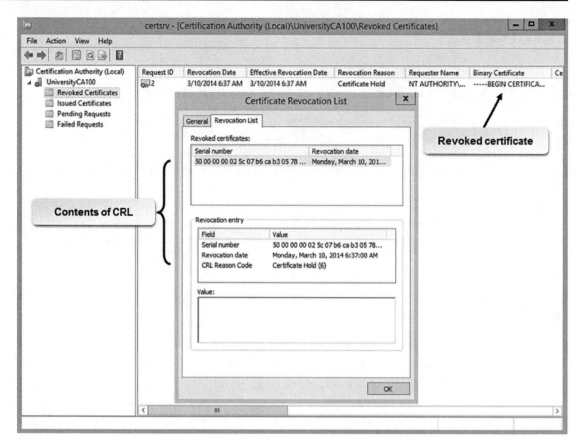

Figure 6-10: A detailed list of all revoked certificates issued by a CA.

CRL Checked By Software

Many software programs, such as email applications, will check the CRL for the status of a certificate before accepting it, and will reject revoked certificates.

Status Checking and Suspensions

In certificate systems that support temporary certificate suspensions as well as permanent certificate revocations, the certificate clients will check for both suspended and revoked certificates and will reject certificates that have been either suspended or revoked.

OCSP

The *Online Certificate Status Protocol (OCSP)* is an HTTP-based alternative to a CRL for checking the status of revoked certificates. OCSP servers, also called responders, accept a request to check a specific certificate's status. The responder uses the certificate's serial number to search for it in the CA's database. The server then sends the certificate's status to the requester.

The main advantage of using OCSP over a CRL is that it lowers overhead. OCSP responses for specific certificate requests contain less data than entire revocation lists, which can benefit both the client and the network. However, because OCSP does not by default encrypt these standard HTTP transmissions, an attacker may be able to glean that a network resource used a specific certificate at a specific time during this OCSP transaction.

 Access the Checklist tile on your LogicalCHOICE course screen for reference information and job aids on How to Revoke Certificates.

ACTIVITY 6-9
Revoking Certificates

Scenario

One of your colleagues in IT thinks that a student has compromised the public and private key pairs on the student registration web server. IT wants to make sure the compromised keys are no longer used. In cases like this, the university's CA security guidelines call on you to revoke the compromised certificate and immediately publish the CRL.

1. Revoke the certificate for the web server.

   a) In the **certsrv** window, select the **Issued Certificates** folder.

   b) Select the certificate that was most recently issued to the web server and select **Action→All Tasks→Revoke Certificate**.

    Note: Scroll to the right and consult the **Certificate Effective Date** column for the most recent certificate with an **Issued Common Name** of Server##.

   c) In the **Certificate Revocation** dialog box, from the **Reason code** drop-down list, select the **Key Compromise** option.

   ### Certificate Revocation [x]

   Are you sure you want to revoke the selected certificate(s)?

   Specify a reason, date and time.

   Reason code:
   [Key Compromise ▼]

   Date and Time:
   [2/ 7/2014 ▦▼] [3:06 PM ▲▼]

   [Yes]   [No]

    Note: Certificates can only be unrevoked if they have a **Reason code** of **Certificate Hold**. Otherwise, the revocation will be permanent.

   d) Select **Yes** to revoke the certificate.

   e) Select the **Revoked Certificates** folder.

   f) Verify that the revoked certificate appears in the **Revoked Certificates** folder.

Request ID	Revocation Date	Effective Revocation Date	Revocation Reason
🔖6	2/7/2014 3:09 PM	2/7/2014 3:06 PM	Key Compromise

2. When will clients know that the certificate has been revoked?
   - ○ When the certificate expires.
   - ○ When they connect to the website.
   - ○ When the CRL is published.
   - ○ When the client requests a new certificate.

3. If an attacker maliciously revokes certificates, how could they be recovered?
   - ○ By renewing the CA certificates.
   - ○ By republishing the CRL.
   - ○ By reissuing the certificates.
   - ○ By restoring the CA from a backup.

4. Publish the CRL manually.
   a) In the **certsrv** window, with the **Revoked Certificates** folder selected, select **Action→All Tasks→Publish**.
   b) In the **Publish CRL** dialog box, select **OK** to confirm that you want to publish a new CRL.

5. Verify that the CRL is current.
   a) Select **Action→Properties** to open the properties for the **Revoked Certificates** folder.
   b) In the **Revoked Certificates Properties** dialog box, select the **View CRLs** tab.
   c) In the **CRLs** section, verify that the CRL with the highest key index is selected.

   > **Note:** The **Effective date** for the current CRL should be the current date and time. The **Next update** is scheduled on the default weekly update schedule.

   d) Select **View CRL**.

CRLs

Key Index	Effective Date	Expiration Date	Publish Status
0	2/7/2014 3:01 PM	2/15/2014 3:21 ...	OK
1	2/7/2014 3:01 PM	2/15/2014 3:21 ...	OK

View CRL

   e) Select the **Revocation List** tab.
   f) From the **Serial number** list, select the entry.
      The **Revocation entry** section displays details about the certificate.
   g) Select **OK** to close the **Certificate Revocation List** dialog box.
   h) In the **Revoked Certificates Properties** dialog box, select **OK** to close it.

ACTIVITY 6-10
Modifying the CRL Publication Interval

Scenario

Your CA is configured with the default weekly publication interval for the CRL. The university's CA security guidelines call for daily publication of the CRL so that revoked certificates may be known quickly, and without placing too much strain on the server. You are responsible for configuring your CA in accordance with the guidelines.

1. Change the publication interval for the CRL.
   a) In the **certsrv** window, open the properties of the **Revoked Certificates** folder.
   b) In the **Revoked Certificates Properties** dialog box, in the **CRL publication interval** section, from the drop-down list, select the **Days** option.

   c) Select **Apply**.
      The **Next update** schedule will change the next time the list is published.
   d) Select **OK** to close the dialog box.

2. Publish the CRL.
   a) With the **Revoked Certificates** folder selected, select **Action→All Tasks→Publish**.
   b) In the **Publish CRL** dialog box, select **OK** to confirm that you want to publish a new CRL.
   c) Open the properties of the **Revoked Certificates** folder.
   d) In the **Revoked Certificates Properties** dialog box, select the **View CRLs** tab, then select **View CRL**.
   e) Verify that the **Next update** is scheduled for one day from the current date. Select **OK** twice.
   f) Close all open windows except **Server Manager**.

Summary

In this lesson, you performed the tasks involved in the day-to-day management of certificates. Regardless of how simple or complex your certificate hierarchy is, you will still need to do different tasks such as install, issue, revoke, renew, recover, and eventually expire certificates. Each of these tasks plays an equally important role in managing certificates.

What types of certificate management functions have you performed or do you plan on performing at your job?

What method of backing up private keys would you prefer to use? Why?

 Note: Check your LogicalCHOICE Course screen for opportunities to interact with your classmates, peers, and the larger LogicalCHOICE online community about the topics covered in this course or other topics you are interested in. From the Course screen you can also access available resources for a more continuous learning experience.

7 Implementing Compliance and Operational Security

Lesson Time: 1 hour, 30 minutes

Lesson Objectives

In this lesson, you will implement compliance and operational security measures. You will:

- Describe physical security issues and principles.

- Describe legal compliance issues and principles.

- Identify security awareness and training requirements.

- Integrate systems and data with third parties.

Lesson Introduction

Now that you have implemented and managed your basic security infrastructure, you will need to make sure that appropriate security procedures and policies are enforced, and rules and regulations are followed. In this lesson, you will identify common compliance issues and related security controls.

Although system and network security are key concerns, you still need to know what areas of the organization are vulnerable to threats. Enforcing operational security across an organization will provide you with the first defense against security threats and will enable regulatory compliance. It is your responsibility as a security professional to provide the right level of support to organizations. Having a strong compliance framework is crucial to gaining the level of security control required to properly protect the employees, systems, and networks within an organization.

TOPIC A

Physical Security

In this lesson, you will acquire the skills to verify your company's compliance with internal and external policies on an ongoing basis. To begin maintaining a complete security infrastructure, make sure that the physical components of your company's security plan are in place. In this topic, you will explore the security measures used to ensure the physical security for an organization.

You can make sure that servers have been secured, access control mechanisms are in place, and all network connections are protected, but all of that effort is wasted if the physical security to those systems is not also properly secured. Part of completely securing an organization's assets is also securing all physical components.

Physical Security Controls

Physical security controls are security measures that restrict, detect, and monitor access to specific physical areas or assets. They can control access to a building, to equipment, or to specific areas, such as server rooms, finance or legal areas, data centers, network cable runs, or any other area that has hardware or information that is considered to have important value and sensitivity. Determining where to use physical access controls requires a risk/benefit analysis and must include the consideration of any regulations or other compliance requirements for the specific types of data that are being safeguarded.

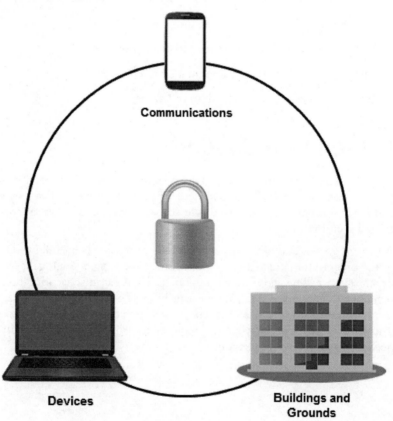

Figure 7–1: Physical security controls.

There are various ways to categorize the different physical security controls:

- **Deterrent** controls discourage attackers from attacking in the first place.

- **Preventive** controls stop an attack before it can cause damage.
- **Detective** controls identify attacks in progress.
- **Compensating** controls support other physical controls.
- **Technical** controls are hardware or software that aid in protecting physical assets.
- **Administrative** controls leverage security policies and are used to train personnel.

> **Note:** Some controls belong to multiple categories, like a surveillance camera that can both deter and detect intrusions.

Physical Security Control Types

There are a number of physical access controls available to ensure the protection of an organization's physical environment.

Physical Security Control	Description
Locks	There are a number of different locks that can be used to prevent unauthorized access to information resources: • Bolting door locks are a traditional lock-and-key method that requires a non-duplicate policy for keys to access a door. • Combination door locks, or cipher locks, use a keypad or dial system with a code or numeric combination to access a door. • Electronic door locks use an access ID card, with an electronic chip or token that is read by the electronic sensor attached to a door. • Biometric door locks are commonly used in highly secure environments. This method uses an individual's unique body features to scan and identify the access permissions for a particular door. • Hardware locks can be attached to a laptop, hard drive, or file cabinet to secure it from being opened or turned on.
Logging and visitor access	Logging should be used at all entrances that are open to the general public. This method requires all visitors to sign in and out when entering and leaving the building. Logging requirements will vary depending on the organization, but should include the following: • Name and company being represented. • Date, time of entry, and time of departure. • Reason for visiting. • Contact within the organization. When possible, one single entry point should be used for all incoming visitors. This decreases the risk of unauthorized individuals gaining access to the building.
Identification systems	Security cards, such as swipe cards or proximity cards, provide identity information about the bearer, which is then checked against an appropriate access list for that location. The cards can be used along with a proximity reader to verify identification and grant access. A security card can also include a picture or some other identification code for a second authentication factor. Security cards should be required for all employees and should be visible at all times.

Physical Security Control	Description
Video surveillance	Video or still-image surveillance from *closed-circuit television (CCTV)* cameras can be put in place to deter or detect unwanted access. These systems can be placed inside and outside the building. All video recording should be saved and stored in a secure environment.
Security guards	Human security guards, armed or unarmed, can be placed in front of and around a location to protect it. They can monitor critical checkpoints and verify identification, allow or disallow access, and log physical entry occurrences. They also provide a visual deterrent and can apply their own knowledge and intuition to potential security breaches.
Signs	Signs are simple and rudimentary, but they nevertheless can be effective against less determined intruders. Beyond basic no trespassing signs, some homes and offices also display signs from the security companies whose services they are currently using. These may convince intruders to stay away.
Bonded personnel	Contracted services personnel, such as cleaning services, should be bonded to protect an organization from financial exposures.
Mantrap doors	A mantrap door system, also referred to as a deadman door, is a system with a door at each end of a secure chamber. An individual enters a secure area through an outer door. The outer door must be closed before an inner door can open. An individual's identity is sometimes verified before they enter the secure area through the first door, and other times while they are confined to the secure area between the two doors. This system also requires that one person enter at a time. This system typically requires two separate authentication processes, with the second one being done while the authenticated person is isolated inside a reinforced enclosure.
Physical barriers	The location of highly secure resources, such as a server room, should not have windows or be visible from the outside of a building. This creates a more secure barrier from the outside. Examples of physical barriers include fencing, barricades, and true floor-to-ceiling wall architectures.
Alarms	Alarms activated by an unauthorized access attempt require a quick response. Locally stationed security guards or police may respond to alarms. These responding individuals may trigger access control devices in the facility to automatically lock.
Motion detection	Sensors that detect motion may trip alarms and alert the authorities to a possible intruder. These sensors can be placed at checkpoints within or outside a building.
Protected distribution	Protected distribution systems are intended to make it difficult for attackers to compromise the physical cabling of a communications network. This is generally achieved by hardening the cables with strong metallic tubing and installing acoustic alarm systems that detect when the cabling is being tampered with. Additionally, protected distribution systems are routinely inspected by qualified personnel for any intrusions that the alarms did not catch.

 Note: For additional information, check out the LearnTO **Apply Physical Controls** presentation from the **LearnTO** tile on the LogicalCHOICE Course screen.

Environmental Exposures

Environmental exposures must be considered when evaluating the overall security of a building. Exposures can include lightning, hurricanes, earthquakes, volcanic eruptions, high winds, and other extreme weather conditions. As a result of any of these exposures, a number of issues may arise:

- Power fluctuations and failures.
- Water damage and flooding.
- Fires.
- Structural damage to the building leading to unauthorized access.

Environmental Controls

There are certain *environmental controls* that can be implemented to help control a facility's physical environment.

Environmental Control	Description
Heating, ventilation, and air conditioning (HVAC) system	An HVAC system controls the environment inside a building: • Humidity and temperature control: Most experts recommend that temperatures in a computer facility should be in the range of 72°–76° Fahrenheit. The relative humidity in the facility should be between 40 percent and 60 percent. High and low temperatures can damage equipment. Low humidity causes static electricity, which can damage the sensitive circuitry of electronics; high humidity causes moisture buildup, which can lead to corrosion. • Positive air pressure is a must. Air should be forced from the facility to keep contaminants out. Filters on HVAC systems keep dust to a minimum and must be changed regularly. • To ensure that HVAC systems are running properly, it is important to monitor them both locally and remotely.
Hot and cold aisle	A method used within data centers and computer rooms to control the temperature and humidity. A hot and cold aisle layout is designed to control the flow of air to or from systems using strategically placed vents and exhaust fans to keep the hardware and room at the desired temperature and humidity.
Electromagnetic interference (EMI) shielding	EMI occurs when a magnetic field builds up around one electrical circuit and interferes with the signal being carried on an adjacent circuit, causing network interference issues resulting in signal noise or errors. EMI shielding is used to prevent electromagnetic transfers from cables and devices by creating a conductive material protective barrier. For example, a shielded cable contains an electromagnetic covering within the cable that directly protects the inner core conductor from producing an electromagnetic discharge.
Alarm control panel	The main control panel for an organization's alarm system should be protected and secured from any type of exposure. The panel must be in a separate location and protected from unauthorized access, and be accessible by the fire department, encased in a waterproof and climate-controlled box, powered by a dedicated circuit, and programmed to function by zone within an organization.

Environmental Control	Description
Fire prevention	The first rule of fire protection is fire prevention. Fires can be prevented by: • Eliminating unnecessary storage items and clutter. • Conducting annual inspections by the fire department, which include an extensive review of computer room controls, all fire suppression systems, and extinguishers within the building. • Installing fireproof walls, and a fireproof floor and ceiling in the computer room, which all have at least a two-hour fire resistance rating. • Using fire-resistant office materials, such as garbage bins, desks, chairs, and window treatments.
Fire detection	Commercial fire detection systems should be connected to a central reporting station where the location of the suspected fire is indicated. In some cases, the detection system or monitoring station is connected directly to a fire department. Various fire detection systems are used to identify the threat of a fire: • Smoke detectors sense the presence of smoke using various scientific methods, such as testing for particles in the air. • Heat sensors are triggered either when a target temperature is reached or when there is a high rate of increase in temperature. • Flame detectors use optical sensors to record incoming radiation at selected wavelengths.
Fire suppression	Fires in computer facilities are especially dangerous. The damage done to computing systems is extremely expensive, and the chemicals used in the machines may emit toxic substances during fires. In some cases, small fires may be extinguished using hand-held fire extinguishers. These systems must be placed in the appropriate locations within a facility and should be inspected regularly. When it is not practical to fight these fires with small extinguishers or to douse fires with water, then special gases should be used to extinguish fires in areas with a large number of computers or servers. Frequently, local jurisdictions mandate water-based fire extinguishing systems, even though gaseous systems often provide more appropriate protection for computer equipment. To satisfy each requirement, organizations are outfitted with both. Here is what occurs: if the gas system does not suppress the fire, the sprinkler system will then activate, but is otherwise maintained as the official back-up extinguisher. The best practice is to contact your local fire authorities when designing a fire suppression system.

Environmental Monitoring

Regularly monitoring the environmental conditions and controls surrounding a building and the hardware stored inside it is important to properly secure and prevent damage to resources. Conditions that can threaten security should be monitored regularly, along with the implementation of necessary security controls. In some instances, constant video monitoring is used to look for environmental issues such as overheating, water, or electricity issues.

Safety

The safety of your employees and your property are also important concerns from a security standpoint. After all, the health of your personnel and the hardware they work with is vital to keeping your operation running at maximum efficiency.

For example, physical controls like fencing and CCTV cameras will deter intruders and keep them from harming your assets. Locks may be placed on doors to hazardous areas, like a warehouse in which heavy machinery is used, in order to protect employees. Proper lighting during the night will keep late workers safe from accidents that occur as a result of poor visibility. For environmental hazards like fire or noxious gas, you need to formulate an escape plan. What is the best way to get all of your personnel out of the building as quickly and calmly as possible? You'll also need to map out the best escape routes in the event of an unsafe situation. However, no amount of written policy will be able to adequately prepare your personnel for such an event, so you should test their preparedness by performing drills.

The wear and tear that *safety controls* are subject to should be a primary concern. You need to make sure that there is no point in time when your personnel and property are left vulnerable. This is why you need to implement *testing controls* to consistently test your fencing, lighting, locks, CCTV cameras, escape plans, etc. If any one of these controls does not meet your standards for safety, you will be able to quickly fix or replace it.

ACTIVITY 7-1
Examining the Components of Physical Security

Scenario

Develetech Industries is relocating its main headquarters to a new building. The Chief Security Officer has asked for your input on the physical security needed to protect the main server room at the new location.

1. What types of physical security controls would you suggest for the main server room?

2. What are some common environmental exposures that you may consider when evaluating the overall security of the new building?

3. What type of environmental controls should the company consider as part of their relocation?

TOPIC B

Legal Compliance

Previously in the course, you identified corporate policies that are designed to meet the internal needs of your organization. But, as a security professional, you may be responsible for meeting the security needs of outside legal authorities as well. In this topic, you will identify security requirements that your company might legally be required to meet.

Legal security compliance requirements can affect your company in a variety of situations. You might work for a company in a publicly regulated industry, such as the nuclear power industry. Your company might have business partnerships with or provide services or products to any one of a number of government agencies. You also have responsibilities to your local municipality for safety and security. As a security professional, you will need to be able to demonstrate that your company is compliant with any or all of these entities' security requirements.

Compliance Laws and Regulations

Compliance is the practice of ensuring that the requirements of legislation, regulations, industry codes and standards, and organizational standards are met. Several controlling authorities need to be recognized to achieve compliance:

- Governmental legislative entities such as national congresses or parliaments and state, provincial, or regional senates or other law-making bodies.
- Governmental regulatory agencies that promulgate rules, regulations, and standards for various industries.
- Industry associations that promulgate rules, regulations, and standards for individual industries.

The effect of laws and regulations on applying security measures can be substantial. Security professionals must review all laws and regulations relevant to the type of business and operation that needs to be secured. Most organizations will have legal requirements that apply to their data systems, processes, controls, and infrastructure. Regulations can affect the way businesses store, transmit, and process data. When securing an organization as a whole, you must review the business' privacy policy and other legal documents that convey business requirements.

Legal Requirements

All organizations must consider their overall or general legal obligations, rights, liabilities, and limitations when creating security policies. Because security incidents can potentially be prosecuted as technology crimes, organizations must be prepared to work with civil authorities when investigating, reporting, and resolving each incident. Information security practices must comply with legal requirements that are documented in other departmental policies, such as human resources. A company's response to a security incident must conform to the company's legal limitations as well as the civil rights of the individuals involved.

In addition to the various local, state, federal, and international legal considerations, organizations in regulated industries, such as utility companies, hazardous material manufacturers, and medical professions, will have to comply with the additional standards and requirements imposed by governmental authorities and professional oversight bodies for each industry. The requirements can vary widely, depending on the industry involved, and are specific for every organization.

When applying security measures to an organization, it is always a good idea to consider industry best practices. Depending on the type of business, best practices will vary.

Types of Legal Requirements

Legal issues can affect different parties within each organization.

Affected Party	Legal Considerations
Employees	• Who is liable for the misuse of email and Internet resources? The organization, the employee, or both? • What is the extent of liability for an organization for criminal acts committed by its employees? • What rights to privacy do employees have regarding electronic communications?
Customers	• What customer data is considered private, and what is considered public? • How will a company protect the privacy and confidentiality of customer information?
Business partners	• Who is liable if data resides in one location (country) and the processing takes place in another location? • Who is responsible for the security and privacy of the information transmitted between an organization and a business partner? The sender or the receiver?

Forensic Requirements

Information security professionals must observe generally accepted forensic practices when investigating security incidents.

Evidence
Collection

Evidence
Preservation

Chain of
Custody

Jurisdiction

Figure 7–2: Forensic requirements.

Forensics Requirement	Description
Evidence collection	Following the correct procedures for collecting evidence from floppy disks, hard drives, smart cards, and other media ensures the integrity of the evidence and prevents tampering. As in any other case, evidence that is improperly collected may not be admissible in court.
Evidence preservation	Criminal cases or even internal security incidents can take months or years to resolve. The company must be able to properly preserve all gathered evidence for a lengthy period of time.
Chain of custody	Whoever gathers and preserves the evidence must also maintain a complete inventory that shows who handled specific items and where they have been stored. This document must be kept secure at all times to prevent tampering. If the chain of custody is broken, it can be difficult, if not impossible, to prosecute a technology crime.

Forensics Requirement	Description
Jurisdiction	Determining exactly who has the right to investigate and prosecute an information technology criminal case can be extremely difficult due to overlapping laws for copyright, computer fraud, and mail tampering. In addition, each country has its own laws, and these laws may vary depending on what part of the country is involved. Organizations are obliged to use due care to determine the appropriate jurisdiction for a security investigation.

ACTIVITY 7-2
Examining Legal Compliance

Data Files

C:\093022Data\Implementing Compliance and Operational Security
\DeveletechAcceptableUsePolicy.rtf

Scenario

As the security administrator for Develetech Industries, you have been assigned the task of determining when appropriate legal action should be taken based on the acceptable use policy (AUP). Use the AUP document to determine if your security policy calls for legal action in the following situations.

---

1. Open and review C:\093022Data\Implementing Compliance and Operational Security \DeveletechAcceptableUsePolicy.rtf.

    a) In File Explorer, navigate to C:\093022Data\Implementing Compliance and Operational Security \DeveletechAcceptableUsePolicy.rtf.

    b) Double-click the file to open it in WordPad.

    c) Review the contents of the file.

2. An employee unintentionally opens an attachment that causes a virus to spread within the organization. Does the policy call for legal action?

3. An employee emails a copy of a new type of encryption software program to a user in a foreign country for testing. Does the policy call for legal action?

4. An employee scans your network for open ports. Does the policy call for legal action?

5. An employee forwards an email that appears to be a Ponzi or Pyramid scheme. Does the policy call for legal action?

6. Two employees have an argument at lunchtime. During the afternoon, one user sends a threatening email to the other. The second employee is afraid to leave the building unescorted that evening. Does the policy call for legal action?

7. Close WordPad and File Explorer.

TOPIC C

Security Awareness and Training

Throughout this course, you have acquired the skills you need to keep your security infrastructure healthy. But security is the responsibility of all the individuals in the organization, not just the professional security team. In this topic, you will learn how to give users the information they need to follow appropriate security practices in their day-to-day work.

Attackers are smart and will take advantage of employees that may not be savvy enough to know they are being solicited for information. Because of this, it is your responsibility to educate or coach your users about their individual security responsibilities. An educated user is the security professional's best partner in preventing security breaches.

Security Policy Awareness

An organization's security policy is created to ensure that all system users comply with the security guidelines and procedures enforced by management. Security professionals should verify that the security policy is accessible and that users are trained in the importance of security awareness within an organization. Regular training sessions and security policy documentation will ensure that users follow the correct procedures when accessing and using system resources and services.

Role-Based Training

In addition to general training for basic security principles and policies, some organizations also implement training based on job roles and organizational responsibilities. For instance, end users might not need training about how to keep budget or personnel information secure, while managers would definitely need to know about restrictions on sharing that sort of data.

Besides role-based technical training, you might establish or encounter role-based training that relates to incident reporting and response.

Personally Identifiable Information

Personally identifiable information (PII) is information that can be used on its own or with other information to identify, contact, or locate a single person, or to identify an individual in context. What constitutes PII will vary depending on the legal jurisdiction.

 Note: The abbreviation PII is widely accepted in the US, but the phrase it abbreviates has four common variants based on word forms for personal (or personally) and identifiable (identifying). These variants are not identical from a legal standpoint. Each term's definition can change depending on the jurisdiction and the reason the term is being used.

PII can include a user's full name, fingerprints, license plate number, phone numbers, street address, driver's license number, and so on.

Classification of Information

To adequately protect information from disclosure and other threats, you need to understand the risks associated with the release or modification of the information. Determining the risk of loss or modification is often measured by labeling the information. Labeling schemes are often known as classifications. The classifications will depend on the type of business and how the data is stored. Classified data can be either hard or soft. Hard data refers to concrete information, such as measurements and facts about an organization. Soft data refers to the organization's ideas, thoughts, and views. All data should be classified and protected accordingly.

Common information classifications include schemes where information is categorized according to the level of sensitivity in the information, such as:

* High, Medium, and Low
* Restricted, Private, and Public
* Confidential, Restricted, and Public

Here are some other terms that you might encounter in information classification schemes.

Classification Scheme Level	Description
Corporate Confidential	Information that should not be provided to individuals outside of the enterprise.
Personal and Confidential	Information of a personal nature that should be protected.
Private	Correspondence of a private nature between two people that should be safeguarded.
Trade Secret	Corporate intellectual property that, if released, will present serious damage to the company's ability to protect patents and processes.
Client Confidential	• Client personal information that, if released, may result in the identity theft of the individual. • Client corporate information or intellectual property. You may need to sign a non-disclosure agreement (NDA) to keep an organization's information about a client confidential.

Employee Education

Information security is not the exclusive responsibility of information professionals. A comprehensive security plan can only succeed when all members of an organization understand the necessary security practices and comply with them. Security professionals are often the ones responsible for educating employees and encouraging their compliance with security policies.

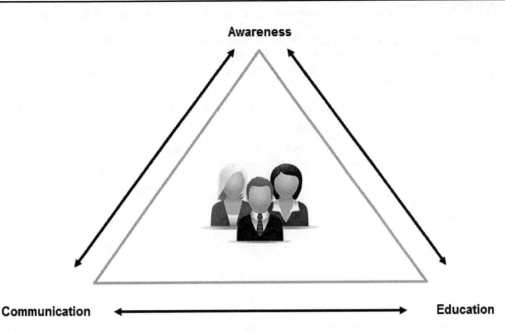

Figure 7–3: The employee education process.

There are three important components that work together in order to ensure proper employee security education.

Step	Explanation
Awareness	Employees must understand the importance of information security and security policies, and have an awareness of the potential threats to security. Threats can include new and upcoming viruses, types of phishing attacks, and zero day exploits. Employees also need to be aware of the role they play to protect an organization's assets and resources. A security professional can create awareness through seminars, email, or information on a company intranet.
Communication	The lines of communication between employees and the security team must remain open. Security professionals can accomplish this by encouraging employees to ask questions and provide feedback on security issues. Also, the security team must take responsibility for keeping the workforce informed of ongoing security concerns and updated best practices and standards.
Education	Employees should be trained and educated in security procedures, practices, and expectations from the moment they walk through the door. Employees are responsible for organizational security the second they join an organization and have access to the physical building and resources, and the intellectual property inside. Education should continue as technology changes and new information becomes available. Education takes many forms, from training sessions to online courses employees can take at work. Educated users are one of your best defenses against social engineering attacks.

Online Resources

A common way to promote employee awareness and training is to provide employees with online access to security-related resources and information. You can provide proprietary, private security information, such as your corporate security policy document, through an organization's intranet. You can also point employees to a number of reputable and valuable security resources on the Internet. However, both you and the employee should be cautious whenever researching information on the Internet. Just because information is posted on a website does not mean it is factual or reliable. Periodically monitor the websites you recommend to your employees to make sure that they are providing worthwhile information, and encourage employees to verify any technical or security-related information with a reliable third party before acting on the information or passing it along to others.

Here are just a few of the information security resources that you can find on the Internet:

- www.microsoft.com/security/default.mspx
- /www.oracle.com/technetwork/topics/security/whatsnew/index.html
- http://tools.cisco.com/security/center/home.x
- www.sans.org
- www.openssh.org
- www.emc.com/domains/rsa/index.htm
- /www.cert.org
- searchsecurity.techtarget.com/
- www.securityfocus.com
- www.entrust.com
- www.ruskwig.com
- www.symantec.com/security_response/index.jsp
- www.mcafee.com
- http://project.honeynet.org
- http://web.mit.edu/kerberos
- http://hoaxbusters.org
- http://vmyths.com
- http://snopes.com

User Security Responsibilities

Because security is most often breached at the end-user level, users need to be aware of their specific security responsibilities and habits.

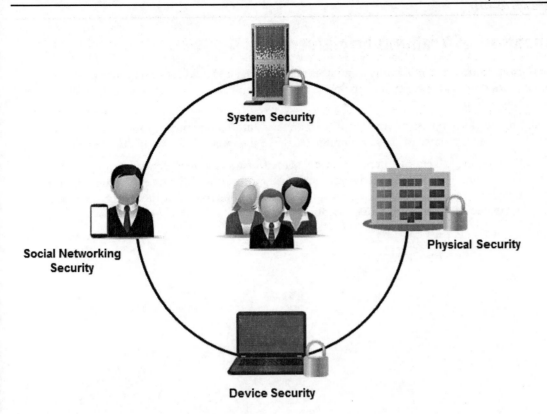

Figure 7-4: User security responsibilities.

Security Area	Employee Responsibilities
Physical security	Employees should not allow anyone in the building without an ID badge. Employees should not allow other individuals to tailgate on a single ID badge. Employees should be comfortable approaching and challenging unknown or unidentified persons in a work area. Access within the building should be restricted to only those areas an employee needs to access for job purposes. Data handling procedures of confidential files must be followed. Employees must also follow clean desk policies to ensure that confidential documents and private corporate information are secured and filed away from plain sight.
System security	Proper password behaviors can be crucial in keeping systems resources secure from unauthorized users. Employees must use their user IDs and passwords properly and comply with the ID and password requirements set forth by management. Password information should never be shared or written down where it is accessible to others. All confidential files should be saved to an appropriate location on the network where they can be secured and backed up, not on a hard drive or removable media device.
Device security	Employees must use correct procedures to log off all systems and shut down computers when not in use. Wireless communication and personally owned devices must be approved by the IT department and installed properly. These devices can be a gateway for attackers to access corporate information and sensitive data. Portable devices, such as laptops and mobile devices, must be properly stored and secured when not in use.
Social networking security	Employees must be made aware of the potential threats and attacks that target social networking and peer-to-peer (P2P) applications and websites. The use of these applications can lead to potential breaches in security on an organization's network. Security policies should include guidelines and restrictions for users of any social networking application or website.

Validation of Training Effectiveness

If an organization invests in security awareness and training, it should also make sure that the training is effective. Effective training helps to ensure compliance and increases the overall security of the organization.

To validate the effectiveness of your security awareness and training programs, you'll need to identify which components of those programs will have the most impact on overall security.

The SANS Securing the Human Program offers some free tools to help organizations establish metrics for measuring impact, or behavioral changes that can be attributed to the training, along with metrics for tracking compliance and ways to assess various risks. For more information, visit **http://www.securingthehuman.org/resources/metrics**.

ACTIVITY 7-3
Examining Security Awareness and Training

Scenario

As the security administrator for Develetech Industries, one of your responsibilities is to coordinate the employee security training and awareness program. The main plant has recently experienced several security incidents involving improper user behavior. IT staff and plant management have come to you for recommendations on how to implement proper employee training procedures to prevent similar problems in the future.

1. A virus has spread throughout your organization, causing expensive system downtime and corrupted data. You find that the virus sent to many users was an email attachment that was forwarded by an employee. The employee that received the original email was fooled into believing the link it contained was a legitimate marketing survey. You quickly determine that this is a well-known email hoax that had already been posted on several hoax-related websites. When questioned, the employee said that he thought it sounded as if it could be legitimate, and he could not see any harm in just trying it. How could better user training and awareness have helped this situation?

2. What specific training steps do you recommend taking in response to this incident?

3. You come in on a Monday morning to find laptops have been stolen from several employees' desks over the weekend. After reviewing videotapes from the security cameras, you find that as an employee exited the building through the secure rear door on Friday night, she held the door open to admit another individual. You suspect this individual was the thief. When you question the employee, she states that the individual told her that he was a new employee who had not yet received his employee badge, that he only needed to be in the building for a few minutes, and that it would save him some time if she could let him in the back door rather than having to walk around to the receptionist entrance. Your security policy states that no one without identification should be admitted through the security doors at any time, but the employee says she was unaware of this policy. You ask her to locate the security policy documents on the network, and she is unable to do so. How could better user education have helped this situation?

4. What user training steps do you recommend taking in response to this incident?

5. One of your competitors has somehow obtained confidential data about your organization. There have been no obvious security breaches or physical break-ins, and you are puzzled as to the source of the leak. You begin to ask questions about any suspicious or unusual employee activity, and you begin to hear stories about a sales representative from out of town who did not have a desk in the office and was sitting down in open cubes and plugging her laptop in to the corporate network. You suspect that the sales representative was really an industrial spy for your competitor. When you ask other employees why they did not ask the sales representative for identification or report the incident to security, the other employees said that, giving their understanding of company policies, they did not see anything unusual or problematic in the situation. You review your security policy documents and, in fact, none of them refer to a situation like this one. How could better user education have helped this situation?

6. What user training steps do you recommend taking in response to this incident?

7. The customer and employee databases include credit card and bank account numbers, governmental tax identification numbers, and other sensitive information. A blog posting hints at the possibility of this information being distributed to unauthorized people, and the media begins calling people at all levels of the organization, trying to confirm or deny the rumor. Current security policies specify that this sort of information needs to be protected, but does not appear to address media enquiries regarding potential breaches. How could better user education have helped in this situation?

8. What user training steps do you recommend taking in response to this incident?

9. How might you suggest that Develetech validate the effectiveness of the user training you've recommended to address these issues?

TOPIC D

Integrate Systems and Data with Third Parties

In this lesson, you've dealt with physical security, legal compliance, and security awareness and training. The final facet of compliance and operational security deals with the sharing of information among organizations. In this topic, you will integrate systems and data with third parties.

Today's business world is one of partnerships and integration. With the advent of so many new technological tools such as social media, more and more organizations find themselves connected to and sharing information with many different entities. The ability to secure these communications while allowing the proper level of access to information is a primary responsibility for any security professional.

Business Partners

A *business partner* is a commercial entity that has a relationship of some sort with another, separate commercial entity. A business partner can be a supplier, customer, agent, reseller, or vendor of similar products or services. Business partnership can be formal, such as a contractual agreement, or informal, but no matter what type of partnership exists, there will always be the need to share information among the business partners.

In order to properly adhere to security protocols, business partners should go through an on-boarding and off-boarding process when the relationship both begins and concludes, respectively. Proper on-boarding involves acclimating partners to the security practices that you expect them to follow. This ensures that there will be a fair balance of responsibility and liability in the partnership. Likewise, when the partnership ends, you should establish an off-boarding process. Both parties should agree to terminate any integration, including loss of cross-organizational access and other controls, that is no longer necessary.

Social Media Networks and Applications

Social media networks and applications such as Facebook, Twitter, LinkedIn, and Yammer are being incorporated into more business scenarios than ever before. Companies leverage the power of these platforms to connect with a more public-facing audience in order to expand their media presence. However, the public nature of social media and related apps often presents a risk to an organization's security. Employees may post sensitive information on a social network that has wider-reaching consequences than simple word-of-mouth. Even on its official web page, a company might reveal more than it should. The openness of social media is also a haven for social engineers who will attempt to deceive employees into compromising security.

Even within private social networks like Yammer, security professionals need to exercise caution. Are your administrators adequately trained on the particular service you're using? Are they given the proper tools to moderate the network? What are some of your privacy considerations as you try to keep sensitive information from leaking? Since you're relying on a third party to provide the service, there will always be a certain measure of control that you lack with social media.

Interoperability Agreements

There are various types of agreements that business entities may rely on to facilitate interoperability. Some of the these agreements are described in the following table.

Agreement Type	Description
Service-level agreement (SLA)	This agreement clearly defines what services are to be provided to the client, and what support, if any, will be provided. Services may include everything from hardware and software to human resources. A strong SLA will outline basic service expectations for liability purposes.
Business partner agreement (BPA)	This agreement defines how a partnership between business entities will be conducted, and what exactly is expected of each entity in terms of services, finances, and security. For security purposes, BPAs should describe exactly what the partners are willing to share with each other, and how any inter-organizational access will be handled.
Memorandum of understanding (MOU)	This type of agreement is usually not legally binding and typically does not involve the exchange money. MOUs are less formal than traditional contracts, but still have a certain degree of significance to all parties involved. They are typically enacted as a way to express a desire for all parties to achieve the same goal in the agreed-upon manner. They are intended to be mutually beneficial without involving courts or money. Because they typically have no legal foundation, MOUs are not the most secure agreement for a partnership.
Interconnection security agreement (ISA)	This type of agreement is geared toward the information systems of partnered entities to ensure that the use of inter-organizational technology meets a certain security standard. Because they focus heavily on security, ISAs are often written to be legally binding. ISAs can also support MOUs to increase their security viability.

on Test (handwritten note in left margin)

Risk Awareness

In any sort of business arrangement or third-party integration, all parties should be aware of the inherent risks involved in the relationship. *Risk awareness* involves being consistently informed about the details of day-to-day interoperability. Likewise, all employees should be trained in spotting risk in their own departments, no matter how large or small. When employees evaluate the role they play in a partnership or social media integration, they will get a better idea of the risks that they are susceptible to. Delegating this responsibility will foster a culture of risk awareness and prepare an organization for risk management.

 Note: Risk management is covered in more depth later in the course.

Data Sharing and Backups

In business partnerships and other third-party relationships, data sharing is often integral to the cooperative process. Allowing a trusted party access to your data will hopefully strengthen the support that they can give you in whatever capacity you deem fit. However, even those you trust in a business arrangement should not necessarily be given total access to the data your organization independently owns. Although you may be able to implement some form of access control to limit what is shared, the human element can render these controls ineffective. You should clearly define what you consider unauthorized sharing based on what data must remain strictly confidential, and caution your employees to abide by these regulations. Any policies that discuss data ownership and sharing with third parties may also include legal ramifications for employees who engage in unauthorized sharing.

A similar concern is how you should handle data backups. You may not want to allow your partners to back up all data that you've shared with them. Some sensitive data is considered volatile and should not be kept in any sort of permanent storage capacity. Data that you share and that a partner backs up may fall into the wrong hands, out of your control.

Guidelines for Securely Integrating Systems and Data with Third Parties

 Note: All Guidelines for this lesson are available as checklists from the **Checklist** tile on the LogicalCHOICE Course screen.

Follow these guidelines for securely integrating systems and data with third parties:

- Consider developing and following procedures for on-boarding and off-boarding business partners as the organizational dynamics change.
- Draft the appropriate interoperability agreement for your security needs when working with partners.
- Follow all security policies and procedures defined in the agreement.
- Review agreement requirements to verify compliance and performance standards.
- Exercise discretion in using social media networks when publishing business information to a wide audience.
- Ensure that employees follow best security practices when using social media.
- Encourage risk awareness in all levels of your organization.
- Clearly define data ownership from the onset of a business arrangement.
- Tightly control data sharing, and caution employees not to engage in unauthorized sharing of data.
- Set rules for backing up volatile data so that it does not fall out of your control.

ACTIVITY 7-4
Integrating Systems and Data with Third Parties

Scenario

Develetech has recently been in talks to establish a business partnership with Mixed Messages Media, a marketing firm that specializes in web design. Develetech's new line of Smart TVs is ready for its initial marketing push, and the company wants to reach its demographic primarily through web-based advertising. As Develetech's security administrator, you need to meet the challenges of this arrangement and ensure that your company's relationship with Mixed Messages Media remains a secure one.

1. Before the partnership with Mixed Messages Media begins, you decide to draft standards for on-boarding and off-boarding of partner employees. What are some of the security issues you need to consider when writing this policy?

2. Now that you've drafted on-boarding and off-boarding policies to share with your partner, you're ready to collaborate with Mixed Messages Media on an interoperability agreement. You want your partnership to be legally binding and focus primarily on keeping Develetech's information infrastructure secure. Which type of agreement would best fulfill these requirements?

   ○ ISA

   ○ MOU

   ○ BPA

   ○ SLA

3. As part of Mixed Messages Media's marketing strategy, they have encouraged their employees to take to various social networks in an effort to spread awareness about Develetech's new line of Smart TVs. These marketing employees are using their own personal social media accounts to publicly divulge information about the product that has not yet been released. As a security administrator, what are your concerns?

4. In Develetech's databases there is a great deal of data regarding the new Smart TVs. In order to effectively communicate their marketing push, Mixed Messages Media needs more than just basic information about the product. They require current finalized hardware specifications, as well as a list of finalized software that the TV runs so that they may better tailor the marketing campaign to the appropriate demographic. What sort of security controls and policies do you need Mixed Messages Media to agree to so that they won't be able to compromise the more secretive data in your databases?

ACTIVITY 7-5
Implementing a Physical Security Policy for an Organization (Optional)

Data Files

C:\093022Data\Implementing Compliance and Operational Security\DeveletechSecurityPolicy.rtf

Scenario

As the security administrator for your organization, you have been assigned the task of implementing a security policy. You are basing your policy, *DeveletechSecurityPolicy.rtf*, on a sample template. Currently, the top priority at your organization is physical security, as someone recently broke into company headquarters and stole hardware and data. You need to protect over $100,000 worth of new equipment that is now centrally stored in your computing center. At the minimum, you will be implementing the following security measures in the computing center:

1. Locks will be placed on computer room doors.
2. Blinds will be installed on windows.
3. No computers will be placed by windows.
4. Locks will be placed on windows.
5. Motion-detection and perimeter intruder alarms will be installed.
6. All contractors will be escorted in and out of the facility.

You need to determine what other security recommendations in the *DeveletechSecurityPolicy.rtf* document your organization should adopt, and you need to enforce the policy once it is finalized.

---

1. Which security level does your organization fall under? Why?

2. Besides using blinds and locks on the windows, what else could you recommend using to secure the windows from unauthorized access?

3. Once the motion-detection alarms are installed, what procedure will you need to follow to verify they are working properly?

4. Given the security requirements of this company and the category of risk the computing center falls into, what other physical security recommendations could you make, based on this document?

Summary

In this lesson, you implemented compliance and operational security, including the best practices and user awareness guidelines used to achieve operational security. With this knowledge, you are better prepared to tackle the common security issues related to physical and environmental security, and also to properly support security policy implementations.

Before attending this course, did you consider environmental issues such as HVAC systems and fire prevention, detection, and suppression as part of your organization's information security initiatives?

How do you think security awareness and training can affect an organization?

 Note: Check your LogicalCHOICE Course screen for opportunities to interact with your classmates, peers, and the larger LogicalCHOICE online community about the topics covered in this course or other topics you are interested in. From the Course screen you can also access available resources for a more continuous learning experience.

8 | Risk Management

Lesson Time: 4 hours

Lesson Objectives

In this lesson, you will manage risk. You will:

- Analyze risk.

- Implement vulnerability assessment tools and techniques.

- Scan for vulnerabilities.

- Identify mitigation and deterrent techniques.

Lesson Introduction

Now that you have taken the steps to secure your systems and networks, you will need to properly manage the risk surrounding those systems and networks. In this lesson, you will analyze the risks, assess vulnerabilities, scan systems, and implement mitigation strategies.

Managing risk plays a major role in ensuring a secure environment for an organization. By assessing and identifying specific risks that can cause damage to network components, hardware, and personnel, you can mitigate possible threats and establish the right corrective measures to avoid possible damage to people or systems.

TOPIC A

Risk Analysis

In the early phases of applying security controls, the focus has been on securing an organization as a whole. You have covered all the main hardware, network, and infrastructure components, and now will review the risk assessment process.

How do you know what to protect your organization against? What constitutes a risk? You need to find out what exactly will help you determine what a risk is on your system or network. If you can foresee and analyze some of those risks, then you can avoid some major issues that can come up later. Risk analysis helps you achieve this objective.

Risk Management

In the information management world, risks come in many different forms. If a risk is not managed correctly, it could result in disclosure, modification, loss, destruction, or interruption of a critical asset. *Risk management* is a cyclical process that includes four phases:

* Identify and assess risks that exist in a system.
* Analyze the potential impact risks will have on a system.
* Formulate a strategy on how to respond to risks.
* Mitigate the impact of risks for future security.

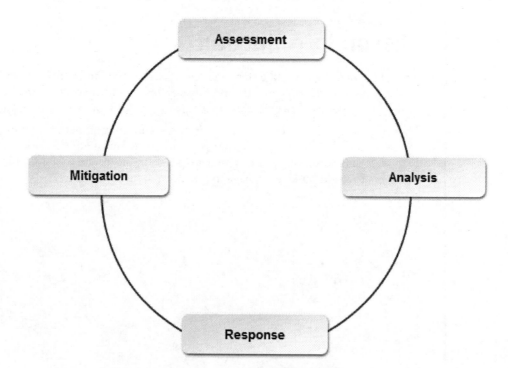

Figure 8–1: The cyclical process of risk management.

Security Assessment Types

Assessing an organization's security infrastructure will determine whether current security measures are acceptable. The three general categories of assessment are described in the following table.

Assessment Type	Description
Risk	A risk assessment is an evaluation of an organization, a portion of an organization, an information system, or system components to assess the security risk. Risk assessments are usually performed as part of the risk analysis process to identify what parts or functions of the business pose the highest risk.
Threat	A threat assessment is an evaluation of known threats to an organization and the potential damage to business operations and systems. Threat assessment is usually performed as part of the risk analysis process, but could be performed at any time to verify that current security controls are still operating successfully, and are detecting and managing threats. An important element in this assessment is determining the path or means by which an attacker can carry out a security attack or *threat vector*.
Vulnerability	A vulnerability assessment is an evaluation used to find security weaknesses within an organization. Vulnerability assessments can be performed on an organization's physical security implementations and all networks, hardware, and software.

Types of Risk

Security risks are often identified as natural, man-made, or system risks, depending on their source. The following table lists examples of each.

Risk Type	Description
Natural	Natural risks are related to weather or other uncontrollable events that are residual occurrences of the activities of nature. Different types of natural disasters include: • Earthquakes • Wildfires • Flooding • Blizzards • Tsunamis • Hurricanes • Tornadoes • Landslides

Risk Type	Description
Man-made	Man-made risks are residual occurrences of individual or collective human activity. Man-made events can be caused intentionally or unintentionally. Intentional man-made attacks include: • Arson • Terrorist attacks • Political unrest • Break-ins • Theft of equipment and/or data • Equipment damage • File destruction • Information disclosure Unintentional man-made risks include: • User computing mistakes • Social networking and cloud computing • Excessive employee illnesses or epidemics • Information disclosure
System	System risks are related to any weakness or vulnerability found within a network, service, application, or device. System risks include: • Unsecured mobile devices • Unstable virtualization environments • Unsecured network devices • Email vulnerabilities, such as viruses and spam • Account management vulnerabilities, such as unassigned privileges

Components of Risk Analysis

Risk is the likelihood that a threat can exploit a vulnerability to cause some type of damage. Therefore, when you perform an analysis to determine if a risk exists, you need to not only identify potential threats, but also determine if there are vulnerabilities in your systems that those threats could exploit. Once you are sure that a risk exists, you can determine the severity of the risk based on how much damage the risk could cause and how likely it is to occur.

Vulnerability–Assessed Threats

Some examples of vulnerability-assessed threats may include the following:

- If a business is located next to railroad tracks and a train derails, leaking toxic fluids, the business might be forced into inactivity for a number of days.
- If key manufacturing staff express their plans to strike, they may threaten to damage equipment beforehand to heighten the impact of their impending actions.
- A key supplier may be unable to provide raw materials for the production of an organization's principal products.

Phases of Risk Analysis

When determining how to protect computer networks, computer installations, and information, *risk analysis* is the security process used for assessing risk damages that can affect an organization.

There are six phases in the risk analysis process, described in the following table.

Risk Analysis Process Phase	Description
1. Asset identification	Identifying the assets that require protection and determining the value of the assets.
2. Vulnerability identification	Identifying vulnerabilities so the analyst can confirm where asset protection problems exist. Locating weaknesses exposes the critical areas that are most susceptible to vulnerabilities. Vulnerability scanning is a method used to determine weaknesses in systems. This method can, however, produce false positives which tend to initiate reasons for concern, even when there are no actual issues or weaknesses in the system.
3. Threat assessment	Once vulnerabilities are understood, the threats that may take advantage of or exploit those vulnerabilities are determined.
4. Probability quantification	Quantifying the likelihood or probability that threats will exploit vulnerabilities.
5. Impact analysis	Once the probabilities are determined, the impact of these potential threats needs to be evaluated. This can include either the impact of recovering from the damage, or the impact of implementing possible preventive measures.
6. Countermeasures determination	Determining and developing countermeasures to eliminate or reduce risks. The countermeasures must be economically sound and provide the expected level of protection. In other words, the countermeasures must not cost more than the expected loss caused by threats that exploit vulnerabilities.

on the Test

Risk Analysis Methods

The following table describes a number of methods that are used to analyze risk.

Method	Description
Qualitative	Qualitative analysis methods use descriptions and words to measure the amount and impact of risk. For example, ratings can be high, medium, or low based on the criteria used to analyze the impact. Qualitative analysis is generally scenario based. A weakness of qualitative risk analysis lies with its sometimes subjective and untestable methodology.
Quantitative	Quantitative analysis is based completely on numeric values. Data is analyzed using historic records, experiences, industry best practices and records, statistical theories, testing, and experiments. This methodology may be weak in situations where risk is not easily quantifiable.
Semi-quantitative	The semi-quantitative analysis method uses a description that is associated with a numeric value. It is neither fully qualitative nor quantitative. This methodology attempts to find a middle ground between the previous two risk analysis types.

Risk Calculation

Risk calculation focuses on financial and operational loss impact and locates threat exploitation indicators in an organization. Risk calculation can be viewed as a formula that takes into account the worth of each asset, the potential impact of each risk, and the likelihood of each threat, and then weighs that against the potential costs of alleviating system vulnerabilities. Organizations may use this process to determine the *single loss expectancy (SLE)* or the *annual loss expectancy (ALE)* for each risk identified. The SLE value represents the financial loss that is expected from a specific adverse event. The ALE value is calculated by multiplying an SLE by its *annual rate of occurrence (ARO)* to determine the total cost of a risk to an organization on an annual basis.

Calculating Risk

A company might calculate that a certain system in its demilitarized zone (DMZ) has almost a 90 percent probability of experiencing a port scan attack on a daily basis. However, although the threat level is high, the company does not consider the system to be at much risk of damage from the threat of a scan. The cost of hardening the system to completely prevent the scan far outweighs the potential losses due to the identified risk.

On the other hand, a company might determine that its server room is at a high risk of complete loss due to a natural disaster and that the cost of such a loss would be catastrophic for the organization. Although the likelihood of the disaster threat is quite low, the overall impact is so great that the company maintains an expensive alternate site that it can switch operations to in the event of such an emergency.

Vulnerability Tables

A simple vulnerability table is often a strategic tool for completing a vulnerability assessment. The following table lists details associated with various vulnerabilities.

Vulnerability	Identification Source	Risk of Occurrence (1 = Low; 5 = High)	Impact Estimate (US Dollars)	Mitigation
Flood damage	Physical plant	5	$95,000	Physical adjustments and flood insurance
Electrical failure	Physical plant	2	$100,000	Generator, Uninterruptible Power Supply (UPS)
Flu epidemic	Personnel	4	$200,000	Flu shots

Using a table allows planners to identify the likelihood of threats or vulnerabilities, record the possible impact, and then prioritize mitigation efforts. Mitigation helps reduce the impact of an exploited vulnerability. A loss of power has a relatively high risk with a reasonable mitigation effort, consisting of a one-time expenditure to purchase a backup generator.

If there were two additional columns in the table, the assessment would be more useful, as in the following example.

Vulnerability	Cost of Mitigation	Vulnerability Impact Post Mitigation
Electrical failure	$500 for generator	$0

By adding these extra columns, business continuity planners would be able to evaluate the vulnerabilities, propose mitigation, and evaluate the vulnerabilities by the residual risks after mitigation.

> **Note:** For additional information, check out the LearnTO **Calculate Risk** presentation from the **LearnTO** tile on the LogicalCHOICE Course screen.

Risk Response Strategies

Once a risk is identified, you may examine a response strategy to determine the appropriate action to take. Multiple strategies may even be combined into a single response. There are five common strategies used, as described in the following table.

Response Strategy	Description
Avoidance	This is used to eliminate the risk altogether by eliminating the cause. This may be as simple as putting an end to the operation or entity that is at risk, like shutting down a server that is a frequent target of attack.
Transference	This is used to allocate the responsibility of risk to another agency, or to a third party, such as an insurance company.
Acceptance	This is the acknowledgement and acceptance of the risk and consequences that come with it, if that risk were to materialize. Acceptance does not mean leaving a system completely vulnerable, but recognizing that the risk involved is not entirely avoidable.
Mitigation	These techniques protect against possible attacks and are implemented when the impact of a potential risk is substantial. Mitigation may come in the form of active defenses like intrusion detection systems (IDSs), or cautionary measures like backing up at-risk data.
Deterrence	This involves applying changes to the conditions to make it less likely or enticing for an attacker to launch an attack. Deterrent factors may include physical security like checkpoints inside and outside of a building. A virtual intruder might be deterred in knowing that a strong system defense may be able to track and identify them to the authorities.

on the exam

Risk Mitigation and Control Types

Risk can be mitigated by implementing the appropriate security controls. The following table describes three major control types

Control Type	Description
Technical controls	Hardware or software installations that are implemented to monitor and prevent threats and attacks to computer systems and services. For example, installing and configuring a network firewall is a type of technical control.
Management controls	Procedures implemented to monitor the adherence to organizational security policies. These controls are specifically designed to control the operational efficiencies of a particular area and to monitor security policy compliance. For example, annual or regularly scheduled security scans and audits to check for compliance with security policies.
Operational controls	Security measures implemented to safeguard all aspects of day-to-day operations, functions, and activities. For example, door locks and guards at entrances are controls used to permit only authorized personnel into a building.
Loss controls	Also called *damage controls*, these are security measures implemented to protect key assets from being damaged. This includes reducing the chances of a loss occurring, and reducing the severity of a loss when one occurs. For example, fire extinguishers and sprinkler systems can reduce property damage in the event of a fire.

on the exam

ACTIVITY 8-1
Examining Risk Analysis

Scenario

Develetech Industries is a well-known home electronics company based in fictional Greene City, Richland. Lately, there have been concerns regarding the security of the server room located on the first floor within the main headquarters building. The high-business-value assets identified in this room are the human resources servers with sensitive employee identification data and the client financial data server. The room is situated next to the main lobby, contains no windows, and is access-controlled with a numeric keypad. Now that you've identified the assets that need protecting, you have been asked to conduct a full risk analysis of the server room's physical security.

---

1. What are some obvious vulnerabilities surrounding the Develetech Industries server room, and what others would you investigate?

2. Based on the known vulnerabilities for the computer room, what potential threats exist?

3. What factors will affect the likelihood of these threats succeeding?

4. What do you think the potential impact would be if an unauthorized access attempt was successful?

5. What risk mitigation strategies would you use in this situation to reduce the risks surrounding the physical access of the server room?

TOPIC B

Implement Vulnerability Assessment Tools and Techniques

To properly assess threats and vulnerabilities, you will have to familiarize yourself with the various tools and techniques required to protect the organization from these threats. In this topic, you will assess threats and vulnerabilities using various tools and techniques.

The first step in building a strong security infrastructure is for you to assess the various threats and vulnerabilities the organization faces. Then, you will be better able to identify and implement the ideal tools and techniques to handle these situations.

Vulnerability Assessment Techniques

Assessing the current state of security implementations for an organization is crucial to ensuring all threats and vulnerabilities have been addressed. The following table describes the common techniques that can be used to carry out security assessments.

Technique	Description
Review the *baseline report*	A baseline report is a collection of security and configuration settings that are to be applied to a particular system or network in the organization. The baseline report is a benchmark against which you can compare other systems in your network. When creating a baseline for a particular computer, the settings you decide to include will depend on its operating system and its function in your organization, and should include manufacturer recommendations.
Perform *code reviews*	Regular code reviews should be conducted for all applications in development. Reviews may be carried out manually by a developer, or automatically using a source code analysis tool. Both methods are useful in identifying potential weaknesses in an application that may eventually lead to an attack if not corrected.
Determine *attack surface*	The attack surface is the combination of all points in a system or application that are exposed and available to attackers. By reducing the points in an attack surface, you will be less vulnerable to possible attacks.
Review the security architecture	A *security architecture review* is an evaluation of an organization's current security infrastructure model and measures. Regular reviews are important to determine if current systems and critical assets are secured properly, and if potential threats and vulnerabilities have been addressed. During this review, areas of concern are targeted and further evaluated to make sure security measures meet the current needs.
Review the security design	Security design reviews are completed before a security implementation is applied. Using the architectural review results, the reviewer can determine if the security solution will in fact fulfill the needs of an organization.

Vulnerability Assessment Tools

When assessing security for your system or systems, there are many software tools that are available. Tools can be found to scan for and detect a very wide range of vulnerabilities and specific hard-to-detect vulnerabilities. By running these tools, you can see exactly what potential attackers would see if they assessed your systems. However, their usefulness to you is dependent on how well you can interpret the results of security assessment tools. When you become acquainted with what to expect and what to look out for in a tool's results, you'll find it easier to remove any vulnerabilities in your system.

The following table lists several different types of tools available for assessing your systems.

Tool Type	Use
Protocol analyzer	Implement to assess traffic on a network and what it reveals about the protocols being used.
Sniffer (packet analyzer)	Implement to capture and assess individual data packets sent over a network.
Vulnerability scanner	Implement this application to assess your systems, networks, and applications for weaknesses.
Port scanner	Implement to assess the current state of all ports on your network, and to detect potential open ports that may pose risks to your organization.
Honeypot / Honeynet	Implement this environment to redirect suspicious activity away from legitimate network systems and onto an isolated system where you can monitor it safely.

Honeypots

A *honeypot* is a security tool that lures attackers away from legitimate network resources while tracking their activities. Honeypots appear and act as legitimate components of the network but are actually secure lockboxes where security professionals can block the intrusion and begin logging activity for use in court, or even launch a counterattack. The act of luring individuals in could potentially be perceived as entrapment or violate the code of ethics of your organization. These legal and ethical issues should be discussed with your organization's legal counsel and human resources department.

Honeypots can be software emulation programs, hardware decoys, or an entire dummy network, known as a *honeynet*. A honeypot implementation often includes some kind of IDS to facilitate monitoring and tracking of intruders. Some dedicated honeypot software packages can be specialized types of IDSs.

> Access the Checklist tile on your LogicalCHOICE course screen for reference information and job aids on How to Implement Vulnerability Assessment Tools and Techniques.

ACTIVITY 8-2
Capturing Network Data with Microsoft Message Analyzer

Data Files
C:\093022Data\Risk Management\MessageAnalyzer64.msi

 Note: Microsoft updates some of their security tools on a regular basis. The version of the tool this activity was written to may not be the same version you are using. If this is the case, the screenshots and object names may be different than what you see in your environment.

Scenario
Before you begin assessing specific vulnerabilities that exist on your network, you want to capture data under normal network traffic conditions. This will give you a baseline to which you can compare any future traffic that may indicate a new weak point in your network.

You will use the Microsoft® Message Analyzer tool to run a capture/trace scenario on your server's link layer. Message Analyzer presents a detailed view of individual protocol messages and is useful for troubleshooting various system problems. Because secure web connections are such a common occurrence on your network, you'll filter the captured network data to show only SSL/TLS messages. You'll then review an individual message to learn more about your network's day-to-day secure operations.

1. Install Microsoft Message Analyzer.
    a) Open File Explorer and navigate to **C:\093022Data\Risk Management**.
    b) Double-click the **MessageAnalyzer64** file.
    c) In the **Microsoft Message Analyzer Setup** window, select **Next**.
    d) On the **End-User License Agreement** page, check the **I accept the terms in the License Agreement** check box and select **Next**.
    e) On the **Custom Setup** page, select **Next**.
    f) On the **Ready to install Microsoft Message Analyzer** page, select **Install**.
    g) When installation completes, select **Finish**.
    h) Open the **Search Charm** and type *message*
    i) Select **Microsoft Message Analyzer** to open it.

    j) In the **Microsoft Message Analyzer** dialog box, select **Do not update items** and select **OK**.

2. Perform a sample capture of network traffic.

a) In Microsoft Message Analyzer, in the navigation pane on the left, select **Capture / Trace**.

b) In the **Trace Scenarios** section, select **Local Link Layer (Windows 8.1/Windows Server 2012 R2)**.

c) At the bottom right of the window, select the **Start With** button.

Microsoft Message Analyzer begins capturing network traffic.

3. Generate HTTPS traffic on the network.
   a) Open Internet Explorer.
   b) In the **Address** bar, enter *https://www.google.com*
   c) In the **Security Alert** dialog box, select **OK**.
   d) Add the site to the trusted sites zone.
   e) If necessary, add **gstatic.com** and **apis.google.com** to the trusted sites zone.

    Note: Google uses the **gstatic.com** domain to host static content like JavaScript and images to reduce bandwidth usage. The **apis.google.com** subdomain handles user interaction with Google's many services.

   f) Verify that you have successfully connected to the Google home page.

4. Stop the capture and review the capture log.
   a) From the taskbar, select **Administrator: Microsoft Message Analyzer** to display the window.
   b) Select **Stop**.

   c) In the **View Filter** group on the ribbon, select in the **Enter a filter expression, such as** text box and type *tcp.port==443* to filter the results by SSL/TLS traffic.

▼ Filter	tcp.port==443		▼	⚡ Remove ▾	▼
🔍 Find			Apply	▼ Library ▾	Quick
Set Mode			Filter	🕘 History ▾	Filter ▾
		View Filter*			

   d) Select **Apply Filter**.
   e) In the list of messages, verify that the messages have either a **Source** or **Destination** that is your server's internal IP address. The IP address in the corresponding column is the address of **google.com** or one of its subdomains.
   f) Verify that the **Module** for each message is either **TCP** or **TLS**.
   g) In the list of messages, select any of the messages to view more details about the SSL/TLS messages you sent and received over the network. The **Details** pane and **Message Data** pane provide unique information for each message.
   h) When you have finished, close Microsoft Message Analyzer without saving the capture.
   i) Close Internet Explorer.

TOPIC C

Scan for Vulnerabilities

You just performed the threat and vulnerability assessment for your business. Based on the findings of the assessment, you may have to intensify your security policies to reduce vulnerabilities. In this topic, you will scan for vulnerabilities.

IT departments in businesses today strive to defend themselves against threats and vulnerabilities to protect the valuable information and intellectual property they possess. When valuable information falls into the wrong hands, it may result in major disruptions to the business. To avoid losing valuable information, IT departments should continually scan for vulnerabilities and threats inside and outside their organizations.

The Hacking Process

Understanding the general steps of the hacking process will help you recognize attacks in progress and stop them before they cause damage. The following table describes each step.

Hacking Step	Description
Footprinting	Also known as *profiling*, in this step, the attacker chooses a target and begins to gather information that is publicly or readily available. With basic tools, such as a web browser and an Internet connection, an attacker can often determine the IP addresses of a company's Domain Name System (DNS) servers; the range of addresses assigned to the company; names, email addresses, and phone numbers of contacts within the company; and the company's physical address. Attackers use dumpster diving, or searching through garbage, to find sensitive information in paper form. The names and titles of people within the organization enable the attacker to begin social engineering to gain even more private information. The Hypertext Markup Language (HTML) code of a company's web page can provide information, such as IP addresses and names of web servers, operating system versions, file paths, and names of developers or administrators. DNS servers are common footprinting targets because, if not properly secured, they can provide a detailed map of an organization's entire network infrastructure.
Scanning	Also called *banner grabbing*, the second step is to scan an organization's infrastructure or systems to see where vulnerabilities might lie. In this step, the attacker may use a network mapping tool such as Nmap or perform a *ping sweep* to determine which host IP addresses in the company's IP address range are active. The attacker will scan the target's border routers, firewalls, web servers, and other systems that are directly connected to the Internet to see which services are listening on which ports and to determine the operating systems and manufacturers of each system. Additionally, the attacker might begin a war dialing campaign to determine if there are any vulnerabilities in the organization's telecommunications system. The attacker might even try war driving, which involves driving up to the company with a laptop and a wireless card to see if there are any wireless access points (APs) to provide a way into the network.
Enumerating	During this step, the attacker will try to gain access to resources or other information, such as users, groups, and shares. The attacker can obtain this information through social engineering, network sniffing, dumpster diving, watching a user log in, or searching for credentials written down at user workstations. If the attacker can obtain a valid user name, he can begin the process of cracking the user's password.

Hacking Step	Description
Attacking	Attacking is the last phase of the hack, in which the hacker attempts to cause damage or a service disruption, or to steal or destroy sensitive information using various hacking tools.

Network Mappers

Network mapping tools are used to explore and gather network layout information from a network. A network map can be used to illustrate the physical connectivity of networks within an organization, and can provide detailed information on hardware, services, and traffic paths.

Ethical Hacking

In *ethical hacking*, a planned and approved attempt is made to penetrate the security defenses of a system in order to identify vulnerabilities. In an ethical hack, a friendly or designated hacker (a white hat) assumes the mindset of an attacker and attempts to breach security using any and all tools and techniques an attacker might employ. It may be performed by an employee on the company's behalf, or by an outside firm contracted by the company.

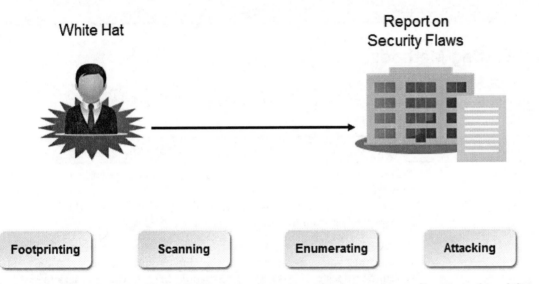

Figure 8-2: An ethical hacker with consent to breach a system in order to discover vulnerabilities.

> **Note:** Performing an ethical hack is a perfect illustration of the classical adage, "Know your enemy." Understanding the hacking process and tools gives organizations a deeper and more practical appreciation of the dangers they can face from unscrupulous attackers.

Vulnerability Scanning and Penetration Testing

When a company tests a computer system or network, it is generally testing a production network that is live; security tests are rarely conducted on offline or test networks. A *vulnerability scan* uses passive tools and security utilities to identify and quantify vulnerabilities within a system, such as lacking security controls and common misconfigurations, but does not directly test the security features of that system. Vulnerability scans may be credentialed, in that they implement credentials in order to ascertain vulnerabilities at the highest privilege levels, or they may be non-credentialed, meaning they run without credentials to see what a hacker would see at a lower level. Like other scanning mechanisms, vulnerability scanners run the risk of producing false positives and false negatives.

A true *penetration test*, or pen test, uses active tools and security utilities to evaluate security by simulating an attack on a system. A penetration test will verify that a threat exists, then will actively test and bypass security controls, and will finally exploit vulnerabilities on the system. Penetration testing is less common and more intrusive than vulnerability scanning. While the information gained from a penetration test is often more thorough, there is a risk that the system may suffer actual damage because of the security breach.

Types of Vulnerability Scans

A vulnerability scan is one of the first steps in either an attack or an ethical hack. There are two main types of vulnerability scans: scans for general vulnerabilities, such as scans for open ports; and application-specific scans, such as a password crack against a particular operating system. You will use different scanning tools depending upon the type of scan you wish to run.

Note: There are a variety of specialized web-based scanning services, such as ShieldsUP® from Gibson Research Corporation, available at **www.grc.com**.

You can also consider registering with security event aggregators, such as **www.dshield.org** or **www.mynetwatchman.com**. They will also analyze your firewall logs and act as fully automated abuse escalation/management systems.

Box Testing Methods

When conducting a penetration test, the organization must examine the different testing methods and determine what information the tester will be given beforehand. The following table describes the three main penetration test types.

Test Type	Description
Black box test	This refers to a situation where the tester is given no specific information about the structure of the system being tested. The tester may know what a system does, but now how it does it. This type of test would fall into the footprinting or scanning phase of the hacking process.
Grey box test	This refers to a situation where the tester has partial knowledge of internal architectures and systems, or other preliminary information about the system being tested. This type of test would fall into the enumerating phase of the hacking process.
White box test	This refers to a situation when the tester knows about all aspects of the system and understands the function and design of the system before the test is conducted. This type of test is sometimes conducted as a follow-up to a black box test to fully evaluate flaws discovered during the black box test. This type of test would fall into the attacking phase of the hacking process.

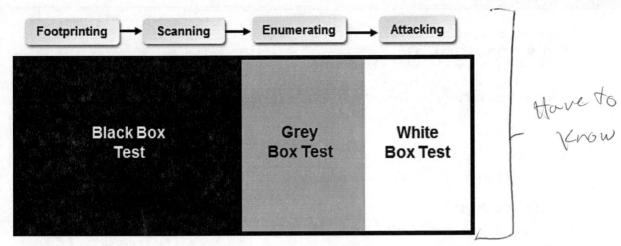

Figure 8–3: The various box testing methods and where they belong in the hacking process.

Security Utilities

Any security or network tool can be used for ethical or unethical purposes. To perform an ethical hack, you will need to use the same tools employed by attackers. Some tools are generally available by downloading them from the Internet, and some must be purchased from vendors. Because tools and utilities are constantly changing, it is important to continually research the available tools and their functions.

There are many different tools available for different security tasks, and some have multiple uses. The following table gives some examples.

Security Utility Type	Typical Tools
Vulnerability scanning	Microsoft Baseline Security Analyzer (MBSA), Nessus®, SAINT, Nmap Security Scanner, GFI LANguard™, OpenVAS
Port scanning	Nmap Security Scanner, Snort, Netcat, SuperScan, ShieldsUP, hping
Password scanning and cracking	John the Ripper, Cain & Abel, THC Hydra, pwdump, Ophcrack, Medusa
Exploits, Trojan horses, and other "stress testers"	Metasploit, Social Engineer Toolkit, w3af, Core Impact, sqlmap
Intrusion detection	Snort, NFR® BackOfficer Friendly, IDScenter, Fport, OSSIM
Network and security administration	Webmin, Tripwire®, Bastille, PuTTY, HiSecWeb
Protocol analyzer, or packet sniffer	Wireshark, NetStumbler, dsniff, OmniPeek, Ettercap, Microsoft Message Analyzer, tcpdump, WinDump, Cain & Abel

 Access the Checklist tile on your LogicalCHOICE course screen for reference information and job aids on How to Scan for Vulnerabilities.

ACTIVITY 8-3
Scanning for Port Vulnerabilities

Data Files

C:\093022Data\Risk Management\nmap-6.40-setup.exe

Before You Begin

You will work with a partner in this activity. The WinPcap driver was already installed in a previous lesson.

Scenario

As Develetech's security administrator, you need to make sure your new Microsoft® Windows Server® 2012 servers are secure by scanning them for open ports. Develetech's IT department has had problems in the past with attackers gaining access to applications on servers by getting through the firewall and accessing open ports on the servers. You have already hardened your servers and now want to check your work.

Before connecting the new Windows Server 2012 R2 servers to your network, you need to make sure not only that the base operating system is hardened, but also that no unnecessary ports are open on the servers to minimize the likelihood of attacks. You are responsible for scanning your Windows Server 2012 R2 computer. You will initiate the scan with Nmap, a port scanning utility. Nmap will identify the common ports that are open on your server, and with this knowledge, you can better account for some of the vulnerabilities in your network.

---

1. Install Nmap.
   a) Open File Explorer and navigate to **C:\093022Data\Risk Management**.
   b) Double-click the **nmap-6.40-setup** file.
   c) In the **Nmap Setup** wizard, select **I Agree**.
   d) On the **Choose Components** page, select **Next**.
   e) On the **Choose Install Location** page, select **Install**.
   f) In the **WinPcap (Nmap) 4.1.2 Setup** message box, select **No**.
   g) When installation of Nmap completes, select **Next**.
   h) On the **Create Shortcuts** page, select **Next**.
   i) Select **Finish** to close the wizard.

2. Use Nmap to scan for open ports on your partner's server.
   a) On the Desktop, double-click the **Nmap - Zenmap GUI** shortcut to open it.

   b) Maximize the **Zenmap** window.
   c) In the **Target** text box, type *Server##*, where *##* is your partner's student number.
   d) Select the **Profile** drop-down list and select **Quick scan**.
   e) In the top right of the **Zenmap** window, select the **Scan** button to start the scan.

3. Examine the scan results.

a) When the scan is complete, verify that several TCP ports were detected as open, indicating several vulnerable areas on your partner's server.

```
Starting Nmap 6.40 ( http://nmap.org ) at 2014-02-10 16:46 Eastern Standard Time
Nmap scan report for Server100 (192.168.37.100)
Host is up (0.00s latency).
Not shown: 88 filtered ports
PORT       STATE SERVICE
21/tcp     open  ftp
53/tcp     open  domain
80/tcp     open  http
88/tcp     open  kerberos-sec
135/tcp    open  msrpc
139/tcp    open  netbios-ssn
389/tcp    open  ldap
443/tcp    open  https
445/tcp    open  microsoft-ds
49153/tcp  open  unknown
49155/tcp  open  unknown
49157/tcp  open  unknown
MAC Address: 24:BE:05:17:83:64 (Hewlett Packard)

Nmap done: 1 IP address (1 host up) scanned in 2.30 seconds
```

b) Close **Zenmap** without saving the report, then close File Explorer.

ACTIVITY 8-4
Scanning for Password Vulnerabilities

Data Files

C:\093022Data\Risk Management\ca_setup.exe

 Note: Cain & Abel is updated regularly. The version of the tool this activity was written to may not be the same version you are using. If this is the case, the screenshots and object names may be different than what you see in your environment.

Before You Begin

WinPcap is installed.

Scenario

Your boss at Develetech has asked that you verify that all client information is secure in order to ensure that no outside attempts to gather clients' confidential financial information will succeed. As part of your security audit, you want to make sure that all users, especially administrators, are using secure passwords and not common dictionary words. Users who have elevated rights and permissions, like administrators, can put an organization at risk if their credentials are especially vulnerable to cracking attempts. You will use Cain & Abel, a common password-cracking utility, to confirm the strength of your employees' passwords.

 Note: You can use Cain & Abel to perform brute force password discovery where it will attempt to determine more secure passwords, meaning those that consist of alphanumeric characters, symbols, and mixed casing. Unfortunately, brute force password detection can take an extremely long time and requires a large amount of computing resources. Since this isn't feasible in a classroom, a dictionary attack is performed in this activity.

1. Install the Cain & Abel utility.
   a) In File Explorer, verify that you are in **C:\093022Data\Risk Management**.
   b) Double-click the **ca_setup** file.
   c) In the **Cain & Abel 4.9.54 Installation** dialog box, on the **Cain & Abel 4.9.54** page, select **Next**.
   d) On the **License Agreement** page, select **Next**.
   e) On the **Select Destination Directory** page, observe that **C:\Program Files (x86)\Cain** is the default location and select **Next**.
   f) On the **Select ProgMan Group** page, select **Next**.
   g) On the **Ready to Install!** page, select **Next**.
   h) When installation completes, select **Finish**.
   i) In the **WinPcap Installation** message box, select **Don't install**.

2. Load the local SAM database.
   a) On the Desktop, double-click the **Cain** shortcut to open it.

Cain

b) In the **Cain** message box, select **OK**.

c) In the **Cain** window, select the **Cracker** tab.

File   View   Configure   Tools   Help

| Decoders | Network | Sniffer | Cracker | Traceroute | CCDU | Wireless | Query |

---

d) In the left pane, select **LM & NTLM Hashes**.

e) On the toolbar, select the **Add to list** plus sign. ✚

f) In the **Add NT Hashes from** dialog box, check the **Include Password History Hashes** check box and select **Next**.

g) Verify that the list of system user names appears in the right pane.

 Note: If the Abel service fails to start, you can safely continue with the rest of the steps in this activity.

3. Scan for the password of the Administrator account.

a) Select the **Administrator** account.

User Name	LM Password	< 8	NT Password	LM Hash	NT Hash
✖ Administrator	* empty *	*		AAD3B435B51...	0E6613E827D6...
🔑 Guest	* empty *	*	* empty *	AAD3B435B51...	31D6CFE0D16...
✖ krbtgt	* empty *	*		AAD3B435B51...	B90FA5860902...

b) Right-click and select **Dictionary Attack→NTLM Hashes**.

c) In the **Dictionary Attack** dialog box, in the **Dictionary** section, right-click and select **Add to list**.

d) In the **Open** dialog box, verify that **C:\Program Files (x86)\Cain** is the current folder, and double-click the **Wordlists** folder.

e) Double-click the **Wordlist** text file.

f) Verify that the **File** column contains the full path to the **Wordlist.txt** file.

Dictionary

File

▦ C:\Program Files (x86)\Cain\Wordlists\Wordlist.txt

 Note: This text file contains hundreds of thousands of words that Cain & Abel uses in various forms to try and crack the password.

g) Select **Start**.

h) Verify that the password of the Administrator is not displayed on completion of the scan, which indicates that the current password is secure from a dictionary attack.

```
                          Dictionary Attack                              [X]

 Dictionary
  File                                                Position
  √ C:\Program Files (x86)\Cain\Wordlists\Wordlist.txt   3456292


 Key Rate                              Options
 [                    ]                 ☑ As Is (Password)
                                       ☑ Reverse (PASSWORD - DROWSSAP)
 Dictionary Position                   ☑ Double (Pass - PassPass)
 [                    ]                 ☑ Lowercase (PASSWORD - password)
                                       ☑ Uppercase (Password - PASSWORD)
                                       ☑ Num. sub. perms (Pass,P4ss,Pa5s,...P45s...P455)
 Current password                      ☐ Case perms (Pass,pAss,paSs,...PaSs...PASS)
 [                    ]                 ☑ Two numbers Hybrid Brute (Pass0....Pass99)

 Attack stopped!
 0 of 1 hashes cracked



                                                    [ Start ]   [ Exit ]
```

i) Select **Exit** to close the **Dictionary Attack** dialog box.
j) Close the **Cain** window and select **Yes** to confirm.

ACTIVITY 8-5
Scanning for General Vulnerabilities

Before You Begin

MBSA 2.3 has been installed. A baseline security scan has been performed.

Scenario

At Develetech, you have already hardened all of your servers and other computer systems, but a new regulation requires that you also perform periodic vulnerability scans to audit system security. Periodic scans will enable you to see what vulnerabilities lie in your network, and also keep track of any changes that have been made to your systems. Because you have Windows Server 2012 R2 servers installed on your network, you already used Microsoft Baseline Security Analyzer as a service scanning tool during the hardening process. Now that you have added various services to your server, you will also use this tool for periodic vulnerability scans so you can compare them to previous scans. Detecting a change in vulnerabilities over time will keep you up-to-date and informed about your servers' security needs.

---

1. Use MBSA to scan your server for vulnerabilities.

   a) On the Desktop, double-click the **Microsoft Baseline Security Analyzer 2.3** shortcut to open it.

   b) In the **Check computers for common security misconfigurations** section, select the **Scan a computer** link.

   c) Verify that your computer name appears in the **Computer name** text box. Uncheck the **Check for SQL administrative vulnerabilities** check box. Uncheck the **Check for security updates** check box.

   d) Select **Start Scan**.

2. Analyze the results of the vulnerability scan.

   a) For any of the results listed, select a **How to correct this** link to open a browser window with more information on potential fixes for system vulnerabilities. When finished examining this information, close the browser window.

   b) Scroll down, and in the **Internet Information Services (IIS) Scan Results** section, under **Administrative Vulnerabilities**, notice that Parent Paths is generating an issue. Parent Paths is disabled by default in IIS 8.5, so this does not pose a security risk; however, the current version of MBSA does not recognize this, so an issue is generated.

Internet Information Services (IIS) Scan Results

Administrative Vulnerabilities

Score	Issue	Result
⊗	Parent Paths	Parent paths are enabled in some web sites and/or virtual directories. What was scanned Result details How to correct this
✓	IIS Lockdown Tool	The IIS Lockdown tool was developed for IIS 4.0, 5.0, and 5.1, and is not needed for new Windows Server 2003 installations running IIS 6.0. What was scanned
✓	Sample Applications	IIS sample applications are not installed. What was scanned
✓	IISAdmin Virtual Directory	IISADMPWD virtual directory is not present. What was scanned
✓	MSADC and Scripts Virtual Directories	The MSADC and Scripts virtual directories are not present. What was scanned

c) At the top left of the window, select the **Back** button twice.

3. Compare the report with the baseline scan.

   a) In the left pane, select the **View security reports** link.

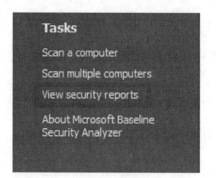

   b) On the **Choose a security scan report to view** page, next to the **Sort order** drop-down list, select the **Click here to see all security reports** link.

   Sort order: | Scan date (descending) ▼ | Click here to see all security reports

   c) From the report list, select the earliest report.

   d) On the **Report Details** page, under **Windows Scan Results**, scroll down to review the report.

   e) In the **Internet Information Services (IIS) Scan Results** section, in the **Administrative Vulnerabilities** section, notice that IIS common files were not installed at the time and were generating an incomplete scan.

   f) At the bottom of the **Microsoft Baseline Security Analyzer 2.3** window, select the **Previous security report** link to compare the changes.

 Previous security report

   g) Close the **Microsoft Baseline Security Analyzer 2.3** window.

TOPIC D

Mitigation and Deterrent Techniques

In the previous topic, you scanned for security threats and vulnerabilities. Scanning for threats and vulnerabilities will help you prevent most of them from materializing. In this topic, you will mitigate and deter threats and vulnerabilities.

No matter how secure a system may be, unfortunate events continue to happen. The IT security team should plan for worst-case scenarios and should have strong mitigation and deterrent techniques in place, should something go wrong.

Security Posture

Security posture is the position an organization takes on securing all aspects of its business. Strong security posture includes an initial baseline configuration for the organization, continuous security monitoring methods and remediation techniques, as well as strict mitigation and deterrent methods.

DLP

Data loss/leak prevention (DLP) is a software solution that detects and prevents sensitive information in a system from being stolen or otherwise falling into the wrong hands. The software actively monitors data in any state—whether in use or at rest—and detects any unauthorized attempts to destroy, move, or copy that data. If any suspicious activity is detected, some DLP software is able to block users from interacting with data in specific ways. For example, a security administrator might put a DLP system in place on the corporate network to detect any attempt to send confidential files over email, and then prevent that email from reaching its destination. In this respect, data loss prevention has the opposite goal of an intrusion detection/prevention system; instead of focusing on inbound attacks, DLP software protects outbound data. The malicious transfer of data from one system to another is called *data exfiltration*.

Data Loss vs. Leakage

Although related, data loss and data leakage are not entirely the same. Data that is leaked is transfered to unauthorized parties, but may still exist in its original form and location. Data that is lost is transfered to unauthorized parties *and* is no longer in its owners' possession.

Detection Controls and Prevention Controls

Detection controls are implemented to monitor a situation or activity, and react to any irregular activities by bringing the issue to the attention of administrators. Prevention controls are similar to detection controls, but instead of just monitoring for irregularities, they can react by blocking access completely—thereby preventing damage to a system, building, or network.

The decision to detect or prevent attacks or unacceptable traffic is based on risk. If there is a high risk of damage to the network or organization due to a Denial of Service (DoS) attack, a prevention control that blocks the attack is most appropriate. Detection controls are best employed when experience shows that little or no threat to network security exists and a warning of possible problems is sufficient. For example, a surveillance camera will monitor and detect when access is attempted, but it cannot prevent access. However, if a guard is placed at the access point, then he or she could not only detect, but also prevent access if it is unauthorized.

Blocking Techniques

Blocking techniques include logging the user off a system or reconfiguring the firewall to block the source.

Risk Mitigation Strategies

Risk mitigation techniques can be applied at many levels of an organization to help guard against potential risk damage. The following table describes some of the most effective techniques.

Technique	Description
Policies and procedures	Policies and procedures can be implemented so an organization can enforce conduct rules among employees. It is crucial for an organization to distribute the appropriate policies in order to reduce the likelihood of damage to assets and to prevent data loss or theft. Policies and procedures can include: • Privacy policy • Acceptable use policy (AUP) • Security policy • Mandatory vacation procedures • Job rotation procedures • Audit policy • Password policy • Separation of duties guidelines • Least privilege guidelines
Auditing and reviews	Perform routine audits to assess the risk of a particular operation and to verify that the current security controls in place are operating properly to secure the organization. Be sure to review existing user rights and permissions to make sure they meet your needs for confidentiality as well as accessibility of information and resources.
Security controls	Proper implementation of the appropriate technical, management, and operational controls is a powerful way to mitigate both general and specific risks.
Change management	Good change management practices can mitigate unintentional internal risks caused by inappropriate alterations to systems, tools, or the environment.
Incident management	Organizations must deal with security incidents as they arise, and good management strategies can mitigate the severity of damage caused by risks.

Types of Mitigation and Deterrent Techniques

There are many different techniques used to both monitor for vulnerabilities and to mitigate issues as soon as they are detected. The more common of these techniques are described in the following table.

Technique	Description
Performance and system monitoring	Performance and system monitoring enable you to monitor and diagnose the system and network for potential problems. In Windows® systems, performance monitoring is available on the **Administrative Tools** menu. This tool can be used to quickly monitor some elements of the operation of your system. You can also gather real-time data, export data to be used in a separate program, send administrative alerts based on predefined criteria, create a performance baseline, detect network issues, and manage server performance.
Monitoring system logs	Reviewing the activity recorded in log files can reveal a great deal about a suspected attack. Log files that should be monitored regularly on a set schedule are: • Event logs • Audit logs • Security logs • Access logs
Manual bypassing of electronic controls	Electronic controls are common in securing an organization's building, server rooms, and other highly secure areas. When the electronic controls have been tampered with and there is a security breach by any unauthorized individual, a manual bypass control should be implemented. This gives authorized personnel the ability to bypass the electronic control and ensure that the area is locked down and remains secure.
Hardening	General hardening procedures should be considered as a mitigation technique. In particular, the following security measures should be enforced to provide a higher level of security: • Disable all unnecessary services. • Ensure that the management interface and applications are properly protected. • Password protect all accounts. • Disable all unnecessary accounts. • Establish appropriate detection and prevention controls based on the needs of the organization.
Applying port security	Properly securing the ports on your network will prevent attackers from carrying out port scanning activities to gain information about your network. Security measures include: • Configuring port authentication (802.1x). • Disabling all unused ports.
Reporting	Regular system reporting procedures should be in place to manage and enhance system capabilities. There are three reporting methods that can be utilized to support mitigation efforts made within a system: • Alarms are used to bring attention to a fault condition in the system. • Alerts are used to communicate that a condition has occurred and needs attention before it shuts down. • Trends are a snapshot of the system performance across a specified time frame.

Technique	Description
Implementing physical security	Applying proper physical security controls and measures can be an effective deterrent technique to discourage attackers from attempting to gain access to the building, grounds, systems, resources, and data. Examples might include fencing, door locks, surveillance cameras and systems, and guards.

Failsafe, Failsecure, and Failopen

Failsafe, *failsecure*, and *failopen* are different ways that systems can be designed to perform when those systems cease to operate or when certain conditions are met. For example, most push lawn mowers are designed with some sort of lever that must be held in position by an operator in order for the blades to function. If that lever is released, the blades stop. This type of failsafe design is implemented to prevent harm to individuals.

A common application of this design consideration is in an organization's physical access control systems. In the event of a power failure, electric door strikes cannot be operated, so they are failsecure devices because they keep doors secured without power. Mechanical crashbars are failsafe devices in that they can be added to the inside of those doors to permit people to safely exit, even though the electric strike has no power. A magnetic lock is an example of a failopen device, as it leaves the door unsecured in the event of a power failure. For example, a school's exterior doors may be designed to failopen so that the fire alarm system could cut power to them to permit students and faculty to exit and emergency responders to get in, whereas the server room might be designed as failsafe/failsecure to permit staff to exit while still keeping unauthorized people out.

ACTIVITY 8-6
Monitoring for Intruders

Data Files

C:\093022Data\Risk Management\portscandetection.txt

Before You Begin

You will work with a partner in this activity. Snort and Nmap are installed.

Scenario

As Develetech's security administrator, you want to make sure your new Windows Server 2012 R2 systems are secure by actively monitoring your system for intruders. The IT department wants to take a proactive approach to security and catch the intruders before they do harm. You have already hardened your servers and scanned for vulnerabilities. Now, you want to be able to actively monitor for intrusions in real time, as well as to log suspicious activity for later analysis.

One common attack vector that malicious users take advantage of is the port scan. As you've seen before, port scans can reveal the many vulnerabilities of a network and are often the precursor to a full-on attack. You'll use Snort as an IDS on your servers to detect a simulated port scanning attack from a client source, then verify that a log file captures the intrusion. Being able to monitor intrusions of this nature will help you to recognize what the attack is and where it's coming from, making it easier for you to mitigate any potential damage done to your system.

---

1. Copy the port scanning rules file to the Snort directory.
   a) In File Explorer, verify that you are in **C:\093022Data\Risk Management**.
   b) Copy the **portscandetection** file to **C:\Snort\rules**.

    Note: This rules file is preconfigured to detect port scans for any protocol and that originate from any internal IP addresses. Any such scans will be recorded in a log file.

2. Run Snort in IDS mode using the port scanning rules.
   a) Right-click the **Start** button and select **Command Prompt**.
   b) At the prompt, enter *cd C:\Snort\bin* to change to the Snort directory.

c) At the prompt, enter *snort -i# -c C:\Snort\rules\portscandetection.txt -l C:\Snort\log* where *#* is your local network adapter's **Index** number.

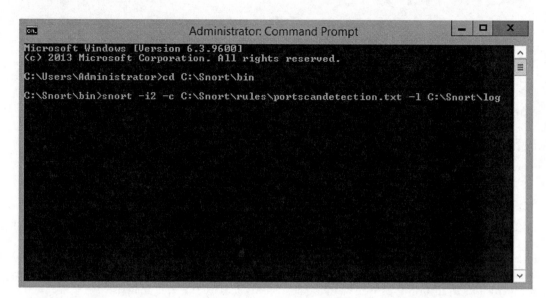

Snort runs in IDS mode using your custom configuration file and outputting to a log file.

3. Run a port scan of your partner's server using Nmap.
   a) Open Nmap.
   b) Maximize the **Zenmap** window.
   c) In the **Target** text box, type *Server##*, where *##* is your partner's student number.
   d) In the **Profile** drop-down list, select **Quick scan**.
   e) Select **Scan**.

4. Verify that your partner's intrusion was detected on your server.
   a) In File Explorer, navigate to **C:\Snort\log**.
   b) Double-click the **portscan** file to open it in Notepad.
   c) Verify that Snort captured and recorded the port scanning attack.

```
Time: 02/11-09:40:45.006338
event_ref: 0
192.168.36.200 -> 192.168.37.100 (portscan) TCP Portscan
Priority Count: 5
Connection Count: 34
IP Count: 1
Scanner IP Range: 192.168.36.200:192.168.36.200
Port/Proto Count: 33
Port/Proto Range: 21:8888
```

The log file records various details about the attack, including:
   • The time of the attack.
   • The source and destination IP addresses of the attack.
   • The type of port scan used in the attack.
   • The number of unique ports scanned in the attack.

5. Close the **Administrator: Command Prompt** window to stop Snort.

6. Close all open windows.

ACTIVITY 8-7
Researching Internet Security Resources (Optional)

Scenario
You have recently been hired to assist the security administrator at a large university. To bring yourself up to speed on the issues, tools, and information you will need in your new job role, you plan to spend some time researching current security information and resources that are available on the Internet.

1. Open your web browser and navigate to the search site of your choice.

2. Search for articles and information related to risk analysis and assessment tools and techniques. Explore the content on some of the sites you find.

3. Search for articles, utilities, and information related to vulnerability assessment tools and techniques. Explore the content on some of the sites you find.

4. Search for articles, utilities, and information related to vulnerability scanning. Explore the content on some of the sites you find.

5. Search for articles, utilities, and information related to vulnerability and risk mitigation. Explore the content on some of the sites you find.

6. Search for any other security-related topics that interest you, or scan recent news items on websites such as **www.krebsonsecurity.com** or **www.securityfocus.com**. You may also wish to scan security user groups like **security.stackexchange.com** for help with implementation and other security-related issues you may have.

Summary

In this lesson, you managed risk in a variety of ways. When risk is identified and managed properly, the possible damage to an organization is decreased substantially. It is your responsibility to analyze risk, and properly assess and determine vulnerabilities for your organization in order to apply the most effective mitigation strategies. With these skills, you will be able to carry out a full risk analysis and apply customized security measures tailored to not only control access, but to also mitigate risk.

What security risks does your organization face, and what methods would you employ in your risk analysis?

What vulnerability assessment tools are you familiar with? What tools do you think you may use in the future?

 Note: Check your LogicalCHOICE Course screen for opportunities to interact with your classmates, peers, and the larger LogicalCHOICE online community about the topics covered in this course or other topics you are interested in. From the Course screen you can also access available resources for a more continuous learning experience.

9 | Troubleshooting and Managing Security Incidents

Lesson Time: 1 hour, 30 minutes

Lesson Objectives

In this lesson, you will troubleshoot and manage security incidents. You will:

- Respond to security incidents.
- Recover from a security incident.

Lesson Introduction

This lesson will cover another phase of the information security cycle. This is the phase that you hope never arrives: your system is under attack, and you need to respond. In this lesson, you will troubleshoot and manage all aspects of a security incident.

You might hope that if you implement security well and monitor vigilantly, you will never have to live through an attack. But attacks are inevitable. Attackers are out there every day, constantly scanning the Internet with automated tools that can uncover and penetrate susceptible systems. No matter how secure your system is, detecting an attack is a question of when, not if. The skills you will learn in this lesson will help you to identify, respond appropriately to, and manage all phases of an incident.

TOPIC A

Respond to Security Incidents

Just as you must secure an organization's infrastructure from attack, you must also plan how you would react if you were directly affected by a computer-related incident. In this topic, you will identify proper computer crime incident response processes and techniques.

The reliability of the evidence collected during an investigation is essential to the success of any future legal proceeding. The intangibility of computer crimes makes the burden of evidence all the more critical. To ensure that your evidence is reliable, you must understand how to appropriately perform investigations and collect substantial proof when incidents of computer crime arise.

Security Incident Management

A *security incident* is a specific instance of a risk event occurring, whether or not it causes damage. Security *incident management* is the set of practices and procedures that govern how an organization will respond to an incident in progress. The goals of incident management are to contain the incident appropriately, and ultimately minimize any damage that may occur as a result of the incident. Incident management typically includes procedures to log and report on all identified incidents and the actions taken in response.

For instance, an organization might create a task force specifically designed to manage all aspects of incident management within the organization. The team carries out all operations using the security governance guidelines and procedures issued by management. The task force is responsible for incident analysis, incident response, incident reporting, and documentation.

Computer Crimes

A *computer crime* is a criminal act that involves using a computer as a source or target, instead of an individual. It can involve stealing restricted information by hacking into a system, compromising national security, perpetrating fraud, conducting illegal activity, or spreading malicious code. It may be committed via the Internet or a private network.

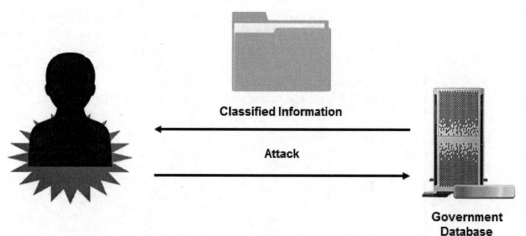

Figure 9–1: A computer crime.

Examples of typical computer crimes include unauthorized access to a computer or network, distributing illegal information via a computer network, and stealing classified information stored on a computer. Phishing and other similar social engineering attacks, if they involve illegal activity, can also be categorized as computer crimes.

IRPs

An *Incident Response Policy (IRP)* is the security policy that determines the actions that an organization will take following a confirmed or potential security breach. The IRP usually specifies:

- Preparation measures like researching known and likely threats.
- Who determines and declares if an actual security incident has occurred.
- How they go about this incident identification.
- What individuals or departments will receive notification.
- How and when they are notified.
- Who will respond to the incident.
- Guidelines for the appropriate response, including mitigation steps to take.
- When the response needs escalation to more qualified personnel.

DEVELETECH

The Wave of the Future

Incident Response Policy

1.0 Overview
This Incident Response Policy includes guidelines and appropriate actions to take following a confirmed or potential security breach. All employees are responsible for taking the appropriate steps, as outlined in this policy, to secure the assets of the organization and avoid major damages in responding to an incident.

2.0 Purpose
To establish guidelines and procedures for responding appropriately to an incident.

3.0 Scope
This policy applies to all Develetech Industries employees who are responsible for responding to an incident, regardless of changes in personnel or job titles.

4.0 Policy Specification
4.1 General
- The incident response team will consist of representatives from the IT and HR departments, and the Chief Security Officer (CSO).
- All incident response information will be made available to employees and managed by the Operations department.
- Employees should be notified on a quarterly basis of any policy changes or updates.
- The HR and Public Relations departments will work together to notify employees, stockholders, and the general public whenever necessary.
- If necessary, seek approval from the Public Relations Director before contacting the media.

4.2 Guidelines
- Call the incident response team.
- The incident response team will notify the Chief Information Officer if the security risk level is high.
- If the security risk level is low to medium, the team will start response procedures as outlined in the Response Plan.
- Manage a mitigation plan when necessary.

Figure 9–2: An IRP.

The incident response will usually involve several departments, and, depending on the severity of the incident, may involve the media. The human resources and public relations departments of an organization generally work together in these situations to determine the extent of the information that will be made available to the public. Information is released to employees, stockholders, and the general public on a need-to-know basis.

In the wake of a security incident, an IRP is a valuable tool for assessing what policies and procedures need to change in an organization based on any lessons learned.

Example

Develetech's IRP is highly detailed in some places, and highly flexible in others. For example, the list of who should respond to an incident is broken down both by job title and by equivalent job function in case a company reorganization causes job titles to change. This same flexibility is given to the department titles. However, the majority of the IRP consists of highly detailed response information that addresses how proper individuals and authorities should be notified of an incident. Since some computer attacks might still be ongoing at the time they are discovered, or since some attacks might take the communications network down entirely, Develetech has made sure that there are multiple lines of secure communication open during the aftermath of an incident.

First Responders

A *first responder* is the first experienced person or a team of trained professionals that arrive on an incident scene. In a non-IT environment, this term can be used to define the first trained person—such as a police officer or firefighter—to respond to an accident, damage site, or natural disaster. In the IT world, first responders can include security professionals, human resource personnel, or IT support professionals.

Security Professional **Human Resources Professional** **IT Support Professional**

Figure 9–3: First responders.

Chain of Custody

The *chain of custody* is the record of evidence handling from collection through presentation in court. The evidence can be hardware components, electronic data, or telephone systems. The chain of evidence reinforces the integrity and proper custody of evidence from collection, to analysis, to storage, and finally to presentation. Every person in the chain who handles evidence must log the methods and tools they used.

Analyze and Store

Collect Evidence **Present in Court**

Figure 9–4: The chain of custody from evidence collection to presentation in court.

Incident Isolation

When computer crimes are reported, one of the first response activities is quarantining affected devices to separate them from the rest of the devices in a system. Separation can be both physical and virtual. Doing this prevents the affected devices from altering other elements of a system, or vice versa. Devices can also be completely removed from the crime location. They are tagged with a chain of custody record to begin the process of making the evidence secure for future presentation in court.

CHFI ✶

Computer Forensics

Computer forensics is the skill that deals with collecting and analyzing data from storage devices, computer systems, networks, and wireless communications and presenting this information as a form of evidence in a court of law. Primarily, forensics deals with the recovery and investigation of potential evidence. Computer forensics is still an emerging field, and so there is little standardization or consistency in practicing it across organizations and courts. Basically, computer forensics is a blend of the elements of law with computer science in analyzing evidence in a way that is permissible in the court of law.

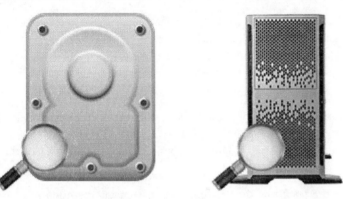

Figure 9–5: A forensic investigation of several types of devices.

Order of Volatility – *Simulation on exam* ✶

Data is volatile, and the ability to retrieve or validate data after a security incident depends on where it is stored in a location or memory layer of a computer or external device. For example, data on backup CDs or thumb drives can last for years, while data in random-access memory (RAM) may last for only nanoseconds.

The order in which you need to recover data after an incident before the data deteriorates, is erased, or is overwritten is known as the *order of volatility*. The general order of volatility for storage devices is:

* Registers, cache, and RAM.
* Network caches and virtual memory.
* Hard drives and flash drives.
* CD-ROMs, DVD-ROMs, and printouts.

Basic Forensic Process

There are four basic phases in a forensic process.

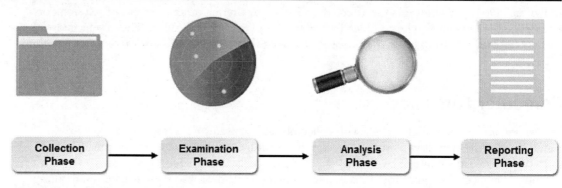

Figure 9–6: The forensic process.

Basic Phase in a Forensic Process	Description
Collection phase	• Identify the attacked system and label it. • Record and acquire details from all related personnel who have access to the system, as well as the evidence material, keeping in mind the integrity of the data.
Examination phase	• Use automated and manual methods to forensically process collected data. • Assess and extract the evidence, keeping in mind the integrity of the data.
Analysis phase	• Analyze the results of the examination phase using methods and techniques permissible by law. • Obtain useful information that justifies the reason for the collection and examination.
Reporting phase	• Report the results of the forensic analysis, including a description of the tools and methods used and why things were done that way. • Brainstorm different ways to improve existing security controls and provide recommendations for better policies, tools, procedures, and other methods in a forensic process.

(handwritten note in left margin: "Process in order")

> **Note:** For additional information, check out the LearnTO **Follow the Forensic Process** presentation from the **LearnTO** tile on the LogicalCHOICE Course screen.

Basic Forensic Response Procedures for IT

Forensic response procedures for IT help security professionals collect evidence from data in a form that is admissible in a court of law.

Forensic Response Procedure	Description
Capture system image	One of the most important steps in computer forensic evidence procedures is to capture exact duplicates of the evidence, also known as forensic images. This is accomplished by making a bit-for-bit copy of a piece of media as an image file with high accuracy.

Forensic Response Procedure	Description
Examine network traffic and logs	Attackers always leave behind traces; you just need to know how and where to look. Logs record everything that happens in an intrusion prevention system (IPS) or intrusion detection system (IDS), and in routers, firewalls, servers, desktops, mainframes, applications, databases, antivirus software, and virtual private networks (VPNs). With these logs, it is possible to extract the identity of hackers and provide the evidence needed.
Capture video	Video forensics is the method by which video is scrutinized for clues. Tools for computer forensics are used in reassembling video to be used as evidence in a court of law.
Record time offset	The format in which time is recorded against a file activity, such as file creation, deletion, last modified, and last accessed, has developed to incorporate a local time zone offset against GMT. This makes it easier for forensics to determine the exact time the activity took place even if the computer is moved from one time zone to another or if the time zone has deliberately been changed on a system.
Take hashes	Federal law enforcement agencies and federal governments maintain a list of files such as files relating to components of Microsoft® Windows® and other application software. The hash codes generated by a file or software can be compared to the list of known file hashes and hacker tools if any are flagged or marked as unknown.
Take screenshots	You should capture screenshots of each and every step of a forensic procedure, especially when you are retrieving evidence using a forensic tool. This will ensure that data present on a compromised system is not tampered with and also provides the court with proof of your use of valid computer forensic methods while extracting the evidence.
Identify witnesses	Courts generally accept evidence if it is seconded by the testimony of a witness who observed the procedure by which the evidence was acquired. A computer forensics expert witness is someone who has experience in handling computer forensics tools and is able to establish the validity of evidence.
Track man hours and expense	When the first incidents of computer crimes occurred, it would usually take less than 40 man hours to complete a forensic investigation because incidents usually involved single computers. Now, with the advances in technology and the advent of new digital media such as voice recorders, cameras, laptop computers, and mobile devices, computer forensics procedures can take up an exponentially greater amount of man hours and expenses. Also, the increase in storage device capacities and encryption affect the amount of man hours that it can take to assess any damage, and consequently increase expenses incurred in any computer forensics investigation. Capturing this expense is part of the overall damage assessment for the incident.

Big Data Analysis

Big data poses a great challenge in the area of forensic analysis. Accurately securing, collecting, and evaluating big data sets is especially difficult because big data implementations often lack a consistent structure and have a variety of different sources. Additionally, because big data is relatively new in practice, there is not much precedent for a forensic investigator to base their analysis off of.

Still, there are general characteristics that you should look for when responding to a data breach, which also apply to big data:

- Unformatted or incorrectly formatted data.
- Incomplete or missing data.
- Invalid data.
- Data that is out of range.
- Data that is duplicated.

Guidelines for Responding to Security Incidents

> **Note:** All Guidelines for this lesson are available as checklists from the **Checklist** tile on the LogicalCHOICE Course screen.

Once an incident has been identified, the response team or security administrator must investigate all aspects of the security crime. Here are some steps you might take to investigate a security crime:

- If an IRP exists, then follow the guidelines outlined to respond to the incident.
- If an IRP does not exist, then determine a primary investigator who will lead the team through the investigation process.
- Determine if the events actually occurred and to what extent a system or process was damaged.
- Document the incident.
- Assess the damage and determine the impact on affected systems.
- Determine if outside expertise is needed, such as a consultant firm.
- Notify local law enforcement, if needed.
- Secure the scene, so that the hardware is contained.
- Collect all the necessary evidence, which may be electronic data, hardware components, or telephony system components. Observe the order of volatility as you gather electronic data from various media.
- Interview personnel to collect additional information pertaining to the crime.
- Report the investigation's findings to the required people.

ACTIVITY 9-1
Responding to Security Incidents

Scenario

As a security administrator for Develetech, you have been asked to join a committee of high-level managers to develop an IRP. Before the committee's first meeting, you prepare to discuss the relevant issues.

1. Based on your own professional or personal experience, what are some examples of typical computer crimes?

2. In your own words, why is it important to have an IRP?

3. What do you think are the most important components in an IRP?

4. In general, do you think it is important to notify employees of common or minor security incidents? Why or why not?

5. Why might you want to alert law enforcement officials of a security incident? Why might you want to notify the media?

6. What forensic techniques would you leverage in response to a network breach?

7. On your Windows Server 2012 R2 computer, access the Internet, and search for sample IRPs. Identify the common guidelines listed in all of them.

TOPIC B

Recover from a Security Incident

Though you spend a great deal of your time ensuring that attacks do not happen, eventually you will have to react to a security incident, fix the damage, and make sure that business can get back to normal as quickly as possible. Not only will you have to accurately assess the damage to your company, but you will also have to report on it. Communication skills are critical if you want to ensure that the incident, or one like it, will not happen again. In this topic, you will recover from a security incident and inform your organization about what happened.

Now that you have responded to a security incident, and have both collected and preserved evidence of an attack, you must help your company return to work. The faster and more efficiently you can recover from a security incident, the less financial damage is suffered, and the more likely that the company can prevent similar incidents from occurring. To fully recover from the incident, you must not only know how to fix the network, but also how to describe the problem to the key decision makers at your company so that future incidents can be avoided.

Basic Incident Recovery Process

The basic process for incident recovery is relatively simple:

1. Assess the level of damage caused by the incident.
2. Recover from the incident.
3. Report the incident.

Figure 9–7: The incident recovery process.

Damage Assessment

During or after a security incident, a damage assessment should be done to determine the extent of damage, the origin or cause of the incident, and the amount of expected downtime. The assessment can also determine the appropriate strategy to employ as you move into the recovery phase.

> **Note:** For additional information, check out the LearnTO **Assess Damage** presentation from the **LearnTO** tile on the LogicalCHOICE Course screen.

Example

Employees at Develetech Industries discovered that its headquarters had a physical security breach, as one of the outside doors was propped open all night. An intern discovered that her desktop computer was missing, and she immediately notified her manager, who called local law enforcement. While waiting for them to arrive, a security professional evacuated the area of the building where the attack was reported, so that employees did not inadvertently disrupt any physical evidence that might remain. They also organized a small group of people to take a quick inventory of any missing hardware; by the time the police arrived, Develetech employees had learned that six computers were stolen.

Recovery Methods

After assessing the damage, you will know the extent of recovery that needs to be done. Many organizations rely on reformatting the system in the case of a rootkit code attack, applying software patches or reloading system software in the case of a virus or malicious code infestation, and restoring backups in the case of an intrusion or backdoor attack. Recovery methods can also involve replacing hardware in the case of a physical security incident.

Example

The IT team at Develetech Industries discovered that the systems in a certain group have been affected by a virus, which is spreading to the computers of other groups. The IT team disconnects the networks that are affected and the networks that are possibly affected. The team then performs a scan of all the systems to find the virus and clean the systems using antivirus and other software. When all the affected systems are clean, they are reconnected to the network and steps are taken to install an IPS.

Incident Reports

An *incident report* is a report that includes a description of the events that occurred during a security incident. Care should be taken to write as much detail relating to an incident as possible, such as the name of the organization, the nature of the event, names and phone numbers of contacts, the time and date of an event, and log information. However, a report should not be delayed because of problems with gathering information. Further probes can be carried out after the report has been written.

Incident Report

Section 1: Incident Description

Date and time detected:	_____	Date and time reported:	_____
Location:	_____	Name of first responder:	_____
System or application affected:	_____	Title of first responder:	_____
Name and contact information for other responders:	_____	Contact information for first responder:	_____

Section 2: Summary of Incident

Incident type detected:

❏	DoS	❏	Unplanned downtime
❏	Unauthorized access or use	❏	Damage to hardware
❏	Malicious code	❏	Other

Tools used to detect the incident: _____

_____

Detailed incident description: _____

_____

_____

_____

_____

Section 3: Notification and Escalation

❏	IS Team	❏	Public Affairs
❏	Local law enforcement	❏	Government regulatory agencies

Figure 9–8: An incident report.

Guidelines for Recovering from a Security Incident

Damage assessment, recovery, and reporting are important in dealing with an incident. Follow these general guidelines during the overall recovery process:

• Some steps you might take while assessing the damage in a security incident:

  • Assess the area of damage to determine the next course of action.

  • Determine the amount of damage to the facility, hardware, systems, and networks.

  • If your company has suffered digital—rather than physical—damage, you may need to examine log files, identify which accounts have been compromised, and identify which files have been modified during the attack.

  • If your company has suffered physical—and not digital—damage, you may need to take a physical inventory to determine which devices have been stolen or damaged, which areas the intruder(s) had access to, and how many devices may have been damaged or stolen.

  • One of the most important and overlooked components of damage assessment is to determine if the attack is over; attempting to react to an attack that is still in progress could do more harm than good.

- Some steps you might take when recovering from a security incident:
  - Replace hardware and network cables in case any have been damaged or stolen.
  - Detect and delete malware and viruses from the affected systems and media.
  - Disconnect the intruded systems from the servers and shut down the server to avoid further intrusions.
  - Disable access to user accounts that have affected the network and search for all the backdoor software installed by the intruder.
  - Establish that your organization is no longer exposed to a threat by scanning the networks and systems using an IDS.
  - Reconnect the servers to the network.
  - Restore the data and network systems from the most recent backup.
  - Replace compromised data and applications, or reformat the system and perform a fresh installation of the operating system.
  - Harden the networks and servers by changing passwords, installing patches, and reconfiguring firewalls and routers.
  - Inform company officials and important stakeholders of the incident, and if an insider was the source of the incident, reprimand the individual responsible according to company policies, or contact law enforcement to take action depending on the extent of the attack.
  - Write a report describing the recovery process. A summary of the report should be saved for use in future security incident responses.
- Some details you may need to capture when reporting a security incident:
  - The name of the organization.
  - The name and phone number of the person who discovered the incident.
  - The name(s) and phone number(s) of first responder(s).
  - The type of event; for instance, a physical attack, malicious code attack, or network attack.
  - The date and time of the event, including the time zone.
  - The source and destination of systems and networks, including IP addresses.
  - The operating system and antivirus software used, and their versions.
  - The methods used to detect the incident; for instance, logs or IDSs.
  - The business impact of the incident.
  - The resolution steps taken.

ACTIVITY 9-2
Recovering from a Security Incident

Scenario

You are a security professional at Develetech Industries. Video surveillance tapes show that there was a physical security breach at the end of the workday yesterday, as an employee let an unauthorized person into the building. It is still the early stages of the investigation, and it is not clear what the attacker was doing there, nor is it clear how or when he left the building. The server rooms were not accessed, and it does not seem that any suspicious network activity occurred, but you are not yet finished going through the logs of all after-hours network activity.

1. This was a weakness in the security of the facility. As an information security professional, why are you involved?

2. What is the first step you need to take in handling this incident?

3. What are the immediate steps you need to take to recover from any damage?

4. Should this incident be reported to the entire company?

5. Should law enforcement be notified?

6. According to the company's risk assessment analysis, unauthorized trespassing was listed as high risk. In composing your report, what are some things you can do to bring that risk down to a more manageable level?

_____

ACTIVITY 9–3
Researching Security Incidents (Optional)

Scenario

In this activity, you will research real-world security incidents and compare them to possible incidents within your own company or organization.

1. Open your web browser and connect to the Internet search site of your choice.

2. Search for *database hacked*. Explore the content on some of the sites you find. Compare the types of data stolen to the types of data that your company stores that involves information on its employees, clients, or partners.

3. Search for *credit card numbers stolen*. Explore the content on some of the sites you find. Compare some of the information you find to the financial risk at your company.

4. Search for *server hacked*. Explore the content on some of the sites you find. Compare the methods of attack that characterize each of the incidents, particularly the complexity of the hack.

5. Search for *Windows vulnerabilities*. Explore the content on some of the sites you find. Are the vulnerabilities that you found unique to a certain kind of server, such as a file server, or a database server?

6. Search for *Unix vulnerabilities*. Explore the content on some of the sites you find. Are the vulnerabilities that you found unique to a certain kind of server, such as a file server, or a database server?

7. Search for *IT disaster*. Explore the content on some of the sites you find. Compare some of the fallout from natural disasters to the types of disasters that are likely in your company's region.

8. Search for *downtime damage*. Explore the content on some of the sites you find. What kind of business would be halted or hindered if your company had a comparable amount of downtime?

9. What are some other specific search terms you can think of that will provide information on IT security incidents? Feel free to research those terms and determine if the resulting information will have relevance to the security requirements in your organization.

Summary

In this lesson, you dealt with the inevitable: a security attack. Try as you might, you will never achieve a network that is impervious to attack, as the methods and techniques that attackers use are constantly changing; a secure network should always be considered a moving target. Ultimately, responding to and recovering from a security incident involves both security and communication skills, since responding to a security incident is a collaborative process that many different job roles take part in.

How many times have you had to consult an IRP, and for what reasons?

What are some good approaches to writing an incident report?

 Note: Check your LogicalCHOICE Course screen for opportunities to interact with your classmates, peers, and the larger LogicalCHOICE online community about the topics covered in this course or other topics you are interested in. From the Course screen you can also access available resources for a more continuous learning experience.

10 | Business Continuity and Disaster Recovery Planning

Lesson Time: 2 hours

Lesson Objectives

In this lesson, you will plan for business continuity and disaster recovery. You will:

- Describe business continuity.

- Plan for disaster recovery.

- Execute DRPs and procedures.

Lesson Introduction

So far in this course, you have dealt with detecting and preventing security risks from affecting a system or network. But sometimes there are cases where the risk that occurs causes such a disruption that it threatens the existence of the business. For an organization to function uninterrupted in these situations, you will need a foolproof plan. In this lesson, you will develop a business continuity plan (BCP) and a disaster recover plan (DRP) so that you can be ready if the worst happens.

Your business depends on the availability of your IT systems, so even the slightest interruption to services can cause you to lose business. When faced with an interruption of services, what do you plan to do? Implementing a strong BCP will help mitigate the overall impact on the business, and a DRP will help you quickly recover sensitive data that has been affected or lost with a negligible loss of revenue.

TOPIC A

Business Continuity

You will need to develop BCPs and DRPs to help minimize losses at your organization. As a security professional, you need to come up with the best possible plan. In this topic, you will describe the importance of business continuity to an organization.

A security system is only as good as its ability to ward off threats and overcome disasters. Therefore, a key component of that system is to have a plan in place so that when disaster strikes, business will still continue in the interim until the issue is fixed. A BCP will help ensure continuous service to customers. As an IT security professional, you may not be responsible for overall business continuity, but you will be an important contributor to the security and IT components of the plan, so a good understanding of the plan, its components, and the process by which it is built is important.

BCPs

A *business continuity plan (BCP)* is a policy that defines how an organization will maintain normal day-to-day business operations in the event of business disruption or crisis. A viable BCP should involve the identification of critical systems and components to ensure that such assets are protected. The BCP also ensures the survival of the organization itself by preserving key documents, establishing decision-making authority, communicating with internal and external stakeholders, and maintaining financial functions. The BCP should address infrastructure issues such as maintaining utilities service, utilizing high-availability or fault-tolerant systems that can withstand failure, and creating and maintaining data backups. The BCP should be reviewed and tested on a regular basis. The plan must have executive support to be considered authoritative; the authorizing executive should personally sign the plan.

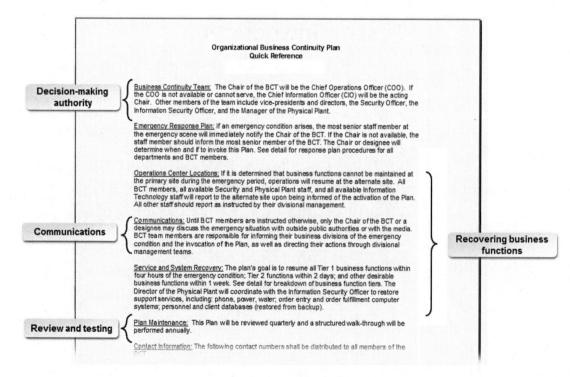

Figure 10-1: A BCP.

BIA

A *business impact analysis (BIA)* is a preparation step in BCP development that identifies present organizational risks and determines the impact to ongoing, business-critical operations and processes if such risks actually occur. BIAs contain vulnerability assessments and evaluations to determine risks and their impact. BIAs should include all phases of the business to ensure a strong business continuation strategy.

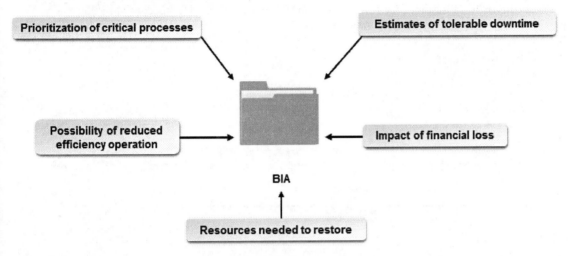

Figure 10–2: BIA.

As a risk is identified, an organization determines the chance of risk occurrence and then determines the quantity of potential organizational damage. For instance, if a roadway bridge crossing a local river is washed out by a flood and employees are unable to reach a business facility for five days, estimated costs to the organization need to be assessed for lost manpower and production.

MTD

Maximum tolerable downtime (MTD) is the longest period of time that a business outage may occur without causing irrecoverable business failure. Each business process can have its own MTD, such as a range of minutes to hours for critical functions, 24 hours for urgent functions, 7 days for normal functions, and so on. MTDs vary by company and event.

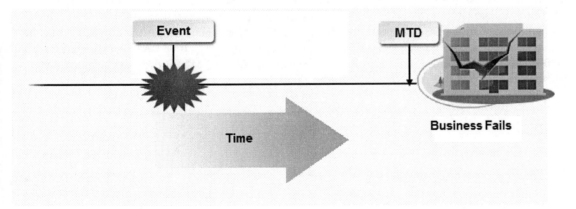

Figure 10–3: MTD.

The MTD limits the amount of recovery time that a business has to resume operations. For example, an organization specializing in medical equipment may be able to exist without incoming manufacturing supplies for three months because it has stockpiled a sizeable inventory. After three months, the organization will not have sufficient supplies and may not be able to manufacture additional products, therefore leading to failure. In this case, the MTD is three months.

RPO

The *recovery point objective (RPO)* is the point in time, relative to a disaster, where the data recovery process begins. In IT systems, it is often the point in time when the last successful backup is performed before a disruptive event occurs.

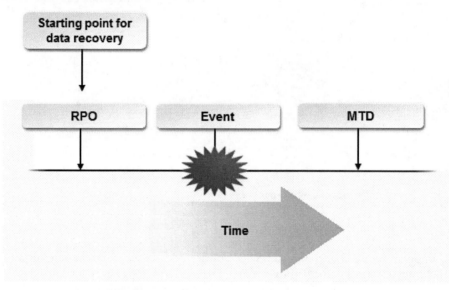

Figure 10-4: An RPO.

For example, if the last backup was executed Sunday afternoon and the failure occurs on the following Tuesday, then the RPO is Sunday afternoon. The latest backup is restored and processing begins to recover all activity from Sunday afternoon to the Tuesday failure point.

RTO

The *recovery time objective (RTO)* is the length of time within which normal business operations and activities can be restored following a disturbance. It includes the necessary recovery time to return to the RPO and reinstate the system and resume processing from its current status. The RTO must be achieved before the MTD. *Mean time to recovery (MTTR)* is the average time taken for a business to recover from an incident or failure and is an offset of the RTO. If MTTR exceeds the given RTO, then business operations need to switch to the alternate site.

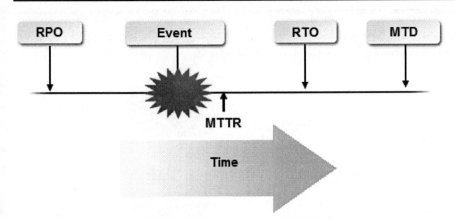

Figure 10-5: An RTO.

Continuity of Operations Plan

A *continuity of operations plan* is the component of the BCP that provides best practices to mitigate risks, and best measures to recover from the impact of an incident. An effective continuity of operations plan can include:

- Auditing of resources, staff, and operational management.
- Auditing storage facilities, data centers, operating systems, and software and applications.
- Auditing networks such as the local area network (LAN) and the wireless area network (WAN), including remote access and authentication systems.
- Analyzing comprehensive risk and vulnerability.
- Creating data backups, recovery methods, and emergency response procedures.
- Establishing a process on how to manage operations during a disaster.

Figure 10-6: Steps in a continuity of operations plan.

Alternate Sites

As part of a BCP, an organization can maintain various types of alternate sites that can be used to restore system functions. A *hot site* is a fully configured alternate network that can be online quickly after a disaster. A *warm site* is a location that is dormant or performs non-critical functions under normal conditions, but which can be rapidly converted to a key operations site if needed. A *cold site* is a predetermined alternate location where a network can be rebuilt after a disaster.

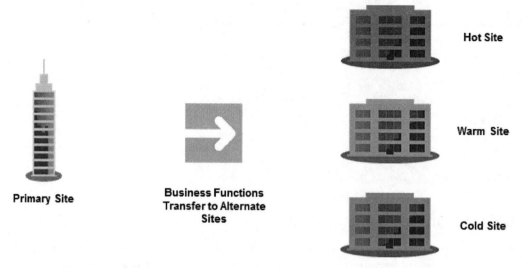

Figure 10–7: Alternate sites.

An example of a hot site would be a secondary operations center that is fully staffed and in constant network contact with the primary center under normal conditions. A warm site might be a customer service center that could be converted quickly to use as a network-maintenance facility, if needed. And a cold site might be nothing more than a rented warehouse with available power and network hookups, where key equipment could be moved and installed in the event of disaster.

IT Contingency Planning

An *IT contingency plan* is a component of the BCP that specifies alternate IT contingency procedures that you can switch over to when you are faced with an attack or disruption of service leading to a disaster for an organization. Interim measures can include operating out of an alternate site, using alternate equipment or systems, and relocating the main systems. The effectiveness of an IT contingency plan depends upon:

- Key personnel understanding the components of the IT contingency plan and when and how it should be initiated when the organization is facing an attack or disruption of service.
- Reviewing a checklist from time to time to see that all the aspects of an IT contingency plan are in place, such as recovery strategies including alternate sites.
- Providing adequate training to employees and management to exercise the contingency plan, and maintaining the plan and reexamining it from time to time.

Orient Key Personnel

Review Checklist

Train and Prepare

Figure 10–8: IT contingency planning.

Succession Planning

A *succession plan* ensures that all key business personnel have one or more designated backups who can perform critical functions when needed. A succession plan identifies the individuals, who they can replace, which functions they can perform, and how they need to be trained.

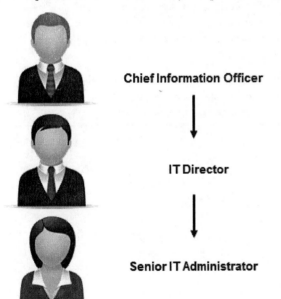

Chief Information Officer

IT Director

Senior IT Administrator

Figure 10–9: Succession planning.

Business Continuity Testing Methods

You can employ various methods to test a BCP, as well as familiarize staff with their duties and responsibilities.

BCP Testing Method	Description
Paper testing methods	Reviewing plan contents. Because they are familiar with the BCP construction, plan developers review the BCP's contents. However, because of their involvement as developers, they often have a limited view of corporate needs that can cause biased opinions.
	Analyzing the solution. Senior management and division and department heads perform an additional analysis to ensure that the business continuity solution fulfills organizational recovery requirements. Because these individuals view the process from a corporate standpoint, they help to confirm that the BCP properly meets expectations.
	Using checklists. Checklists confirm whether the BCP meets predetermined, documented business needs.
Performing walkthroughs	Walkthroughs specifically focus on each BCP phase. Planners and testers walk through the individual steps to validate the logical flow of the sequence of events as a group.
Parallel testing	This test is used to ensure that systems perform adequately at any alternate offsite facility, without taking the main site offline.
	Simulations effectively test the validity and compliance of the BCP. In a simulation, each part of the plan is executed, with the exception of replicating and causing an outage. Although calls are made and specific actions are taken, the real event response is simulated.
	Simulations are instrumental in verifying design flaws, recovery requirements, and implementation errors. By identifying these solution discrepancies, process improvements can be applied that help ensure high-level plan maintenance.
Cutover	This test mimics an actual business disruption by shutting down the original site to test transfer and migration procedures to the alternate site, and to test operations in the presence of an emergency.

ACTIVITY 10-1
Discussing Business Continuity Planning

Scenario

As a security administrator at Develetech, you have been invited to a working lunch to discuss the development schemes, contingency requirements, and other components involved in business continuity planning.

1. As the security administrator, you are responsible for ensuring that your BCP coincides with the organization's needs. What are your goals while establishing a BCP? (Select all that apply.)

   ☐ Preserve important documents.

   ☐ Establish decision-making authority.

   ☐ Analyze fault tolerance.

   ☐ Maintain financial functions.

2. Your organization is located in an area where there is a threat of hurricanes. As a member of the BCP team, you need to determine what effect there would be if a hurricane halted business activities at your organization. Which BCP component is this an example of?

   ○ Continuity of operations

   ○ BIA

   ○ IT contingency planning

   ○ Succession planning

3. Which part of the plan specifies interim sites and systems you can switch to following a disaster?

   ○ RPO

   ○ BIA

   ○ IT contingency plan

   ○ Succession plan

4. You recommend the company pay a small monthly rental fee for a warehouse with phone and power hookups to use as a:

   ○ Hot site

   ○ Cold site

   ○ Warm site

5. You and your colleague have just performed a walkthrough of the plan that would be put into effect in the event of a Denial of Service (DoS) attack on your company website. The two of you think that you need to perform more rigorous tests to ensure the effectiveness of the BCP. What are some other testing methods you might want to recommend?

TOPIC B

Plan for Disaster Recovery

You know that your organization needs to have a plan for overall business continuity so that business operations can continue with little or no interruption in a disaster. As part of that plan, as an IT security professional, you need to ask specific technical questions such as, "what about the sensitive data that has been lost or damaged in the attack?" In this topic, you will develop a plan for disaster recovery.

Disaster recovery planning is crucial for the security of large business systems. In order for organizations to ensure the safety of information systems, they must be proactive and develop an effective DRP to make sure that if there were ever a major system attack or environmental event, sensitive information can be protected or, at the worst, recovered.

DRPs

A *disaster recovery plan (DRP)* is a plan that prepares an organization to react appropriately if the worst were to happen, be it a natural or a man-made disaster, and provides the means to recover from such disaster. DRPs help organizations to recover from an incident without the loss of much time and money. The plan's most important concern, however, is the safety of personnel. A DRP can include:

- A list and contact information of individuals responsible for recovery.
- An inventory of hardware and software.
- A record of important business and customer information that you would require to continue business.
- A record of procedure manuals and other critical information such as the BCP and IT contingency plans.
- Specifications for alternate sites.

Figure 10-10: A DRP.

Note: The contents of a BCP and DRP overlap, and the terms are sometimes used interchangeably.

Fault Tolerance

Fault tolerance is the ability of a network or system to withstand a foreseeable component failure and continue to provide an acceptable level of service. There are several categories of fault tolerance measures, including those that protect power sources, disks and data storage, and network components. Fault tolerant systems often employ some kind of duplication or redundancy of resources to maintain functionality if one component is damaged or fails.

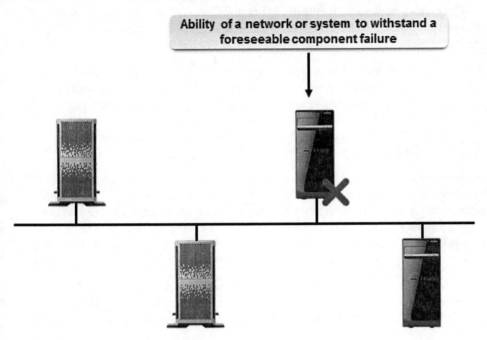

Figure 10–11: Fault tolerance.

Redundancy Measures

Mean time to failure (MTTF) is the rating that predicts the length of time that a device or component is expected to be operational. MTTF is generally used to evaluate the reliability of devices and components that are not repaired.

Mean time between failures (MTBF) is the rating on a device or devices that predicts the expected time between failures. Based on the MTTF and/or MTBF of a system, you must consider and plan for the necessary redundancy measures.

Failure Point	Redundancy Measure
Disks	The *Redundant Array of Independent Disks (RAID)* standards are a set of vendor-independent specifications mostly for fault tolerant configurations on multiple-disk systems. If one or more of the disks fail, data can be recovered from the remaining disks. RAID can be implemented through operating system software, but hardware-based RAID implementations are more efficient and are more widely deployed. There are several RAID levels, each of which provides a different combination of features and efficiencies. RAID levels are identified by number; RAID 0, RAID 1, and RAID 5 are the most common. All RAID forms except for RAID 0 reduce the threat of loss due to disk failures and provide protection.

Failure Point	Redundancy Measure
Circuits	To reduce the damage caused by the loss of a communications circuit in a data network, a backup circuit should be made available and installed to serve as a redundant connection. The backup circuit may be used on either an on-demand basis or all the time. If the primary circuit is interrupted, the network continues to operate on the second, or backup, circuit on a limited performance basis.
Servers	Server clustering allows servers to work together to provide access, ensuring minimal data loss from a server failure. Should one of the servers in the cluster fail, the remaining servers, or server, will assume the responsibilities, but with the possibility of decreased performance. When the failed server is restored, it will integrate back into the cluster and reinstate with a minimal noticeable shift in performance.
Routers	*Router redundancy* is the technique of deploying multiple routers in teams to limit the risk of routing failure should a router malfunction. The routers in a redundant environment share common configurations and act as one to route and control information. They communicate with each other to determine if everything is functioning well. If a redundant router fails, the remaining routers assume the load and sustain the routing process.
General hardware	Keeping used or spare parts on hand for emergencies is good practice. You should be aware that there could be some security or backward-compatibility issues with some of the spare parts (such as wireless routers, decommissioned laptops, slower central processing units [CPUs], or old switches). Periodically add spare parts to your network to test them; in the event of an emergency, they can be the difference between shutting down business or operating at a reduced—but acceptable—level.
Power supplies	A recent feature of power supplies is to include two or more units built into one system with capabilities for each to supply power to the entire system. If one of the units fails, then by means of a hot swap built into the server, the other unit supplies power.
Network adapters	Systems can also be supplied with built-in redundant network adapters that automatically hot-swap if one fails.

Note: There are various resources you can consult for more information on RAID and RAID levels, including the websites of various RAID solution vendors.

High Availability

High availability is a rating that expresses how closely systems approach the goal of providing data availability 100 percent of the time while maintaining a high level of system performance. High-availability systems are usually rated as a percentage that shows the proportion of expected uptime to total time. Some of the methods used in achieving this include clustering, load balancing, and redundancy measures.

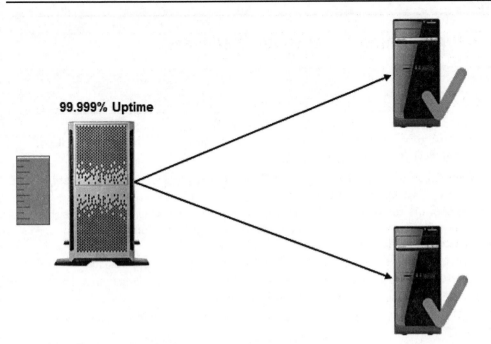

Figure 10-12: High availability.

An uptime rating of 99.999% or "five nines" is a very high level of availability, resulting in less than six minutes of downtime per year. "Six nines," or 99.9999% uptime, results in around 30 seconds of downtime per year, but comes with an associated proportional increase in cost.

DRP Testing and Maintenance

Every DRP should be tested periodically as part of its implementation, and your DRP development process should include an evaluation phase to ensure its effectiveness. You can use testing methods and evaluation techniques similar to those used to evaluate a BCP, or you can use emergency planning exercises such as those developed by the U.S. Federal Emergency Management Agency (FEMA). FEMA recognizes and recommends several types of exercises that you can use to evaluate DRPs.

Exercise Type	Description
Walkthroughs, workshops, and orientation seminars	Often used to provide basic awareness and training for disaster recovery team members, these exercises describe the contents of BCPs, DRPs, and other plans, and the roles and responsibilities outlined in those plans.
Tabletop exercises	Discussion-based sessions where disaster recovery team members discuss their roles in emergency situations, as well as their responses to particular situations.
Functional exercises	Action-based sessions where employees can validate DRPs by performing scenario-based activities in a simulated environment.
Full-scale exercises	Action-based sessions that reflect real situations, these exercises are held onsite and use real equipment and real personnel as much as possible. Full-scale exercises are often conducted by public agencies, but local organizations might be asked to participate.

For more information about emergency preparedness, visit **http://www.ready.gov/business**.

After the plan has been completed, you should review it at least yearly and make any maintenance-level changes required based on the results of the review as well as the results of periodic testing.

Guidelines for Planning for Disaster Recovery

> **Note:** All Guidelines for this lesson are available as checklists from the **Checklist** tile on the LogicalCHOICE Course screen.

To plan for disaster recovery, you must properly assess your organization's current state of readiness, and you must know when and how to improve any limitations of the current strategy. Keep the following guidelines in mind:

- If your organization has not tested the BCP or DRP recently, do so. Conduct several offline scenarios that use only backup resources.
- If you are creating or improving the BCP and/or DRP, research any available templates that might help guide you. Websites such as **www.disasterrecoveryforum.com** or **www.disasterrecoveryworld.com** are good places to begin.
- Ensure that there are redundancy measures in place for servers, power supplies, and your ISP.
- Verify that the company has access to spare hardware and peripherals for emergency use, and that the devices are secure enough to conduct business with.
- Review any service level agreements (SLAs) that are in place so that you have an idea of what constitutes acceptable downtime.
- Create a line of communication that does not make use of company resources, so it does not break should the company lose power after hours. Do the same in the event that the city or regional power is down.
- Identify and document all single points of failure, as well as any up-to-date redundancy measures.
- Make sure that the company's redundant storage is secure.
- Be sure that your DRP includes provisions for regular tests of the plan. You might want to schedule a "fire drill," where one day, all managers are moved to an offsite location, unannounced. This helps to simulate a disaster or emergency, which does not always provide ample warning.
- Employees must receive training to understand the importance of the DRP.

ACTIVITY 10-2
Creating a DRP

Scenario

You are a security professional at Develetech Industries, which has just experienced a huge growth spurt. With a growing roster of employees, a larger network infrastructure, and more remote network access by traveling employees, the company has decided that it has outgrown its original security policies. You have been asked to create the company's first DRP.

1. Which are common components that should be in Develetech Industries' DRP? (Select all that apply.)

   ☐ A list of employees' personal items.

   ☐ Contact information for key individuals.

   ☐ An inventory of important hardware and software.

   ☐ Plans to reconstruct the network.

2. Develetech Industries is willing to set aside some capital to install a fault tolerance system. What can you suggest?

3. Assume that Develetech Industries is located in a climate and location identical to the company you work for now. What are some unique geographical or weather-related conditions you might need to account for, but that might not be a consideration for other companies?

4. Assume that a high-level manager has expressed some dissatisfaction with the notion of a "fire drill" to test the company's preparedness for a disaster; it seems he is leery of so much paid time being used in an unproductive way, and he wonders if you cannot just write a detailed plan instead. What are some things you can mention to help persuade him that such an unannounced drill is necessary?

5. Once you have the DRP and other components in place, what do you do to make sure it works smoothly?

TOPIC C

Execute DRPs and Procedures

Even though you know how important it is to create and test a DRP, the true test of a plan is putting it into effect in a real disaster situation. In this topic, you will execute a DRP and its procedures.

What is the use of a good DRP if it is not well executed? Knowing who to contact and knowing how to execute a DRP in the best way possible will help get business back up and running in no time and avoid all unnecessary losses to the organization.

The Disaster Recovery Process

The disaster recovery process includes several steps to properly resume business operations after a disruptive event.

Disaster Recovery Step	Description
Notify stakeholders	Stakeholders should be informed of a business-critical disaster. They may consist of senior management, board members, investors, clients, suppliers, employees, and the public. Different categories of stakeholders are notified at different times, and the level of detail follows the notification procedures in your policy.
Begin emergency operations	The DRP should contain detailed steps regarding specific emergency services. An incident manager should be appointed to assume control of the situation and ensure the safety of personnel.
Assess the damage	A damage assessment should be conducted to determine the extent of incurred facility damages, to identify the cause of the disaster if it is unclear, and to estimate the amount of expected downtime. This assessment can also determine the appropriate response strategy. For instance, a full recovery to a remote site may not be warranted if damage is limited to parts of the business that do not threaten operational functions.
Assess the facility	It is necessary to assess the current facility's ability to continue being the primary location of operation. If the facility has been adversely affected and has suffered significant losses, relocating to an alternate site may be the best option.
Begin recovery process	Once you have notified stakeholders, performed the initial emergency operations, and assessed the damage and the facility's ability to function, then it is time to start the recovery process.

The Recovery Team

The *recovery team* is a group of designated individuals who implement recovery procedures and control recovery operations in the event of an internal or external disruption to critical business processes. The recovery team immediately responds in an emergency and restores critical business processes to their normal operating capacity, at the remote or recovery site, once key services and information systems are back online. Team members might include systems managers, systems administrators, security administrators, facilities specialists, communications specialists, human resources staff, and legal representatives.

Figure 10-13: The recovery team provides immediate response.

Secure Recovery

The BCP or DRP must include provisions for securely recovering data, systems, and other sensitive resources. This might mean designating a trusted administrator to supervise the recovery, as well as documenting the steps and information needed to restore the processes, systems, and data needed to recover from the disaster, and instructions for continuing operations either at the primary site or an alternate site. The secure recovery process should be reviewed and tested on a regular basis.

Figure 10-14: Secure recovery procedures.

Backup Types and Recovery Plans

The process of recovering data from a backup varies depending on the backup types that were included in the original backup plan. There are three main types of backups.

Backup Type	Description
Full backup	All selected files, regardless of the state of the archived bit, are backed up. The *archive bit* is a file property that essentially indicates whether the file has been modified since it was last backed up. A full backup then clears the archive bit.
Differential backup	All selected files that have changed since the last full backup are backed up. A differential backup does not clear the archive bit. When differential backups are used, you must restore the last full backup plus the most recent differential backup.

Backup Type	Description
Incremental backup	All selected files that have changed since the last full or differential backup are backed up. It clears the archive bit. An incremental backup typically takes less time to perform than a differential backup because it includes less data. When incremental backups are used, you must restore the last full backup plus all subsequent incremental backups.

Backout Contingency Plans

A *backout contingency plan* is a documented plan that includes specific procedures and processes that are applied in the event that a change or modification made to a system must be undone. The plan may include key individuals, a list of systems, backout time frames, and the specific steps needed to fully undo a change. Part of the plan may also include a backup plan that may be deployed as part of the backout processes and procedures.

Backout Contingency Plan

Project Name:_____   Project Number:_____
Project Version:_____   Document Creation Date:_____
Document Author(s):_____

Project Leader:_____   Permission Given By:_____

Revision History

Document Author(s)	Version Number	Revision Date	Summary of Changes

Backout Plan Summary

As part of the backout plan at Develetech Industries, a SAN-based snapshot of the database volumes of the Exchange Server application is taken and archived using the .tar file format, and will be stored for one (1) month.

During this time, if the organization experiences any issues that affect the new Exchange Server application, they will be able to roll back the application to an earlier time. However, if any issues occur after a month, the organization must use a different workaround, as the backout plan is effective for only one (1) month.

Develetech Industries can also present fresh SAN volumes to copy data from the snapshots of the database volumes of the Exchange Server application. The .tar files can be extracted to their respective

Figure 10-15: A backout contingency plan.

Secure Backups

Backing up sensitive or important data is only part of the solution, as that backup also needs to be secure. Storing copies of sensitive or critical information is a sensible security practice, and should not simply be limited to a secondary hard disk, a Compact Disc-Recordable (CD-R), or a tape archive. A backup can be considered most secure if it is offline and offsite, and stored in an environment that is physically locked and protected from environmental intrusions such as fire or water.

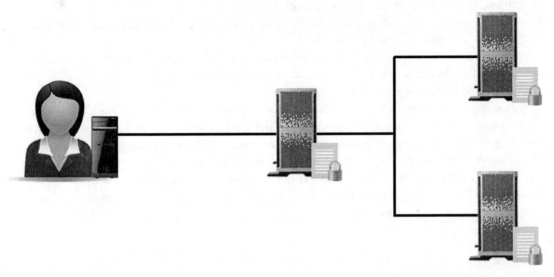

Figure 10–16: Secure backups.

Backup Storage Locations

The magnetic tapes or other physical media used to create data backups must be stored securely, but must remain accessible in case the data is needed. Many organizations employ both onsite and offsite backup storage. The onsite storage location is for the most recent set of backups, so that they can be accessed quickly if a data restoration is needed during normal operations. The offsite location is a secure, disaster-resistant storage facility where the organization keeps either a duplicate or an older backup set to protect it against any damage caused by disaster conditions at the primary site.

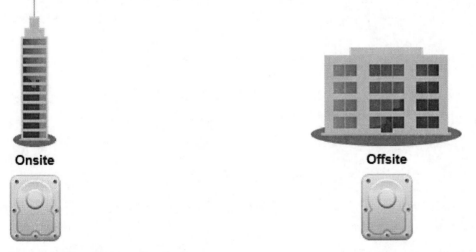

Figure 10–17: Backup storage locations.

Guidelines for Executing DRPs and Procedures

To execute DRPs and procedures, you need to ensure that the DRPs are in place and can be readily implemented in the event of a disaster. Keep the following guidelines in mind:

- The organization needs to identify the team that will handle the disaster situation, including the incident manager.
- Each disaster recovery team member must have clearly laid out roles and responsibilities and must be easily accessible to the other employees.
- Employees must be aware of the members of the disaster recovery team and must know who they need to contact in the event of a disaster.
- The disaster recovery team must work out a backup plan for the incident that will ensure that the continuity of the business is not affected as an aftermath of the disaster.
- Inform stakeholders as specified in your DRP.
- Roll out emergency services, such as an alternate site, under the control of the incident manager.
- The damage to the main site should be assessed, and the recovery team should be brought in to repair any physical damage and assess the extent to which the main site can be restored.
- A restoration of the backup should be done of all files that have been compromised or deleted.
- Decisions should be made to purchase or replace missing system elements.
- Once the recovery process is completed, document the steps taken and save a report to be used in case of another recovery process.

ACTIVITY 10–3
Executing DRPs and Procedures

Scenario

Develetech's chief information security officer has asked for your assistance to execute the best possible DRP and procedures to get the company's systems back up and running as quickly as possible.

---

1. **What should you keep in mind while choosing a good recovery team?**

    ○ Include individuals who can do an analysis of the damage that the crisis has caused to the organization.

    ○ Include individuals who can implement the proper procedures in response to the disruption to critical business processes.

    ○ Include individuals who can record the history of the evidence of a computer crime from collection, to presentation in court, to return or disposal.

    ○ Include individuals who determine how much money and effort will go into a recovery plan.

2. **You have been assigned to perform a secure recovery; what does your task include?**

3. **You have to decide on the kind of backup source you will use to recover data and restore function to the business in the least possible time. What type of backup could you choose?**

4. **What types of backup storage locations can you suggest to store data for your company?**

ACTIVITY 10-4
Researching Business Continuity and Disaster Recovery (Optional)

Scenario
You are the information security officer and your organization needs your help in reviewing and implementing business continuity and disaster recovery. You will research BCPs and DRPs and compare them to the existing plans within your own company or organization so that you can improve the plans already in place.

1. Open your web browser and connect to the Internet search site of your choice.

2. Search for *business continuity plans* and *business continuity testing methods*. Explore the content on some of the sites you find. Compare these findings to the plans in place in your organizations, if you are familiar with them, or to the needs your organization might have.

3. Search for *business impact analysis*. Explore the content on some of the sites you find. Compare these findings to the BIA procedures in place in your organization, if you are aware of them. Suggest ways to improve them, or suggest how BIA should be approached in your organization.

4. Search for *continuity of operations plans*. Explore the content on some of the sites you find. Compare these findings to the continuity of operations plan in place in your organization, if you have one, and suggest ways to improve the plan. Or, consider what your organization's plan should include.

5. Search for *disaster recovery plans* and *disaster recovery plan testing*. Explore the content on some of the sites you find. Compare these findings to your organization's plan and suggest what your organization's plan should include.

6. Search for *IT contingency plans* and *succession planning*. Explore the content on some of the sites you find. Compare these findings to the plans in place in your organization, if you are aware of them. Suggest ways to improve your organization's plans or ways IT contingency or succession planning should be approached.

7. Search for *fault tolerance* and *redundancy measures*. Explore the content on some of the sites you find. Compare these findings to the fault tolerance systems and redundancy measures already in place in your organization, if you are aware of them. Suggest ways to improve fault tolerance and redundancy measures or ways these measures should be approached.

8. Search for *alternate sites*. Explore the content on some of the sites you find. What kind of site would best suit your organization? A cold site, warm site, or hot site? Are there different functions within your organization with different needs?

9. What are some other specific search terms you can think of that will provide assistance with implementing BCPs and DRPs? Feel free to research those terms and determine if the resulting information will have relevance to the planning requirements in your organization.

Summary

In this lesson, you developed a BCP and a DRP so that your organization's processes will be uninterrupted and continuous, or recovered as soon as possible after a disaster.

What risks are prevalent in your field of expertise, and how do you prevent them?

What kind of alternate site does your organization maintain? Why?

 Note: Check your LogicalCHOICE Course screen for opportunities to interact with your classmates, peers, and the larger LogicalCHOICE online community about the topics covered in this course or other topics you are interested in. From the Course screen you can also access available resources for a more continuous learning experience.

Course Follow-Up

Congratulations! You have completed the *CompTIA® Security+® (Exam SY0-401)* course. You have gained the skills and information you will need to implement and monitor security on hosts, networks, applications, and operating systems, and respond to security breaches.

You also covered the objectives that you will need to prepare for the CompTIA Security+ (Exam SY0-401) certification examination. If you combine this class experience with review, private study, and hands-on experience, you will be well prepared to demonstrate your security expertise both through professional certification and with solid technical competence on the job.

What's Next?

Your next step after completing this course will probably be to prepare for and obtain your CompTIA Security+ certification. In addition, there are a number of advanced security courses and certifications that you might want to pursue following the CompTIA Security+ (Exam SY0-401) course, including CompTIA Advanced Security Practitioner (CASP) certification, CompTIA Mobility+® certification, and CompTIA Mobile App Security+ certification for Android™ or iOS development. You might also wish to pursue further technology-specific training in operating system or network design, implementation and support, or in application development and implementation.

You are encouraged to explore computer and network security further by actively participating in any of the social media forums set up by your instructor or training administrator through the **Social Media** tile on the LogicalCHOICE Course screen.

A | Mapping Course Content to CompTIA® Security+® Exam SY0-401

Obtaining CompTIA® Security+® certification requires candidates to pass exam SY0-401. This table describes where the objectives for exam SY0-401 are covered in this course.

Domain and Objective	Covered In
Domain 1.0 Network Security	
1.1 Implement security configuration parameters on network devices and other technologies.	Lesson 3, Topic C; Lesson 4, Topic A
• Firewalls	
• Routers	Lesson 3, Topic C; Lesson 4, Topic A
• Switches	Lesson 4, Topic A
• Load Balancers	Lesson 4, Topic A
• Proxies	Lesson 4, Topic A
• Web security gateways	Lesson 4, Topic A
• VPN concentrators	Lesson 4, Topic A
• NIDS and NIPS (Behavior based, Signature based, Anomaly based, Heuristic)	Lesson 4, Topic A
• Protocol analyzers	Lesson 4, Topic A
• Spam filter	Lesson 4, Topic A
• UTM security appliances (URL filter, Content inspection, Malware inspection)	Lesson 4, Topic D
• Web application firewall vs. network firewall	Lesson 4, Topic A
• Application aware devices (Firewalls, IPS, IDS, Proxies)	Lesson 4, Topic A
1.2 Given a scenario, use secure network administration principles.	Lesson 4, Topic D
• Rule-based management	

Domain and Objective	Covered In
• Firewall rules	Lesson 3, Topic C; Lesson 4, Topic A
• VLAN management	Lesson 4, Topic D
• Secure router configuration	Lesson 4, Topic D
• Access control lists	Lesson 4, Topic D
• Port Security	Lesson 4, Topic D
• 802.1x	Lesson 4, Topic E
• Flood guards	Lesson 4, Topic D
• Loop protection	Lesson 4, Topic D
• Implicit deny	Lesson 4, Topic D
• Network separation	Lesson 4, Topic D
• Log analysis	Lesson 4, Topic D
• Unified Threat Management	Lesson 4, Topic D
1.3 Explain network design elements and components. • DMZ	Lesson 4, Topic B
• Subnetting	Lesson 4, Topic B
• VLAN	Lesson 4, Topic B
• NAT	Lesson 4, Topic B
• Remote Access	Lesson 4, Topic B
• Telephony	Lesson 4, Topic B
• NAC	Lesson 4, Topic B
• Virtualization	Lesson 4, Topic B
• Cloud Computing (Platform as a Service, Software as a Service, Infrastructure as a Service, Private, Public, Hybrid, Community)	Lesson 4, Topic B
• Layered security/Defense in depth	Lesson 3, Topic A
1.4 Given a scenario, implement common protocols and services.	Lesson 4, Topic C
• Protocols (IPSec, SNMP, SSH, DNS, TLS, SSL, TCP/IP, FTPS, HTTPS, SCP, ICMP, IPv4, IPv6, iSCSI, Fibre Channel, FCoE, FTP, SFTP, TFTP, TELNET, HTTP, NetBIOS)	
• Ports (21, 22, 25, 53, 80, 110, 139, 143, 443, 3389)	Lesson 4, Topic C
• OSI relevance	Lesson 4, Topic B

Domain and Objective	Covered In
1.5 Given a scenario, troubleshoot security issues related to wireless networking.	Lesson 4, Topic E
• WPA	
• WPA2	Lesson 4, Topic E
• WEP	Lesson 4, Topic E
• EAP	Lesson 4, Topic E
• PEAP	Lesson 4, Topic E
• LEAP	Lesson 4, Topic E
• MAC filter	Lesson 4, Topic E
• Disable SSID broadcast	Lesson 4, Topic E
• TKIP	Lesson 4, Topic E
• CCMP	Lesson 4, Topic E
• Antenna placement	Lesson 4, Topic E
• Power level controls	Lesson 4, Topic E
• Captive portals	Lesson 4, Topic E
• Antenna types	Lesson 4, Topic E
• Site surveys	Lesson 4, Topic E
• VPN (over open wireless)	Lesson 4, Topic E

Domain and Objective	Covered In
Domain 2.0 Compliance and Operational Security	
2.1 Explain the importance of risk related concepts.	Lesson 8, Topic A
• Control types (Technical, Management, Operational)	
• False positives	Lesson 8, Topic C
• False negatives	Lesson 8, Topic C
• Importance of policies in reducing risk (Privacy policy, Acceptable use, Security policy, Mandatory vacations, Job rotation, Separation of duties, Least privilege)	Lesson 8, Topic D
• Risk calculation (Likelihood, ALE, Impact, SLE, ARO, MTTR, MTTF, MTBF)	Lesson 8, Topic A; Lesson 10, Topic A; Lesson 10, Topic B
• Quantitative vs. qualitative	Lesson 8, Topic A
• Vulnerabilities	Lesson 1, Topic A; Lesson 8, Topic A
• Threat vectors	Lesson 8, Topic A
• Probability/threat likelihood	Lesson 8, Topic A

Domain and Objective	Covered In
• Risk-avoidance, transference, acceptance, mitigation, deterrence	Lesson 8, Topic A
• Risks associated with Cloud Computing and Virtualization	Lesson 8, Topic A
• Recovery time objective and recovery point objective	Lesson 10, Topic A
2.2 Summarize the security implications of integrating systems and data with third parties.	Lesson 7, Topic D
• On-boarding/off-boarding business partners	
• Social media networks and/or applications	Lesson 7, Topic D
• Interoperability agreements (SLA, BPA, MOU, ISA)	Lesson 7, Topic D
• Privacy considerations	Lesson 7, Topic D
• Risk awareness	Lesson 7, Topic D
• Unauthorized data sharing	Lesson 7, Topic D
• Data ownership	Lesson 7, Topic D
• Data backups	Lesson 7, Topic D
• Follow security policy and procedures	Lesson 7, Topic D
• Review agreement requirements to verify compliance and performance standards	Lesson 7, Topic D
2.3 Given a scenario, implement appropriate risk mitigation strategies.	Lesson 8, Topic D
• Change management	
• Incident management	Lesson 8, Topic D
• User rights and permissions reviews	Lesson 8, Topic D
• Perform routine audits	Lesson 8, Topic D
• Enforce policies and procedures to prevent data loss or theft	Lesson 8, Topic D
• Enforce technology controls (Data Loss Prevention [DLP])	Lesson 8, Topic D
2.4 Given a scenario, implement basic forensic procedures.	Lesson 9, Topic A
• Order of volatility	
• Capture system image	Lesson 9, Topic A
• Network traffic and logs	Lesson 9, Topic A
• Capture video	Lesson 9, Topic A
• Record time offset	Lesson 9, Topic A
• Take hashes	Lesson 9, Topic A

Domain and Objective	Covered In
• Screenshots	Lesson 9, Topic A
• Witnesses	Lesson 9, Topic A
• Track man hours and expense	Lesson 9, Topic A
• Chain of custody	Lesson 9, Topic A
• Big data analysis	Lesson 9, Topic A
2.5 Summarize common incident response procedures.	Lesson 9, Topic A
• Preparation	
• Incident identification	Lesson 9, Topic A
• Escalation and notification	Lesson 9, Topic A
• Mitigation steps	Lesson 9, Topic A
• Lessons learned	Lesson 9, Topic A
• Reporting	Lesson 9, Topic A
• Recovery/reconstitution procedures	Lesson 10, Topic C
• First responder	Lesson 9, Topic A
• Incident isolation (Quarantine, Device removal)	Lesson 9, Topic A
• Data breach	Lesson 9, Topic A
• Damage and loss control	Lesson 8, Topic A
2.6 Explain the importance of security related awareness and training.	Lesson 7, Topic C
• Security policy training and procedures	
• Role-based training	Lesson 7, Topic C
• Personally identifiable information	Lesson 7, Topic C
• Information classification (High, Medium, Low, Confidential, Private, Public)	Lesson 7, Topic C
• Data labeling, handling, and disposal	Lesson 1, Topic E; Lesson 7, Topic C
• Compliance with laws, best practices and standards	Lesson 1, Topic E; Lesson 7, Topic B; Lesson 7, Topic C
• User habits (Password behaviors, Data handling, Clean desk policies, Prevent tailgating, Personally owned devices)	Lesson 7, Topic C
• New threats and new security trends/alerts (New viruses, Phishing attacks, Zero day exploits)	Lesson 7, Topic C
• Use of social networking and P2P	Lesson 7, Topic C
• Follow up and gather training metrics to validate compliance and security posture	Lesson 7, Topic C

Domain and Objective	Covered In
2.7 Compare and contrast physical security and environmental controls.	Lesson 7, Topic A
• Environmental controls (HVAC, Fire suppression, EMI shielding, Hot and cold aisles, Environmental monitoring, Temperature and humidity controls)	
• Physical security (Hardware locks, Mantraps, Video surveillance, Fencing, Proximity readers, Access list, Proper lighting, Signs, Guards, Barricades, Biometrics, Protected distribution [cabling], Alarms, Motion detection)	Lesson 7, Topic A
• Control types (Deterrent, Preventive, Detective, Compensating, Technical, Administrative)	Lesson 7, Topic A
2.8 Summarize risk management best practices.	Lesson 8, Topic A; Lesson 10, Topic A; Lesson 10, Topic B; Lesson 10, Topic C
• Business continuity concepts (Business impact analysis, Identification of critical systems and components, Removing single points of failure, Business continuity planning and testing, Risk assessment, Continuity of operations, Disaster recovery, IT contingency planning, Succession planning, High availability, Redundancy, Tabletop exercises)	
• Fault tolerance (Hardware, RAID, Clustering, Load balancing, Servers)	Lesson 4. Topic A; Lesson 10, Topic B
• Disaster recovery concepts (Backup plans/policies, Backup execution/frequency, Cold site, Hot site, Warm site)	Lesson 10, Topic A; Lesson 10, Topic C
2.9 Given a scenario, select the appropriate control to meet the goals of security.	Lesson 1, Topic B
• Confidentiality (Encryption, Access controls, Steganography)	
• Integrity (Hashing, Digital signatures, Certificates, Non-repudiation)	Lesson 1, Topic B
• Availability (Redundancy, Fault tolerance, Patching)	Lesson 1, Topic B
• Safety (Fencing, Lighting, Locks, CCTV, Escape plans, Drills, Escape routes, Testing controls)	Lesson 7, Topic A

Domain and Objective	Covered In
Domain 3.0 Threats and Vulnerabilities	
3.1 Explain types of malware.	Lesson 2, Topic B
• Adware	
• Virus	Lesson 2, Topic B
• Spyware	Lesson 2, Topic B
• Trojan	Lesson 2, Topic B

Domain and Objective	Covered In
• Rootkits	Lesson 2, Topic B
• Backdoors	Lesson 2, Topic C
• Logic bomb	Lesson 2, Topic B
• Botnets	Lesson 2, Topic B
• Ransomware	Lesson 2, Topic B
• Polymorphic malware	Lesson 2, Topic B
• Armored virus	Lesson 2, Topic B
3.2 Summarize various types of attacks.	Lesson 2, Topic D
• Man-in-the-middle	
• DDoS	Lesson 2, Topic D
• DoS	Lesson 2, Topic D
• Replay	Lesson 2, Topic D
• Smurf attack	Lesson 2, Topic D
• Spoofing	Lesson 2, Topic D
• Spam	Lesson 2, Topic A
• Phishing	Lesson 2, Topic A
• Spim	Lesson 2, Topic A
• Vishing	Lesson 2, Topic A
• Spear phishing	Lesson 2, Topic A
• Xmas attack	Lesson 2, Topic D
• Pharming	Lesson 2, Topic A
• Privilege escalation	Lesson 1, Topic B
• Malicious insider threat	Lesson 2, Topic A
• DNS poisoning and ARP poisoning	Lesson 2, Topic D
• Transitive access	Lesson 2, Topic D
• Client-side attacks	Lesson 2, Topic C
• Password attacks (Brute force, Dictionary attacks, Hybrid, Birthday attacks, Rainbow tables)	Lesson 2, Topic C
• Typo squatting/URL hijacking	Lesson 2, Topic A
• Watering hole attack	Lesson 2, Topic C
3.3 Summarize social engineering attacks and the associated effectiveness with each attack.	Lesson 2, Topic A
• Shoulder surfing	

Domain and Objective	Covered In
• Dumpster diving	Lesson 2, Topic A
• Tailgating	Lesson 2, Topic A
• Impersonation	Lesson 2, Topic A
• Hoaxes	Lesson 2, Topic A
• Whaling	Lesson 2, Topic A
• Vishing	Lesson 2, Topic A
• Principles (reasons for effectiveness) (Authority, Intimidation, Consensus/Social proof, Scarcity, Urgency, Familiarity/liking, Trust)	Lesson 2, Topic A
3.4 Explain types of wireless attacks.	Lesson 2, Topic E
• Rogue access points	
• Jamming/interference	Lesson 2, Topic E
• Evil twin	Lesson 2, Topic E
• War driving	Lesson 2, Topic E
• Bluejacking	Lesson 2, Topic E
• Bluesnarfing	Lesson 2, Topic E
• War chalking	Lesson 2, Topic E
• IV attack	Lesson 2, Topic E
• Packet sniffing	Lesson 2, Topic E
• Near field communication	Lesson 2, Topic E
• Replay attacks	Lesson 2, Topic E
• WEP/WPA attacks	Lesson 2, Topic E
• WPS attacks	Lesson 2, Topic E
3.5 Explain types of application attacks.	Lesson 2, Topic C
• Cross-site scripting	
• SQL injection	Lesson 2, Topic C
• LDAP injection	Lesson 2, Topic C
• XML injection	Lesson 2, Topic C
• Directory traversal/command injection	Lesson 2, Topic C
• Buffer overflow	Lesson 2, Topic C
• Integer overflow	Lesson 2, Topic C
• Zero day	Lesson 2, Topic C
• Cookies and attachments	Lesson 2, Topic C

Domain and Objective	Covered In
• LSO (Locally Shared Objects)	Lesson 2, Topic C
• Flash Cookies	Lesson 2, Topic C
• Malicious add-ons	Lesson 2, Topic C
• Session hijacking	Lesson 2, Topic D
• Header manipulation	Lesson 2, Topic C
• Arbitrary code execution/remote code execution	Lesson 2, Topic C
3.6 Analyze a scenario and select the appropriate type of mitigation and deterrent techniques.	Lesson 8, Topic D
• Monitoring system logs (Event logs, Audit logs, Security logs, Access logs)	
• Hardening (Disabling unnecessary services, Protecting management interfaces and applications, Password protection, Disabling unnecessary accounts)	Lesson 8, Topic D
• Network security (MAC limiting and filtering, 802.1x, Disabling unused interfaces and unused application service ports, Rogue machine detection)	Lesson 4, Topic A; Lesson 4, Topic D; Lesson 4, Topic E
• Security posture (Initial baseline configuration, Continuous security monitoring, Remediation)	Lesson 8, Topic D
• Reporting (Alarms, Alerts, Trends)	Lesson 8, Topic D
• Detection controls vs. prevention controls (IDS vs. IPS, Camera vs. guard)	Lesson 8, Topic D
3.7 Given a scenario, use appropriate tools and techniques to discover security threats and vulnerabilities.	Lesson 8, Topic A
• Interpret results of security assessment tools	
• Tools (Protocol analyzer, Vulnerability scanner, Honeypots, Honeynets, Port scanner, Passive vs. active tools, Banner grabbing)	Lesson 8, Topic B; Lesson 8, Topic C
• Risk calculations (Threat vs. likelihood)	Lesson 8, Topic A
• Assessment types (Risk, Threat, Vulnerability)	Lesson 8, Topic A
• Assessment technique (Baseline reporting, Code review, Determine attack surface, Review architecture, Review designs)	Lesson 8, Topic B
3.8 Explain the proper use of penetration testing versus vulnerability scanning.	Lesson 8, Topic C
• Penetration testing (Verify a threat exists, Bypass security controls, Actively test security controls, Exploiting vulnerabilities)	

Domain and Objective	Covered In
• Vulnerability scanning (Passively testing security controls, Identify vulnerability, Identify lack of security controls, Identify common misconfigurations, Intrusive vs. non-intrusive, Credentialed vs. non-credentialed, False positive)	Lesson 8, Topic C
• Black box	Lesson 8, Topic C
• White box	Lesson 8, Topic C
• Gray box	Lesson 8, Topic C

Domain and Objective	Covered In
Domain 4.0 Application, Data, and Host Security	
4.1 Explain the importance of application security controls and techniques.	Lesson 3, Topic B
• Fuzzing	
• Secure coding concepts (Error and exception handling, Input validation)	Lesson 3, Topic B
• Cross-site scripting prevention	Lesson 3, Topic B
• Cross-site Request Forgery (XSRF) prevention	Lesson 3, Topic B
• Application configuration baseline (proper settings)	Lesson 3, Topic B
• Application hardening	Lesson 3, Topic B
• Application patch management	Lesson 3, Topic B
• NoSQL databases vs. SQL databases	Lesson 3, Topic B
• Server-side vs. Client-side validation	Lesson 3, Topic B
4.2 Summarize mobile security concepts and technologies.	Lesson 3, Topic D
• Device security (Full device encryption, Remote wiping, Lockout, Screen-locks, GPS, Application control, Storage segmentation, Asset tracking, Inventory control, Mobile device management, Device access control, Removable storage, Disabling unused features)	
• Application security (Key management, Credential management, Authentication, Geo-tagging, Encryption, Application whitelisting, Transitive trust/ authentication)	Lesson 3, Topic D
• BYOD concerns (Data ownership, Support ownership, Patch management, Antivirus management, Forensics, Privacy, On-boarding/off-boarding, Adherence to corporate policies, User acceptance, Architecture/ infrastructure considerations, Legal concerns, Acceptable use policy, On-board camera/video)	Lesson 3, Topic D

Domain and Objective	Covered In
4.3 Given a scenario, select the appropriate solution to establish host security.	Lesson 3, Topic C
• Operating system security and settings	
• OS hardening	Lesson 3, Topic C
• Anti-malware (Antivirus, Anti-spam, Anti-spyware, Pop-up blockers)	Lesson 3, Topic C
• Patch management	Lesson 3, Topic C
• White listing vs. black listing applications	Lesson 3, Topic C
• Trusted OS	Lesson 3, Topic C
• Host-based firewalls	Lesson 3, Topic C
• Host-based intrusion detection	Lesson 4, Topic A
• Hardware security (Cable locks, Safe, Locking cabinets)	Lesson 3, Topic C
• Host software baselining	Lesson 3, Topic C
• Virtualization (Snapshots, Patch compatibility, Host availability/elasticity, Security control testing, Sandboxing)	Lesson 3, Topic C
4.4 Implement the appropriate controls to ensure data security.	Lesson 3, Topic C
• Cloud storage	
• SAN	Lesson 3, Topic A
• Handling big data	Lesson 3, Topic A
• Data encryption (Full disk, Database, Individual files, Removable media, Mobile devices)	Lesson 3, Topic A
• Hardware based encryption devices (TPM, HSM, USB encryption, Hard drive)	Lesson 3, Topic A
• Data in-transit, Data at-rest, Data in-use	Lesson 3, Topic A
• Permissions/ACL	Lesson 3, Topic A
• Data policies (Wiping, Disposing, Retention, Storage)	Lesson 3, Topic A
4.5 Compare and contrast alternative methods to mitigate security risks in static environments.	Lesson 3, Topic C
• Environments (SCADA, Embedded [Printer, Smart TV, HVAC control], Android, iOS, Mainframe, Game consoles, In-vehicle computing systems)	
• Methods (Network segmentation, Security layers, Application firewalls, Manual updates, Firmware version control, Wrappers, Control redundancy and diversity)	Lesson 3, Topic C

Domain and Objective	Covered In
Domain 5.0 Access Control and Identity Management	
5.1 Compare and contrast the function and purpose of authentication services.	Lesson 5, Topic A
• RADIUS	
• TACACS+	Lesson 5, Topic A
• Kerberos	Lesson 5, Topic A
• LDAP	Lesson 5, Topic A
• XTACACS	Lesson 5, Topic A
• SAML	Lesson 5, Topic A
• Secure LDAP	Lesson 5, Topic A
5.2 Given a scenario, select the appropriate authentication, authorization, or access control.	Lesson 1, Topic B
• Identification vs. authentication vs. authorization	
• Authorization (Least privilege, Separation of duties, ACLs, Mandatory access, Discretionary access, Rule-based access control, Role-based access control, Time of day restrictions)	Lesson 1, Topic B
• Authentication (Tokens, Common access card, Smart card, Multi-factor authentication, TOTP, HOTP, CHAP, PAP, Single sign-on, Access control, Implicit deny, Trusted OS)	Lesson 1, Topic B; Lesson 1, Topic C; Lesson 5, Topic A
• Authentication factors (Something you are, Something you have, Something you know, Somewhere you are, Something you do)	Lesson 1, Topic B; Lesson 1, Topic C
• Identification (Biometrics, Personal identification verification card, User name)	Lesson 1, Topic B; Lesson 1, Topic C
• Federation	Lesson 5, Topic B
• Transitive trust/authentication	Lesson 3, Topic D
5.3 Install and configure security controls when performing account management, based on best practices.	Lesson 5, Topic B
• Mitigate issues associated with users with multiple accounts/roles and/or shared accounts	
• Account policy enforcement (Credential management, Group policy, Password complexity, Expiration, Recovery, Disablement, Lockout, Password history, Password reuse, Password length, Generic account prohibition)	Lesson 5, Topic B
• Group based privileges	Lesson 5, Topic B
• User assigned privileges	Lesson 5, Topic B
• User access reviews	Lesson 5, Topic B

Domain and Objective	Covered In
• Continuous monitoring	Lesson 5, Topic B

Domain and Objective	Covered In
Domain 6.0 Cryptography	
6.1 Given a scenario, utilize general cryptography concepts.	Lesson 1, Topic D
• Symmetric vs. asymmetric	
• Session keys	Lesson 1, Topic D
• In-band vs. out-of-band key exchange	Lesson 1, Topic D
• Fundamental differences and encryption methods (Block vs. stream)	Lesson 1, Topic D
• Transport encryption	Lesson 3, Topic A
• Non-repudiation	Lesson 1, Topic B
• Hashing	Lesson 1, Topic D
• Key escrow	Lesson 6, Topic E
• Steganography	Lesson 1, Topic D
• Digital signatures	Lesson 1, Topic D
• Use of proven technologies	Lesson 1, Topic D
• Elliptic curve and quantum cryptography	Lesson 1, Topic D
• Ephemeral key	Lesson 1, Topic D
• Perfect forward secrecy	Lesson 1, Topic D
6.2 Given a scenario, use appropriate cryptographic methods.	Lesson 2, Topic E; Lesson 4, Topic E
• WEP vs. WPA/WPA2 and preshared key	
• MD5	Lesson 1, Topic D
• SHA	Lesson 1, Topic D
• RIPEMD	Lesson 1, Topic D
• AES	Lesson 1, Topic D
• DES	Lesson 1, Topic D
• 3DES	Lesson 1, Topic D
• HMAC	Lesson 1, Topic D
• RSA	Lesson 1, Topic D
• Diffie-Hellman	Lesson 1, Topic D
• RC4	Lesson 1, Topic D

Domain and Objective	Covered In
• One-time pads	Lesson 1, Topic D
• NTLM	Lesson 1, Topic D
• NTLMv2	Lesson 1, Topic D
• Blowfish	Lesson 1, Topic D
• PGP/GPG	Lesson 3, Topic A
• TwoFish	Lesson 1, Topic D
• DHE	Lesson 1, Topic D
• ECDHE	Lesson 1, Topic D
• CHAP	Lesson 5, Topic A
• PAP	Lesson 5, Topic A
• Comparative strengths and performance of algorithms	Lesson 1, Topic D
• Use of algorithms/protocols with transport encryption (SSL, TLS, IPSec, SSH, HTTPS)	Lesson 3, Topic A
• Cipher suites (Strong vs. weak ciphers)	Lesson 1, Topic D
• Key stretching (PBKDF2, Bcrypt)	Lesson 1, Topic D
6.3 Given a scenario, use appropriate PKI, certificate management, and associated components.	Lesson 6, Topic A; Lesson 6, Topic F
• Certificate authorities and digital certificates (CA, CRLs, OCSP, CSR)	
• PKI	Lesson 6, Topic A
• Recovery agent	Lesson 6, Topic E
• Public key	Lesson 1, Topic D; Lesson 6, Topic A
• Private key	Lesson 1, Topic D; Lesson 6, Topic A
• Registration	Lesson 6, Topic A
• Key escrow	Lesson 6, Topic E
• Trust models	Lesson 6, Topic A

Solutions

ACTIVITY 1–1: Identifying Information Security Concepts and Components

1. As an information security officer, what are the information security goals that you need to keep in mind while defining the protection you will need? (Select all that apply.)

   - ☑ Prevention
   - ☐ Auditing
   - ☑ Recovery
   - ☑ Detection

2. Which of these are vulnerabilities? (Select all that apply.)

   - ☑ Improperly configured software
   - ☑ Misuse of communication protocols
   - ☑ Damage to hardware
   - ☐ Lengthy passwords with a mix of characters

3. Describe the differences between a threat, vulnerability, and risk.

   A: Answers will vary, but may include: A threat is any potential violation of security policies or procedures. A vulnerability is any condition that leaves a system open to attack. A risk is an exposure to the chance of damage or loss, and it signifies the likelihood of a hazard or dangerous threat.

ACTIVITY 1–2: Discussing Information Security Controls

1. What are the three most fundamental goals of computer security?

   - ☑ Confidentiality
   - ☐ Auditing
   - ☑ Integrity
   - ☐ Privilege management
   - ☑ Availability

2. A biometric handprint scanner is used as part of a system for granting access to a facility. Once an identity is verified, the system checks and confirms that the user is allowed to leave the lobby and enter the facility, and the electronic door lock is released. Which security controls are being used in this situation? (Select all that apply.)

- ☑ Authentication
- ☑ Authorization
- ☑ Access control
- ☐ Auditing

3. Katie's handprint is matched against a record in the system that indicates that she has been assigned clearance to view the contents of secret documents. Later, at her desk, she tries to connect to a folder that is marked Top Secret, and access is denied. Which type of access control is being used?

- ◉ MAC
- ○ DAC
- ○ RBAC
- ○ Rule-Based Access Control

4. At the end of the day, security personnel can view electronic log files that record the identities of everyone who entered and exited the building along with the time of day. Which type of security control is this?

- ○ Authentication
- ○ Authorization
- ○ Access control
- ◉ Auditing

5. An administrator of a large multinational company has the ability to assign object access rights and track users' resource access from a central administrative console. Users throughout the organization can gain access to any system after providing a single user name and password. Which type of security control is this?

- ○ Auditing
- ○ Security labels
- ◉ Privilege management
- ○ Confidentiality

ACTIVITY 1-3: Discussing Authentication Methods

1. Brian works in your IT department. To access his laptop, he inserts his employee ID card into a special card reader. This is an example of:

- ○ User name/password authentication.
- ○ Biometrics.
- ◉ Token-based authentication.
- ○ Mutual authentication.

2. To access the server room, Brian places his index finger on a fingerprint reader. This is an example of:
   - ○ Password authentication.
   - ○ Token-based authentication.
   - ◉ Biometric authentication.
   - ○ Multi-factor authentication.

3. To withdraw money from an automatic teller machine, Nancy inserts a card and types a four-digit PIN. This incorporates what types of authentication? (Select all that apply.)
   - ☑ Token-based
   - ☑ Password
   - ☐ Biometrics
   - ☑ Multi-factor
   - ☐ Mutual

4. What is the best description of token-based authentication?
   - ○ It relies on typing a code.
   - ○ It relies on a card and a PIN.
   - ○ It relies on a user's physical characteristics.
   - ◉ It relies on a card being inserted into a card reader.

5. What is an example of a "what you do" authentication factor?
   - ○ Fingerprint or handprint recognition
   - ○ ID card and PIN
   - ◉ Keystroke pattern recognition
   - ○ Geolocation
   - ○ User name and password

6. True or False? Mutual authentication protects clients from submitting confidential information to an insecure server.
   - ☑ True
   - ☐ False

7. How does multi-factor authentication enhance security?

   A: Because the attacker must obtain at least two authentication factors, not just one, in order to breach the system. This can be particularly difficult with biometrics, or "who you are" authentication, where at least one of the factors is a unique physical characteristic of an individual.

ACTIVITY 1–4: Discussing Cryptography Fundamentals

1. Which algorithm is a hashing encryption algorithm?
   - ◉ SHA
   - ○ AES
   - ○ RSA
   - ○ 3DES

2. Which of the following is a specific set of actions used to encrypt data?

   ○ Steganography

   ○ Key

   ◉ Cipher

   ○ Digital signature

3. True or False? A digital signature is an application of hashing encryption, because the signature is never transformed back to cleartext.

   ☑ True

   ☐ False

4. What are the distinctions between an encryption algorithm and a key?

   A: The encryption algorithm is the general rule or instruction set applied to the data to transform it to ciphertext. The key is the actual value used by the algorithm. A different key value results in different ciphertext, although the basic encryption process is the same.

5. What is a potential drawback of symmetric encryption?

   A: The need to share the key between the two parties creates the potential for key compromise or loss.

6. What makes public key encryption potentially so secure?

   A: The keys are not shared between the parties.

7. Considering that hashing encryption is one-way and the hash is never decrypted, what makes hashing encryption a useful security technique?

   A: Because two parties can hash the same data and compare hashes to see if they match, hashing can be used for data verification in a variety of situations, including password authentication. Hashes of passwords, rather than the passwords themselves, can be sent between the two parties. A hash of a file or a hash code in an electronic message can be verified by both parties after information transfer.

8. Which asymmetric encryption algorithm uses a temporary key?

   ○ RSA

   ○ RC4

   ◉ DHE

   ○ RIPEMD

   ○ ECC

9. What are the common components of a cipher suite? (Select all that apply.)

   ☑ Message authentication code algorithm

   ☐ Ephemeral key

   ☑ Bulk encryption algorithm

   ☑ Pseudorandom function

   ☑ Key exchange algorithm

10. True or false? A session key is equivalent to a static key.

    ☐ True

    ☑ False

11. **Give at least one example of a key-stretching implementation.**

    A: Responses might vary, but could include key-derivation functions such as bcrypt and PBKDF2.

ACTIVITY 1–5: Examining a Security Policy

---

2. **What type of policy document is this?**
   - ○ Acceptable use policy
   - ○ Audit policy
   - ○ Extranet policy
   - ◉ Password policy
   - ○ Wireless standards policy

3. **Which standard policy components are included in this policy? (Select all that apply.)**
   - ☑ Policy statement
   - ☑ Standards
   - ☑ Guidelines
   - ☐ Procedures

4. **How often must system-level administrators change their passwords to conform to this policy?**

   A: The password policy states that administrator passwords should be changed monthly to remain secure.

5. **To conform to this policy, how often must regular system users change their passwords?**

   A: The password policy states that regular system users should change their passwords every three months to stay secure.

6. **According to this policy, what is the minimum character length for a password, and how should it be constructed?**

   A: Eight characters is the minimum length for security purposes, and you should include numbers and special characters to make it more secure.

7. **According to this policy, why is "password1" not a good choice for a password?**

   A: It contains a common usage word that is also found in dictionaries.

ACTIVITY 2–1: Identifying Social Engineering Attacks

---

1. **Social engineering attempt or false alarm? A supposed customer calls the help desk and states that she cannot connect to the e-commerce website to check her order status. She would also like a user name and password. The user gives a valid customer company name, but is not listed as a contact in the customer database. The user does not know the correct company code or customer ID.**
   - ☑ Social engineering attempt
   - ☐ False alarm

2. Social engineering attempt or false alarm? The VP of sales is in the middle of a presentation to a group of key customers and accidentally logs off. She urgently needs to continue with the presentation, but forgets her password. You recognize her voice on the line, but she is supposed to have her boss make the request according to the company password security policy.

   ☐ Social engineering attempt

   ☑ False alarm

3. Social engineering attempt or false alarm? A new accountant was hired and would like to know if he can have the installation source files for the accounting software package, so that he can install it on his computer himself and start work immediately. Last year, someone internal compromised company accounting records, so distribution of the accounting application is tightly controlled. You have received all the proper documentation for the request from his supervisor and there is an available license for the software. However, general IT policies state that the IT department must perform all software installations and upgrades.

   ☐ Social engineering attempt

   ☑ False alarm

4. Social engineering attempt or false alarm? Christine receives an instant message asking for her account name and password. The person sending the message says that the request is from the IT department, because they need to do a backup of Christine's local hard drive.

   ☑ Social engineering attempt

   ☐ False alarm

5. Social engineering attempt or false alarm? Rachel gets an email with an attachment that is named NewVirusDefinitions.vbs. The name in the email is the same as the IT software manager, but the email address is from an account outside the company.

   ☑ Social engineering attempt

   ☐ False alarm

6. Social engineering attempt or false alarm? A user calls the help desk stating that he is a phone technician needing the password to configure the phone and voice-mail system.

   ☑ Social engineering attempt

   ☐ False alarm

7. Social engineering attempt or false alarm? A vendor team requests access to the building to fix an urgent problem with a piece of equipment. Although the team has no work order and the security guard was not notified of the visit, the team members are wearing shirts and hats from the preferred vendor.

   ☑ Social engineering attempt

   ☐ False alarm

8. Social engineering attempt or false alarm? The CEO of Develetech needs to get access to market research data immediately. You definitely recognize her voice, but a proper request form has not been filled out to modify the permissions. She states that normally she would fill out the form and should not be an exception, but she urgently needs the data.

   ☐ Social engineering attempt

   ☑ False alarm

9. Social engineering attempt or false alarm? A purchasing manager is browsing a list of products on a vendor's website when a window opens claiming that software has detected several thousand files on his computer that are infected with viruses. Instructions in the official-looking window indicate the user should click a link to install software that will remove these infections.

   ☑ Social engineering attempt

   ☐ False alarm

ACTIVITY 2-2: Identifying Types of Malware

---

1. While using your computer, an app window displays on your screen and demands that you pay a fine or be reported to the authorities. You try closing the window, but you're unable to. The other processes on your computer seem to be unavailable, so you try rebooting your machine. When your computer loads, the app window demanding payment pops back up and essentially locks you out of your computer's functions. What type of malware has infected your computer?

   ○ Trojan horse

   ◉ Ransomware

   ○ Adware

   ○ Botnet

   If students answer adware, remind them that spyware actually monitors their computer usage, and that spam email is not considered malicious software.

2. Checking your email over a period of a week, you notice something unusual: the spam messages that you've been receiving all seem to be trying to sell you something closely related to the websites you happened to visit that day. For example, on Monday you visited a subscription news site, and later that day you noticed a spam email that solicited a subscription to that very news site. On Tuesday, you browsed to an online retailer in order to buy a birthday gift for your friend. The same gift you were looking at showed up in another spam email later that night. What type of malware has infected your computer?

   ○ Adware

   ◉ Spyware

   ○ Ransomware

   ○ Logic bomb

3. You open up your favorite word processing app. As it opens, a window pops up informing you that an important file has just been deleted. You close the word processing app and open up a spreadsheet app. The same thing happens—another file is deleted. The problem continues to spread as you open up several more apps and each time, a file is deleted. What type of malware has infected your system?

   ○ Botnet

   ○ Spyware

   ○ Adware

   ◉ Virus

4. Early in the day, someone claiming to be a coworker sends you an email with an attachment. The sender indicates the attachment is an updated spreadsheet, so you download it. You don't open the file right away, but instead go on to do other work. Not long after, you find that your computer is running unusually slow. Restarting doesn't seem to fix the problem, as your computer slows down so much that any apps you try to use begin locking up and crashing. Realizing that you may have been a victim of social engineering, you delete the supposed spreadsheet from your computer. Doing so eventually stabilizes your machine. What type of malware had infected your computer?

   ● Trojan horse

   ○ Virus

   ○ Botnet

   ○ Spyware

5. What primary characteristic do polymorphic and armored viruses share?

   ○ Smaller file size than typical viruses

   ● Harder to detect than typical viruses

   ○ More destructive than typical viruses

   ○ Spread faster than typical viruses

ACTIVITY 2-3: Identifying Software Attacks

1. Kim, a help desk staffer, gets a phone call from Alex in human resources stating that he cannot log on. Kim looks up the account information for Alex and sees that the account is locked. This is the third time the account has locked this week. Alex insists that he was typing in his password correctly. Kim notices that the account was locked at 6 A.M.; Alex says he was in a meeting at a client's site until 10 A.M. today. This could be a(n):

   ● Password attack.

   ○ Backdoor attack.

   ○ Application attack.

2. Your customer database was recently compromised and much of its data was corrupted. The database administrator, Carly, pulls the log files for you to review. Shortly before the corruption was detected, the log files list various bogus SQL statements being entered into the database. This could be a(n):

   ○ Password attack.

   ○ Backdoor attack.

   ● Application attack.

3. Your file server has been performing sluggishly, and several times a day it is entirely unreachable. You've ruled out traffic spikes and insufficient hardware as the cause, and your antivirus software detects no signs of an infection. You review the usage logs on the server and notice that an administrator account logs in and out remotely several times per day. You've discussed the matter with everyone in IT that is currently authorized to access the file server, and none of them seem to recognize this account. You determine that this unknown administrator account is being used to gain entry into your file server to disrupt its normal operations. This could be a(n):

   ○ Password attack.

   ● Backdoor attack.

   ○ Application attack.

ACTIVITY 2–4: Classifying Network–Based Threats

1. While you are connected to another host on your network, the connection is suddenly dropped. When you review the logs at the other host, it appears as if the connection is still active. This could be a(n):
   - ○ IP spoofing attack.
   - ○ Replay attack.
   - ○ Man-in-the-middle attack.
   - ◉ Session hijacking attack.

2. Your e-commerce web server is getting extremely slow. Customers are calling stating that it is taking a long time to place an order on your site. This could be a(n):
   - ○ DNS poisoning attack.
   - ◉ DoS attack.
   - ○ Eavesdropping attack.
   - ○ ARP poisoning attack.

3. Tina, the network analysis guru in your organization, analyzes a network trace capture file and discovers that packets have been intercepted and retransmitted to both a sender and a receiver during an active session. This could be a(n):
   - ○ IP spoofing attack.
   - ○ Session hijacking attack.
   - ○ Replay attack.
   - ◉ Man-in-the-middle attack.

4. Your intranet webmaster, Tim, has noticed an entry in a log file from an IP address that is within the range of addresses used on your network. But, Tim does not recognize the computer name as valid. Your network administrator, Deb, checks the DHCP server and finds out that the MAC address is not similar to any in their list of MAC addresses in that particular domain. This could be a(n):
   - ◉ ARP poisoning attack.
   - ○ Replay attack.
   - ○ Man-in-the-middle attack.
   - ○ Session hijacking attack.

5. Instead of connecting to your web server IP address, when you enter your website's URL into your browser, it brings you to a site that looks similar to yours but at a completely different IP address. While on this site, your antivirus software alerts you to a possible malware infection. This could be a(n):
   - ◉ DNS poisoning/hijacking attack.
   - ○ Replay attack.
   - ○ ARP poisoning attack.
   - ○ Session hijacking attack.

ACTIVITY 2-5: Discussing Wireless Security, Threats, and Vulnerabilities

1. John is given a laptop for official use and is on a business trip. When he arrives at his hotel, he turns on his laptop and finds a wireless access point with the name of the hotel, which he connects to for sending official communications. He may become a victim of which wireless threat?

   ○ Jamming

   ○ War driving

   ○ Bluesnarfing

   ◉ Evil twins

2. A new administrator in your company is in the process of installing a new wireless device. He is called away to attend an urgent meeting before he can secure the wireless network, and without realizing it, he forgot to switch the device off. A person with a mobile device who is passing the building takes advantage of the open network and hacks the network. Your company may become vulnerable to which type of wireless threat?

   ○ Jamming

   ◉ War driving

   ○ Bluesnarfing

   ○ Rogue access point

3. Every time Margaret decided to work at home, she would get frustrated with the poor wireless connection. But when she gets to her office, the wireless connection seems normal. What might have been one of the factors affecting Margaret's wireless connection when she worked at home?

   ○ Bluesnarfing

   ◉ Jamming

   ○ IV attack

   ○ Evil twins

4. Chuck, a sales executive, is attending meetings at a professional conference that is also being attended by representatives of other companies in his field. At the conference, he uses his smartphone with a Bluetooth headset to stay in touch with clients. A few days after the conference, he finds that competitors' sales representatives are getting in touch with his key contacts and influencing them by revealing what he thought was private information from his email and calendar. Chuck is a victim of which wireless threat?

   ○ Packet sniffing

   ○ Bluejacking

   ◉ Bluesnarfing

   ○ Rogue access point

5. You've tasked Joel, one of your network specialists, with configuring new wireless routers in the building in order to extend the range of your network. Which of the following wireless encryption protocols should you remind Joel to use in order to keep your network secure?

   ○ WPA

   ◉ WPA2 with WPS disabled

   ○ WPA2 with WPS enabled

   ○ WEP

ACTIVITY 2-6: Identifying Physical Threats and Vulnerabilities

1. A disgruntled employee removes the UPS on a critical server system and then cuts power to the system, causing costly downtime. This physical threat is a(n): (Select all that apply.)

   - ☑ Internal threat.
   - ☐ External threat.
   - ☑ Man-made threat.
   - ☐ False alarm.

2. A power failure has occurred due to a tree branch falling on a power line outside your facility, and there is no UPS or generator. This physical threat is a(n): (Select all that apply.)

   - ☐ Internal threat.
   - ☑ External threat.
   - ☐ Man-made threat.
   - ☑ False alarm.

3. A backhoe operator on a nearby construction site has accidentally dug up fiber optic cables, thus disabling remote network access. This physical threat is a(n): (Select all that apply.)

   - ☐ Internal threat.
   - ☑ External threat.
   - ☑ Man-made threat.
   - ☐ False alarm.

4. While entering the building through the rear security door, an employee realizes he has left his car keys in his car door lock. He has already swiped his badge to open the door, so he props it open with his briefcase while he returns to his car to retrieve his keys. He has the door in view at all times and no one else enters while the door is propped open. He locks the door behind him once he is in the building. This is a(n): (Select all that apply.)

   - ☑ Internal threat.
   - ☐ External threat.
   - ☑ Man-made threat.
   - ☑ False alarm.

ACTIVITY 3-1: Managing Data Security

1. Why should Develetech invest in data security?

   A: Implementing proper data security throughout the organization will not only protect sensitive data from being stolen, but also will protect an employee's personal information from unauthorized access. Data cannot be bought back.

2. What data encryption method should you implement when you need to send data for Develetech's annual earnings report as an attachment in an email from your mobile device to the board of directors?

   - ○ Database encryption
   - ◉ Email encryption
   - ○ Mobile device encryption
   - ○ Full disk encryption

3. **How can data leakage affect the organization, and how could it be prevented?**

   A: Data leakage occurs unintentionally through normal user activities without the users knowing they are compromising the security of data. Because of this, it is crucial for Develetech to ensure that users are aware of what data leakage is, and how they can better prevent it from happening.

ACTIVITY 3-3: Managing Application Security

1. Develetech has a new public-facing website that includes forums for customers to discuss the company's products and any technical issues they may be having. You've received reports that several forum users had their accounts hijacked. These hijacked accounts started spamming the forums, which led to them being banned. In your investigation, you noticed that all of the users that were impersonated had either commented on or simply visited a specific forum thread. In this thread, a user invoked an HTML script in their comment. This could be a(n):

   ○ XSRF attack.

   ◉ Stored XSS attack.

   ○ Reflected XSS attack.

   ○ Fuzzing test.

2. The IT department's engineering team is currently developing a mobile app that gives customers another interface for accessing Develetech's online store. You are one of the app's beta testers and are looking for any security vulnerabilities. During your test, you select a product that is on sale and the app crashes. As it crashes, a message pops up that reveals information about what kind of database the app was attempting to connect to and how the data is supposed to be referenced. You determine that this is information that an attacker can easily use to their advantage. This is an example of:

   ○ Insufficient input validation.

   ○ Poor database management.

   ○ Insufficient XSS and XSRF prevention.

   ◉ Poor error/exception handling.

3. Using this mobile app, customers will be able to log in with individual accounts. When customers create an account with the app, they enter personal information into a standard registration form. To prevent an attacker from injecting malicious code into the account database, you should implement which of the following security techniques in your app? (Select all that apply.)

   ○ Patch management

   ◉ Client-side input validation

   ◉ Server-side input validation

   ○ Error/exception handling

4. In evaluating the mobile app, your IT team has decided to migrate the existing SQL database to a NoSQL database to greater facilitate the web app experience for customers. What security concerns do you need to remind your team of for this transition?

   A: Answer will vary, but may include the fact that any account may have complete access to the entire database. This is problematic in terms of authorization, as the team may want to limit some accounts to only certain data sets. Likewise, credentials may not be required at all for access to the database. The IT team should also realize that data is not necessarily encrypted when it is stored in a NoSQL database, which, depending on how sensitive the data is, could be a significant risk.

ACTIVITY 3-5: Hardening a Server

4. According to general system hardening guidelines, what additional software should you install to combat malware on all systems?

   ○ Security Configuration Wizard

   ◉ Antivirus software

   ○ A firewall

   ○ Database software

ACTIVITY 3-6: Managing Mobile Security

1. What are some of the security concerns you have about the common mobile devices you use or support?

   A: Concerns will vary, but may include mobile devices that are lost or stolen are at greater risk to be used in a malicious way to gain unauthorized access; the use of personal mobile devices when accessing and sending company email, servers, or services; and some mobile devices may not be equipped with the right level of security features or encryption functionality needed to ensure the right level of security.

2. Develetech policy requires that you ensure your smartphone is secured from unauthorized access in case it is lost or stolen. To prevent someone from accessing data on the device immediately after it has been turned on, what security control should be used?

   ○ GPS tracking

   ○ Device encryption

   ◉ Screen lock

   ○ Sanitization

3. An employee's car was recently broken into, and the thief stole a company tablet that held a great deal of sensitive data. You've already taken the precaution of securing plenty of backups of that data. What should you do to be absolutely certain that the data doesn't fall into the wrong hands?

   ○ Remotely lock out access.

   ◉ Remotely wipe and sanitize the device.

   ○ Encrypt the device.

   ○ Enable GPS to track the device.

4. You begin noticing that, more and more often, employees at Develetech are using their own personal devices to get work done in the office. To address this new challenge to security, you decide to draft an acceptable use policy that employees must agree to. What sort of protocols and controls should you include in this policy to address the BYOD phenomenon in your organization?

   A: There are many different concerns as far as BYOD goes. Students may suggest defining a clear legal stance in the acceptable use policy so that employees know who owns company data, and how that data may or may not be used with their mobile devices. It would also benefit the organization's security if the policy encourages employees to install antivirus software and be mindful of any security patches. The policy should also address employees' concerns about privacy.

5. Develetech is developing a mobile app for internal use only. This app needs to provide a great deal of security, as it will work with sensitive company data. What security controls should you instruct your engineers to implement in the design of the app?

   A: Some controls to consider are: enforcing data encryption and proper key management. This will keep data secure in both transit and rest states. If the app has users log in to accounts, their credentials should be managed properly, especially if they will be transmitted over the Internet. Providing strong authentication will help prevent unauthorized users from accessing the app's services. The app might also benefit from being selective when it comes to communicating with others apps. Only apps that are absolutely trusted should be allowed to interface with Develetech's app.

6. Pair up with a partner who has a different mobile device and examine the security features on that mobile device. Use the main menu to open the security settings.

7. Look at the specific security settings for each device such as the screen lock feature, device encryption options, and GPS tracking features. Compare the available settings on each device.

ACTIVITY 4-3: Examining Network Design Components

1. In what situation might you want to install a DMZ on your network?

   A: Answers may vary, but could include providing an FTP server for the public to download from, while separating access to that server from the rest of your internal network. Others may point to the need to section off mail servers behind a DMZ that send and receive external email messages. Services like VoIP and web access may also be beneficial to the network with DMZ protection.

2. What is the role of NAT on a network?

   A: You use NAT to conceal your internal network's IP addressing scheme from the public Internet. To do so, you configure a router with a single public IP address on its interface that connects to the Internet. Then, you configure the router's second interface with a private, non-routable IP address. NAT then translates between the public and private IP addressing schemes.

3. Which telephony technology allows telephone, email, fax, web, and computer actions to be integrated to work together?
   - ○ PBX
   - ○ VoIP
   - ◉ CTI
   - ○ DMZ

4. Develetech is in the testing phase of a new accounting application and needs to verify its functionality on various operating systems before deploying it to customers, but is dealing with hardware availability issues. What network design component would you suggest in this scenario?

   A: Answers may vary, but should include virtualization technology. This option allows you to install a number of operating system versions on the same computer.

5. The CEO of Develetech proposes establishing cloud computing technology to centralize the services and software that employees use every day. However, he stipulates that security is a priority due to the sensitive and confidential nature of the data that the company deals with. You also know that resources are unlikely to be shared with any competitors. What cloud computing deployment model do you suggest to him?

   ○ Hybrid
   ○ Community
   ◉ Private
   ○ Public

ACTIVITY 4-7: Securing a File Server

5. EFS encrypts files and folders on an individual basis, whereas BitLocker encrypts an entire drive. In what situation(s) might you use EFS instead of BitLocker?

   A: Answers may vary, but if you only want to share a specific file or folder with others while still maintaining the security of encryption, EFS may be the preferable choice. Encrypting an entire drive can take a significant amount of time, and once encrypted, the drive may suffer from decreased performance.

ACTIVITY 6-4: Securing Network Traffic with Certificates

5. Why did the connection fail?

   ◉ Because the server now requires secure communications.
   ○ Because you typed an invalid URL.
   ○ Because you did not log on.
   ○ Because the certificate has expired.

6. How can you connect successfully?

   ○ By using the SFTP protocol.
   ◉ By using the HTTPS protocol.
   ○ By using a certificate to authenticate the user.
   ○ By logging on as a different user.

ACTIVITY 6-9: Revoking Certificates

2. When will clients know that the certificate has been revoked?

   ○ When the certificate expires.
   ○ When they connect to the website.
   ◉ When the CRL is published.
   ○ When the client requests a new certificate.

3. If an attacker maliciously revokes certificates, how could they be recovered?

   ○ By renewing the CA certificates.

   ○ By republishing the CRL.

   ○ By reissuing the certificates.

   ◉ By restoring the CA from a backup.

ACTIVITY 7-1: Examining the Components of Physical Security

1. What types of physical security controls would you suggest for the main server room?

   A: Answers will vary, but should be focused on access controls surrounding the room such as door locks with identification systems, surveillance systems, and possibly an alarm system.

2. What are some common environmental exposures that you may consider when evaluating the overall security of the new building?

   A: Answers will vary depending on the specific environment a building is in, but common exposures could include water damage and flooding, power failures, and fires.

3. What type of environmental controls should the company consider as part of their relocation?

   A: Answers will vary, but should include proper fire prevention, detection, and suppression controls. These systems will most likely be standard and will be implemented according to the fire code guidelines set forth by the local fire department, but other special fire suppression systems may be needed to appropriately secure the organization's most sensitive assets, such as any server rooms and data centers.

ACTIVITY 7-2: Examining Legal Compliance

2. An employee unintentionally opens an attachment that causes a virus to spread within the organization. Does the policy call for legal action?

   A: According to section 4.3, there is no call for legal action against the employee in this situation because the employee was unaware of the virus. However, disciplinary action may be taken to be sure the user understands the "extreme caution" provision in section 4.2. The only legal action that may be considered is against the individual who actually sent the virus.

3. An employee emails a copy of a new type of encryption software program to a user in a foreign country for testing. Does the policy call for legal action?

   A: According to section 4.3, depending on your locality and the destination country, this may be a legal violation of export control laws, and legal action might be taken.

4. An employee scans your network for open ports. Does the policy call for legal action?

   A: According to section 4.3, there is no call for legal action in this situation. However, disciplinary action may be taken.

5. An employee forwards an email that appears to be a Ponzi or Pyramid scheme. Does the policy call for legal action?

   A: According to section 4.3, the policy does not call for legal action in this situation. However, disciplinary action may be taken.

6. Two employees have an argument at lunchtime. During the afternoon, one user sends a threatening email to the other. The second employee is afraid to leave the building unescorted that evening. Does the policy call for legal action?

    A: According to section 4.3, hostile or threatening messages could be considered a form of harassment, which could be subject to legal action.

ACTIVITY 7-3: Examining Security Awareness and Training

1. A virus has spread throughout your organization, causing expensive system downtime and corrupted data. You find that the virus sent to many users was an email attachment that was forwarded by an employee. The employee that received the original email was fooled into believing the link it contained was a legitimate marketing survey. You quickly determine that this is a well-known email hoax that had already been posted on several hoax-related websites. When questioned, the employee said that he thought it sounded as if it could be legitimate, and he could not see any harm in just trying it. How could better user training and awareness have helped this situation?

    A: If the employees had been aware of the dangers of opening email attachments, and had been more knowledgeable about how to identify email hoaxes, it is unlikely that the virus would have spread as far. If the initial employee, in particular, had been better informed, you might have been able to keep the virus out of your organization altogether.

2. What specific training steps do you recommend taking in response to this incident?

    A: Because this was a widespread incident, your response must include better security awareness for all users. You could distribute or prominently post a notice regarding the incident, or review proper guidelines for opening email attachments and for identifying email hoaxes. You could distribute links to common hoax-debunking websites to make it easy for employees to research possible hoaxes. You could also review your new-hire training procedures to be sure they include information on email security.

3. You come in on a Monday morning to find laptops have been stolen from several employees' desks over the weekend. After reviewing videotapes from the security cameras, you find that as an employee exited the building through the secure rear door on Friday night, she held the door open to admit another individual. You suspect this individual was the thief. When you question the employee, she states that the individual told her that he was a new employee who had not yet received his employee badge, that he only needed to be in the building for a few minutes, and that it would save him some time if she could let him in the back door rather than having to walk around to the receptionist entrance. Your security policy states that no one without identification should be admitted through the security doors at any time, but the employee says she was unaware of this policy. You ask her to locate the security policy documents on the network, and she is unable to do so. How could better user education have helped this situation?

    A: Regardless of the specific policy, if the employee had been informed and been made more aware of some common-sense security guidelines, she might have not admitted the stranger without question.

4. What user training steps do you recommend taking in response to this incident?

    A: This seems to be an isolated incident, so you should be sure to address it with the employee in question and the employee's manager, by reviewing all security policies with her and emphasizing the possible consequences of her actions. You should probably also post all security policies and best practices in an easily accessible location on the network and send out a company-wide reminder about them. However, because this employee never even attempted to refer to the policy, the inaccessibility of the policy documents was not a contributing factor in this incident. Finally, you should review your new-hire security training procedures from time to time to be sure they include common-sense tips and guidelines on building security.

5. One of your competitors has somehow obtained confidential data about your organization. There have been no obvious security breaches or physical break-ins, and you are puzzled as to the source of the leak. You begin to ask questions about any suspicious or unusual employee activity, and you begin to hear stories about a sales representative from out of town who did not have a desk in the office and was sitting down in open cubes and plugging her laptop in to the corporate network. You suspect that the sales representative was really an industrial spy for your competitor. When you ask other employees why they did not ask the sales representative for identification or report the incident to security, the other employees said that, giving their understanding of company policies, they did not see anything unusual or problematic in the situation. You review your security policy documents and, in fact, none of them refer to a situation like this one. How could better user education have helped this situation?

   A: In this case, it is not apparent that there were any problems in the education process. Users were aware of the presence of policy documents, but the documents themselves were inadequate because they did not deal with the dangers of this type of situation.

6. What user training steps do you recommend taking in response to this incident?

   A: You need to update your network acceptable use policy to make it clear what kind of authorization an individual needs in order to access the corporate network from within the building. You also need to disseminate this new information to all employees. You might want to follow this up in a few weeks or months with a staged attack of a similar nature, to see how employees respond.

7. The customer and employee databases include credit card and bank account numbers, governmental tax identification numbers, and other sensitive information. A blog posting hints at the possibility of this information being distributed to unauthorized people, and the media begins calling people at all levels of the organization, trying to confirm or deny the rumor. Current security policies specify that this sort of information needs to be protected, but does not appear to address media enquiries regarding potential breaches. How could better user education have helped in this situation?

   A: In this case, there may not have been problems with the education process, as the policy documents did not deal with handling media enquiries.

8. What user training steps do you recommend taking in response to this incident?

   A: You need to consider implementing role-based training to protect personally identifiable information and to designate which employees have the responsibility for alerting customers, employees, and the public of a potential security breach.

9. How might you suggest that Develetech validate the effectiveness of the user training you've recommended to address these issues?

   A: Answers will vary, but might include: identifying and tracking the number of computers affected by malware, tracking which employees have taken security training, and requiring that employees sign off on security policies and changes to the policies.

ACTIVITY 7-4: Integrating Systems and Data with Third Parties

1. Before the partnership with Mixed Messages Media begins, you decide to draft standards for on-boarding and off-boarding of partner employees. What are some of the security issues you need to consider when writing this policy?

   A: Answers may vary, but the issues surrounding on-boarding could be that you need a way to ensure that Mixed Messages Media's employees can adapt to your own organization's security policies; that there will be a fair division of responsibility amongst employees in both companies; and that there is no imbalance of liability should something go wrong. For off-boarding, you should establish a process for winding down a partnership; agree to terminate any integration with third parties; and remove any access that was granted to these parties.

2. Now that you've drafted on-boarding and off-boarding policies to share with your partner, you're ready to collaborate with Mixed Messages Media on an interoperability agreement. You want your partnership to be legally binding and focus primarily on keeping Develetech's information infrastructure secure. Which type of agreement would best fulfill these requirements?

   ◉ ISA

   ○ MOU

   ○ BPA

   ○ SLA

3. As part of Mixed Messages Media's marketing strategy, they have encouraged their employees to take to various social networks in an effort to spread awareness about Develetech's new line of Smart TVs. These marketing employees are using their own personal social media accounts to publicly divulge information about the product that has not yet been released. As a security administrator, what are your concerns?

   A: Answers may vary, but social media opens up a great deal of risk to an organization because of how quickly and ubiquitously information can spread. Depending on how much the marketing employees know about the new TVs, they may accidentally let some information slip that they should not have. This could give a competitor an edge, or, if the information they divulge is about a feature that hasn't been finalized, this could cause consumer confusion if that feature is dropped upon release. Also, social networks are rife with social engineering. The security training you gave to your own employees may not have been given to the marketing firm's employees. This means that they could be much more susceptible to social engineering tactics, and any compromise on their end may reach your own organization.

4. In Develetech's databases there is a great deal of data regarding the new Smart TVs. In order to effectively communicate their marketing push, Mixed Messages Media needs more than just basic information about the product. They require current finalized hardware specifications, as well as a list of finalized software that the TV runs so that they may better tailor the marketing campaign to the appropriate demographic. What sort of security controls and policies do you need Mixed Messages Media to agree to so that they won't be able to compromise the more secretive data in your databases?

   A: Answers may vary, but before you begin sharing, you need to remind Mixed Messages Media that Develetech retains full ownership of all data regarding the Smart TVs. You may want to set up some form of authentication and access control for a select few marketing employees that need continual access to your hardware and software specs. These employees should be limited to only accessing this type of information, and denied access to anything else. You should also caution your employees at Develetech who have wider access not to share any information with the marketing firm that you have deemed off-limits. Finally, depending on the nature of these specs, you may want to prohibit Mixed Messages Media from creating backups of the data that they receive—any backups will be handled by you and your team.

ACTIVITY 7-5: Implementing a Physical Security Policy for an Organization (Optional)

1. Which security level does your organization fall under? Why?

    A: According to section 3.2.4 of the policy, the organization is in security level 4, due to the monetary value of the equipment you need to protect in a single location.

2. Besides using blinds and locks on the windows, what else could you recommend using to secure the windows from unauthorized access?

    A: According to section 3.3 of the policy, you could install obscurity filming or even metal bars.

3. Once the motion-detection alarms are installed, what procedure will you need to follow to verify they are working properly?

    A: According to section 3.3 of the policy, you will need to perform a walk test to verify that the alarms have been installed correctly.

4. Given the security requirements of this company and the category of risk the computing center falls into, what other physical security recommendations could you make, based on this document?

    A: Answers may vary; for example, the escorted contractors should give 48 hours of notice on what they will be doing. Computers could be placed at least 5 feet from external windows.

ACTIVITY 8-1: Examining Risk Analysis

1. What are some obvious vulnerabilities surrounding the Develetech Industries server room, and what others would you investigate?

    A: Answers will vary, but the obvious vulnerability is the room's close proximity to the main lobby. Other vulnerabilities you might notice are the type of walls installed around the room. You can verify that they extend from floor to ceiling and that they do not contain large vents that could be used as access points. You might check to see if there are other doors to the room and if they are secured.

2. Based on the known vulnerabilities for the computer room, what potential threats exist?

    A: While there may be many specific threats, the main concern here is that visitors coming and going could easily view the type of physical access control used to get into the computer room. Another potential threat is that visitors could be in a position to see the access code being entered and could use it to gain access themselves.

3. What factors will affect the likelihood of these threats succeeding?

    A: There are several factors to consider: how much guest traffic the lobby receives on any given day; how many authorized employees tend the lobby; how conspicuous the server room itself looks; how easy it is to see the numeric keypad from afar; whether or not employees are discrete about revealing what's on the servers; how sought-after the data on the servers is by rival companies; and so on.

4. **What do you think the potential impact would be if an unauthorized access attempt was successful?**

   A: The impact would be large in this case, due to what is stored inside the server room. Unauthorized users could gain access to the sensitive data stored in the servers and use this against the organization and therefore demolish the organization's credibility. In a monetary sense, the company could lose revenue if customer data is analyzed by a competitor to glean certain trade secrets.

5. **What risk mitigation strategies would you use in this situation to reduce the risks surrounding the physical access of the server room?**

   A: Answers will vary, but may include implementing better security controls, such as operational controls, including a server room security guard. Another possibility would be to simply relocate the servers to a more secure and remote area of the building.

ACTIVITY 9-1: Responding to Security Incidents

1. **Based on your own professional or personal experience, what are some examples of typical computer crimes?**

   A: Responses might include: unauthorized access to a computer or network; distributing illegal information via a computer network; stealing classified information stored on a computer; and social engineering attacks that involve illegal activity.

2. **In your own words, why is it important to have an IRP?**

   A: Answers will vary, but generally, an IRP is important because it will help reduce confusion during a security incident by detailing who should respond to an incident and in what fashion, and it will minimize the impact such an incident will have on an organization.

3. **What do you think are the most important components in an IRP?**

   A: Answers will vary, but may include the definition of an incident, the classification of the incident's urgency level, and the process flow of the incident response (reporting the incident, determining how to investigate it, and reviewing the effectiveness of the response).

4. **In general, do you think it is important to notify employees of common or minor security incidents? Why or why not?**

   A: Answers will vary. You should notify the employees when an incident affects safety, workflows, or job responsibilities. It is not recommended or appropriate to advertise or publicize problems outside of need-to-know requirements.

5. **Why might you want to alert law enforcement officials of a security incident? Why might you want to notify the media?**

   A: Answers will vary, but generally, you would want to notify law enforcement if the incident was serious enough to have a financial impact or other consequence that might warrant a criminal investigation. You might notify the media to warn other companies to protect against a specific type of attack or if the incident had any effects on the organization that might be important to stockholders.

6. **What forensic techniques would you leverage in response to a network breach?**

   A: Answers will vary, but your first move should be to assess your hardware's order of volatility so that you don't lose time-sensitive data. You should then consider capturing an image of any system that was affected by the intrusion, allowing you to essentially "freeze" the evidence in place. Additionally, you'll want to examine network traffic logs, especially anything that was detected by an IDS. This may point you to the method of the attack, or even the origin. You can also record time offsets to narrow down exactly when the intrusion took place.
   If you have a favorite example of an IRP on the web, direct students to it. You can then focus classroom discussion on that specific policy.

7. On your Windows Server 2012 R2 computer, access the Internet, and search for sample IRPs. Identify the common guidelines listed in all of them.

   A: Answers will vary, but an IRP will specify who determines and declares if an actual incident has occurred, who should be notified about an incident and when, who will respond to an incident, and guidelines for appropriate response procedures that have been tested.

ACTIVITY 9-2: Recovering from a Security Incident

1. This was a weakness in the security of the facility. As an information security professional, why are you involved?

   A: Answers will vary, but some companies make no distinction between the physical infrastructure and IT, especially since the actual security used to maintain a secure building requires implementing and maintaining a network infrastructure. For example, the video surveillance camera that caught images of the trespasser needs a network to send its images to be monitored or stored. Another reason is that the physical network infrastructure or its devices are fairly vulnerable in this case, even if it is not clear what the attacker was doing there, or if the attack happened off-camera. Any recommendations for how the company can recover from this type of attack will likely involve increased technological security or surveillance, both of which will fall into the job duties of an IT security professional.

2. What is the first step you need to take in handling this incident?

   A: The first step would be for you to assess the extent of damage caused. Check if any critical systems were damaged or if network cables were unplugged. If no external damage is visible, then you need to scan the systems to see if any files were deleted or if malware or backdoor programs were installed. After finding any possible damage, you need to calculate the time it will take to repair the damage caused.

3. What are the immediate steps you need to take to recover from any damage?

   A: Answers will vary, but you need to replace hardware if it was damaged or stolen and delete malware that has been injected into systems. Disconnect the affected systems if they are capable of spreading viruses, and inform officials of your plans to recover from the incident. When you know that your systems are no longer exposed to any threats, then you can reconnect them back to the servers and restore the necessary backup to continue operations.

4. Should this incident be reported to the entire company?

   A: The company security policy most likely prohibits allowing unauthorized visitors into the building. If this is the case, then this highlights a serious vulnerability, and reviewing the acceptable use policy (AUP) and end user policy with the entire company might be in order. Even if the security policy makes no mention of allowing visitors into the building, it would be a good time to review the security policy and best practices with the entire staff. On the other hand, there is a potential downside to this, as alerting employees of this incident might alarm them unnecessarily.

5. Should law enforcement be notified?

   A: Yes. While the types of crimes that require legal intervention might be different in your region, this type of attack does constitute trespassing, which is illegal.

6. According to the company's risk assessment analysis, unauthorized trespassing was listed as high risk. In composing your report, what are some things you can do to bring that risk down to a more manageable level?

   A: Answers will vary, but may include recommendations such as mantraps, keypads, or smart cards required at all access points, and more explicit guidelines in the security policy for unauthorized personnel.

ACTIVITY 10-1: Discussing Business Continuity Planning

1. As the security administrator, you are responsible for ensuring that your BCP coincides with the organization's needs. What are your goals while establishing a BCP? (Select all that apply.)

   ☑ Preserve important documents.

   ☑ Establish decision-making authority.

   ☐ Analyze fault tolerance.

   ☑ Maintain financial functions.

2. Your organization is located in an area where there is a threat of hurricanes. As a member of the BCP team, you need to determine what effect there would be if a hurricane halted business activities at your organization. Which BCP component is this an example of?

   ○ Continuity of operations

   ◉ BIA

   ○ IT contingency planning

   ○ Succession planning

3. Which part of the plan specifies interim sites and systems you can switch to following a disaster?

   ○ RPO

   ○ BIA

   ◉ IT contingency plan

   ○ Succession plan

4. You recommend the company pay a small monthly rental fee for a warehouse with phone and power hookups to use as a:

   ○ Hot site

   ◉ Cold site

   ○ Warm site

5. You and your colleague have just performed a walkthrough of the plan that would be put into effect in the event of a Denial of Service (DoS) attack on your company website. The two of you think that you need to perform more rigorous tests to ensure the effectiveness of the BCP. What are some other testing methods you might want to recommend?

   A: Parallel testing and cutover testing.

ACTIVITY 10-2: Creating a DRP

1. Which are common components that should be in Develetech Industries' DRP? (Select all that apply.)

   ☐ A list of employees' personal items.

   ☑ Contact information for key individuals.

   ☑ An inventory of important hardware and software.

   ☑ Plans to reconstruct the network.

2. Develetech Industries is willing to set aside some capital to install a fault tolerance system. What can you suggest?

   A: Answers may vary, but you can suggest implementing a better RAID standard, backup circuits, server clustering, spare hardware, and a redundant power supply.

3. Assume that Develetech Industries is located in a climate and location identical to the company you work for now. What are some unique geographical or weather-related conditions you might need to account for, but that might not be a consideration for other companies?

   A: Answers will vary, but you some locales might be particularly concerned with natural disasters such as hurricanes, tornadoes, river flooding, ice storms, heavy snowfall, and so on.

4. Assume that a high-level manager has expressed some dissatisfaction with the notion of a "fire drill" to test the company's preparedness for a disaster; it seems he is leery of so much paid time being used in an unproductive way, and he wonders if you cannot just write a detailed plan instead. What are some things you can mention to help persuade him that such an unannounced drill is necessary?

   A: Answers will vary, but should contain some reference to the cost of being unprepared. If a company were to never test their DRP or BCP, then how does one really know if they will work? A company might be spending a lot of money on non-billable projects during a "fire drill," but such a drill could ensure that business is actually able to continue if disaster struck the company. You can also mention the legal ramifications or liability exposure of being unprepared for a disaster situation.

5. Once you have the DRP and other components in place, what do you do to make sure it works smoothly?

   A: Answers may vary, but you can perform a walkthrough or parallel testing, and when you are sure it all works well, you can even perform a cutover. Also make sure there is a system in place to review the plan annually and make any maintenance-level changes.

ACTIVITY 10-3: Executing DRPs and Procedures

1. What should you keep in mind while choosing a good recovery team?

   ○ Include individuals who can do an analysis of the damage that the crisis has caused to the organization.

   ◉ Include individuals who can implement the proper procedures in response to the disruption to critical business processes.

   ○ Include individuals who can record the history of the evidence of a computer crime from collection, to presentation in court, to return or disposal.

   ○ Include individuals who determine how much money and effort will go into a recovery plan.

2. You have been assigned to perform a secure recovery; what does your task include?

   A: As a designated and trusted officer, you need to supervise the recovery, making sure to document each step taken, noting the information needed to restore the processes and system. You might also note the data that is needed to recover from the disaster, and important instructions to maintain the continuity of operations.

3. You have to decide on the kind of backup source you will use to recover data and restore function to the business in the least possible time. What type of backup could you choose?

   A: It depends on what your best backup source is. Usually you want the backup source that is most current and accessible. Rebuilding data directly from a RAID array is preferred; if that is not possible, use a local backup, then an offsite backup.

4. **What types of backup storage locations can you suggest to store data for your company?**

    A: Answers may vary, but can include an onsite storage location where the most recent set of backups are stored so they can be accessed quickly for use in normal day-to-day operations. You may also choose a disaster-resistant offsite location to securely store a duplicate backup of all data present and past.

Glossary

3DES
(Triple DES) A symmetric encryption algorithm that encrypts data by processing each block of data three times, using a different DES key each time.

802.11
A family of specifications developed by the IEEE for wireless LAN technology.

802.11a
A fast, secure, but relatively expensive protocol for wireless communication. The 802.11a protocol supports speeds up to 54 Mbps in the 5 GHz frequency.

802.11ac
A wireless communication protocol that improves upon 802.11n by adding wider channels to increase bandwidth.

802.11b
The first specification to be called Wi-Fi, 802.11b is the least expensive wireless network protocol used to transfer data among computers with wireless network cards, or between a wireless computer or device and a wired LAN. The 802.11b protocol provides for an 11 Mbps transfer rate in the 2.4 GHz frequency.

802.11g
A specification for wireless data throughput at the rate of up to 54 Mbps in the 2.4 GHz band that is a potential replacement for 802.11b.

802.11n
A wireless standard for home and business implementations that adds QoS features and multimedia support to 802.11a and 802.11b.

802.1x
An IEEE standard used to provide a port-based authentication mechanism over a LAN or wireless LAN.

access control
In security terms, the process of determining and assigning privileges to various resources, objects, and data.

Access Control List
See ACL.

account federation
The practice of linking a single account across many different management systems.

account management
A common term used to refer to the processes, functions, and policies used to effectively manage user accounts within an organization.

account phishing
In social networking, an attack where an attacker creates an account and gets on the friends list of an individual just to try to obtain information about the individual and their circle of friends or colleagues.

account policy
A document that includes an organization's user account management guidelines.

account privileges
Permissions granted to users that allow them to perform various actions such as creating, deleting, and editing files, and also accessing systems and services on the network.

accountability
In security terms, the process of determining who to hold responsible for a particular activity or event.

accounting
In security terms, the process of tracking and recording system activities and resource access.

ACL
(Access Control List) In a DAC access control scheme, this is the list that is associated with each object, specifying the subjects that can access the object and their levels of access.

Active Directory
The standards-based directory service from Microsoft that runs on Microsoft Windows servers.

Address Resolution Protocol
See ARP.

Advanced Encryption Standard
See AES.

adware
Software that automatically displays or downloads advertisements when it is used.

AES
(Advanced Encryption Standard) A symmetric 128-, 192-, or 256-bit block cipher based on the Rijndael algorithm developed by Belgian cryptographers Joan Daemen and Vincent Rijmen and adopted by the U.S. government as its encryption standard to replace DES.

ALE
(annual loss expectancy) The total cost of a risk to an organization on an annual basis.

all-in-one security appliance
A single network device that is used to perform a number of security functions to secure a network.

annual loss expectancy
See ALE.

annual rate of occurrence
See ARO.

anomaly-based monitoring
A monitoring system that uses a database of unacceptable traffic patterns identified by analyzing traffic flows.

anti-malware software
A category of software programs that scan a computer or network for known viruses, Trojans, worms, and other malicious software.

anti-spam
A program that will detect specific words that are commonly used in spam messages.

anti-spyware
Software that is specifically designed to protect systems against spyware attacks.

antivirus software
An application that scans files for executable code that matches specific patterns that are known to be common to viruses.

API
(application programming interface) A mechanism that defines how software elements interact with each other.

application attacks
Attacks that are targeted at web-based and other client-server applications.

application aware device
A network device that manages information about any application that connects to it.

application blacklisting
The practice of preventing undesirable programs from running on a computer, computer network, or mobile device.

application programming interface
See API.

application whitelisting
The practice of allowing approved programs to run on a computer, computer network, or mobile device.

arbitrary code execution
An attack that exploits an application vulnerability into allowing the attacker to execute commands on a user's computer.

archive bit
A file property that essentially indicates whether the file has been modified since the last back up.

armored virus
A virus that is able to conceal its location or otherwise render itself harder to detect by anti-malware programs.

ARO
(annual rate of occurrence) How many times per year a particular loss is expected to occur.

ARP
(Address Resolution Protocol) The mechanism by which individual hardware MAC addresses are matched to an IP address on a network.

ARP poisoning
A method in which an attacker with access to the target network redirects an IP address to the MAC address of a computer that is not the intended recipient.

asymmetric encryption
A two-way encryption scheme that uses paired private and public keys.

attachment attack
An attack where the attacker can merge malicious software or code into a downloadable file or attachment on an application server so that users download and execute it on client systems.

attack
Any technique that is used to exploit a vulnerability in any application on a computer system without the authorization to do so.

attack surface
The portion of a system or application that is exposed and available to attackers.

attackers
A term for users who gain unauthorized access to computers and networks for malicious purposes.

attacking
The final phase of a hack in which the attacker steals data, disrupts traffic, or damages systems.

auditing
The practice of examining logs of what was recorded in the accounting process.

authentication
In security terms, the process of validating a particular individual or entity's unique credentials.

authorization
In security terms, the process of determining what rights and privileges a particular entity has.

availability
The fundamental security goal of ensuring that systems operate continuously and that authorized persons can access data that they need.

backdoor
A mechanism for gaining access to a computer that bypasses or subverts the normal method of authentication.

backdoor attack
A type of attack where the attacker creates a software mechanism to gain access to a system and its resources. This can involve software or a bogus user account.

backout contingency plan
A documented plan that includes specific procedures and processes that are applied in

the event that a change or modification made to a system must be undone.

banner grabbing
See scanning.

baseline report
A collection of security and configuration settings that are to be applied to a particular system or network in the organization.

BCP
(business continuity plan) A policy that defines how normal day-to-day business will be maintained in the event of a business disruption or crisis.

bcrypt
A key-derivation function based on the Blowfish cipher algorithm.

behavior-based monitoring
A monitoring system that detects changes in normal operating data sequences and identifies abnormal sequences.

BIA
(business impact analysis) A BCP preparatory step that identifies present organizational risks and determines the impact to ongoing, business-critical operations if such risks actualize.

big data
Collections of data that are so large and complex that they cannot be managed using traditional database management tools.

biometrics
Authentication schemes based on individuals' physical characteristics.

birthday attack
A type of password attack that exploits weaknesses in the mathematical algorithms used to encrypt passwords, in order to take advantage of the probability of different password inputs producing the same encrypted output.

black box test
A test in which the tester is given no information about the system being tested.

black hat
A hacker who exposes vulnerabilities for financial gain or for some malicious purpose.

blacklisting
See application blacklisting.

block cipher
A type of symmetric encryption that encrypts data one block at a time, often in 64-bit blocks. It is usually more secure, but is also slower, than stream ciphers.

Blowfish
A freely available 64-bit block cipher algorithm that uses a variable key length.

bluejacking
A method used by attackers to send out unwanted Bluetooth signals from smartphones, mobile phones, tablets, and laptops to other Bluetooth-enabled devices.

bluesnarfing
A process in which attackers gain access to unauthorized information on a wireless device using a Bluetooth connection.

Bluetooth
A short-range wireless radio network transmission medium usually used between two personal devices, such as between a mobile phone and wireless headset.

botnet
A set of computers that has been infected by a control program called a bot that enables attackers to exploit the computers to mount attacks.

BPA
(business partner agreement) An agreement that defines how a business partnership will be conducted.

bring your own device
See BYOD.

brute force attack
A type of password attack where an attacker uses an application to exhaustively try every possible alphanumeric combination to try cracking encrypted passwords.

buffer overflow
A type of DoS attack that exploits fixed data buffer sizes in a target piece of software by sending data that is too large for the buffer.

business continuity plan
See BCP.

business impact analysis
See BIA.

business partner
A commercial entity that has a relationship with another, separate commercial entity.

business partner agreement
See BPA.

BYOD
(bring your own device) The practice in which employees bring their own personal devices (usually mobile) into the office and use them for work-related purposes.

CA
(Certificate Authority) A server that can issue digital certificates and the associated public/ private key pairs.

CA hierarchy
A single CA or group of CAs that work together to issue digital certificates.

CAC
(Common Access Card) See smart cards.

captive portal
A web page that a client is automatically directed to when connecting to a network, usually through public Wi-Fi.

CBC encryption
(Cipher Block Chaining encryption) A block encryption model where before a block is encrypted, information from the preceding block is added to the block. In this way, you can be sure that repeated data is encrypted differently each time it is encountered.

CCMP
(Counter Mode with Cipher Block Chaining Message Authentication Code Protocol) An AES cipher-based encryption protocol used in WPA2.

CCTV
(closed-circuit television) Surveillance cameras that do not openly broadcast signals.

Certificate Authority
See CA.

certificate management system
A system that provides the software tools to perform the day-to-day functions of a PKI.

certificate repository database
A database containing digital certificates.

Certificate Revocation List
See CRL.

certificate signing request
See CSR.

CFB encryption
(Cipher Feedback mode encryption) A block encryption model that allows encryption of partial blocks rather than requiring full blocks for encryption.

chain of custody
The record of evidence history from collection, to presentation in court, to disposal.

Challenge Handshake Authentication Protocol
See CHAP.

change management
A systematic way of approving and executing change in order to ensure maximum security, stability, and availability of information technology services.

CHAP
(Challenge Handshake Authentication Protocol) An encrypted remote access authentication method that enables connections from any authentication method requested by the server, except for PAP and SPAP unencrypted authentication.

CIA triad
(confidentiality, integrity, availability) The three principles of security control and management: confidentiality, integrity, and availability. Also known as the information security triad or triple.

cipher
The rule, system, or mechanism used to encrypt or decrypt data.

Cipher Block Chaining encryption
See CBC encryption.

Cipher Feedback mode encryption
See CFB encryption.

cipher suite
A collection of symmetric and asymmetric encryption algorithms commonly used in SSL/TLS connections.

ciphertext
Data that has been encoded with a cipher and is unreadable.

cleartext
The unencrypted form of data. Also known as plaintext.

clickjacking
An attack that forces a user to unintentionally click a link. An attacker uses opaque layers or multiple transparent layers to trick a user.

client–side attacks
Attacks that exploit the trust relationship between a client and the server it connects to.

closed–circuit television
See CCTV.

cloud computing
A method of computing that relies on the Internet to provide the resources, software, data, and media needs of a user, business, or organization.

code reviews
An evaluation used in identifying potential weaknesses in an application.

cold site
A predetermined alternate location where a network can be rebuilt after a disaster.

compliance
The practice of ensuring that the requirements of legislation, regulations, industry codes and standards, and organizational standards are met.

computer crime
A criminal act that involves the use of a computer as a source or target, instead of an individual.

computer forensics
A skill that deals with collecting and analyzing data from storage devices, computer systems, networks, and wireless communications and presenting this information as a form of evidence in the court of law.

computer telephony integration
See CTI.

confidentiality
The fundamental security goal of keeping information and communications private and protecting them from unauthorized access.

continuity of operations plan
A plan that includes best practices to mitigate risks and attacks and the best measures to recover from an incident.

controls
The countermeasures that you need to put in place to avoid, mitigate, or counteract security risks due to threats or attacks.

cookie
A small piece of text saved on a computer by a web browser that consists of one or more name-value pairs holding bits of information useful in remembering user preferences.

cookie manipulation
An attack where an attacker injects a meta tag in an HTTP header making it possible to modify a cookie stored in a browser.

correction controls

Controls that help to mitigate a consequence of a threat or attack from hazardously affecting the computer system.

counter mode encryption

See CTR encryption.

Counter Mode with Cipher Block Chaining Message Authentication Code Protocol

See CCMP.

cracker

A user who breaks encryption codes, defeats software copy protections, or specializes in breaking into systems.

credential manager

An application that stores passwords in an encrypted database for easy retrieval by the appropriate user.

CRL

(Certificate Revocation List) A list of certificates that are no longer valid.

cross-site request forgery

See XSRF.

cross-site scripting

See XSS.

cryptography

The science of hiding information.

cryptoprocessors

Microprocessors that provide cryptographic functions.

CSR

(certificate signing request) A message sent to a certificate authority in which a resource applies for a certificate.

CTI

(computer telephony integration) Telephony technology that incorporates telephone, email, web, and computing infrastructures.

CTR encryption

(counter mode encryption) A block encryption model that is similar to OFB and uses a counter as input.

cyberterrorist

A hacker that disrupts computer systems in order to spread fear and panic.

DAC

(Discretionary Access Control) In DAC, access is controlled based on a user's identity. Objects are configured with a list of users who are allowed access to them. An administrator has the discretion to place the user on the list or not. If a user is on the list, the user is granted access; if the user is not on the list, access is denied.

damage controls

See loss controls.

data

A general term for the information assets of a person or organization. In a computer system, data is generally stored in files.

Data Encryption Standard

See DES.

data exfiltration

The malicious transfer of data from one system to another.

data leakage

Gaining access to data through unintentional methods that could lead to data loss or theft.

data loss/leak prevention

See DLP.

data sanitization

The method used to repeatedly delete and overwrite any traces or bits of sensitive data that may remain on a device after data wiping has been done.

data security

The security controls and measures taken in order to keep an organization's data safe and accessible and to prevent unauthorized access.

data wiping

A method used to remove any sensitive data from a mobile device and permanently delete it.

DDoS attack

(Distributed Denial of Service attack) A network attack in which an attacker hijacks or manipulates multiple computers (through the use of zombies or drones) on disparate networks to carry out a DoS attack.

deciphering

The process of reversing a cipher.

decryption

A cryptographic technique that converts ciphertext back to cleartext.

defense in depth

A comprehensive approach to layered security that is intended to slow an attack.

demilitarized zone

See DMZ.

Denial of Service attack

See DoS attack.

DES

(Data Encryption Standard) A symmetric encryption algorithm that encrypts data in 64-bit blocks using a 56-bit key, with 8 bits used for parity.

detection

The act of determining if a user has tried to access unauthorized data, or scanning the data and networks for any traces left by an intruder in any attack against the system.

detection controls

Controls that are implemented to monitor a situation or activity, and react to any irregular activities by bringing the issue to the attention of administrators.

device

A piece of hardware such as a computer, server, printer, or smartphone.

DH

(Diffie-Hellman) A cryptographic protocol that provides for secure key exchange.

DHCP

(Dynamic Host Configuration Protocol) A protocol used to automatically assign IP addressing information to IP network computers.

DHE

(Diffie-Hellman Ephemeral) A cryptographic protocol that is based on Diffie-Hellman and that provides for secure key exchange by using ephemeral keys.

Diameter

An authentication protocol that allows for a variety of connection types, such as wireless.

dictionary attack

A type of password attack that automates password guessing by comparing encrypted passwords against a predetermined list of possible password values.

differential backup

A backup that backs up all files in a selected storage location that have changed since the last full backup.

Diffie–Hellman

See DH.

Diffie–Hellman Ephemeral

See DHE.

digital certificate

An electronic document that associates credentials with a public key.

digital signature

An encrypted hash value that is appended to a message to identify the sender and the message.

directory service

A network service that stores identity information about all the objects in a particular network, including users, groups, servers, client computers, and printers.

directory traversal
An attack that allows access to commands, files, and directories that may or may not be connected to the web document root directory.

disaster recovery plan
See DRP.

Discretionary Access Control
See DAC.

Distributed Denial of Service attack
See DDoS attack.

DLP
(data loss/leak prevention) Software that stops data in a system from being stolen.

DMZ
(demilitarized zone) A small section of a private network that is located between two firewalls and made available for public access.

DNS
(Domain Name System) The service that maps names to IP addresses on most TCP/IP networks, including the Internet.

DNS hijacking
An attack in which an attacker sets up a rogue DNS server. This rogue DNS server responds to legitimate requests with IP addresses for malicious or non-existent websites.

DNS poisoning
An attack in which an attacker exploits the traditionally open nature of the DNS system to redirect a domain name to an IP address of the attacker's choosing.

Domain Name System
See DNS.

DoS attack
(Denial of Service attack) A network attack in which an attacker disables systems that provide network services by consuming a network link's available bandwidth, consuming a single system's available resources, or exploiting programming flaws in an application or operating system.

drive-by download
A program that is automatically installed on a computer when you access a malicious site, even without clicking a link or giving consent.

drone
See zombie.

DRP
(disaster recovery plan) A plan that prepares the organization to react appropriately in a natural or a man-made disaster and provides the means to recover from a disaster.

dumpster diving
A human-based attack where the goal is to reclaim important information by inspecting the contents of trash containers.

Dynamic Host Configuration Protocol
See DHCP.

EAP
(Extensible Authentication Protocol) An authentication protocol that enables systems to use hardware-based identifiers, such as fingerprint scanners or smart card readers, for authentication.

eavesdropping attack
A network attack that uses special monitoring software to gain access to private communications on the network wire or across a wireless network. Also known as a sniffing attack.

ECB encryption
(Electronic Code Block encryption) A block encryption model where each block is encrypted by itself. Each occurrence of a particular word is encrypted exactly the same.

ECC
(elliptic curve cryptography) An asymmetric encryption technique that leverages the algebraic structures of elliptic curves over finite fields.

ECDHE
(Elliptic Curve Diffie-Hellman Ephemeral) A cryptographic protocol that is based on Diffie-Hellman and that provides for secure key

exchange by using ephemeral keys and elliptic curve cryptography.

EFS
(Encrypting File System) Microsoft Windows NTFS-based public key encryption.

electromagnetic interference
See EMI.

Electronic Code Block encryption
See ECB encryption.

elliptic curve cryptography
See ECC.

Elliptic Curve Diffie–Hellman Ephemeral
See ECDHE.

EMI
(electromagnetic interference) A disruption of electrical current that occurs when a magnetic field around one electrical circuit interferes with the signal being carried on an adjacent circuit.

enciphering
The process of applying a cipher.

Encrypting File System
See EFS.

encryption
A security technique that converts data from plain, or cleartext form, into coded, or ciphertext form so that only authorized parties with the necessary decryption information can decode and read the data.

encryption algorithm
See cipher.

enumerating
The stage of the hacking process in which the attacker will try to gain access to users and groups, network resources, shares, applications, or valid user names and passwords.

environmental controls
A system or device that is implemented to prevent or control environmental exposures or threats.

ethical hacking
Planned attempts to penetrate the security defenses of a system in order to identify vulnerabilities.

evil twin attack
In social networking, an attack where an attacker creates a social network account to impersonate a genuine user, becoming friends with others and joining groups, and thus getting access to various types of personal and professional information. In wireless networking, a type of rogue access point at a public site that is configured to look like a legitimate access point in order to tempt a user to choose to connect to it.

Extensible Authentication Protocol
See EAP.

eXtensible Markup Language
See XML.

failopen
A control that provides open access when a system fails.

failsafe
A control that provides user safety when a system fails.

failsecure
A control that provides security when a system fails.

fault tolerance
The ability of a network or system to withstand a foreseeable component failure and continue to provide an acceptable level of service.

FCoE
(Fibre Channel over Ethernet) Fibre Channel implementations that use high-speed Ethernet networks to transmit and store data.

Fibre Channel
A protocol that implements links between data storage networks using special-purpose cabling to increase performance and reliability.

Fibre Channel over Ethernet
See FCoE.

File Transfer Protocol
See FTP.

File Transfer Protocol Secure
See FTPS.

firewall
A software or hardware device that protects a system or network by blocking unwanted network traffic.

first responder
The first person or team to respond to an accident, damage site, or natural disaster in an IT company.

Flash cookies
See LSO.

flood guard
A tool used by network administrators and security professionals to protect resources from flooding attacks, such as DDoS attacks.

footprinting
The stage of the hacking process in which the attacker chooses a target organization or network and begins to gather information that is publicly available. Also called profiling.

FTP
(File Transfer Protocol) A communications protocol that enables the transfer of files between a user's workstation and a remote host.

FTP over SSH
A secure version of FTP that uses an SSH tunnel to encrypt files in transit.

FTP–SSL
See FTPS.

FTPS
(File Transfer Protocol Secure) A protocol that combines the use of FTP with additional support for TLS and SSL.

full backup
A backup that backs up all selected files regardless of the state of the archived bit.

fuzzing
A testing method used to identify vulnerabilities and weaknesses in applications, by sending the application a range of random or unusual input data and noting failures and crashes.

gain
The reliable connection range and power of a wireless signal, measured in decibels.

geolocation
The process of identifying the real-world geographic location of an object, often by associating a location such as a street address with an IP address, hardware address, Wi-Fi positioning system, GPS coordinates, or some other form of information.

GNU Privacy Guard
See GPG.

GPG
(GNU Privacy Guard) A free open-source version of PGP that provides the equivalent encryption and authentication services.

grey box test
A test in which the tester may have knowledge of internal architectures and systems, or other preliminary information about the system being tested.

grey hat
A hacker who exposes security flaws in applications and operating systems without consent, and does so for the greater good instead of maliciously.

group based privileges
Privileges that are assigned to an entire group of users within an organization.

group policy
A centralized configuration management feature available for Active Directory on Windows Server systems.

guessing
A human-based attack where the goal is to guess a password or PIN through brute force means or by using deduction.

guidelines
Suggestions for meeting a policy standard or best practices.

hackers
Users who excel at programming or managing and configuring computer systems, and have the skills to gain access to computer systems through unauthorized or unapproved means.

hacktivist
A hacker motivated by the desire for social change.

hardening
A security technique in which the default configuration of a system is altered to protect the system against attacks.

hardware attack
An attack that targets a computer's physical components and peripherals, including its hard disk, motherboard, keyboard, network cabling, or smart card reader.

Hardware Security Module
See HSM.

hardware-based encryption devices
A device or mechanism that provides encryption, decryption, and access control.

hash
The value that results from hashing encryption. Also known as hash value or message digest.

hash value
See hash.

Hash-based Message Authentication Code
See HMAC.

hashing encryption
One-way encryption that transforms cleartext into a coded form that is never decrypted.

header manipulation
An attack where the attacker manipulates the header information that is passed between web servers and clients in HTTP requests.

heating, ventilation, and air conditioning
See HVAC system.

heuristic monitoring
A monitoring system that uses known best practices and characteristics in order to identify and fix issues within the network.

high availability
A rating that expresses how closely systems approach the goal of providing data availability 100 percent of the time while maintaining a high level of system performance.

HMAC
(Hash-based Message Authentication Code) A method used to verify both the integrity and authenticity of a message by combining cryptographic hash functions, such as MD5 or SHA-1, with a secret key.

HMAC-based one-time password
See HOTP.

hoax
An email-based or web-based attack that tricks the user into performing undesired actions, such as deleting important system files in an attempt to remove a virus, or sending money or important information via email or online forms.

honeynet
An entire dummy network used to lure attackers.

honeypot
A security tool used to lure attackers away from the actual network components. Also called a decoy or sacrificial lamb.

host availability

The ability of a host to remain accessible despite any system changes it needs to adapt to.

host elasticity

See host availability.

host-based firewall

Software that is installed on a single system to specifically guard against networking attacks.

host/personal firewalls

Firewalls installed on a single or home computer.

hot and cold aisle

A method used within data centers and server rooms as a temperature and humidity control method.

hot site

A fully configured alternate network that can be online quickly after a disaster.

hotfix

A patch that is often issued on an emergency basis to address a specific security flaw.

HOTP

(HMAC-based one-time password) An algorithm that generates a one-time password using a hash-based authentication code to verify the authenticity of the message.

HSM

(Hardware Security Module) A cryptographic module that can generate cryptographic keys.

HTTP

(Hypertext Transfer Protocol) A protocol that defines the interaction between a web server and a browser.

HTTPS

(Hypertext Transfer Protocol Secure) A secure version of HTTP that supports e-commerce by providing a secure connection between a web browser and a server.

HVAC system

(heating, ventilation, and air conditioning) A system that controls the air quality and flow inside a building.

hybrid password attack

An attack that utilizes multiple attack methods, including dictionary, rainbow table, and brute force attacks when trying to crack a password.

Hypertext Transfer Protocol

See HTTP.

Hypertext Transfer Protocol Secure

See HTTPS.

IaaS

(Infrastructure as a Service) A method that uses the cloud to provide any or all infrastructure needs.

ICMP

(Internet Control Message Protocol) An IP network service that reports on connections between two hosts.

ICMP flood

A type of DoS attack that exploits weaknesses in ICMP. Specific attacks include Smurf attacks and ping floods.

identification

In security terms, the process of attaching a human element to an authentication.

identity management

An area of information security that is used to identify individuals within a computer system or network.

identity theft

A crime that occurs when an individual's personal information or data is stolen and used by someone other than the authorized user.

IDS

(intrusion detection system) A software and/or hardware system that scans, audits, and monitors the security infrastructure for signs of attacks in progress.

IM
(instant messaging) A type of communication service which involves a private dialogue between two persons via instant text-based messages over the Internet.

impersonation
A type of spoofing in which an attacker pretends to be someone they are not, typically an average user in distress, or a help desk representative.

implicit deny
The principle that establishes that everything that is not explicitly allowed is denied.

incident management
Practices and procedures that govern how an organization will respond to an incident in progress.

incident report
A description of the events that occurred during a security incident.

Incident Response Policy
See IRP.

incremental backup
A back up that backs up all files in a selected storage location that have changed since the last full or differential backup.

information security
The protection of available information or information resources from unauthorized access, attacks, thefts, or data damage.

information security triad
See CIA triad.

Infrastructure as a Service
See IaaS.

initialization vector
See IV.

input validation
Any technique used to ensure that the data entered into a field or variable in an application is within acceptable bounds for the object that will receive the data.

instant messaging
See IM.

integer overflow
An attack in which a computed result is too large to fit in its assigned storage space, leading to crashing, corruption, or triggering a buffer overflow.

integrity
The fundamental security goal of ensuring that electronic data is not altered or tampered with.

interconnection security agreement
See ISA.

interference
Within wireless networking, the phenomenon by which radio waves from other devices interfere with the 802.11 wireless signals.

Internet Control Message Protocol
See ICMP.

Internet Protocol Security
See IPSec.

Internet Small Computer System Interface
See iSCSI.

intrusion
An instance of an attacker accessing your computer system without the authorization to do so.

intrusion detection system
See IDS.

intrusion prevention system
See IPS.

IP version 4
See IPv4.

IP version 6
See IPv6.

IPS
(intrusion prevention system) An inline security device that monitors suspicious network and/or system traffic and reacts in real time to block it.

IPSec
(Internet Protocol Security) A set of open, non-proprietary standards that you can use to secure data through authentication and encryption as the data travels across the network or the Internet.

IPv4
(IP version 4) An Internet standard that uses a 32-bit number assigned to a computer on a TCP/IP network.

IPv6
(IP version 6) An Internet standard that increases the available pool of IP addresses by implementing a 128-bit binary address space.

IRP
(Incident Response Policy) The security policy that determines the actions that an organization will take following a confirmed or potential security breach.

ISA
(interconnection security agreement) A agreement that focuses on securing technology in a business relationship.

iSCSI
(Internet Small Computer System Interface) A protocol that implements links between data storage networks using IP.

IT contingency plan
An alternate plan that you can switch over to when faced with an attack or disruption of service.

IV
(initialization vector) A technique used in cryptography to generate random numbers to be used along with a secret key to provide data encryption.

IV attack
An attack where the attacker is able to predict or control the IV of an encryption process, thus giving the attacker access to view the encrypted data that is supposed to be hidden from everyone else except the user or network.

jamming
See interference.

job rotation
The principle that establishes that no one person stays in a vital job role for too long a time period.

Kerberos
An authentication system in which authentication is based on a time-sensitive ticket-granting system. It uses an SSO method where the user enters access credentials that are then passed to the authentication server, which contains the allowed access credentials.

key
In cryptography, a specific piece of information that is used in conjunction with an algorithm to perform encryption and decryption.

key escrow
A method for backing up private keys to protect them while allowing trusted third parties to access the keys under certain conditions.

key escrow agent
A third party that maintains a backup copy of private keys.

key exchange
Any method by which cryptographic keys are transferred among users, thus enabling the use of a cryptographic algorithm.

key generation
An asymmetric encryption process of generating a public and private key pair using a specific application.

key stretching
A technique that strengthens potentially weak cryptographic keys, such as passwords or passphrases created by people, against brute force attacks.

keystroke authentication
A type of authentication that relies on detailed information that describes exactly when a keyboard key is pressed and released as someone types information into a computer or other electronic device.

L2TP

(Layer Two Tunneling Protocol) The de facto standard VPN protocol for tunneling PPP sessions across a variety of network protocols such as IP, Frame Relay, or ATM.

Layer Two Tunneling Protocol

See L2TP.

layered security

An approach to securing systems that incorporates many different avenues of defense.

LDAP

(Lightweight Directory Access Protocol) A simple network protocol used to access network directory databases, which store information about authorized users and their privileges as well as other organizational information.

LDAP injection

An attack that targets web-based applications by fabricating LDAP statements that typically are created by user input.

LDAPS

(Lightweight Directory Access Protocol Secure) A method of implementing LDAP using SSL/TLS encryption.

LEAP

(Lightweight Extensible Authentication Protocol) Cisco Systems' proprietary EAP implementation.

least privilege

The principle that establishes that users and software should only have the minimal level of access that is necessary for them to perform the duties required of them.

Lightweight Directory Access Protocol

See LDAP.

Lightweight Directory Access Protocol Secure

See LDAPS.

Lightweight Extensible Authentication Protocol

See LEAP.

load balancer

A network device that performs load balancing as its primary function.

load balancing

The practice of spreading out the work among the devices in a network.

locally shared object

See LSO.

lockout

A method of restricting access to data on a device without deleting that data.

log

A record of significant events. In computing, it is using an operating system or application to record data about activity on a computer.

logging

The act of creating a log.

logic bomb

A piece of code that sits dormant on a target computer until it is triggered by the occurrence of specific conditions, such as a specific date and time. Once the code is triggered, the logic bomb "detonates," performing whatever action it was programmed to do.

loss controls

Security measures implemented to prevent key assets from being damaged.

LSO

(locally shared object) Data stored on a user's computer after visiting a website that uses Adobe Flash Player. These can be used to track a user's activity.

M of N scheme

A mathematical control that takes into account the total number of key recovery agents (N) along with the number of agents required to perform a key recovery (M).

MAC

(Mandatory Access Control) A system in which objects (files and other resources) are assigned security labels of varying levels, depending on the object's sensitivity. Users are assigned a security level or clearance, and when they try to access an object, their clearance is compared to the object's security label. If there is a match, the user can access the object; if there is no match, the user is denied access.

MAC address
(Media Access Control address) A unique physical address assigned to each network adapter board at the time of manufacture.

MAC filtering
The security technique of allowing or denying specific MAC addresses from connecting to a network device.

MAC limiting
The security technique of defining exactly how many different MAC addresses are allowed access to a network device.

malicious add-on
An add-on that is meant to look like a normal add-on, except that when a user installs it, malicious content will be injected to target the security loopholes that are present in a web browser.

malicious code attack
A type of software attack where an attacker inserts malicious software into a user's system.

malicious insider threat
A threat originating from an employee in an organization who performs malicious acts, such as deleting critical information or sharing this critical information with outsiders, which may result in a certain amount of losses to the organization.

malware
Malicious code, such as viruses, Trojans, or worms, which is designed to gain unauthorized access to, make unauthorized use of, or damage computer systems and networks.

man-in-the-middle attack
A form of eavesdropping where the attacker makes an independent connection between two victims and steals information to use fraudulently.

management controls
Procedures implemented to monitor the adherence to organizational security policies.

Mandatory Access Control
See MAC.

mandatory vacations
Periods of time in which an employee must take time off from work so that their activities may be subject to a security review.

mantrap
A physical security control system that has a door at each end of a secure chamber.

maximum tolerable downtime
See MTD.

MD4
(Message Digest 4) This hash algorithm, based on RFC 1320, produces a 128-bit hash value and is used in message integrity checks for data authentication.

MD5
(Message Digest 5) This hash algorithm, based on RFC 1321, produces a 128-bit hash value and is used in IPSec policies for data authentication.

mean time between failures
See MTBF.

mean time to failure
See MTTF.

mean time to recovery
See MTTR.

media
A method that connects devices to the network and carries data between devices.

Media Access Control address
See MAC address.

memorandum of understanding
See MOU.

message digest
See hash.

Message Digest 4
See MD4.

Message Digest 5
See MD5.

MOU
(memorandum of understanding) An informal business agreement that is not legally binding and does not involve the exchange of money.

MTBF
(mean time between failures) The rating on a device or devices that predicts the expected time between failures.

MTD
(maximum tolerable downtime) The longest period of time a business can be inoperable without causing the business to fail irrecoverably.

MTTF
(mean time to failure) The length of time a device or component is expected to remain operational.

MTTR
(mean time to recovery) The average time taken for a business to recover from an incident or failure.

multi-factor authentication
Any authentication scheme that requires validation of at least two of the possible authentication factors.

multifunction network device
Any piece of network hardware that is meant to perform more than one networking task without having to be reconfigured.

mutual authentication
A security mechanism that requires that each party in a communication verifies its identity.

NAC
(Network Access Control) The collection of protocols, policies, and hardware that govern access on devices to and from a network.

NAS
(Network Access Server) A RADIUS server configuration that uses a centralized server and clients.

NAT
(Network Address Translation) A simple form of Internet security that conceals internal addressing schemes from the public Internet by translating between a single public address on the external side of a router and private, non-routable addresses internally.

Near Field Communication
See NFC.

NetBIOS
A simple, broadcast-based naming service.

Network Access Control
See NAC.

Network Access Server
See NAS.

network adapter
Hardware that translates the data between the network and a device.

Network Address Translation
See NAT.

network analyzer
See protocol analyzer.

Network Basic Input Output System
See NetBIOS.

network intrusion detection system
See NIDS.

network intrusion prevention system
See NIPS.

network operating system
Software that controls network traffic and access to network resources.

network-based firewalls
A hardware/software combination that protects all the computers on a network behind the firewall.

NFC

(Near Field Communication) A mobile device communication standard that operates at very short range, often through physical contact.

NIDS

(network intrusion detection system) A system that uses passive hardware sensors to monitor traffic on a specific segment of the network.

NIPS

(network intrusion prevention system) An active, inline security device that monitors suspicious network and/or system traffic and reacts in real time to block it.

non-repudiation

The security goal of ensuring that the party that sent a transmission or created data remains associated with that data and cannot deny sending or creating that data.

NoSQL database

A database that provides data storage and retrieval in a non-relational manner.

NT LAN Manager

See NTLM.

NTLM

(NT LAN Manager) An authentication protocol created by Microsoft for use in its products.

OCSP

(Online Certificate Status Protocol) An HTTP-based alternative to a certificate revocation list that checks the status of certificates.

OFB encryption

(Output Feedback mode encryption) A block encryption model that converts a block cipher into a stream cipher, which is fed back as input of a block cipher.

off-boarding

Ensuring that employees or partners leaving an organization or business relationship do not pose a security risk.

on-boarding

Bringing new employees or business partners up to speed on security protocols.

one-time password

See OTP.

Online Certificate Status Protocol

See OCSP.

Open Directory

The directory service that ships as part of Mac OS X Server.

Open Systems Interconnection model

See OSI model.

operational controls

Security measures implemented to safeguard all aspects of day-to-day operations, functions, and activities.

order of volatility

The order in which volatile data should be recovered from various storage locations and devices following a security incident.

orphaned accounts

User accounts that remain active even after the employees have left the organization.

OSI model

(Open Systems Interconnection model) A method of abstracting how different layers of a network structure interact with one another.

OTP

(one-time password) A password that is generated for use in one specific session and becomes invalid after the session ends.

Output Feedback mode encryption

See OFB encryption.

P2P

(peer-to-peer) A network that has a broadcast application architecture that distributes tasks between peer systems who have equal privileges, and in which resource sharing, processing, and communications controls are decentralized.

P2P attacks

Attacks that are launched by malware propagating within a P2P architecture to launch DoS attacks.

PaaS
(Platform as a Service) A method that uses the cloud to provide any platform-type services.

packet sniffing
An attack on wireless networks where an attacker captures data and registers data flows in order to analyze what data is contained in a packet.

PAP
(Password Authentication Protocol) A remote access authentication service that sends user IDs and passwords as cleartext.

password attack
Any type of attack in which the attacker attempts to obtain and make use of passwords illegitimately.

Password Authentication Protocol
See PAP.

password stealer
A type of software that can capture all passwords and user names entered into the IM application or social networking site that it was designed for.

Password–Based Key Derivation Function 2
See PBKDF2.

patch
A small unit of supplemental code meant to address either a security problem or a functionality flaw in a software package or operating system.

patch management
The practice of monitoring for, evaluating, testing, and installing software patches and updates.

PBKDF2
(Password-Based Key Derivation Function 2) A key derivation function used in key stretching to make potentially weak cryptographic keys such as passwords less susceptible to brute force attacks.

PCBC encryption
(Propagating or Plaintext Cipher Block Chaining encryption) A block encryption model that causes minimal changes in the ciphertext while encrypting or decrypting.

PEAP
(Protected Extensible Authentication Protocol) Similar to EAP-TLS, PEAP is an open standard developed by a coalition made up of Cisco Systems, Microsoft, and RSA Security.

peer–to–peer
See P2P.

penetration test
A method of evaluating security by simulating an attack on a system.

perfect forward secrecy
A property of public key cryptographic systems that ensures that any session key derived from a set of long-term keys cannot be compromised if one of the keys is compromised at a future date.

permanent DoS attack
A type of DoS attack that targets the hardware of a system in order to make recovery more difficult.

personal identification verification card
Any physical token like a smart card that is used in identification and authentication.

personally identifiable information
See PII.

PGP
(Pretty Good Privacy) A method of securing emails created to prevent attackers from intercepting and manipulating email and attachments by encrypting and digitally signing the contents of the email using public key cryptography.

pharming
An attack in which a request for a website, typically an e-commerce site, is redirected to a similar-looking, but fake, website.

phishing
A type of email-based social engineering attack, in which the attacker sends email from a spoofed source, such as a bank, to try to elicit private information from the victim.

phlashing
See permanent DoS attack.

physical security
The implementation and practice of various control mechanisms that are intended to restrict physical access to facilities.

physical security controls
Implemented security measures that restrict, detect, and monitor access to specific physical areas or assets.

PII
(personally identifiable information) The pieces of information that a company uses or prefers to use to identify or contact an employee.

ping floods
A common name for ICMP flood attack. It is a type of DoS attack in which the attacker attempts to overwhelm the target system with ICMP Echo Request (ping) packets.

ping sweep
A scan of a range of IP addresses to locate active hosts within the range.

PKCS
(Public Key Cryptography Standards) A set of protocol standards developed by a consortium of vendors to send information over the Internet in a secure manner using a PKI.

PKCS #10—Certification Request Syntax Standard
A PKCS that describes the syntax used to request certification of a public key and other information.

PKCS #7—Cryptographic Message Syntax Standard
A PKCS that describes the general syntax used for cryptographic data such as digital signatures.

PKI
(Public Key Infrastructure) A system that is composed of a CA, certificates, software, services, and other cryptographic components, for the purpose of enabling authenticity and validation of data and/or entities.

plaintext
Un-encoded data. Also known as cleartext.

Platform as a Service
See PaaS.

PMI
(Privilege Management Infrastructure) An implementation of a particular set of privilege management technologies.

Point-to-Point Protocol
See PPP.

Point-to-Point Tunneling Protocol
See PPTP.

policy statement
An outline of the plan for an individual security component.

polymorphic malware
A virus that is able to alter its decryption module each time it infects a new file.

pop-up
A window or frame that loads and appears automatically when a user connects to a particular web page.

pop-up blockers
Software that prevents pop-ups from sites that are unknown or untrusted and prevents the transfer of unwanted code to the local system.

port scanning attack
An attack where an attacker scans your systems to see which ports are listening in an attempt to find a way to gain unauthorized access.

ports
The endpoints of a logical connection that client computers use to connect to specific server programs.

PPP
(Point-to-Point Protocol) The VPN protocol that is an Internet standard for sending IP datagram packets over serial point-to-point links.

PPTP
(Point-to-Point Tunneling Protocol) A VPN protocol that is an extension of the PPP remote access protocol.

Pretty Good Privacy
See PGP.

prevention
The security approach of blocking unauthorized access or attacks before they occur.

prevention controls
Controls that can react to anomalies by blocking access completely, thereby preventing damage to a system, building, or network.

private key
The component of asymmetric encryption that is kept secret by one party during two-way encryption.

private root CA
A root CA that is created by a company for use primarily within the company itself.

privilege bracketing
The task of giving privileges to a user only when needed and revoking them as soon as the task is done.

privilege management
The use of authentication and authorization mechanisms to provide an administrator with centralized or decentralized control of user and group role-based privilege management.

Privilege Management Infrastructure
See PMI.

procedures
Instructions that detail specifically how to implement a policy.

profiling
See footprinting.

Propagating or Plaintext Cipher Block Chaining encryption
See PCBC encryption.

protected distribution
A method of securing the physical cabling of a communications infrastructure.

Protected Extensible Authentication Protocol
See PEAP.

protocol
Software that controls network communications using a set of rules.

protocol analyzer
This type of diagnostic software can examine and display data packets that are being transmitted over a network.

proxy server
A system that isolates internal networks from the Internet by downloading and storing Internet files on behalf of internal clients.

public key
The component of asymmetric encryption that can be accessed by anyone.

Public Key Cryptography Standards
See PKCS.

Public Key Infrastructure
See PKI.

public root CA
A root CA that is created by a vendor for general access by the public.

quantum cryptography
A type of encryption based on quantum communication and quantum computation.

qubit
In quantum cryptography, a unit of data that is encrypted by entangling data with a sub-atomic particle such as a photon or electron that has a particular spin cycle. A qubit is the equivalent of a bit in computing technology.

RA

(Registration Authority) An authority in a PKI that processes requests for digital certificates from users.

RACE Integrity Primitives Evaluation Message Digest

See RIPEMD.

RADIUS

(Remote Authentication Dial-In User Service) A standard protocol for providing centralized authentication and authorization services for remote users.

RAID

(Redundant Array of Independent Disks) A set of vendor-independent specifications for fault tolerant configurations on multiple-disk systems.

rainbow tables

Sets of related plaintext passwords and their hashes.

ransomware

An attack in which an attacker takes control of a user's system or data and demands a payment for return of that control.

RBAC

(Role-Based Access Control) A system in which access is controlled based on a user's role. Users are assigned to roles, and network objects are configured to allow access only to specific roles. Roles are created independently of user accounts.

RC

(Rivest Cipher) A series of variable key-length symmetric encryption algorithms developed by Ronald Rivest.

recovery

The act of recovering vital data present in files or folders from a crashed system or data storage devices when data has been compromised or damaged.

recovery agent

An individual with the necessary credentials to decrypt files that were encrypted by another user.

recovery point objective

See RPO.

recovery team

A group of designated individuals who implement recovery procedures and control the recovery operations in the event of an internal or external disruption to critical business processes.

recovery time objective

See RTO.

Redundant Array of Independent Disks

See RAID.

reflected attack

An attack where the attacker poses as a legitimate user and sends information to a web server in the form of a page request or form submission.

reflected DoS attack

A type of DoS attack that uses a forged source IP address when sending requests to a large number of computers. This causes those systems to send a reply to the target system, causing a DoS condition.

Registration Authority

See RA.

remote access

The ability to connect to systems and services from an offsite or remote location using a remote access method.

Remote Authentication Dial–In User Service

See RADIUS.

remote code execution

See arbitrary code execution.

replay attack

A type of network attack where an attacker captures network traffic and stores it for retransmission at a later time to gain unauthorized access to a network.

reputation
The public's opinion of a particular company based on certain standards.

resource
Any virtual or physical components of a system that have limited availability. A physical resource can be any device connected directly to a computer system. A virtual resource refers to any type of file, memory location, or network connection.

RIPEMD
(RACE Integrity Primitives Evaluation Message Digest) A message digest algorithm that is based on the design principles used in MD4.

risk
An information security concept that indicates exposure to the chance of damage or loss, and signifies the likelihood of a hazard or dangerous threat.

risk analysis
The security management process for addressing any risk or economic damages that affect an organization.

risk awareness
The process of being consistently informed about the risks in one's organization or specific department.

risk management
The practice of managing risks from the initial identification to mitigation of those risks.

Rivest Cipher
See RC.

Rivest Shamir Adelman
See RSA.

rogue access point
An unauthorized wireless access point on a corporate or private network, which allows unauthorized individuals to connect to the network.

rogue machine
An unknown or unrecognized device that is connected to a network, often for nefarious purposes.

Role-Based Access Control
See RBAC.

rollup
A collection of previously issued patches and hotfixes, usually meant to be applied to one component of a system, such as the web browser or a particular service.

root CA
The top-most CA in the hierarchy and consequently, the most trusted authority in the hierarchy.

rootkit
Software that is intended to take full or partial control of a system at the lowest levels.

router
A device that connects multiple networks that use the same protocol.

router redundancy
A technique for employing multiple routers in teams to limit the risk of routing failure should a router malfunction.

RPO
(recovery point objective) The point in time, relative to a disaster, where the data recovery process begins.

RSA
The first successful algorithm to be designed for public key encryption. It is named for its designers, Rivest, Shamir, and Adelman.

RTO
(recovery time objective) The length of time within which normal business operations and activities must be restored following a disturbance.

Rule-Based Access Control
A non-discretionary access control technique that is based on a set of operational rules or restrictions.

rule-based management
The use of operational rules or restrictions to govern the security of an organization's infrastructure.

S-box
A relatively complex key algorithm that when given the key, provides a substitution key in its place.

SaaS
(Software as a Service) A method that uses the cloud to provide application services to users.

safety controls
Security measures implemented to protect personnel and property from physical harm.

SAML
(Security Assertion Markup Language) An XML-based data format used to exchange authentication information between a client and a service.

sandboxing
The practice of isolating an environment from a larger system in order to conduct security tests safely.

SCADA system
(supervisory control and data acquisition) A type of industrial control system that monitors and controls industrial processes such as manufacturing and fabrication, infrastructure processes such as power transmission and distribution, and facility processes such as energy consumption and HVAC systems.

scanning
The phase of the hacking process in which the attacker uses specific tools to determine an organization's infrastructure and discover vulnerabilities.

schema
A set of rules in a directory service for how objects are created and what their characteristics can be.

SCP
(Secure Copy Protocol) A protocol that is used to securely transfer computer files between a local and a remote host, or between two remote hosts, using SSH.

script kiddie
An inexperienced hacker with limited technical knowledge who relies on automated tools to hack.

Secure Copy Protocol
See SCP.

Secure FTP
See FTP over SSH.

Secure Hash Algorithm
See SHA.

Secure LDAP
See LDAPS.

Secure Shell
See SSH.

Secure Socket Tunneling Protocol
See SSTP.

Secure Sockets Layer
See SSL.

security architecture review
An evaluation of an organization's current security infrastructure model and security measures.

Security Assertion Markup Language
See SAML.

security auditing
Performing an organized technical assessment of the security strengths and weaknesses of a system.

security baseline
A collection of security configuration settings that are to be applied to a particular host in the enterprise.

security incident
A specific instance of a risk event occurring, whether or not it causes damage.

security policy
A formalized statement that defines how security will be implemented within a particular organization.

security posture
The position an organization takes on securing all aspects of its business.

separation of duties
The principle that establishes that no one person should have too much power or responsibility.

service pack
A collection of system updates that can include functionality enhancements, new features, and typically all patches, updates, and hotfixes issued up to the point of the release of the service pack.

service-level agreement
See SLA.

session hijacking attack
An attack where the attacker exploits a legitimate computer session to obtain unauthorized access to an organization's network or services.

session key
A single-use symmetric key used in encrypting messages that are in a series of related communications.

SFTP
(Simple File Transfer Protocol) An early unsecured file transfer protocol that has since been declared obsolete.

SHA
(Secure Hash Algorithm) A hash algorithm modeled after MD5 and considered the stronger of the two because it produces a 160-bit hash value.

shoulder surfing
A human-based attack where the goal is to look over the shoulder of an individual as he or she enters password information or a PIN.

signature-based monitoring
A monitoring system that uses a predefined set of rules provided by a software vendor to identify traffic that is unacceptable.

Simple File Transfer Protocol
See SFTP.

Simple Network Management Protocol
See SNMP.

single loss expectancy
See SLE.

single sign-on
See SSO.

sinkhole attack
An attack in which all traffic on a wireless network is funneled through a single node.

site survey
The collection of information on a location for the purposes of building the most ideal infrastructure.

SLA
(service-level agreement) A business agreement that outlines what services and support will be provided to a client.

SLE
(single loss expectancy) The financial loss expected from a single adverse event.

smart cards
Devices similar to credit cards that can store authentication information, such as a user's private key, on an embedded microchip.

Smurf attacks
A common name for ICMP flood attacks. These are a type of DoS attack in which a ping message is broadcast to an entire network on behalf of a victim computer, flooding the victim computer with responses.

snapshot
The state of a virtual system at a specific point in time.

sniffer

A device or program that monitors network communications on the network wire or across a wireless network and captures data.

sniffing attack

A network attack that uses special monitoring software to gain access to private communications on the network wire or across a wireless network. Also known as an eavesdropping attack.

SNMP

(Simple Network Management Protocol) An application-layer service used to exchange information between network devices.

social engineering attack

A type of attack where the goal is to obtain sensitive data, including user names and passwords, from network users through deception and trickery.

Software as a Service

See SaaS.

software attack

Any attack that targets software resources, including operating systems, applications, protocols, and files.

source code

Software code that is generated by programming languages, which is then compiled into machine code to be executed by a computer. Access to source code enables a programmer to change how a piece of software functions.

spam

An email-based threat that floods the user's inbox with emails that typically carry unsolicited advertising material for products or other spurious content, and which sometimes deliver viruses. It can also be utilized within social networking sites such as Facebook and Twitter.

spam filters

Programs used to read and reject incoming messages that contain target words and phrases used in known spam messages.

spear phishing

An email-based or web-based form of phishing which targets particularly wealthy individuals. Also known as whaling.

spim

An IM-based attack just like spam but which is propagated through instant messaging instead of through email.

spoofing

A human-based or software-based attack where the goal is to pretend to be someone else for the purpose of identity concealment. Spoofing can occur in IP addresses, MAC addresses, and email.

spyware

Surreptitiously installed malicious software that is intended to track and report the usage of a target system or collect other data the author wishes to obtain.

SQL

(Structured Query Language) A programming and query language common to many large-scale database systems.

SQL injection

An attack that injects an SQL query into the input data directed at a server by accessing the client side of the application.

SSH

(Secure Shell) A protocol for secure remote logon and secure transfer of data.

SSL

(Secure Sockets Layer) A security protocol that uses certificates for authentication and encryption to protect web communication.

SSO

(single sign-on) An aspect of privilege management that provides users with one-time authentication to multiple resources, servers, or sites.

SSTP

(Secure Socket Tunneling Protocol) A protocol that uses the HTTP over SSL protocol and encapsulates an IP packet with a PPP header and then with an SSTP header.

standards
Definitions of how adherence to a policy will be measured.

static environment
An operating system or other environment that is not updated or changed.

steganography
The practice of attempting to obscure the fact that information is present.

storage segmentation
The process of dividing data storage along certain predefined lines.

stored attack
An attack where an attacker injects malicious code or links into a website's forums, databases, or other data.

stream cipher
A relatively fast type of encryption that encrypts data one bit at a time.

strong password
A password that meets the complexity requirements that are set by a system administrator and documented in a password policy.

Structured Query Language
See SQL.

subnetting
The division of a large network into smaller logical networks.

subordinate CAs
Any CAs below the root in the hierarchy.

succession plan
A plan that ensures that all key business personnel have one or more designated backups who can perform critical functions when needed.

supervisory control and data acquisition system
See SCADA system.

switch
A device that has multiple network ports and combines multiple physical network segments into a single logical network.

symmetric encryption
A two-way encryption scheme in which encryption and decryption are both performed by the same key. Also known as shared-key encryption.

SYN flood
A type of DoS attack in which the attacker sends multiple SYN messages initializing TCP connections with a target host.

tabletop exercise
An emergency planning exercise that enables disaster recovery team members to meet and discuss their roles in emergency situations, as well as their responses in particular situations.

TACACS
(Terminal Access Controller Access Control System) Provides centralized authentication and authorization services for remote users.

TACACS+
Cisco's extension to the TACACS protocol that provides multi-factor authentication.

tailgating
A human-based attack where the attacker will slip in through a secure area following a legitimate employee.

takeover attack
A type of software attack where an attacker gains access to a remote host and takes control of the system.

TCB
(Trusted Computing Base) The hardware, firmware, and software components of a computer system that implement the security policy of a system.

TCP/IP
(Transmission Control Protocol/Internet Protocol) A non-proprietary, routable network protocol suite that enables computers to communicate over all types of networks.

technical controls

Hardware or software installations that are implemented to monitor and prevent threats and attacks to computer systems and services.

telephony

Technology that provides voice communications through devices over a distance.

Temporal Key Integrity Protocol

See TKIP.

Terminal Access Controller Access Control System

See TACACS.

testing controls

Security measures that verify whether or not certain security techniques meet the standards set for them.

TFTP

(Trivial File Transfer Protocol) An insecure, limited version of FTP used primarily to automate the process of configuring boot files between computers.

threat

Any potential damage to an asset.

threat vector

The path or means by which an attacker compromises security.

time of day restrictions

Security controls that restrict the periods of time when users are allowed to access systems, which can be set using a group policy.

timed HMAC–based one–time password

See TOTP.

TKIP

(Temporal Key Integrity Protocol) A security protocol created by the IEEE 802.11i task group to replace WEP.

TLS

(Transport Layer Security) A security protocol that uses certificates and public key cryptography for mutual authentication and data encryption over a TCP/IP connection.

tokens

Physical or virtual objects that store authentication information.

TOS

(Trusted Operating System) The operating system component of the TCB that protects the resources from applications.

TOTP

(timed HMAC-based one-time password) An improvement on HOTP that forces one-time passwords to expire after a short period of time.

TPM

(Trusted Platform Module) A specification that includes the use of cryptoprocessors to create a secure computing environment.

transitive access

Access given to certain members in an organization to use data on a system without the need for authenticating themselves.

transitive access attack

An attack that takes advantage of the transitive access given in order to steal or destroy data on a system.

transitive trust

When a trust relationship between entities extends beyond its original form.

Transmission Control Protocol/ Internet Protocol

See TCP/IP.

transport encryption

The technique of encrypting data that is in transit, usually over a network like the Internet.

Transport Layer Security

See TLS.

Triple DES

See 3DES.

Trivial File Transfer Protocol

See TFTP.

Trojan horse
An insidious type of malware that hides itself on an infected system and can pave the way for a number of other types of attacks.

trust model
A CA hierarchy.

Trusted Computing Base
See TCB.

Trusted Operating System
See TOS.

Trusted Platform Module
See TPM.

tunneling
A data-transport technique in which a data packet is encrypted and encapsulated in another data packet in order to conceal the information of the packet inside.

Twofish
A symmetric key block cipher, similar to Blowfish, consisting of a block size of 128 bits and key sizes up to 256 bits.

typo squatting
See URL hijacking.

UDP flood
A type of DoS attack in which the attacker attempts to overwhelm the target system with UDP ping requests. Often the source IP address is spoofed, creating a DoS condition for the spoofed IP.

unified threat management
See UTM.

URL filtering
The inspection of files and packets to block restricted websites or content.

URL hijacking
An attack in which an attacker registers a domain name with a common misspelling of an existing domain, so that a user who misspells a URL they enter into a browser is taken to the attacker's website.

URL shortening service
An Internet service that makes it easier to share links on social networking sites by abbreviating URLs.

user assigned privileges
Privileges that are assigned to a system user and can be configured to meet the needs of a specific job function or task.

UTM
(unified threat management) The process of centralizing various security techniques into a single device.

virtual local area network
See VLAN.

virtual private network
See VPN.

virtualization
A class of technology that separates computing software from the hardware it runs on via an additional software layer, allowing multiple operating systems to run on one computer simultaneously.

virus
A self-replicating piece of code that spreads from computer to computer by attaching itself to different files.

vishing
Voice phishing, a human-based attack where the attacker extracts information while speaking over the phone or leveraging IP-based voice messaging services (VoIP).

VLAN
(virtual local area network) A point-to-point physical network that is created by grouping selected hosts together, regardless of their physical location.

Voice over IP
See VoIP.

VoIP
(Voice over IP) A term used for a technology that enables you to deliver telephony communications over a network by using the IP protocol.

VPN

(virtual private network) A private network that is configured within a public network, such as the Internet.

VPN concentrator

A single device that incorporates advanced encryption and authentication methods in order to handle a large number of VPN tunnels.

VPN protocols

Protocols that provide VPN functionality.

vulnerability

Any condition that leaves a system open to harm.

vulnerability scan

An assessment that identifies and quantifies weaknesses within a system, but does not test the security features of that system.

WAP

(Wireless Application Protocol) A protocol designed to transmit data such as web pages, email, and newsgroup postings to and from wireless devices such as mobile phones, smartphones, and tablets over very long distances, and display the data on small screens in a web-like interface.

war chalking

Using symbols to mark off a sidewalk or wall to indicate that there is an open wireless network which may be offering Internet access.

war driving

The act of searching for instances of wireless LAN networks while in motion, using wireless tracking devices like mobile phones, smartphones, tablets, or laptops.

warm site

A location that is dormant or performs non-critical functions under normal conditions, but which can be rapidly converted to a key operations site if needed.

watering hole attack

An attack in which an attacker targets a specific group, discovers which websites that group frequents, then injects those sites with malware. At least one member of the group will be infected, possibly compromising the group itself.

web application-based firewalls

A firewall that is deployed to secure an organization's web-based applications and transactions from attackers.

web security gateway

A software program used primarily to block Internet access to a predefined list of websites or category of websites within an organization or business.

WEP

(Wired Equivalent Privacy) A deprecated protocol that provides 64-bit, 128-bit, and 256-bit encryption using the RC4 algorithm for wireless communication that uses the 802.11a and 802.11b protocols.

whaling

See spear phishing.

white box test

A test in which the tester knows about all aspects of the systems and understands the function and design of the system before the test is conducted.

white hat

A hacker who exposes security flaws in applications and operating systems with an organization's consent so that they can fix them before the problems become widespread.

whitelisting

See application whitelisting.

Wi-Fi Protected Access

See WPA.

Wi-Fi Protected Setup

See WPS.

WIDS

(wireless intrusion detection system) A system that uses passive hardware sensors to monitor traffic on a specific segment of a wireless network.

Windows security policies
Configuration settings within the Windows operating systems that control the overall security behavior of the system.

WIPS
(wireless intrusion prevention system) An active, inline security device that monitors suspicious network and/or system traffic on a wireless network and reacts in real time to block it.

Wired Equivalent Privacy
See WEP.

Wireless Application Protocol
See WAP.

wireless intrusion detection system
See WIDS.

wireless intrusion prevention system
See WIPS.

wireless security
Any method of securing your wireless LAN network to prevent unauthorized access and data theft while ensuring that authorized users can connect to the network.

Wireless Transport Layer Security
See WTLS.

worm
A self-replicating piece of code that spreads from computer to computer without attaching to different files.

WPA
(Wi-Fi Protected Access) A wireless encryption protocol that generates a 128-bit key for each packet sent. Superseded by WPA2.

WPA2
See WPA.

WPS
(Wi-Fi Protected Setup) An insecure feature of WPA and WPA2 that allows enrollment in a wireless network based on an 8-digit PIN.

WTLS
(Wireless Transport Layer Security) The security layer of a wireless AP and the wireless equivalent of TLS in wired networks.

XML
(eXtensible Markup Language) A widely adopted markup language used in many documents, websites, and web applications.

XML injection
An attack that injects corrupted XML query data so that an attacker can gain access to the XML data structure and input malicious code or read private data.

XSRF
(cross-site request forgery) A type of application attack where an attacker takes advantage of the trust established between an authorized user of a website and the website itself.

XSS
(cross-site scripting) A type of application attack where the attacker takes advantage of scripting and input validation vulnerabilities in an interactive website to attack legitimate users.

XTACACS
An extension to the original TACACS protocol.

zero day exploit
A hacking attack that occurs immediately after a vulnerability is identified, when the security level is at its lowest.

zombie
A computer that has been infected with a bot and is being used by an attacker to mount a DDoS attack. Also called a drone.

Index

N

093022S rev 1.0
ISBN-13 978-1-4246-2232-0
ISBN-10 1-4246-2232-8